PAGE 36 | **ON THE ROAD**

YOUR COMPLETE DESTINATION GUIDE
In-depth reviews, detailed listings
and insider tips

Accommodation > p175

Hania
p38

Rethymno
p77

Iraklio
p109

Lasithi
p148

PAGE 249 | **SURVIVAL GUIDE**

VITAL PRACTICAL INFORMATION TO
HELP YOU HAVE A SMOOTH TRIP

Language

THIS EDITION WRITTEN AND RESEARCHED BY

Andrea Schulte-Peevers
Chris Deliso, Des Hannigan

welcome to
Crete

Bewitching Scenery

Crete is in many respects the culmination of the Greek experience. Nature here has been as prolific as Picasso in his prime. There's something undeniably artistic in the way the landscape unfolds, from the sun-drenched beaches in the north to rugged canyons spilling into a cove-riddled and cliff-studded south coast. In between, valleys cradle moody villages, and round-shouldered hills are the overture to often snow-dabbed mountains. Take it all in on a driving tour or venture outdoors and trek through Europe's longest gorge, hike to the cave where Zeus was born, cycle among orchards on the Lasithi Plateau or simply plant your footprints on a sandy beach.

Rich Historical Tapestry

Crete's natural beauty is equalled only by the richness of its history. The island is the birthplace of the first advanced society on European soil, the Minoans, who ruled over much of the Aegean some 4000 years ago. You'll find vestiges of this mysterious civilisation all over, including the famous Palace of Knossos. At the crossroads of three continents, Crete has been coveted and occupied by consecutive invaders. History imbues the air in the old towns of Hania and Rethymno, where labyrinthine lanes – laid out by the Venetians – are lorded over by mighty fortresses, and where gorgeously restored Renaissance mansions rub rafters with mosques and Turkish bathhouses.

GARETH MCCORMACK/LONELY PLANET IMAGES

Crete is a magical quilt of splendid beaches, ancient treasures and landscapes encompassing vibrant cities and dreamy villages, where locals will share with you their traditions, wonderful cuisine and generous spirit.

(left) Parasols and sunbathers at Marble Beach
(below) Mural at the Palace of Knossos

MARIA BREUER/IMAGEBROKER

Hundreds of chapels, churches and monasteries – often with Byzantine roots – attest to the influence of the Orthodox Church. Many still sport magnificent frescoes, especially the Church of Panagia Kera in Lasithi, while others, such as Moni Arkadiou near Rethymno, played key historic roles during the Ottoman era and WWII.

Culture, Cuisine & Character

In the end, though, it's humans – not bricks and mortar – that create the most vivid memories. Crete's spirited people champion their unique culture and customs, and time-honoured traditions remain a dynamic part of the island's soul. Meeting regular folk gossiping in *kafeneia* (coffee houses), preparing their Easter feast, tending to their sheep or celebrating during their many festivals is what makes a visit to Crete so special. And if you're a traveller on the gourmet trail, you'll delight in the distinctive farm-fresh and organic cuisine served in tavernas across the island. In fact, the Cretan diet is among the healthiest in the world. Be sure to pair your meal with an excellent local wine and, to cap it off, a fiery shot of *raki*.

❯Crete

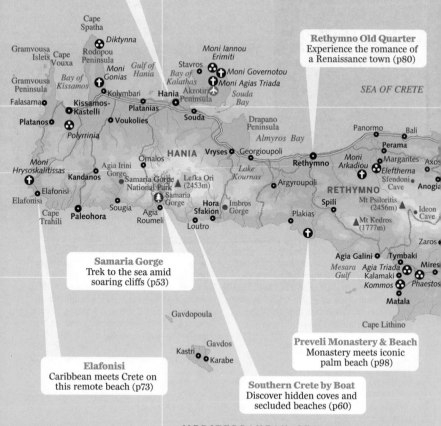

N 0 ———— 20 km
   0 ———— 12 miles

MEDITERRANEAN

SEA

Hania Old Town
Drift around this historic
harbour town (p41)

Rethymno Old Quarter
Experience the romance of
a Renaissance town (p80)

Cape
Spatha

Diktynna

Moni Iannou
Erimiti

SEA OF CRETE

Gramvousa
Islets   Cape
Vouxa   Rodopou
         Peninsula
Gramvousa   Moni   Gulf of   Stavros Moni Governotou
Peninsula Bay of Gonias   Hania   Bay of
          Kissamos   Kolymbari Kalathas Moni Agias Triada
Falasarna   Hania   Akrotiri
         Kissamos-   Peninsula Souda
         Kastelli   Platanias   Bay
Platanos   Souda
          Voukolies
        Polyrrinia   Drapano
                                    Peninsula   Panormo   Bali
                            Vryses   Almyros Bay   Perama
                   Omalos   HANIA   Georgioupoli Rethymno Moni   Margarites Axos
Moni   Agia Irini   Lake   Arkadiou Eleftherna
Hrysoskalitissas Gorge   Kournas   Sfendoni Anogia
         Kandanos   Samaria Gorge Lefka Ori   Argyroupoli RETHYMNO Cave
                    National Park (2453m)   Mt Psiloritis
Elafonisi Elafonisi   Samaria   Imbros Spili   (2456m)   Ideon
         Sougia   Gorge   Hora   Gorge   Mt Kedros Cave
Cape   Paleohora Agia   Sfakion Plakias   (1777m)
Trahili   Roumeli Loutro   Zaros
                                                  Agia Galini Tymbaki Mires
                                         Mesara Agia Triada Phaestos
Samaria Gorge   Gulf   Kalamaki
Trek to the sea amid   Kommos
soaring cliffs (p53)   Matala

                                         Cape Lithino

Gavdopoula   **Preveli Monastery & Beach**
                                         Monastery meets iconic
         Gavdos   palm beach (p98)
     Kastri Gavdos
         Karabe

Elafonisi
Caribbean meets Crete on   **Southern Crete by Boat**
this remote beach (p73)   Discover hidden coves and
                             secluded beaches (p60)

MEDITERRANEAN SEA

24° E

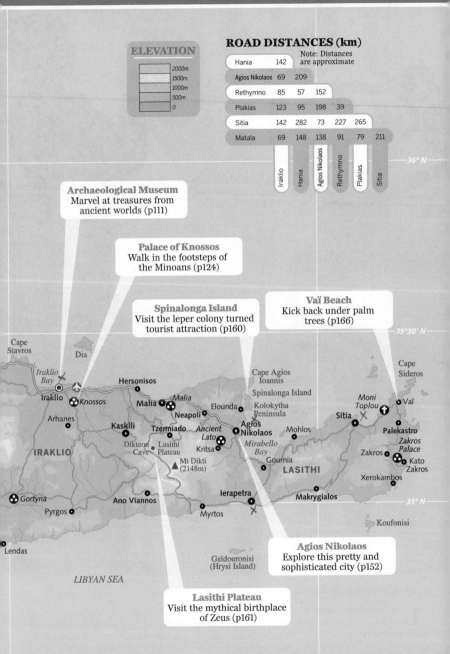

ELEVATION

2000m
1500m
1000m
500m
0

ROAD DISTANCES (km)

Note: Distances are approximate

	Iraklio	Hania	Agios Nikolaos	Rethymno	Plakias	Sitia
Hania	142					
Agios Nikolaos	69	209				
Rethymno	85	57	152			
Plakias	123	95	198	39		
Sitia	142	282	73	227	265	
Matala	69	148	138	91	79	211

Archaeological Museum
Marvel at treasures from ancient worlds (p111)

Palace of Knossos
Walk in the footsteps of the Minoans (p124)

Spinalonga Island
Visit the leper colony turned tourist attraction (p160)

Vaï Beach
Kick back under palm trees (p166)

Agios Nikolaos
Explore this pretty and sophisticated city (p152)

Lasithi Plateau
Visit the mythical birthplace of Zeus (p161)

Cape Stavros

Dia

Iraklio Bay

Iraklio

Knossos

Arhanes

Hersonisos

Malia

Neapoli

Kasklli

Tzermiado

Dikteon Cave

Lasithi Plateau

Kritsa

Mt Dikti (2148m)

Ancient Lato

Elounda

Kolokytha Peninsula

Cape Agios Ioannis

Spinalonga Island

Agios Nikolaos

Mirabello Bay

Mohlos

Gournia

LASITHI

Cape Sideros

Moni Toplou

Sitia

Vaï

Palekastro

Zakros Palace

Zakros

Kato Zakros

Xerokambos

IRAKLIO

Gortyna

Pyrgos

Ano Viannos

Myrtos

Ierapetra

Makrygialos

Koufonisi

Lendas

Gaïdouronisi (Hrysi Island)

LIBYAN SEA

36° N

35°30' N

35° N

34°30' N

25°E

26° E

12 TOP EXPERIENCES

Palace of Knossos

1 Rub shoulders with the ghosts of the Minoans, a Bronze Age people that attained an astonishingly high level of civilisation and ruled large parts of the Aegean from its capital in Knossos some 4000 years ago. Until the site's excavation in the early 20th century, an extraordinary wealth of frescoes, sculptures, jewellery, seals and other remnants lay buried under the Cretan soil. Despite a controversial partial reconstruction, Knossos remains one of the most important archaeological sites in the Mediterranean and is Crete's most-visited tourist attraction (p123).

2 An Aladdin's cave of treasures spanning thousands of years, this extraordinary museum (p111) opens a fascinating window onto the ancient world. Prime billing goes to the world's largest and finest Minoan collection but, once the main museum reopens, a veritable feast of findings from other periods will also be on display. A visit will enrich your understanding of Knossos and the other famous archaeological sites throughout the island. If you see only one museum in Crete, make it this one.

Hania Old Town

3 Regardless of the crowds, you can't help but feel enthralled by Hania's old town (p41), where Greek and Ottoman flourishes in the form of churches and minarets burst from a sturdy Venetian base. The winding old streets conceal charming boutique hotels and some of the island's best dining options. The ever-so-slightly Parisian Splantzia quarter has leafy cafes and shops offering hard-to-find traditional goods. At sunset, the view over the protected bay, studded with its lighthouse, is sublime.

Elafonisi

4 It's the beach everyone promises to see while in Crete, though not everyone manages to fulfil the promise, nestled as it is deep in the wild southwest of the island, beyond the craggy mountains and little villages. Elafonisi (p73) is a long sandy stretch known for its sparkling, clear waters and pink-and-tan sands. It gets busy in high summer, but in autumn, when the visitors disappear, it is heavenly. When you wade out to Elafonisi's tiny tidal island and feel the warm southern winds... Is this Crete, or the Caribbean?

KATJA KREDER/ IMAGEBROKER ©

Samaria & Other Western Gorges

5 The gaping gorge of Samaria (p53), starting at Omalos and running down through an ancient riverbed to the Libyan Sea, is the most-trod canyon in Crete – and with good reason. The magnificent gorge is home to varied wildlife, soaring birds of prey and a dazzling array of wildflowers in spring. It's a full-day's walk (about six hours down), and you'll have to start early, but the scenery is certainly worth the sore feet. To get more solitude, try lesser-known gorges such as Trypiti (p56) and Aradena (p27), running roughly parallel to Samaria. Samaria Gorge, below

GARETH MCCORMACK/LONELY PLANET IMAGES ©

Rethymno Old Quarter

6 Traffic fades to a quiet hum in the labyrinthine lanes of this historic quarter (p80) with its charismatic Renaissance-era Venetian buildings sprinkled with exotic features from the Turkish period. Embark on an aimless wander and you'll find wonderful surprises: a romantic flower-filled courtyard, perhaps, or an idyllic plaza, a cafe in an Ottoman bathhouse or a Venetian mansion turned boutique hotel. Don't miss a spin around the massive fortress and cap your old-quarter exploration with dinner in one of the many excellent restaurants.

Southern Crete by Boat

7 This is for escapists, beach lovers and adventurers – and it's so easy! Large sections of southern Crete's mountainous coast are accessible only by boat, and this hop-on, hop-off service (p65) allows you to see some remarkable sites, such as the glittering jewel of Loutro, tucked between secluded beaches, and laid-back Sougia, with its friendly folk and fresh seafood. The beginning and end of the voyage – Paleohora and Hora Sfakion – represent two of the most iconic (and affordable) towns in Crete, full of rugged individuals and live Cretan music.

Spinalonga Island

8 Fast becoming one of Greece's most iconic sights, this one-time leper colony (p160) has shot to stardom, thanks to the best-selling romantic novel *The Island*, by British writer Victoria Hislop. The book was adapted as a Greek television series (*To Nisi*) that has won critical acclaim for its atmospheric take on Spinalonga's powerful history. You may have to share the experience with fellow admirers, but Spinalonga, with its ruins of Venetian fortifications and reconstructed buildings of the period described in the novel, is both moving and inspiring.

Moni Preveli & Preveli Beach

9 Get high on the knockout views from this 17th-century monastery in its lofty aerie above the Libyan Sea, then descend down to Preveli Beach (p98), whose rare grove of palm trees makes it one of Crete's most celebrated sandy strips. There's fantastic swimming, but in peak season you won't be alone. The monastery itself (p97) has repeatedly entered the tomes of history, the last time during WWII when the local abbot facilitated the evacuation of 5000 Allied soldiers trapped in Crete during the Nazi occupation.

Agios Nikolaos

10 Agios Nikolaos (p152) is now established as one of the nicest towns in Crete. The setting on the Gulf of Mirabello – the Venetians' 'beautiful view' – is a winner, and the town's pleasing layout around a small harbour and circular lake adds to the appeal. You can relax by day around the lakeside cafes and then enjoy the night-time scene when an influx of visitors from nearby resorts mixes happily with modish young locals in the harbourside bars.

DIMITRY KOVYAZIN/ALAMY ©

Vaï Beach

12 This is where the South Seas take a break in Crete on an exotic beach of golden sand backed by a deep forest of palm trees (p166). Vaï means 'palm frond' in the local dialect and the palms are said to have sprouted from date stones cast away by Roman soldiers or pirates. Vaï is a popular place, of course, but on the quieter edges of summer it's a pleasure and during busy times just follow your nose to either end of the beach for less-crowded options.

KATJA KREDER/IMAGEBROKER ©

Lasithi Plateau & Dikteon Cave

11 Getting to the Lasithi Plateau (p161) can feel like a *Jack and the Beanstalk* trip as the main access routes climb relentlessly from sea level through ever-steepening bends on scenic roads. The plateau bursts into view with some drama and you realise that the green expanse before you is more plain than plateau, surrounded as it is by soaring mountains. The fairy-tale theme continues at the famous Dikteon Cave (p162), the mythical birthplace of Zeus and a cathedral-like cavernous space full of fantastical limestone features. Zeus may be long gone, but the Olympian spirit lingers on.

need to know

Currency
» euro (€)

Language
» Greek

When to Go

Hania
GO May–Jun & Sep

Knossos
GO Oct–May

Zaros
GO May–Sep

Agios Nikolaos
GO Jun–Aug

Matala
GO May–Jun & Sep–Oct

Warm to hot summers, mild winters

High Season
(Jul & Aug)

» Queues at big sights, heavy traffic, busy beaches

» Prices for lodgings are at their peak

» *Meltemi* winds can make sandy beaches unpleasant

» Hot days, but balmy evenings and warm sea for swimming

Shoulder (Apr–Jun & Sep–Oct)

» Best time for hiking and outdoor activities

» Moderate temperatures, smaller crowds

» Wildflowers in springtime, grape harvest in autumn

» Lower rates and wide availability for lodgings

Low Season
(Nov–Mar)

» Sights, attractions and restaurants scale back their hours; beach resorts close down

» No crowds at major sights

» Highest chance of rain

Your Daily Budget

Budget less than
€50

» Hostel, camping or basic hotel: €10–25

» Use public transport to get around

» Put together picnics with local produce from markets

» Stick to house wine and filling mezedhes in tavernas

Midrange
€50–150

» Apartment or double room in midrange hotel: €40–90

» Lunch and dinner in nice tavernas with wine

» Hire a car to get around

Top End over
€120

» Double room in boutique hotel or beach resort: from €120

» Lunch at high-end tavernas, dinner at gourmet restaurants in prime locations

Money

» ATMs widely available in cities, towns and larger villages. Visa and MasterCard accepted in cities and tourist centres.

Visas

» Generally not required for stays of up to 90 days (or at all for EU nationals); some nationalities need a Schengen Visa (p256).

Mobile Phones

» European and Australian phones work. Slip in a Greek SIM card to call with a cheaper local number.

Accommodation

» Full range of lodging options, from hostels to villas, apartments to business hotels, guesthouses to beach resorts. Book ahead in summer. See p175.

Web...

» ...
.exp...
gene...

» Inf...
.infocr...
to Top 1...
related v...

» Interkr...
.interkriti.c...
Compreher...
guide to the...

» Lonely Pla...
.lonelyplanet.c...
/crete) Destina...
information, hot...
bookings, travell...
forum and more.

» Crete Region (w...
.crete-region.gr)
Official government site.

...xchange Rates

...ralia	A$1	€0.75
...la	C$1	€0.72
	¥100	€0.87
	NZ$1	€0.57
	UK£1	€1.14
	US$1	€0.70

...xchange rates see www.xe.com.

...nt Numbers

	☎166
	☎100
...ce	☎10400
...le	☎30
...code	☎00

Arriving in Crete

» **Nikos Kazantzakis International Airport, Iraklio** (p122)
Bus No 1 to Iraklio city centre: every 10 minutes from 6.15am to 10.45pm (€1.10).
Taxis into Iraklio: €7 to €10.
All international car hire agencies have outlets at the airport.

Driving in C...

Driving is on the right and overtaking on the left; the steering wheel is on the left side of the car. Away from the main highways, roads are paved but often narrow and winding; some are still unpaved and only suitable for 4WD – especially in the more remote areas in the south. Most road signs are in Greek and Latin letters, except in far-flung mountain areas. Unless posted otherwise, speed limits are 120km/h on highways, 90km/h on other major roads and 50km/h in built-up areas. Seatbelts are compulsory in the front and back. Outside built-up areas, traffic on a main road has right of way at intersections, while in towns, vehicles coming from the right have right of way. The blood-alcohol limit is 0.05%; anything over 0.08% is considered a criminal offence.

if you like...

Bewitching Beaches

Virgin strands, romantic coves, exotic lagoons or long sandy sweeps – no matter where you are in Crete, you're rarely far from a glorious beach hemmed in by clear waters glistening in shades from deep blue to iridescent green.

Balos Go tropical on this incredibly photogenic lagoon-like sandy beach (p70)

Vaï Watch out for falling dates as you revel in Europe's largest natural palm forest (p166)

Preveli Beach Crete's 'other' famous palm beach at the confluence of river and sea amid cave-combed cliffs (p98)

Falasarna Take in splendid sunsets on this long, sandy ribbon (p71)

Agios Pavlos For crowd-free tanning, point the compass to the massive sand dunes spilling down into this isolated south-coast beach (p98)

Gaïdouronisi (Hrysi Island) Count the shades of blue and green as you contemplate the shimmering waters lapping this island just off Ierapetra (p173)

Islands

As Greece's largest island, Crete sometimes feels like a country all by itself. If you're in the mood for the classic island vibe, catch a boat to these offshore escapes.

Spinalonga You can feel the poignant, powerful history of this haunting island, even among the summertime crowds (p160)

Gavdos The southernmost spot in Europe; catch it outside busy August for a genuine sense of happy isolation (p66)

Gaïdouronisi (Hrysi Island) Check out the lovely beaches and cedar trees of Gaïdouronisi, also known as Hrysi, the Golden Island (p173)

Elafonisi Pink sands and warm waters extending across shallow isles make this Crete's most magical beach (p73)

Imeri Gramvousa This tiny island on the remote western Gramvousa Peninsula is crowned by a ruined Venetian castle, while the cerulean waters at the nearby Balos lagoon – where the Mediterranean and the Sea of Crete mix – are simply picture-perfect (p70)

Enchanting Villages

There is no simpler pleasure than strolling around a charismatic village laced with time-worn lanes, peppered with ancient churches and anchored by a square where locals gather to exchange gossip.

Hora Sfakion This whimsical southern port boasts larger-than-life characters and a long and colourful history (p56)

Argyroupoli Devour trout while surrounded by rushing natural springs in this ancient mountain village (p87)

Mohlos Minoan antiquity meets seashore vibes and some of Crete's best tavernas (p163)

Kritsa In the heart of the mountains, Kritsa offers fine craftwork and an atmospheric old town (p157)

Myrthios See if you can spot Africa from this whitewashed village high above the Libyan Sea (p98)

Amari A higgledy-piggledy pile in the heart of the pastoral Amari Valley (p95)

Theriso Up in thick forest just south of Hania, this historically significant mountain village is a great place to recharge the batteries (p50)

STEFAN KIEFER/IMAGEBROKER

» Cycling towards the Lefka Ori (White Mountains) near Vamos

PLAN YOUR TRIP IF YOU LIKE...

15

Food & Drink

Gourmets will be in heaven in Crete, where 'locavore' is not a trendy concept but a way of life. This is especially true in rural areas, where tavernas often have their own farm producing meat, cheese, olive oil, *raki* and wine.

Wine Sample fine vintages on a tasting tour of the Iraklio Wine Country, Crete's largest wine-growing region (p131)

Organic farming Visit a showcase of traditional, organic farming at the enchantingly located Agreco Farm (p89)

Herbs Cretan hillsides are redolent with the smell of sage, thyme and other herbs. Find out their medicinal purposes while visiting a herb shop in Maroulas (p88)

Mountain Taverns The village tavern, one of the delights of travelling through Crete, is experiencing a revival, especially in Rethymno (p80)

Beer Brink's is the only brewery in Crete and a good one at that (p96)

Outdoor Adventures

No matter what gets you off that couch, you'll be able to pursue it in the water or on land. There's plenty to do from spring to autumn, with each season offering its own special delights.

Climb Mt Psiloritis For the ultimate fitness fix, escape the summer heat atop Crete's highest peak (p93)

Cycle the Lasithi Plateau Strap on your helmet and cycle among orchards, fields and windmills (p161)

Rock climb at Kapetaniana Fire up the adrenalin as you rock around the cliffs and clefts with expert guides (p143)

Windsurf in Palekastro Catch Crete's wildest winds at Kouremenos Beach, the island's top boarding venue (p167)

Hike the Aradena Gorge Trek to the Libyan Sea through this serene and spectacular cousin of the Samaria Gorge (p59)

Take on the Waves At pristine Falasarna beach, crash headlong into the breakers rolling in from the open Med (p71)

Museums

Museums are windows to the past that serve to enlighten and entertain us. Crete has plenty of these eye-openers. Venture beyond the must-dos like the Iraklio Archaeological Museum and you'll be surprised what other delights await.

Nikos Kazantzakis Museum Discover what the famous Cretan writer was up to when not writing *Zorba the Greek* (p132)

Maritime Museum of Crete A Minoan ship replica and other testaments to maritime greatness in a Venetian shipyard (p42)

Ierapetra Archaeological Collection Marvel at a marble Persephone and abstract images on ancient clay coffins (p170)

Lychnostasis Museum Time travel to a traditional Cretan village (p144)

Museum of Cretan Ethnology A fascinating immersion into centuries of Cretan daily life (p139)

Museum of Traditional Musical Instruments Ross Daily's collection, packed with fun, precious and rare sound machines (p132)

month by month

January

Winter is the time when Cretans have the island pretty much to themselves. Views of the snow-capped mountains are tremendous, but cold and windy weather makes this a good month for museums and churches.

New Year's (Feast of St Basil)

A day of gift-giving, singing, dancing, feasting and the slicing of the *vasilopita* cake. The person who gets the piece of cake with the hidden coin is promised a lucky year.

Epiphany

On 6 January, seas, lakes and rivers are blessed by a priest who then tosses a cross into the water. The brave soul who retrieves it can expect a year of good luck.

February

It's not as sweltering as Rio, but Cretan Carnival is still a good excuse for a big party. Blossoming almond trees hint at impending springtime. Stock up on the freshly pressed crop of olive oil.

Carnival

Pre-Lent is celebrated with three weeks of dancing, masquerade balls, games and treasure hunts, culminating in a grand street parade on the last Sunday. The biggest party is in Rethymno.

March

Winter will soon be a distant memory as days get longer and sunny days more frequent. No swimming yet, but a great chance to see the sights without the crowds.

Independence Day

25 March is a double whammy: military parades and dancing commemorate the beginning of the 1821 War of Independence, while the Feast of the Annunciation celebrates the day when Mary discovered she was pregnant.

April

A painters' palette of wildflowers blankets the island as locals prepare for the big Easter feast, giving you a chance to experience Cretan hospitality at its finest.

Easter

This is the most important religious holiday in Greece. Endeavour to attend some of the Orthodox Easter services, which include a candle-lit procession on Good Friday evening and fireworks at midnight on Easter Saturday.

May

Sunny weather and moderate temperatures make May the perfect month for walking, cycling and island explorations. The countryside is redolent with thyme, sage and other aromatic herbs.

May Day

1 May sees a mass exodus to the countryside. During picnic excursions, wildflowers are gathered and made into wreaths to

decorate houses. Since this is also International Labour Day, the bigger cities stage demonstrations.

 ### Battle of Crete Anniversary

This epic battle and the Cretan resistance are commemorated during the last week of May with ceremonies, re-enactments, athletic events and folk dancing. The biggest celebrations are in Hania and Rethymno.

June

The start of summer, so time to head for the beaches before they get crowded. Gourmets rejoice in the bounty of fresh, local produce in the markets.

 ### Navy Week

Navy Week honours Crete's relationship with the sea with music, dancing, swimming and sailing. Held in late June in even-numbered years, celebrations are especially big in Soudha, near Hania.

July

Peak season starts, so you better be the gregarious type. Definitely prebook if you're coast-bound or else escape the heat by heading for the hills and their traditional villages. Strong winds are common.

 ### Renaissance Festival

Top international talent descends upon Rethymno for two weeks of theatre, dance and music from the Renaissance period.

Iraklio Summer Festival

Renowned local and international performers (from the Bolshoi Ballet to the Vienna State Opera) come to this high-calibre festival of dance, music, theatre and cinema, held from July to mid-September.

August

It's hot, hot, hot! The height of the festival season spills over from July when the sea is at its balmiest and ripe melons, figs, peaches and cherries jam-pack markets. It's still windy.

 ### Assumption Day

15 August, the day Mary ascended to heaven, is a major celebration that sees everyone on the move back to their villages for family reunions. Expect curtailed services and heavy traffic.

October

Still a great month weatherwise, but with hardly any crowds. Winds die down and the harvest of sun-plump grapes kicks into high gear. Also a good time for exploring Crete's natural beauty on foot.

 ### Ohi Day

A simple 'no' (ohi in Greek) was Prime Minister Metaxas' famous response when Mussolini demanded free passage through Greece for his troops on 28 October 1940. The date is now a national holiday with remembrance services, parades, feasting and dance.

November

Tourist resorts all but shut down in early November as the weather gets cooler and more unpredictable. The air is clear and mountains start receiving a dusting of snow. In the villages, the *raki* distilling season peaks.

 ### Moni Arkadiou Anniversary

Patriotism kicks into high gear from 7 to 9 November during the anniversary of the explosion at Moni Arkadiou, a key holiday in Crete.

December

Days are short and quite cold, making this month a good time for indoor activities. Bring an umbrella.

 ### Christmas

Although not as important as Easter, Christmas is still celebrated with religious services and feasting. Western influences, including trees, decorations and gift-giving, are a fairly recent phenomenon.

itineraries

Whether you've got six days or 60, these itineraries provide a starting point for the trip of a lifetime. Want more inspiration? Head online to lonelyplanet.com /thorntree to chat with other travellers.

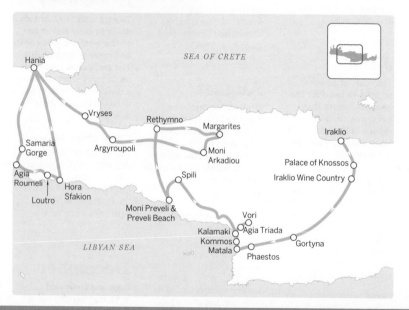

Two Weeks
Essential Crete

> Bookended by two great cities, this route is a roller-coaster of natural and sightseeing treasures. Spend a few days in **Iraklio** checking out the superb museums before heading to the **Palace of Knossos**, and enjoying the fruits of the **Iraklio Wine Country**. Next, stake out a base near Matala to combine trips to Roman **Gortyna**, the Minoan palaces of **Phaestos** and **Agia Triada** and the outstanding museum at **Vori** with swimming at **Kommos** and **Kalamaki** beaches.

Travelling west, lunch in **Spili** en route to **Moni Preveli** and picture-postcard **Preveli Beach** before steering north to soulful **Rethymno**. Spend two days wandering this Venetian maze and another few exploring the countryside, perhaps steering towards **Moni Arkadiou**, the pottery village of **Margarites** or the mountain village of **Argyroupoli**.

Head west via **Vryses** to **Hania**, your next base. When you've had your fill of this historic beauty, take the early bus to **Samaria Gorge** and trek to **Agia Roumeli** for the boat to **Loutro**. Next morning, take the boat to **Hora Sfakion** and bus back to Hania.

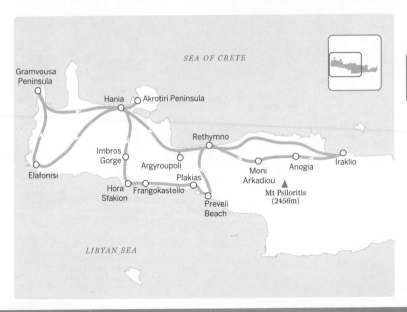

SEA OF CRETE

Gramvousa
Peninsula

Hania   Akrotiri Peninsula

Rethymno

Imbros
Gorge   Argyroupoli

Elafonisi   Plakias   Moni   Anogia   Iraklio
Arkadiou

Hora   Frangokastello
Sfakion   Mt Psiloritis
Preveli   (2456m)
Beach

LIBYAN SEA

10 Days
Central to West Crete

This trip presents you with the mother lode of soul-stirring attractions, including the unspoiled southern coast, higgledy-piggledy mountain villages and spirit-lifting culture in Crete's two most attractive towns. Kick off your trip in **Iraklio**, taking in the archaeological museum and imposing fortress, before steering west to quaint **Anogia**, where ancient traditions thrive at the foot of Mt Psiloritis. Continue west via the pottery village of Margarites to **Moni Arkadiou**, site of one of the bloodiest moments in Crete's struggle for independence from the Turks. Spend the next day in stately **Rethymno**, taking your sweet time ambling around its bewitching mix of Turkish and Venetian buildings serenaded by a lordly 16th-century fortress.

From Rethymno push on to the south coast, where the lively beach town of **Plakias** makes an ideal base for exploring nearby secluded beaches, including palm-studded **Preveli Beach**, stunningly located at the mouth of a rugged gorge.

Heading west, make a pit stop at the seaside fortress of **Frangokastello** before plunging on to **Hora Sfakion**, where you can hop on a boat and explore the remote villages along this beautiful stretch of coast. Continue north from Hora Sfakion via a steep road towards the Lefka Ori (White Mountains) and make time for a hike through spectacular **Imbros Gorge**. Push on to the north coast and linger a night or two in **Hania**, with its beautiful harbour, grand fortress, ambience-packed old town and interesting museums. It's also a good base for visiting the **Akrotiri Peninsula**, which has some fine monasteries and the famous beach at Stavros, where the key dance scene in *Zorba the Greek* was filmed.

Hania also makes a good launch pad for exploring the far western reaches of Crete. Take the circular route southwest via Kolymbari and the Innahorion villages to the westernmost tip of the island at **Elafonisi**, which beckons with pink-shimmering sandy beaches. Pushing back north via the coastal road, make a detour to the **Gramvousa Peninsula**, accented by the spectacular lagoonlike beach at Balos.

Returning back to Iraklio via Hania, consider making a quick detour to the springs of **Argyroupoli** before taking the coastal road east of Rethymno via peaceful Panormo and busy Bali.

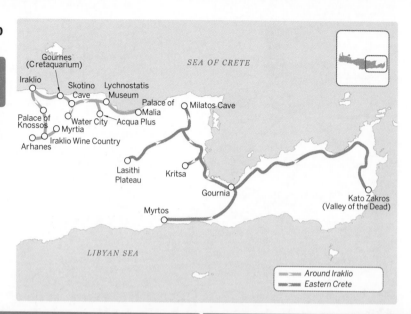

One Week
Eastern Crete

Go ahead, indulge in a few days of hedonistic resort life on the beach, in the bars and at the buffet. But when you're ready to tear yourself away, there's an entire world of discoveries waiting for you, and all can be done as easy day trips by car. Gorgeous scenery is the ticket on the **Lasithi Plateau**, high on the upper decks of the Dikti mountains, where wind power once drove the sails of thousands of windmills. Or simply lose yourself along the winding roads north of **Myrtos**, where bare mountains crowned with coxcombs of rock rise from green woods. If you're keen on history, drop by **Milatos Cave**, site of a vicious 1823 massacre of villagers by Turkish besiegers, yet which today is a serene and absorbing corner of rural Crete. To satisfy artistic cravings, steer towards the **Church of Panagia Kera** near Kritsa for a feast of fabulous frescoes. Archaeology fans can indulge their passion at the Late Minoan site of **Gournia**. Key sites on the eastern coast are the palace of **Kato Zakros** and the **Valley of the Dead**, where the awesome landscape overwhelms the human element.

One Week
Around Iraklio

Iraklio is the perfect base from which to access many of Crete's most famous sights and relaxation spots, even without your own vehicle. Crete's largest city itself beckons with top-notch museums, a Venetian fortress, a colourful street market, lively nightlife and some excellent dining. Once you've had your urban fill, hop on a bus for the quick ride to the **Palace of Knossos** for a 3D introduction to Minoan society, then apply what you've learned on a visit to the **Palace of Malia** on another day. Culture overdose? Commune with aquatic creatures at the state-of-the-art **Cretaquarium**, near Gournes, or keep cool while whooshing down the slides at **Acqua Plus** or **Water City** water parks. Nearby, you can get a glimpse of traditional Cretan life at the kooky open-air **Lychnostatis Museum**. If you have your own wheels, designate a driver and spend a day sampling the local vintages of the **Iraklio Wine Country**, with stops at the Nikos Kazantzakis Museum in **Myrtia** and the moody Minoan vestiges in **Arhanes**. Adventurous types could steer towards spooky **Skotino Cave** – bring a torch.

Hiking & Outdoor Activities

Best Coastal Hike

Delve into the past among Hellenistic, Roman and Byzantine ruins at Lissos on the 14.5km hike from Paleohora to Sougia.

Best Birdwatching

The marshes, lakes and rivers at Georgioupoli throng with migrant birds such as kingfishers and egrets.

Best Off-road Bike Trip

Get high along mountain trails between the Lasithi Plateau and the Katharo Plateau.

Best Bungee Jumping

The Aradena Gorge scoops top prize for the best-bungee tick.

Best Horse Riding

Exhilarating coastal and inland riding treks around Malia and through the Dikti mountains.

Best Gorge Walk

Eastern Crete's Zakros Gorge (otherwise known as the Valley of the Dead) is only 4km in length, but packs in all that's best in gorge walking.

Planning Your Trip

Get outdoors and active in Crete and you'll experience the rewards of this stunning island beyond the relaxed pleasures of sun and sand. Crete's rugged terrain, soaring mountains, dramatic gorges and wild coastline beyond the resorts make for an adventurer's paradise, and such is the relative ease of access to these splendid wilderness areas that you can sample just about every outdoor activity available through selective day trips.

If you're keen to sample a more edgy and exhilarating take on outdoor sport, opportunities for active and challenging holidays have increased on Crete, with several specialist operators running activities on the island. There are excellent horse-riding trails, and more extreme pursuits, including rock climbing, canyoning and bungee jumping, are available with experienced guides and instructors.

Luxuriate on Crete's superb beaches, of course, but take off now and then for some life-fulfilling experiences on the wild side of this wonderful island.

When to Go

You can follow walking routes on the island's hills and mountains and along the unspoiled coastlines at all times of the year, although, for the higher mountains, experience and full equipment is required during the winter period. While Crete is a veritable

THE E4 ROUTE

The trans-European E4 walking trail starts in Portugal and ends in Crete. In Crete, the trail picks up at the port of Kissamos in the west and ends – after 320km – on the pebbly shore of Kato Zakros in eastern Crete. Enthusiasts planning to tackle the Cretan leg can do it in a minimum of three weeks, allowing for 15km per day, or more comfortably in four weeks allowing for stops and/or shorter hiking trips. You can, of course, tackle only sections of the route if your time is limited or if you just want to walk the most interesting parts. However, you will need to make important decisions early on as the trail splits into two distinct sections through western Crete: the coastal route and the alpine route.

Making Your Way

Hikers tackling the E4 trail need to do some planning. While there is nearly always accommodation within the range of a six- to seven-hour daily hike, some of it will need to be arranged beforehand – particularly the mountain refuges (see p25), for which you might need to pick up keys.

The E4 trail is marked throughout its length with black and yellow posts and signs, but is not always well-maintained: paths are overgrown and in many sections signs are hard to find. The three-volume GPS-compatible 1:100.000 scale touring maps by **Anavasi** (210 321 8104; www.anavasi.gr) show the E4 across Crete, but its walking maps cover sections in greater detail (at a scale of 1:25,000) for the Lefka Ori (Sfakia and Pahnes), Samaria/Sougia, Mt Psiloritis and Zakros-Vaï.

The E4 can be a lonely trail and there is no food (and little water) along most of the route – it is always wise to get local advice before setting off.

Web Guides

CreteTravel.com (www.cretetravel.com/Activities/E4_walking_path.htm)
Completely Crete (www.completely-crete.com/E4-path.html)

paradise for hikers, walking is not much fun between July and August, when the temperatures can reach 40°C. Spring and autumn are the best times for great walks and serious hikes through beautiful gorges or along scenic coastal paths and alpine trails, while cycling, even for a day, is a rewarding way to explore Crete's country byways and off-road tracks.

Hiking

Crete offers an enormous variety of options for keen hikers and trekkers that pass through remote villages, across plains and into gorges. There are a few detailed English-language guides in publication and local booklets are beginning to appear. Check out www.discoveronfoot.com for some excellent walking guidebooks to Crete. Trails are not too well marked, although things are improving, especially as local interest grows. Many visitors may opt for a guided hike or a short off-road stroll, but experienced walkers will find plenty to test and stimulate them.

Walking the Gorges

Crete's numerous gorges attract hikers from all over the world. The walks can be a breathtaking and sometimes hard-going experience. The bonuses include the sheer pleasure of the spectacular surroundings, the aroma of wild herbs and flowers, shaded picnic spots and the potential for spotting wildlife.

Preparation

Most gorge walks require a fairly decent level of fitness. A few require only straight-forward walking, although tough footwear and a fair degree of stamina are still needed. Several demand some rock-scrambling experience and agility. The most extreme, such as the mighty Ha Gorge, require serious canyoning and rock-climbing abilities and the services of a competent guide.

Getting Around

Gorge walking will involve a bit of planning if you have your own transport. You will either have to walk back the same way

despite the mountainous terrain. While it is possible to cycle from one end of Crete to the other and barely raise a sweat, north-south routes and the southern coast are likely to test your stamina and fortitude. In contrast, the escarpment villages and valleys of the north coast and the Mesara Plain of the south do allow for some relatively flat cycling experiences on surfaced roads. Crete, of course, is an off-road mountain-biker's dream.

Bike Touring

Plateau tours (especially around the Lasithi Plateau) are big business, with specialist companies transporting bikes up to the plateau to save you the gruelling 'Tour de France' haul up from the coast. There are also more extreme biking options and eight-day tours covering more than 650km.

Several companies offer tours (see boxed text, p27) for all levels of experience and fitness, including specialist small operators such as **Odysseas the Cyclist** (✆28310 58178; odysseasthecyclist@hotmail.com) in Rethymno, who conducts organised and custom tours. Mountain bike tours start from €50 per day.

On Your Own

Independent cyclists coming to Crete with their own bikes are advised to bring sturdy touring bikes with multiple gears. You can hire mountain bikes for about €8 to €20 per day from a range of places around the island.

More Information

Until recently there was a dearth of biking guides to Crete and though it's still a good idea to join a tour, there is an excellent online cycling guide at www.rethymnon.gr (follow the Tourism link) detailing 22 cycling routes throughout the Rethymno prefecture, complete with useful gradient graphs.

Canyoning, Climbing & Bungee Jumping

While Crete doesn't offer the kind of stunning alpine terrain that's found in Austria or Switzerland, the island does have a large number of mountains and established mountaineering clubs. Each prefecture has its own club, which maintain the E4 trail and mountain refuges. They are all members of the association of Greek Mountaineering Clubs (EOS) and organise regular climbing, walking, speleology and skiing excursions around Crete, which visitors are welcome to join.

» **Mountaineering Club of Hania** (✆28210 74560; www.interkriti.org/orivatikos /hania1.htm; Tzanakaki 90, Hania)

» **Mountaineering Club of Iraklio** (✆2810 227 609, 8.30-10.30pm; www.interkriti.org /orivatikos/orivat.html; Dikeosynis 53, Iraklio)

» **Mountaineering Club of Lasithi** (✆28970 23230)

» **Mountaineering Club of Rethymno** (✆28310 57766; www.eos.rethymnon.com; Dimokratias 12, Rethymno) Lists excursions on its website.

MOUNTAINEERING CLUB REFUGES

NAME	LOCATION	ALTITUDE	CAPACITY (BEDS)	EOS
Kallergi	Near the Samaria Gorge	1680m	50	Hania
Katsiveli-Svourihtis	Svourihtis foothills	1970m	25	Hania
Limnarkarou	Lasithi Plateau	1350m	15	Lasithi
Prinos	Asites, East Psiloritis	1100m	45	Iraklio
Tavris	Plateau of Askyfou	1200m	42	Hania
Toubotos Prinos	Mt Psiloritis	1500m	28	Rethymno
Volikas	Volikas Keramion	1400m	40	Hania

Canyoning

Canyoning is a developing sport in Crete and should not be confused with gorge walking. Most canyoning routes require serious rock-climbing and/or caving experience, including the ability to abseil (rappel) under your own control. Most routes also require swimming ability and experience of constricted water flows. There is no shortage of wild and challenging canyons on the island. The well-organised Cretan Canyoning Association (☎6997090307; www.canyon .gr) has equipped more than 50 gorges in southern Crete with abseil and belay bolt anchors and guide wires. One of the most awe-inspiring is the mighty Ha Gorge (see boxed text) near Mt Thripti in eastern Crete. The Association's website has useful information and a published guide to Crete's canyons. It organises regular excursions and also runs beginners' courses. Canyoning is not a 'thrill-seeker's' day out and you should be certain of your capabilities before getting involved. If you're new to the sport, you should always be accompanied by an experienced canyoning guide.

The multilingual *Canyoning in Crete*, by Yiannis Bromirakis (Road Editions 2007), covers many of Crete's newly accessible gorges in fine detail with maps and drawings.

Rock Climbing

Rock climbing is also on the increase in Crete. Southern Iraklio is one of the most popular areas for climbing, particularly the stunning cliffs around Kapetaniana and Mt Kofinas on the southern flanks of the Asteroussia mountains (p143). The Agiofarango Gorge (p142) near Matala is another popular climbing spot, while many new venues are being developed around Crete, including around Samaria, Plakias, Loutro and Malia. The offshoot sport of deep water soloing – traversing sea cliffs unroped directly above deep water – has potential around Hora Sfakion. Unless you are experienced, you are advised to contact local organisations before attempting any form of rock climbing. The website www.climbincrete.com has plenty of information and some entertaining articles including an account of an early descent of the Ha Gorge.

OUTDOOR ADVENTURES IN CRETE

The following companies run a range of organised hikes, biking and other outdoor activities in Crete. Guided walks start from €44 per day and €500 per week including accommodation, transfers and meals.

Axas Outdoor Activities (☎2810 871 239; axas@yahoo.gr) Run by walking and nature enthusiast Dimitris Kornaros. Specialises in custom tours to off-the-beaten-track locations. Based in Profitis Ilias near Iraklio.

Cretan Adventures (☎2810 332 772; www.cretanadventures.gr; Evans 10, Iraklio) Organises hiking and trekking tours, mountain biking and other specialist and extreme activities.

Happy Walker (☎/fax 28310 52920; www.happywalker.com; Tobazi 56, Rethymno) Runs a range of walks from March to November, including summer walks in the Omalos Plateau and Lefka Ori.

Korifi Tours (☎28930 41440; www.korifi.de) Hiking and climbing tours around Kapetaniana, in southern Iraklio. Based in Kapetaniana.

Nature & Adventure (☎28310 54135, 6977541550; www.nat-adv.gr) Based in Rethymno. Organises daily walks and other activities including horse riding, mountain biking, rock climbing and paragliding.

Strata Walking Tours (☎28220 24336; www.stratatours.com) In Kissamos, offering anything from leisurely day trips to seven- to 15-day walking tours to the south coast.

Trekking Hellas (☎210 331 0323; www.trekking.gr) One of the biggest mainland operators running out of Athens. Runs extensive activities in Crete.

Trekking Plan (☎/fax 28210 60861; www.cycling.gr) This outfit at Agia Marina, 10km west of Hania, will take you hiking, rock climbing, abseiling (rappelling) and mountain biking in western Crete.

Bungee Jumping

High above the Aradena Gorge, on the south coast, is a spectacular bungee-jumping location, the highest bungee-jumping bridge in Greece and the second-highest in Europe. Thrill seekers can jump 138m into the narrow gorge from the bridge that crosses over the canyon. Jumps are held every weekend from June to September by **Liquid Bungy** (📞6937615191; www.bungy.gr; per jump €100).

Other Activities

Golf

Crete has a few nine-hole golf courses, but the island's only 18-hole pro course is the **Crete Golf Club** (📞28920 26000; www.crete -golf.com) in Hersonisos. This desert-style, par-72 course has been designed to blend in with the environment. The course is quite tough and also has a double-ended driving range, a golf academy and club house. It's not for casual hackers, however. A nine-hole round in summer costs €50, an 18-hole round €80 (excluding clubs or buggies).

Horse Riding

Several places in Crete offer horse riding and guided trail rides through the countryside. The most impressive operation is **Odysseia Stables** (📞28970 51080; www .horseriding.gr) above Avdou, at the foot of Mt Dikti. These stables have excellent facilities (including accommodation) and run anything from two-hour beginners' rides to three-day rides on the Lasithi Plateau and week-long trails through the Dikti mountains to the south coast. Typical prices range from €20 for a one-hour beach ride, €35 for a two-hour hack, €65 for a day trip and from €539 for eight-day courses including accommodation and meals. An eight-day trek up to the Lasithi Plateau area costs about €990.

Zoraida's Horseriding (📞28250 61745; www.zoraidas-horseriding.com), in Georgioupoli, offers beach and nature trails, including day safaris and a six-day course for advanced riders, and **Melanouri Horse Farm** (📞2892045040; www.melanouri.com) in Pitsidia, near Matala, runs rides through the surrounding region.

Water Sports

In the Swim

Falasarna
Enjoy a fabulous sunset swim at this lovely west-coast beach where crystal-clear waters fill sandy coves.

Matala
Swim off a golden beach where Bob Dylan and Joni Mitchell once hung out.

Elafonisi
Explore Crete's quasi-tropical paradise with exquisite lagoons and the offshore Elafonisi Island.

Olous
Swim with history around the causeway that links mainland Elounda to the Kolokytha Peninsula.

Gaïdouronisi (Hrysi Island)
Take a boat trip to this semi-tropical island off Crete's southeast coast that sports idyllic beaches and sparkling water.

Vaï Beach
Visit this palm tree paradise where the best swimming is out of season.

Going Coastal

Crete may seem like a country in its own right, but it is emphatically an island and is rather neatly defined as such, with its long north and south coasts boxed off by short east and west shorelines. The result is a range of sea conditions that lend themselves to all sorts of water sports.

What to Do

You can start with the 'fun sports' on the main organised beaches where everything is on offer, including waterskiing, jet-skiing, pedalos, banana boats, and doughnut or ringo rides (in which you're towed at speed across the water in an inflatable ring or raft). The most spectacular beachside trip is parasailing, which can be done singly or in tandem. Some of these outings can be quite costly, but they're hard to resist and there's certainly a lot of fun to be had in rocking around on a big yellow inflatable with a gang of like-minded others.

On Crete's northern coast, you'll find a water-sports centre attached to most luxury hotels, and they are usually open to non-residents.

The more specialised water sports available in Crete include scuba diving and snorkelling, windsurfing, kayaking and sailing. With diving and windsurfing, there are specific areas where ideal conditions prevail and there are numerous commercial operators who organise trips and rent equipment.

WATER WISE

The sea can still be a hostile environment even when flat calm and lapping a Greek beach. All water sports can be potentially dangerous. The more specialised sports such as diving and kayaking are usually well regulated and clients are accompanied by qualified instructors. You should, however, always check your operators' certification. With beach sports such as parasailing, make sure that whoever is operating the facility has full certification and a good safety record. Ringo rides are best left to capable youngsters with good swimming abilities! Parents should also keep an eye on teenagers when jet skis are up for hire. By law, operators must exercise strict checks on age limits and that no drink has been taken.

When to Go

» **Water temperature** Over 20°C from May until November and reaches as high as 27°C in August.

» **Summer** Fabulous heat and sunshine, day after day, and the best place to be is in the sea, although you won't be the only one loving it.

» **Spring and Autumn** Bookend seasons when the island is often at its loveliest, and dazzling wildflowers and aromatic herbs grace the coast.

» **Meltemi** The summertime *meltemi* (dry northerly) wind is ideal for windsurfing but can sometimes be uncomfortable on exposed beaches where it blows the sand about.

Diving & Snorkelling

The sea off much of Crete's coastline is a paradise for snorkelling and diving. There is nothing quite like cruising gently through water that can be as clear as air with visibility at times well over 30m.

For many years there were restrictions on diving anywhere in Greece due to fears of potential damage to ancient undersea ruins and because of the very real problem of theft of ancient artefacts from the seabed. Diving interests and the tourism lobby pushed for a sensible easing of the restrictions and in 2005 the Greek government opened up most Greek waters to recreational diving, with the exception of about 100 important archaeological sites. Some permitted recreational dive sites have ancient walls, fallen columns and large amphorae, the giant urns once used for storing wine, olive oil and grain.

The most popular region for diving is Crete's north coast, where accessibility and sea conditions are more favourable, but many diving outfits also operate on south coast sites where there is a distinct upping of the ante on diving's sense of adventure.

Some of the more interesting easy snorkelling is around the sunken city of Olous near Elounda (p158), which can be accessed from the shore. Bali and Panormo (p100), Ammoudara and Malia (p145), Plakias (p94) and Paleohora (p61) are popular diving sites.

Several diving centres offer courses from beginners to PADI-certification. It's wise to call at least a day in advance to book a dive.

Dive Operators

» **Agia Pelagia** Stay Wet Diving Center (☑2897 042 683; www.staywet.gr)

» **Agios Nikolaos** Happy Divers (☑28410 82546; www.happydivers.gr) On the beach of the Coral Hotel and at Plaka and Elounda. Crete Underwater Center (☑28410 22406; www.creteunderwatercenter.com) In the Mirabello Hotel. Pelagos Dive Centre (☑28410 24376; www.divecrete.com) In the Minos Beach Art Hotel.

» **Bali** Hippocampos (☑28340 94193; www.hippocampos.com) Near the port.

» **Hania** Blue Adventures Diving (☑28210 40608; www.blueadventuresdiving.gr; Daskalogianni 69)

» **Iraklio** Diver's Club (☑2810 811 755; www.diversclub-crete.gr; Agia Pelagia); Stay Wet Diving Center (☑2897 042 683; www.staywet.gr; Mononaftis)

» **Plakias** Kalypso Rock's Palace Dive Center (☑28310 20990; www.kalypsodivingcenter.com; Eleftheriou Venizelou 42); Dive Together Crete (☑28320 32313, 6974031441; http://crete.dive2gether.com; Dimos Finika); Phoenix Diving Club (☑28320 31206; www.scubacrete.com)

UNDERSEA UTOPIA

The diving landscape of Crete is superb with a fascinating mix of natural features, rocks, reefs, caverns, cliffs and shining sand. Sea life on view includes the beautiful 'wallpaper' of marine plants, red and green algae, corals, sea anemones and sponges that coat undersea rocks and reefs, while the often variegated volcanic rocks of Crete create a kaleidoscope of undersea colour. You stand a good chance of spotting a roll-call of favourite fish and crustaceans including octopus, cuttlefish, squid, sea horses, lobster, moray, scorpionfish, snapper, bream and even stingrays.

» **Rethymno** Paradise Diving Center (☑28310 26317; www.diving-center.gr; Eleftheriou Venizelou 57)

Sea Kayaking

Crete's south coast has become increasingly popular for sea-kayaking trips. Between Paleohora and Hora Sfakion, especially, the coast is dramatic and fascinating and there are plenty of places to pull ashore at remote beaches and coves. However, there are not many kayaking operators on Crete and the tendency is for multi-day expeditions catering for groups, with accommodation included along the way. It's worth enquiring about day trips, however, and you may even be able to hire a canoe for the day if you have evidence of personal expertise. Some trips combine kayaking with hiking. Check out:

» **Hania Alpine Travel** (☑28210 50939, 6932252890; www.alpine.gr; Boniali 11-19) Based in Hania.

» **Loutro Nature Maniacs** (☑28250 91017; www.naturemaniacs.com) Runs sea kayaking along the south coast.

» **Driros Beach** (☑6944932760; www.spinalonga -windsurf.com) At Plaka, near Elounda. Rents kayaks by the hour and day.

Windsurfing

Windsurfing, or sailboarding, as the dedicated call it, is one of the most exhilarating of all water sports. It is not an easy sport to master although, even for beginners, some success can be achieved in a first lesson. A lot of practice, however, and much skill is needed before you get anywhere near the spectacular freestyle and wave jumping of the experts. But even in the early stages of learning, this is an exciting sport and enjoying it off the beautiful beaches of Crete is a bonus. Stand up, hang on and fly!

The best windsurfing in Crete is at Kouremenos Beach (p167), north of Palekastro in Sitia. Kouremenos is affected by the *meltemi*, the summer wind that can blow fiercely throughout the Aegean, and this wind coupled with a local funnelling effect creates some ideal windsurfing conditions. Windsurfing is also good in Almyrida (p75), near Hania.

For more information about windsurfing in Greece check out the Hellenic Windsurfing Association (☑2103 230 330; Filellinon St, Athens).

Key local operators:

» **Driros Beach** (☑6944932760; www.spinalonga -windsurf.com) At Plaka, near Elounda.

» **Freak Windsurf** (☑28430 61116, 6979254967; www.freak-surf.com) At Kouremenos.

Yachting

To sail round Crete on a well-found yacht is a glorious experience, but unless you are an experienced yachting fan with your own boat, the answer is usually a charter trip. Some companies in Crete do offer daily sailing excursions and most commercial tourist offices will have information on sailing. Try:

» **Amazing Sailing in Crete** (☑6944586475; www.amazingsailingingreece .com) Based in Elounda.

» **Chania Sailing** (☑28210 72790, 6936869912; www.chaniasailing.com; Nerokourou 129) Based in Hania.

Travel with Children

Sun, sea and sand – and other children – are the main ingredients of a happy family holiday – at least as far as the kids are concerned. But in Crete, parents can mix the seaside with a number of other attractions that entertain and inform, and that can be tailored to fit the whole family.

Crete for Kids

Throughout Crete, as in most parts of Greece, children are revered. It all goes back to village life and to the close-knit values that were required for simple survival throughout Crete's long and often difficult history. You'll find that this terrific interest and affection for children will extend to your kids in tavernas, cafes and villages.

Beaches

Most big resorts have developed beside accessible, shallow and easily serviced swathes of clean sand and can be relied on to meet all expectations for family fun. You need to be more careful at isolated beaches and coves that may have potential hazards such as hidden reefs and offshore currents.

Hikes, Bikes & Horses

Holidays are for taking it easy, but there's nothing like a bit of outdoor action and Crete is bursting at the seams with potential. Apart from the more strenuous gorge and mountain walks, such as Samaria, there are numerous options to suit the family. You

SAFETY

Crete is generally safe from physical hazards but there are some aspects of life that may catch you off guard, especially where children are concerned.

» Be careful on roads where there are no pavements or where parked cars obstruct movement.

» At night watch out for unlit minor roadworks, cavities in pavements and protruding masonry.

» Always watch youngsters in ancient sites, especially castles, where there may be no safety fences.

» If hiring a car, check for agencies that have child seats available and fit the seats yourself.

can go with a local guide or simply opt for a short there-and-back along one of the more accessible gorges or take a gentler stroll around a mountain village. The same goes for cycling, while the horse-riding establishments featured in the guide are excellent for tailoring sessions to all ages.

Museums & Attractions

The very word museum may sound the death knell of interest for under-tens – never mind teenagers – but several of Crete's museums have sections aimed at youngsters. One of the best is Iraklio's Natural History Museum, where the Discovery Centre is aimed entirely at kids and is crammed with interactive features.

Another excellent attraction is the splendid Cretaquarium, where youngsters will love the shark tank, the jellyfish tank and the hands-on pool. The nearby beach is a bonus.

Eating Out

Greek tavernas, especially in villages, are kid friendly and many offer child-sized portions. Greek cuisine may not always appeal to youngsters (there's always *patties tighanites*, aka chips, as well as fast food), but dining out in Crete can be a good way to encourage them towards healthy eating. Some mezedhes dishes that kids might grow to love include: *tiropitakia* – cheese parcels in filo pastry; *gigantes* – lima beans cooked in a delicious

sauce; *salingaria* – snails with onion and tomato; dolmadhes – flavoured rice wrapped in vine leaves; and *saganaki* – skillet-fried cheese.

Children's Highlights
Awesome Beaches

» **Elafonisi** Fun bathing in tiny lagoons amid beautiful surroundings.

» **Bali** A series of accessible coves with all services.

» **Kato Gouves** Rock pools and clear water for young explorers.

» **Vaï** Palm tree paradise; quietest outside August.

» **Paleohora** Choice of two town beaches with safe bathing.

Outdoor Adventures

» **Boat trips** Along Hania's south coast or round Elounda in Lasithi.

» **Hiking** Short sections of easy gorges like Zakros or Agia Irini.

» **Kite flying** On quiet beaches.

» **Horse riding** At Avdou, below the Lasithi Plateau.

» **Caves** Visit Dikteon Cave on the Lasithi Plateau or Skotino Cave near Hersonisos.

Interactive Attractions

» **Water City** Enjoy the water fun park at Anopoli, southeast of Iraklio.

» **Natural History Museum** Visit the exciting children's section in Iraklio's imaginative museum.

» **Agora** Browse through Hania's lively daily market.

» **Cretaquarium** Get close and personal with magical sea creatures near Iraklio.

» **Fortezza** Explore Rethymno's Venetian fortress.

» **Aqua World Aquarium** See finny fish and slithery snakes at Hersonisos.

Planning
When to Go

Crete means fun in the sun, and for teens the summer season has the most going for it. For younger kids and toddlers, however, it's worth thinking about spring, early summer and autumn as being the time to go; the sun is not too strong, but temperatures should be pleasantly warm.

Accommodation

Big resort-style hotels tend to open later than independent accommodation (many as late as June), but they are usually a good bet since the best of them take children into account. There are some excellent small family hotels and pensions in the smaller resorts, however, and these can often be a great option.

Accommodation is cheaper in the off seasons, potentially quieter, and locals have more time to chat.

Don't Forget

» Sunscreen – and plenty of it!

» Portable change mat and hand-wash gel – nappy-changing facilities are rare.

regions at a glance

The birthplace of Zeus, Crete is a vast and multifaceted island whose sun-blessed landscape is a quilt of soaring mountains, dramatic gorges and stunning beaches.

The north coast, with its nearly uninterrupted strip of beach resorts, has great infrastructure and gets the most visitors.

The rugged interior, by contrast, is largely untouched by mass tourism. A dreamy mosaic of sleepy villages, terraced vineyards and fertile valleys, dotted with Byzantine churches and historic monasteries, the interior invites exploration at a leisurely pace.

Those with a sense of adventure will be enchanted by the largely untamed south, where serpentine roads dead-end in isolated coves tucked within indented coastlines, and the landscape is sliced by steep gorges where rare plants and animals thrive.

Hania

History ✓✓✓
Beaches ✓✓
Activities ✓✓✓

Venetian Chic

The splendid Venetian port of Hania is bursting with colour and the faded pomp appropriate to the former maritime empire of Venice. Trace your way down the massive stone walls, past the arsenals and shipyards (now housing stylish galleries), and gaze over the waterfront, drink in hand.

Crystal-Clear Seas

Embraced by the open Mediterranean (next stop, Spain!) western Crete has pristine, crystal-clear waters, heated to almost tropical temperatures on shallow sandy beaches like Elafonisi, Balos and Falasarna.

Ultimate Survival

The White Mountains south of Hania comprise Crete's wildest terrain, interspersed with deep gorges, labyrinthine caves and raw cliffs. Whether you're after white-knuckle driving, rock climbing or even (way) off-piste skiing in winter, this is the place to go.

p38

Rethymno

History ✓✓
Beaches ✓✓
Scenery ✓✓✓

History
All phases of Cretan history are omnipresent in Rethymno, whose eponymous main town is itself a pretty pastiche of Venetian and Ottoman architecture. A cave associated with Zeus, monasteries that stood firm against the Turks, and mountain villages drenched in age-old traditions will leave you wanting more.

Remote Shores
There's something otherworldly about Rethymno's corrugated south coast, where craggy inlets embrace perfect little beaches that are often footprint-free. This is the place to dig your toes in the sand and indulge in island dreams.

Jaw-Dropping Views
Lorded over by Crete's highest peak, the often snow-capped Mt Psiloritis, Rethymno will delight shutterbugs with dazzling vistas of dramatic gorges, tranquil valleys and velvety hills blanketed with olive groves, vineyards and wildflowers.

p77

Iraklio

Ancient Sites ✓✓✓
Beaches ✓✓
Kids' Activities ✓✓✓

Minoan Marvels
Endowed with the greatest concentration of Minoan ruins, Iraklio is a mecca for archaeology fans. Stand in awe of the achievements of Europe's oldest civilisation when surveying the palaces of Knossos, Malia, Phaestos and Agia Triada, plus scores of minor sites.

Life's a Beach
No matter whether you like your sandy strand infused with a party vibe or quiet and remote, there's a beach waiting for you to spread your towel.

Childish Delights
Not only do Cretans love kids, in Iraklio they've also come up with myriad ways to entertain them in grand style, be it by letting them frolic in or out on the sea or by taking them to enchanting aquariums, adrenalin-packed water parks, placid playgrounds and hands-on museums.

p109

Lasithi

Ancient Sites ✓✓✓
Beaches ✓✓
Hiking ✓✓

Lesser-Known Minoans
Lasithi may not have the painted and polished ruins of Knossos, but the Minoan sites of Gournia and Kato Zakros evoke a sometimes deeper awareness. Their wild surroundings and the haunting sense of a lost world fire the imagination towards a more personal sense of place and of the past.

Beyond the Main Beach
Lasithi's beaches are generally free of too much organised lounging, although famous venues, such as the palm-lined Vaï, draw thick summer crowds. However, there are many hidden coves and small sandy bays where you can still capture a happy sense of pleasurable isolation.

High Hiking
Some of Crete's finest mountains dominate the Lasithi skyline. Their airy summits and deep gorges offer superb hiking and trekking and put you amid the heady scents of wildflowers and aromatic herbs.

p148

Look out for these icons:

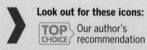 Our author's recommendation

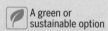 A green or sustainable option

 No payment required

See the Index for a full list of destinations covered in this book.

On the Road

Hania Χανιά

Includes »

Best Places to Eat

» Portes (p47)

» Kyma (p64)

» Kouzina E.P.E. (p47)

» Papadakis (p69)

» Platanos (p58)

Best Places to Stay

» Hotel Doma (p178)

» Milia (p64)

» Casa Delfino (p178)

» Stavroula Palace (p183)

Why Go?

The west of Crete stands apart in so many ways. Full of big mountains, grandiose legends and memorials to great battles past, it is presided over by the preening (but slightly melancholic) port city of Hania, once Venice's jewel of a capital and full of arty boutique hotels, galleries and great eateries. But there's much more to this region: it boasts the grandest gorge in Europe, the continent's southernmost possession (tranquil Gavdos, a remote island nearer to Africa than Greece), and mountain villages hardly affected by modernity. The steep mountains that ripple across the west and into the southern sea guarantee that the region generally remains untouched by the excesses of tourism. The offbeat, sometimes gruff, but always hospitable west Cretans have stayed true to form too – from the olive oil to the moustachioed elders, if you want to see the traditional Crete, Hania and the west is definitely the place.

When to Go

Cretan summers are hot, hot, hot – if you're looking for buzzing crowds, nightlife and crowded beaches, come in July and August.

Spring is a great time to visit for outdoor activities, as the climate's temperate and the mountain wildflowers are in full splendour.

The autumn months are slightly quieter, but the weather is still lovely and the waters – having warmed all summer – are positively tropical, making September ideal for luxuriating on the sands.

Winters are short (but often rainy), though thrill-seeking skiers will find great off-piste adventures in the Lefka Ori (White Mountains).

Getting Around

Hania town is easily navigable on foot, and getting around the wider area is easy too. Air-conditioned KTEL buses depart Hania regularly for other towns and villages in the region, plus the major beaches, and towns elsewhere in Crete. As prices have crept up, however, buses are only economical for solo travellers – for several people planning on doing lots of local travel, hiring a car makes more sense (you can pick it up and drop it off wherever you decide, too).

THREE PERFECT DAYS

Day One

Rise early to beat the crowds and contemplate Hania's **Venetian harbour** with a coffee, then visit the fascinating **Byzantine & Post-Byzantine Collection of Hania** and the **Naval Museum** by the Venetian **Firkas Fortress** before enjoying a quick *mayirefta* (ready-cooked) lunch in the spiffy Splantzia quarter. Then take a drive past olive groves to the superlative beach of **Falasarna**, on the western edge of the island. You'll be back in time for dinner at one of Hania's posh outdoor eateries, with wine and grilled octopus under the stars.

Day Two

Burn off the pounds gained from excessive Cretan cookery with a full-day march through **Samaria Gorge**. The early-morning drive (or bus) leads to **Omalos**, where Europe's grandest canyon sprawls southward. Along the way, look out for the elusive *kri-kri* (Crete's shy wild goat) up in the cliffs, and watch the birds of prey circle in the hope of nibbling on a heatstruck hiker. After wriggling through the Iron Gates (Sidiroportes), the gorge's narrowest point, you'll find salvation at **Agia Roumeli**, where the boat goes to **Hora Sfakion** for the bus back to Hania.

Day Three

From the offbeat southwestern beach town of **Paleohora**, a morning boat trip to **Elafonisi** leaves you a full day to savour the splendid sands of variegated tones, and the Libyan Sea's lapping warm waters. The afternoon boat has you back in plenty of time for a hearty dinner of roast lamb and wild greens, before indulging in Paleohora's fun nightlife (often, live Cretan music played on the bouzouki and *lyra*, a kind of violin).

Accommodation

For sleeping options throughout this region, please see the Accommodation chapter (p175).

DON'T MISS

Azogires, north of Paleohora, is a memorable village with a deep gorge, good-humoured locals, caverns once inhabited by ascetics, and wooded waterfalls said to be haunted by wickedly flirtatious Nereids.

Best Beaches

» Elafonisi (p73) – sublime southwestern beach famed for its pink sands

» Balos (p70) – stunningly clear lagoon of translucent blues and greens, on the Gramvousa Peninsula

» Falasarna (p71) – the most fun waves in the west slam into this long, sandy beach

Best Gorges

» Samaria Gorge (p53) – the biggest and most popular

» Trypiti Gorge (p56) – less visited, but tougher

» Imbros Gorge (p55) – a thickly forested, shorter cousin of Samaria

Resources

» www.chania.gr

» www.eoshanion.gr

» www.west-crete.com

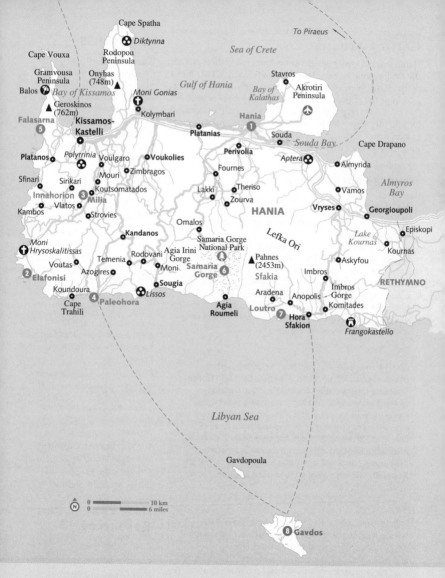

Hania Highlights

1 Take in Hania's splendid **Venetian harbour** (p41) with a coffee on the waterfront

2 Luxuriate on the fine sands of **Elafonisi** (p73) in the remote southwest

3 Get back to nature up in the mountains at Crete's prime ecospot, the traditional settlement of **Milia** (p64)

4 Enjoy live violin- and bouzouki-driven Cretan music in its natural habitat in **Paleohora** (p61), in Hania's southwest

5 Battle the waves at Crete's most entertaining beach, **Falasarna** (p71) on the northwestern coast

6 Soldier on down **Samaria**

Gorge (p53) on the 16km hike to the southern sea

7 Go by boat to escape the masses in the sparkling southern hamlet of **Loutro** (p60)

8 Get (really) away from it all on the sparsely populated island of **Gavdos** (p66), 65km south of Paleohora

HANIA XANIA

POP 55,850

Hania is Crete's most evocative city, with its pretty Venetian quarter, criss-crossed by narrow lanes, culminating at a magnificent harbour. Remnants of Venetian and Turkish architecture abound, with old town houses now restored, transformed into atmospheric restaurants and boutique hotels.

Although all this beauty means the old town is deluged with tourists in summer, it's still a great place to unwind. Excellent local handicrafts mean there's good shopping, too, with the most authentic found in the Splantzia quarter. Along Zambeliou, Theotokopoulou and Angelou streets, roofless Venetian buildings have been turned into outdoor restaurants. Pockmarked with galleries and museums, the Venetian harbour is a good place for a stroll.

Crete's second-biggest city, Hania is also the major transit point for hikers walking Samaria Gorge, and is the main transport hub for all western destinations.

History

The important Minoan settlement of Kydonia was centred on the hill to the east of Hania's harbour, between Akti Tombazi and Karaoli Dimitriou. Kydonia was destroyed along with the rest of Crete's Minoan civilisation in 1450 BC, but was rebuilt and later flourished as an ancient Greek city state during Hellenistic times. It continued to prosper under Roman and Byzantine rule.

Hania, along with the rest of Crete, was claimed by the rising power of Venice following the Fourth Crusade (1204), and the city was renamed La Canea. After briefly losing the city to their Genoese rivals in 1266, the Venetians finally wrested it back in 1290. They constructed massive fortifications to protect the city from pirates, making the city a key strategic hub in their Mediterranean trading empire for three-and-a-half centuries.

In 1645 Hania was captured by the Ottoman Empire, after a two-month siege. The Turks made it the seat of the Turkish Pasha until they were forced out finally in 1898. During the Tourkokratia (Turkish occupation of Greece), the city's churches were converted into mosques and the architectural style of the town changed, becoming more oriental, with wooden walls, latticed windows and minarets (two survive today).

When Crete became independent of Turkish rule in 1898, Hania was declared the island's capital by Europe's Great Powers. It remained so until 1971, when the administration was transferred to Iraklio.

The WWII Battle of Crete largely took place along the coast to the west of Hania. The town itself was heavily bombed during WWII, particularly around Ancient Kydonia, but enough of the old town survives for it to be regarded as Crete's most beautiful city.

⊙ Sights

Venetian Harbour
HISTORICAL SITE

The massive fortifications built by the Venetians to protect their city remain impressive. The best-preserved section is the western wall, running from the **Firkas Fortress** to the **Siavo Bastion**. It was part of a defensive system begun in 1538 by engineer Michele Sanmichele, who also designed Iraklio's defences. Entrance to the fortress is via the gates next to the Naval Museum. From the top of the bastion you can enjoy some fine views of the old town.

The **Venetian lighthouse** at the entrance to the harbour has been restored, though the new lighting along the sea wall could have been more subtle. It's a pleasant 1.5km walk around the sea wall to get there, especially in the early evening (you can cheat by taking the barge from the Fortezza cafe).

On the eastern side of the inner harbour you will see the prominent **Mosque of Kioutsouk Hasan** (also known as the Mosque of Janissaries), which has been restored and houses regular exhibitions.

Archaeological Museum
MUSEUM

(⏹28210 90334; Halidon 30; admission €2; ☺8.30am-3pm Tue-Sun, to 7.30pm May-Oct but call to confirm) Hania's Archaeological Museum is housed in the superb 16th-century Venetian Church of San Francisco that became a

ROAD DISTANCES (km)

	Omalos	Hora Sfakion	Kissamos	Paleohora
Hora Sfakion	114			
Kissamos	98	124		
Paleohora	131	157	51	
Hania	44	70	54	87

WANT MORE?

Head to Lonely Planet (www.lonely planet.com/greece/crete/hania) for planning advice, author recommendations, traveller reviews and insider tips.

mosque under the Turks, a movie theatre in 1913 and a munitions depot for the Germans during WWII. The museum houses a well-displayed collection of finds from western Crete dating from the neolithic to the Roman eras. Artefacts from 3400 to 1200 BC, to the left as you enter the museum, include tablets with Linear A script. There is also some exquisite pottery from the Geometric Age (1200–800 BC) and a case of bull figurines. Among the Hellenistic and Roman exhibits, the statue of Diana is particularly impressive. A marble fountain in the pretty courtyard decorated with lions' heads testifies to the Venetian tradition, while the Turkish fountain is a relic from the building's days as a mosque.

A combined ticket with the Byzantine & Post-Byzantine Collection of Hania costs €3.

Naval Museum   MUSEUM
(☑28210 91875; Akti Koundourioti; admission €3; ☻9am-7pm Mon-Fri, 9am-4pm Sat, 10am-6pm Sun) The Naval Museum has an interesting collection of model ships dating from the Bronze Age, and naval instruments, paintings, photographs and memorabilia from the Battle of Crete. It is housed in the Firkas Fortress, once the old Turkish prison.

Maritime Museum of Crete   MUSEUM
(☑28210 91875; Akti Defkaliona; admission €2; ☻10am-2pm & 5-9pm) Housed in the former Venetian shipyards *(neoria)*, this museum documents ancient and traditional shipbuilding through pictures and replicas – including the authentic replica of a Minoan ship that sailed from Crete to Athens for the Athens 2004 Olympics ceremonies.

FREE Neorio tou Moro   ART GALLERY
(☑28210 40265; Akti Defkaliona; ☻11am-2pm & 7-10pm) Just beyond the Maritime Museum, the Neorio tou Moro is a hip new art gallery that opened in 2011, with temporary modern art exhibits. It's housed in another classic Venetian shipyard (sharing

the space with Hania's long-established Sailing Club), and at the time of writing there were plans for concerts to be held in the space too.

Byzantine & Post-Byzantine Collection of Hania   MUSEUM
(☑28210 96046; Theotokopoulou; admission €2; ☻8.30am-3pm Tue-Sun) The Byzantine museum is in the impressively restored Church of San Salvatore. It has a small but fascinating collection of artefacts, icons, jewellery and coins, including a fine segment of a mosaic floor for an early-Christian basilica and a prized icon of St George slaying the dragon. The building has a mixed bag of interesting architectural features from its various occupiers.

A combined ticket with the Archaeological Museum costs €3.

Cretan House Folklore Museum   MUSEUM
(☑28210 90816; Halidon 46; admission €2; ☻9.30am-3pm & 6-9pm) Hania's interesting Folklore Museum contains a selection of crafts and implements including weavings with traditional designs.

FREE Historical Museum and Archives   MUSEUM
(☑28210 52606; Sfakianaki 20; ☻9am-1pm Mon-Fri) The Historical Museum and Archives of Hania, about a five-minute walk southeast of the old quarter, traces Crete's war-torn history with a series of exhibits focusing on the struggle against the Turks. There are also exhibits relating to the German occupation and a folklore collection.

FREE Great Arsenal   ART GALLERY
(☑28210 40101; www.kam-arsenali.gr; Plateia Katehaki) The stunningly restored Venetian arsenal is now home to the Centre for Mediterranean Architecture, which hosts regular events and exhibitions.

Etz Hayyim Synagogue   SYNAGOGUE
(Parodos Kondylaki; www.etz-hayyim-hania.org; ☻10am-8pm Tue-Fri, 5-8pm Sun, 10am-3pm & 5-8pm Mon) The restored synagogue has a moving memorial to the Jews of Hania who were annihilated by the Nazis.

Municipal Art Gallery   ART GALLERY
(☑28210 92294; www.pinakothiki-chania.gr; Halidon 98; admission €2, free Wed; ☻10am-2pm & 7-10pm Mon-Fri, 10am-2pm Sat) Hania's three-level art gallery hosts exhibitions of modern Greek art.

ΦΟΡΟΛΟΓΙΚΗ ΑΠΟΔΕΙΞΗ
ΕΝΑΡΞΗ
ΠΟΤΑ-ΜΠΑΧΑΡΙΚΑ
ΠΑΡΑΔΟΣΙΑΚΑ ΠΡΟΙΟΝΤΑ
ΕΜΜ. Κ. ΣΤΑΘΑΚΗΣ
ΟΔΟΣ 1866 ΑΡ.12 ΗΡΑΚΛΕΙΟ

ΑΦΜ:063609316

ΔΟΥ ΗΡΑΚΛΕΙΟΥ

ΤΗΛ.2810-281343

Α/Α ΦΗΜ:01 ΧΕΙΡΙΣΤΗΣ 1
ΚΥΡ 10- 5-2015 - 11:53

ΠΟΤΑ 23%	€ 7,00	23.00%
ΜΠΑΧΑΡΙΚΑ	€ 11,00	13.00%
ΜΠΑΧΑΡΙΚΑ	€ 2,20	13.00%
ΜΠΑΧΑΡΙΚΑ	€ 2,00	13.00%

4 ΣΥΝΟΛΟ   € 22,20

ΜΕΤΡΗΤΑ   € 22,20

ΣΥΝΟΛ. ΠΟΣΟΤΗΤΑ: 4
ΠΛΗΘΟΣ ΑΠΟΔ.   16
ΠΡΟΟΔ. ΑΠΟΔ.   2218
          DCB 14000963
ΠΑΗΣ
D3A50D3C1D465C915AEC
688C0D4021D373A9790B

ΦΟΡΟΛΟΓΙΚΗ ΑΠΟΔΕΙΞΗ-ΛΗΞΗ
ΕΥΧΑΡΙΣΤΟΥΜΕ
THANK YOU

ΦΟΡΟΛΟΓΙΚΗ ΑΠΟΔΕΙΞΗ
ΕΝΑΡΞΗ
ΠΟΤΑ-ΜΠΑΧΑΡΙΚΑ
ΠΑΡΑΔΟΣΙΑΚΑ ΠΡΟΙΟΝΤΑ
ΕΜΜ Κ ΣΤΑΒΑΚΗΣ
ΟΛΟΣ 1866 ΑΡ. 12 ΗΡΑΚΛΕΙΟ

ΑΦΜ 063609316
ΔΟΥ ΗΡΑΚΛΕΙΟΥ

ΤΗΛ 2810-281343

Α-Α ΦΗΜ 01 ΧΕΙΡΙΣΤΗΣ 1
ΚΥΡ 10-5-2015 - 11 53

ΠΟΤΑ 23%   € 7,00 23 00%
ΜΠΑΧΑΡΙΚΑ € 11,00 13 00%
ΜΠΑΧΑΡΙΚΑ € 2,20 13 00%
ΜΠΑΧΑΡΙΚΑ € 2 00 13 00%

4 ΣΥΝΟΛΟ   € 22,20

ΜΕΤΡΗΤΑ   € 22.20

ΣΥΝΟΛ ΠΟΣΟΤΗΤΑ   4
ΠΛΗΘΟΣ ΑΠΟΔ   18
ΠΡΟΟΔ ΑΠΟΔ   2218
DCB 14000963

ΠΑΗΤΣ
D3A500302104503C315AEG
E8BC00402109734879Q8

ΦΟΡΟΛΟΓΙΚΗ ΑΠΟΔΕΙΞΗ-ΛΗΞΗ
ΕΥΧΑΡΙΣΤΟΥΜΕ
THANK YOU

FREE Monastiri Tou Karolou ART GALLERY
(28210 50172; Daliani 22; 11am-late, closed Sun) Along Daliani, you will see one of Hania's two remaining **minarets** and pass this restored 16th-century structure. In addition to the courtyard cafe, which hosts occasional live music and cultural events, the old monastery is now the home, atelier and hairdressing salon of Hania's famous formerly Paris-based celebrity hairdresser-cum-sculptor Karolos Kambelopoulos. There are sometimes art exhibits on the 2nd floor too.

Church of Agios Nikolaos CHURCH
(Plateia 1821; 7am-noon & 4-7pm) Hania's other remaining minaret, past a *kafeneio* (coffee house) on Plateia 1821, is quite memorably attached to this church. Towering over the church's opposite end is a bell tower. Strung along in the air across the centre of it all are flapping, intertwined flags of Greece and Byzantium, a cheery display of blues and yellows that seems to festively reassert the final victory of Orthodoxy over both former occupiers, the schismatic Venetians and the infidel Turks.

The church's foundations were laid in 1205 by Venetians, but Franciscan monks (in 1320) can probably be credited with the massive structure's curving ceiling and array of stained-glass windows, which filter a beautiful, kaleidoscopic flood of colour across the floor in late afternoon. In 1645 the Ottomans made the church into a mosque, but the Orthodox Church recovered it in 1918. Nearby you can see the restored Venetian **Church of San Rocco**.

Eleftherios Venizelos Residence & Museum MUSEUM
(28210 56008; Plateia Helena Venizelou; admission €2; 11.30am-1.30pm daily, plus 6-8pm Mon-Fri) Some 1.5km east of the old town, in the Halepa neighbourhood, the Eleftherios Venizelos Residence & Museum preserves the great statesman's home in splendid fashion, with original furnishings, maps and other information. Staff provide a guided tour. Take a public bus, or taxi (€3 to €6), to get there. Hours are reduced in winter.

FREE Ancient Kydonia ANCIENT SITE
You can see excavation works at the site of Ancient Kydonia to the east of the old harbour at the junction of Kanevaro and Kandaloneou. There are recently discovered ancient dwellings to see, plus general info about Minoan civilisation.

As much of Kydonia's ruins lie beneath the modern city, excavations have been limited and thus yielded fewer impressive finds than at Iraklio-area Minoan sites such as Knossos and Phaestos; nevertheless, the discovery of clay tablets with Linear B script has led archaeologists to believe that Kydonia was both a palace site and an important town. In 2004, some 50 Late Minoan graves were found in the Agios Ioannis area, part of the cemetery of Ancient Kydonia. Excavations are continuing.

Agora MARKET
Hania's magnificent covered Agora (Municipal Market) has some excellent eateries (see p48) and is worth a visit even if you don't want to shop. Sadly, the central bastion of the city wall was demolished to make way for this fine 1911 cruciform creation, modelled after the market in Marseille.

Activities

Those looking for free information on all outdoor sports, including serious climbing in the Lefka Ori, mountain refuges and the E4 trail, should first visit the Hania branch of the Greek Mountaineering Association, EOS (28210 44647; www.eoshanion.gr; Tzanakaki 90; 8.30am-10pm). Along with providing information, EOS also runs regular weekend excursions.

Hiking, Climbing & Cycling
Trekking Plan HIKING, CYCLING
(28210 60861; www.cycling.gr; Agia Marina) In Agia Marina, 8km southwest of the old town, Trekking Plan offers hikes to Agia

---

HANIA FOR CHILDREN

If your five-year-old has lost interest in Venetian architecture, head to the **public garden** between Tzanakaki and Dimokratias, where there's a playground, and a shady cafe (but alas, no more goats or zoo). Six kilometres south of town the giant water park **Limnoupolis** (28210 33246; Varypetro; day pass adult/6-12yr €17/12, afternoon pass €12/9; 10am-7pm) has enough slides and rides to keep kids amused, and cafes and pool bars for adults. Buses leave regularly from the KTEL bus station (€2.10).

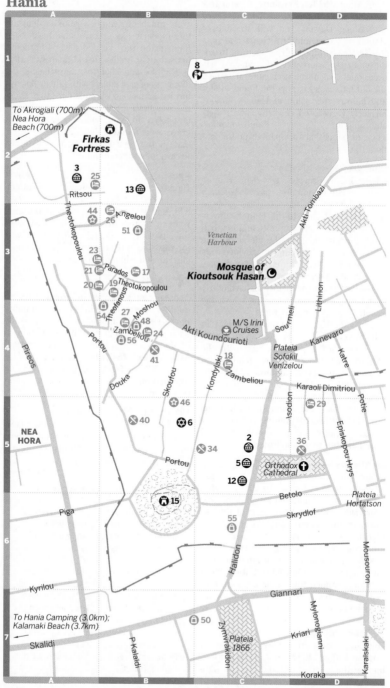

Firkas Fortress

To Akrogiali (700m);
Nea Hora
Beach (700m)

3 🏛

25 🍴

Ritsou

13 🏛

44 ⭐

Angelou

26 🍴

51 🔒

Theotokopoulou

23 🍴

21 🍴 Parados 🍴 17

20 🍴 Theotokopoulou

19 🍴

54 🔒 Theofanous

27 🍴 Moshou

48 🍴

Zambeliou

56 🔒 24

41 ❌

Venetian Harbour

Mosque of Kioutsouk Hasan ☪

Akti Tombazi

M/S Irini Cruises

Akti Koundourioti

Plateia Sofokil Venizelou

18

Zambeliou

Sourmeli

Lithinou

Kanevaro

Karaoli Dimitriou

Katre

Potie

Isodion

29 🍴

36 ❌

Skoufou

Kondylaki

46 ⚽

40 ❌

6 ⚽

34 ❌

2 🏛

5 🏛

12 🏛

Orthodox Cathedral ✛

Episkopou Hrys

Betolo

Plateia Hortatson

NEA HORA

Pireos

Portou

Douka

Portou

🏰 **15**

Piga

55 🔒

Skrydlof

Mousouron

Halidon

To Hania Camping (3.0km);
Kalamaki Beach (3.7km)

Kyrilou

Skalidi

P Kalaidi

Giannari

50 🔒

Zymvrakidon

Plateia 1866

Mylonogianni

Kriari

Karaiskaki

Koraka

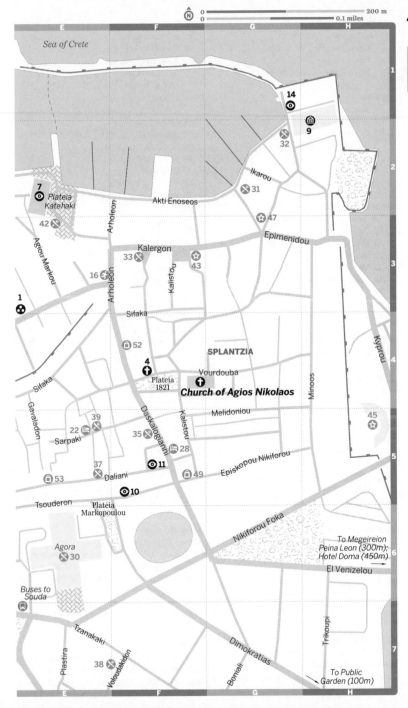

Sea of Crete

200 m
0.1 miles

14

9

32

7
Plateia
Katehaki

42

31

Ikarou

Akti Enoseos

47

Epimenidou

Agiou Markou

Arholeon

Kalergon

33

Kalistou

16

43

Arholeon

1

Sifaka

52

SPLANTZIA

Kyprou

Minoos

4
Plateia
1821

Vourdouba

Church of Agios Nikolaos

45

Sifaka

Gavaladon

Daskalogianni

Kalistou

Melidoniou

39

22

Sarpaki

35

28

37

11

49

Episkopou Nikiforou

53

Daliani

Tsouderon

10

Plateia
Markopoulou

Nikiforou Foka

To Megeireion
Peina Leon (300m);
Hotel Doma (450m)

Agora

30

El Venizelou

Buses to
Souda

Plastira

Tzanakaki

Voloudakidon

38

Dimokratias

Bonibali

Trikoupi

To Public
Garden (100m)

Irini and Imbros Gorges, and climbs of Mt Gingilos, as well as canyoning, rappelling, rock climbing, and kayaking and mountain-biking tours.

Alpine Travel   HIKING
(☏28210 50939; 6932252890; www.alpine.gr; Boniali 11-19) Organises a range of ecotourism, mountaineering and hiking programs.

Hellas Bike Tours   CYCLING
(☏28210 60858; www.hellasbike.net; Agia Marina) In Agia Marina, this group hires out bikes and leads half- and full-day bike tours around the region.

Diving

Blue Adventures Diving   DIVING
(☏28210 40608; www.blueadventuresdiving.gr; Arholeon 11) This outfit offers a PADI certifi-cation course (€370) and daily diving trips around Hania (two dives €75), including beginner dives. There are also snorkelling trips and cruise options if you just want to go along for the ride.

Swimming

The town beach at **Nea Hora** is crowded but generally clean if you need to cool off and get some rays, while that of Koum Kapi is less used (and less clean). For better swimming, keep heading west and you'll come to the beaches (in order) of **Agioi Apostoli**, **Hrysi Akti** and **Kalamaki** (about 3.5km). There are regular local buses heading there and all the way to Platanias and beyond.

👉 Tours

Boat excursions from the harbour access the tiny nearby islands of Agii Theodoroi and Lazaretto and the Gulf of Hania, though all are arguably overpriced. Several operators offer half-hour or one-hour cruises or rides on murky glass-bottomed boats, but they are hardly worth it.

M/S Irini   BOAT TRIPS
(☑28210 52001; cruises €15, sunset cruises €8, under 7yr free) Runs a variety of daily cruises on a lovely 1930s cruiser, including free snorkelling gear, and sunset cruises with complimentary fruit and *raki*.

F/B Alexandros   BOAT TRIPS
(☑28210 71514) Runs daily cruises around Souda Bay that stop at caves and beaches.

🎉 Festivals & Events

In summer, the municipality hosts cultural events around the city, including in the public gardens and at the **open-air theatre** (www .chania.gr) on the outskirts of the city walls (on Kyprou), which has regular music and theatrical performances.

Hania commemorates the **Battle of Crete anniversary** with athletics competitions, folk dancing and ceremonial events during the last week of May.

✖ Eating

Hania has some of the finest restaurants in Crete, some housed in roofless Venetian ruins. As might be expected, most of the prime-position waterfront tavernas are generally mediocre, overpriced and fronted by annoying touts – head for the quieter backstreets for the best food and grog.

TOP CHOICE **Portes**   CRETAN €€
(Portou 48; mains €6-9) Many locals will agree that this is the best place in town for creative Cretan cooking with an international flourish. For years friendly Irishwoman Susanna has been serving exquisite Cretan meals at this superb restaurant in a quiet street in the old town. Try her divine *gavros* (marinated small fish), wild snails, stuffed fish baked in paper, tasty meatballs with leek and tomato,

or pretty much anything from the specials board.

Kouzina E.P.E.   CRETAN €
(Daskalogianni 25; mayirefta €3-7; ⊙noon-8pm) This cheery, bright lunch spot in the Splantzia quarter is a local favourite away from the crowds, serving nourishing *mayirefta* (ready-cooked meals) and grills. The playful name means 'Limited Liability Restaurant', but there's no reason for concern – everything is great, from the sardines and pasticcio to the roast marinated vegetables and veal *stifadho* (veal cooked with onions in a tomato purée).

Megeireion Peina Leon   GREEK €
(El Venizelou 86; mezedhes €3-7; ⊙10am-1am) This friendly place up in the quiet Halepa neighbourhood has great ambience, with big, wood-silled glass doors and original tiled floors. Take your pick from a selection of home-cooked meals including the soft *horta* (wild greens) in olive oil and lemon, mixed cooked vegetables, or stuffed peppers with rice. It also serves the new Cretan-produced beers from Rethymno.

Tamam   GREEK €€
(Zambeliou 49; mains €6-10) Housed in an old *hammam* (Turkish baths), Tamam offers Greek fare with an appropriately Ottoman flourish. Along with a superb selection of vegetarian specialities – try the spicy avocado dip on potato (€6.50) – there are Turkish-inspired dishes such as the *tas kebab* (veal with spices and yoghurt) or the Beyendi chicken with creamy aubergine purée.

Thalassino Ageri   SEAFOOD €€€
(Vivilaki 35; top fish per kg €55; ⊙dinner) It can be tricky to find, but this solitary fish taverna in a tiny port among the ruins of Hania's old tanneries is one of the best eateries in Crete. As well as the superb setting, it has fresh fish and excellent mezedhes such as tender octopus in wine vinegar and melt-in-your-mouth *kalamari* (calamari, squid), as well as a delicious fisherman's salad. Take a taxi or follow El Venizelou around the coast, turning left at Noel St as soon as you veer away from the coast.

Oasis   FAST FOOD €
(Vouloudakidon 2; souvlakia €2; ⊙Mon-Sat, shopping hr only) There are plenty of snack-food and souvlaki places on Halidon, but locals swear by the undeniably tasty souvlakia at

the tiny, old-style Oasis. (As elsewhere in western Crete, specify souvlaki 'kalamaki' to get souvlaki, small cubes of meat grilled on a skewer, instead of *gyros*, meat slivers cooked on a vertical rotisserie.)

Mesogeiako GREEK €
(Daliani 36; mezedhes €3.50-6; ☺6pm-1am) Near the minaret in the revitalised Spantzia quarter, this trendy *mezedhopoleio* (restaurant specialising in mezedhes) serves an array of classic and more creative dishes. Try the fried zucchini flowers, aubergines, pork meatballs and its excellent *raki*.

Doloma GREEK €
(Kalergon 8; mayirefta €4.50-7; ☺Mon-Sat) This unpretentious restaurant tucked behind the harbour is half-hidden amid the vines and foliage surrounding the outdoor terrace. The traditional cooking is faultless. Pick from the various trays of *mayirefta* casseroles and bakes cooked daily, and sample from a good array of local wines.

L'Artigiano Gelateria ICE CREAM €
(Athinagora Plateia; €1.80-4) There is almost always a queue for this very tasty homemade Italian gelati: it has the seal of approval from visitors and locals alike.

Ela CRETAN €€
(Kondylaki 47; mains €8-16; ☺noon-1am) This 14th-century building was a soap factory, then a school, distillery and cheese-processing plant. Now Ela serves up a decent array of Cretan specialities, such as goat with artichokes, while roving musicians create a lively ambience. The tacky board outside tells you it's in every guidebook, but the accolades are not undeserved.

Apostolis I & II SEAFOOD €€€
(Akti Enoseo; fish per kg €40-55) In the quieter eastern harbour, this is a well-respected place for fresh fish and Cretan dishes in two separate buildings. Apostolis II is the more popular as the owner reigns there, but the other store has the same menu at marginally cheaper prices. A seafood platter for two, including salad, is €30. Service is friendly and efficient, and there's a good wine list and harbour setting.

Agora MARKET €
(Municipal Market; ☺8.30am-2pm Mon, Wed & Sat, 8.30am-1.30pm & 6-9pm Tue, Thu & Fri) Hania's famous covered market is a good-value place for self-caterers to stock up on supplies, as well as stop for lunch. It's also good for take-home purchases such as spices, honey, olive oils and wines.

To Karnagio GREEK €€
(Plateia Katehaki 8; Cretan specials €7-12) This is a popular place with outdoor tables near the Great Arsenal. There is a good range of seafood (try the grilled cuttlefish) and classic Cretan dishes, such as octopus *stifadho* (octopus in red tomato and wine sauce), plus a fine wine list.

Pigadi tou Tourkou MIDDLE EASTERN €€
(Sarpaki 1-3; mains €10-14.50; ☺dinner, closed Mon-Tue) Features from this former *hammam*, including the well it's named after ('Well of the Turk'), are incorporated into the cosy design of this popular restaurant, which has dishes inspired by Crete, Morocco and the Middle East. Try the *yiaourtlou* kebab (beef kebab on pitta with Greek yoghurt).

🍷 Drinking & Entertainment

The harbour's lively and prominent waterfront bars and clubs around the mosque are mostly patronised by tourists. There are some lively bars in the streets of the old town. Those seeking real clubs should head 9km to 11km westward out of town to the otherwise unremarkable package tour areas of Agia Marina and Platanias. The most popular clubs at the latter are **Villa Mercedes**, **Utopia** and **Milos**, with top-name DJs, while **Oceanos** is the clubbing fave in Agia Marina.

Fagotto LIVE MUSIC
(Angelou 16; ☺7pm-2am Jul-May) A Hania institution housed in a restored Venetian building, Fagotto offers the smooth sounds of jazz and light rock and blues. Jazz paraphernalia includes a saxophone beer tap. Note that it gets busy only after 10pm.

Synagogi LOUNGE BAR
(Skoufou 15) Housed in a roofless Venetian building that was once a synagogue, this popular lounge bar is a laid-back place to relax and take it all in.

Café Kriti LIVE MUSIC
(Kalergon 22; ☺8pm-late) Also known as Lyra-kia, this rough-and-ready joint features an eclectic, somewhat contrived decor involving saws, pots, ancient sewing machines and animal heads. It delivers live Cretan music (though it is aimed more at tourists than locals).

Ta Duo Lux

CAFE, BAR

(Sarpidona 8; ☺10am-late) Further along the harbour, the arty cafe-bar Ta Duo Lux remains a perennial favourite hang-out for a younger alternative crowd and is popular day and night. Along this strip you will also find Bororo and Hippopotamos.

Koukouvagia

BAR

(Venizelos Graves) If you have wheels, take a 4km drive up the hill to where the great statesman Eleftherios Venizelos is buried. The owl-themed cafe and bar (with an extraordinary owl decor collection) enjoys panoramic views of Hania. It's a cool place to hang out on summer nights. The pitta creations are excellent, as is the large selection of cakes and desserts.

🛍 Shopping

Hania offers some good shopping, especially in the backstreets, particularly around Theotokopoulou. Skrydlof was once the place for authentic Cretan leather boots, but is now more a melange of imported sandals, belts and bags. A very few authentic shops for speciality Cretan items survive, most of them in the Splantzia quarter.

There's also an outdoor *laïki* (street market) on Saturday mornings from 7am to 2pm on Minoos and another market on the waterfront west of the Firkas Fortress on Thursdays.

Most stores in the old town tend to stay open until at least 11pm, while the new town shopping district keeps regular shop hours (see p250).

Crete is famous for its foodstuffs and almost everyone will want to take something home with them. However, those seeking the best local olive oils and thyme honey – typically, sold not in snazzy packaging with silly submerged twigs, but in big unmarked bottles – will find better quality (and prices) at humble local shops in the villages rather than at speciality shops in the cities.

Karistianis

CLOTHING

(Skalidi 9-11) This is the place to go for serious outdoor clothing and hiking shoes; its more hard-core army supply store across the road also sells camping and climbing gear.

Miden Agan

FOOD & DRINK

(Daskalogianni 70; ☺10am-3.30pm Mon & Wed, 10am-2.15pm & 6.15-10pm Tue & Thu-Sat) Food-and-wine lovers are spoiled for choice at this excellent shop, which stocks more than 800 Greek wines, as well as its own wine and liquors. There's a variety of beautifully packaged local traditional gourmet deli foods, including olive oil and honey and its own line of spoon sweets (try the white pumpkin).

Exantas Art Space

SOUVENIRS

(cnr Zambeliou & Moschon; ☺10am-2pm & 6pm-11pm) This classy store has great postcards with old photos, lithographs and engravings, handmade gifts, Cretan music as well as a good range of travel, coffee-table and art books.

Mediterraneo Bookstore

BOOKS

(Akti Koundourioti 57) On the waterfront, this bookshop sells an extensive range of English-language novels and books on Crete, as well as international press.

Giorgos Paterakis

HANDICRAFTS

(Episkopou Nikoforou 13) From a tiny shop in Splantzia, Giorgos is the last maker of authentic Cretan leather boots (€200 to €300 a pair) in town. Cretan men don these knee-length creations typically for weddings, traditional dance and other special occasions, though the sturdy, waterproof nature of the boots makes them sought after by shepherds too.

Nikos Boulamas

HANDICRAFTS

(Daliani 52) It takes four different artisans to make a traditional Cretan knife, and local artisan Nikos Boulamas specialises in crafting the blades that make these deluxe souvenirs go for over €1000. Beware other shops offering real traditional knives – most are just hawking cheap imports passed off as the real thing.

Pelekanakis

BOOKS

(Halidon 98) This classic Hania bookshop sells driving and hiking maps, guidebooks and otherwise hard-to-find books about Crete in 11 languages.

Paraoro

HANDICRAFTS

(Theotokopoulou 16) Stamatis Fasoularis' distinctive series of metal boats are functional as well as decorative, such as his nifty steamship oil burner. The workshop also has unique ceramics by artist Yiorgos Vavatsis, including his trademark skewed drink ware. Bigger gallery pieces are exhibited upstairs.

WORTH A TRIP

THERISO

For a day trip or an alternative route to Omalos, you can take the scenic road to Theriso, 14km from Hania, famous for its connection with Eleftherios Venizelos and the late-19th-century revolutionary period in Crete. Go via the village of Perivolia. This spectacular drive follows a running stream through a green oasis and the 6km Theriso Gorge. At the foot of the Lefka Ori (White Mountains), at 500m above sea level, the village was the site of historical battles against the Turks. These days it is popular for its fine tavernas that host marathon Sunday lunches.

Two tavernas vie for top billing. **O Leventis** has a lovely courtyard under a giant canopy of plane trees and makes a delicious and sizeable *kreatotourta* (local meat pie), while **O Antartis** also makes excellent mezedhes and Cretan food.

Just past the village on your right, there is a small **Museum of National Resistance** with an eerie monument outside paying tribute to a female resistance fighter. The old millstone was used by Turkish occupiers in 1821 to crush Chrysi Tripiti to death in the local olive press.

A steep and winding road takes you through rugged mountain terrain and around an ever-changing landscape of plane, olive, orange, eucalypt and pine trees through the villages of **Zourva** and **Meskla** to **Lakki**, where you can continue to Omalos or head back to Hania.

Roka Carpets   HANDICRAFTS
(Zambeliou 61) This is one of the few places in Crete where you can buy genuine, hand-woven goods (though not antique rugs). You can watch the amiable Mihalis Manousakis and his wife weave wondrous rugs on a 400-year-old loom, using methods that have remained essentially unchanged since Minoan times.

Information

Emergency
Tourist police (☑28210 73333; Kydonias 29; ⊙8am-2.30pm) At the Town Hall.

Internet Access
Wi-fi internet is now widely available for free in public spaces, and at most hotels, restaurants, cafes and bars.
Triple W (cnr Valadinon & Halidon; per hr €2; ⊙24hr) Extensive facilities and high-speed access.
Vranas Internet (Agion Deka 10; per hr €2; ⊙9.30am-1am) Full set-up and air-con.

Medical Services
Hania Hospital (☑28210 22000; Mournies) Located south of town – take a local bus, or a taxi (€8 to €10).

Money
Most banks are in the new city, around Plateia Markopoulou, but there are a few ATMs in the old town on Halidon, including **Alpha Bank** (cnr Halidon & Skalidi) and Citibank. There are numerous places to change money outside banking hours. **National Bank of Greece** (cnr Tzanakaki & Giannari) has a 24-hour exchange machine.

Post
Post office (Peridou 10; ⊙7.30am-8pm Mon-Fri, 7.30am-2pm Sat)

Tourist Information
Municipal tourist office (☑28210 36155; tourism@chania.gr; Kydonias 29; ⊙8am-2.30pm) Located at the Town Hall, it provides helpful practical information and maps. The info booth behind the mosque in the Old Harbour also tends to be manned between noon and 2pm.

Travel Agencies
Diktynna Travel (☑28210 41458; www .diktynna-travel.gr; Arhontaki 6) Organises a range of cultural and ecotourism activities, including cooking classes.
Tellus Travel (☑28210 91500; Halidon 108; www.tellustravel.gr; ⊙8am-11pm) This major Hania agency hires cars, changes money, arranges air and boat tickets, accommodation and excursions.

Websites
www.chania.gr The Municipality of Hania's website is worth a look for information on the city and cultural events.
www.chania-guide.gr Good information on Hania city and prefecture.

❶ Getting There & Away

Air

Hania's **airport** (☑28210 83800) is 14km east of town on the Akrotiri Peninsula.

Aegean Airlines (☑28210 63366; www .aegeanair.com) Four daily flights to Athens (€76 to €123) and one to Thessaloniki (€125 to €135). Booking online at the official Aegean website often gives you a better fare selection depending on what day of the week and period of travel.

Olympic Air (☑28210 58005; www.olympicair .com; Tzanakaki 88) Five daily flights to/from Athens (€76 to €106). Also four flights per week to/from Thessaloniki (€130 to €150).

Boat

Hania's main port is at Souda, 7km southeast of town and site of a NATO base. There are frequent buses to Hania (€1.65), as well as taxis (€9). The **Port Police** (☑28210 89240) can provide ferry information.

ANEK (☑28210 27500; www.anek.gr; Plateia Sofokli Venizelou) Has a daily boat at 9pm from Piraeus to Hania (€33, nine hours) and at 1am from Hania to Piraeus. In July and August there is also a morning ferry from Piraeus (€33). For drivers, car tickets are €78.

Bus

Hania's bus station is on Kydonias, two blocks southwest of Plateia 1866.

Although air-conditioned, buses tend to be slow, stopping to pick up everyone who flags them down along the way. In summer, buses depart from Hania's **bus station** (☑28210 93052) during the week for many destinations, (see table below).

Check with the bus station for off-peak services.

❶ Getting Around

To/From the Airport

From Hania bus station, there are three buses per day to the airport (€2.30, 20 minutes), though sometimes more depending on specific days of the week (check locally). A taxi to or from the airport costs €20 (plus €2 per bag).

Bus

Local **blue buses** (☑28210 27044) meet the ferries at the port of Souda, just near the dock. In Hania, the bus to Souda (€1.65) leaves from outside the food market. Buses for the western beaches leave from the main bus station on Plateia 1866 and go as far as Panormo (€2.60). Local buses also congregate around Plateia Markopoulou and are a good way to get to further suburbs such as Halepa in just a couple of minutes (€1.10). Buy tickets from the coin-operated machine by the stop.

Car, Motorcycle & Bicycle

Most car- and motorcycle-hire outlets are on Halidon, but the companies at Agia Marina are competitive and can bring cars to Hania. Most of the old town is pedestrian only. The best place to park is in the free parking area near the Firkas Fortress (turn right off Skalidi at the sign to the big supermarket car park on Pireos and follow the road down to the waterfront). Some of the new-town streets have paid street parking; check for signs.

Europrent (☑28210 27810; Halidon 87)

Tellus Travel (☑28210 91500; www .tellustravel.gr; Halidon 108)

Left Luggage

KTEL Bus Station (Kydonias 73-77; per bag, per day €2) Will store extra bags for a nominal fee (useful for those wishing to lighten their load before the Samaria Gorge hike).

DESTINATION	DURATION	FARE	FREQUENCY
Elafonisi	2½hr	€11	1 daily
Falasarna	1½hr	€7.60	3 daily
Hora Sfakion	1hr 40min	€7.60	3 daily
Iraklio	2¾hr	€13.80	half-hourly
Kissamos-Kastelli	1hr	€4.70	13 daily
Kolymbari	45min	€3.30	half-hourly
Lakki	1¾hr	€2.60	2 daily
Moni Agias Triadas	30min	€2.30	2 daily
Omalos (for Samaria Gorge)	1hr	€6.90	3 daily
Paleohora	1hr 50min	€7.60	4 daily
Rethymno	1hr	€6.20	half-hourly
Sougia	1hr 50min	€7.10	2 daily
Stavros	30min	€2.10	3 daily

AKROTIRI PENINSULA
ΧΕΡΣΟΝΗΣΟΣ ΑΚΡΩΤΗΡΙ

The Akrotiri (ak-roh-*tee*-ree) Peninsula, to the northeast of Hania, is a barren, hilly stretch of rock covered with scrub. It has a few coastal resorts, Hania's airport, a massive NATO naval base on Souda Bay and two interesting monasteries. There are few buses and the poorly signposted roads can make it a difficult region to explore, but if you have a car it makes an interesting day trip where you can combine a swim and lunch with a visit to the monasteries. If you want to stay at the beach instead of Hania town, Kalathas and Stavros are a much quieter alternative to the package-tour strip west of town.

The beach settlement of **Kalathas**, 10km north of Hania, has two sandy beaches lined by pine trees. It is the preferred weekend haunt of Haniots, many of whom own summer and weekend houses nearby.

Three kilometres north of Kalathas is the small beach settlement of **Tersanas**, signposted off the main Kalathas–Stavros road.

Stavros, 6km north of Kalathas, is little more than a scattering of houses and a few restaurants and hotels. The main cove is a narrow strip of sandy beach dominated by a mammoth rock – it famously served as the dramatic backdrop for the final dancing scene in the classic movie *Zorba the Greek*. It can get crowded, but the sheltered cove is your best bet on a windy day.

The area's major cultural site, the impressive 17th-century **Moni Agias Triadas** (admission €2; ⊙8am-7pm), is a visitor-friendly monastery. It was founded by the Venetian monks Jeremiah and Laurentio Giancarolo, who were converts to the Orthodox faith. There was a religious school here in the 19th century and it is still an active monastery with a rich library. The church is worth visiting for its altarpiece as well as its Venetian-influenced domed facade. There is a small museum and a store selling the monastery's fine wine, oil and *raki*.

The 16th-century **Moni Gouvernetou** (Our Lady of the Angels; ⊙9am-noon & 5-7pm Mon, Tue & Thu, 5-11am & 5-8pm Sat & Sun), 4km north of Moni Agias Triadas, may date as far back as the 11th century, from a time when an inland sanctuary was an attractive refuge from coastal pirates. The building itself is disappointingly plain, but the church inside has an ornate sculptured Venetian facade.

The monastery was attacked and burnt down during the War of Independence but the monks were warned and managed to save the treasures (though not themselves) and had them shipped off to Mount Athos in northern Greece. The monastery is now run by four monks from the Holy Mountain who keep a strict regime and have banned tour buses. Visitors must park in the car park before the monastery and be dressed respectfully while on the grounds (they do not provide long pants or skirts) or they will be asked to leave. Swimming in the cove below is not permitted.

From Moni Gouvernetou, it's a 2km or so walk (uphill on the way back) to the path leading down to the coast to the ruins of **Moni Ioannou Erimiti** (also known as Moni Katholikou). In disuse for many centuries, the monastery is dedicated to St John the Hermit, who lived in the cave behind the ruins, at the bottom of a rock staircase. Near the entrance to the cave there's a small pond of water believed to be holy. When St John died in the cave, his 98 disciples are said to have died with him. His skull is kept in the monastery and brought out for a special service the first Sunday of every month.

On the eastern side of the peninsula is the pleasant beach of **Marathi**, a lovely spot past the military base with two sandy coves and turquoise waters on either side of a small pier. The ruins of **Ancient Minoa** are next to the car park. Marathi gets crowded with local families at weekends and has a couple of tavernas. Further south along this coastline is another nice swimming and snorkelling spot at **Loutraki**.

On the western beach at Stavros, you can stop for a drink at the **Sun Set Beach Bar**, tucked under a huge tree with a shady timber deck and thatched umbrellas evoking the tropics. It also serves a range of local and international-style snacks. Or, if on the beach in Marathi, try the dependable seafood assortment available at **Patrelantonis**. Well regarded by locals and visitors alike, this fish taverna by the beach under the shady tamarisk trees is a good bet for a lazy summer lunch.

⊙ Getting There & Away

There are three buses daily to Stavros beach (€2.10) that stop at Kalathas. There are two buses daily, at 6.30am and 2.15pm, to Moni

Agias Triadas (€2.30, 30 minutes). If coming by car from Hania follow signs to the airport and branch off at the turn-offs from there.

SFAKIA & LEFKA ORI
ΣΦΑΚΙΑ & ΛΕΥΚΑ ΟΡΙ

The memorable drive from Hania to Hora Sfakion – descending through the mountains on numerous loop-back turns overlooking the sea – is one of the most stunning sights in Crete. And it does put an exclamation point on the island's most celebrated region. The mountainous province of Sfakia extends from the Omalos Plateau down to the southern coast, and has some of the island's most spectacular sights, including Samaria (sa-ma-*ria*) Gorge, the Lefka Ori (White Mountains) and Mt Gingilos (2080m) in the rugged interior.

The interior of Sfakia is known for being the only part of Crete never subdued by the Arabs, Venetians or Turks. It was the centre of resistance during the island's long centuries of domination by foreign powers, its steep ravines and hills making effective hideaways for Cretan revolutionaries. The Sfakian people are renowned for their proud fighting spirit, and have a colourfully tragic history of clan vendettas (a very rare occurrence today, however). In general, the Sfakiots are more regarded by other Greeks as a bit ornery, and a bit fascinating for their strong attachment to local roots and dialect.

The website www.sfakia-crete.com has useful information on Sfakia, while the memoir of British linguistics professor and long-time visitor Peter Trudgill, *In Sfakia: Passing Time in the Wilds of Crete* (Lycabbetus Press, 2008), makes for excellent background on the culture and history of the region, gleaned from the author's 35 years of experience in Sfakia.

Hania to Omalos Χανιά Προς Ομαλός

The road from Hania to the beginning of Samaria Gorge is varied and, in places, spectacular. After heading through orange groves to the village of **Fournes**, a left fork leads to **Meskla**, twisting and turning along a gorge offering beautiful views. Although the bottom part of the town is not particularly attractive, with boarded-up buildings, the road becomes more scenic as it winds uphill to the modern, multicoloured **Church of the Panagia**. Next to it is a 14th-century chapel built on the foundations of a 6th-century basilica that might have been built on an even earlier Temple of Aphrodite. At the entrance to the town a sign directs you to the **Chapel of the Metamorfosis Sotiros** (Chapel of the Transfiguration of the Saviour) that contains 14th-century frescoes. The fresco of the Transfiguration on the south wall is particularly impressive.

The main road continues to the unspoilt village of **Lakki** (*la*-kee), 24km from Hania, which affords stunning views wherever one looks. The village was a centre of resistance during both the uprising against the Turks and against the Germans in WWII.

Rooms for Rent Nikolas (☑28210 67232; Lakki; d €35) has comfortable, simple rooms above a taverna, with magnificent views over the valley.

Omalos Ομαλός
POP 30

Most tourists only hurry through Omalos, 36km south of Hania, on their way to Samaria Gorge, but this plateau settlement deserves more of your time. During summer, the air is bracingly cool here compared with the steamy coast and there are some great mountain walks in the area offering magnificent views. After the morning Samaria rush, there's hardly anyone on the plateau except goats and shepherds.

Omalos is little more than a few hotels on either side of the main road cutting through the plateau. The village is practically deserted in winter. The town is about 4km before the entrance to Samaria Gorge.

❶ Getting There & Away

There are three daily buses to Omalos from Hania (one hour, €6.90). If you want to hike the gorge and return to your room (and luggage) in Omalos, you can take the afternoon (4.45pm) boat from Agia Roumeli to Sougia (€6.30, 45 minutes) and get a taxi back to Omalos for about €45.

Samaria Gorge Φαράγγι της Σαμαριάς

Hiking through **Samaria Gorge** (☑28210 67179; admission €5; ⊙6am-3pm 1 May–mid-Oct) is considered one of the 'must-do' singular experiences of Crete, and it attracts both

Samaria Gorge ⓝ

0 ▬▬ 2 km
0 ▬▬ 1 mile

Omalos Plateau
Kallergi Hut
Xyloskalo
Mt Gingilos (2080m)
Mt Volakias (2115m)
Samaria Gorge National Park
Mt Avlimaniko (1858m)
Samaria
St Maria of Egypt Church
Mt Psiristra (1766m)
Samaria Gorge
Iron Gates (Sidiroportes)
Agia Roumeli
Agia Roumeli
Libyan Sea

serious hikers and the less committed. Despite the crowds – more than 170,000 people walk the gorge each year, averaging out to 1000 per day in high season – a hike through this stupendous gorge is still an experience to remember.

At 16km, Samaria Gorge is supposedly the longest in Europe. It begins just below the Omalos Plateau, carved out by the river that flows between the peaks of Mts Avlimaniko (1858m) and Volakias (2115m). Its width varies from 150m to 3m and its vertical walls reach 500m at their highest points. The gorge has an incredible number of wildflowers, which are at their best in April and May.

It is also home to a large number of endangered species, including the Cretan wild goat, the *kri-kri*. The gorge was made a national park in 1962 to save the *kri-kri* from extinction. You are unlikely to see too many of these shy animals, which show a marked aversion to hikers.

An early start (before 8am) helps to avoid the worst of the crowds, but during July and August even the early bus from Hania to the top of the gorge can be packed. There's no spending the night in the gorge, so you are going to have to complete the hike in the time allocated. If you are not sure if you are fit enough, you could try the shorter

(it's about half the length) but nonetheless picturesque Imbros Gorge.

The hike from **Xyloskalo** (the name of the steep stone pathway with wooden rails that gives access to the gorge), to Agia Roumeli on the coast takes from about four hours for the sprinters to six hours for the strollers. Early in the season it's sometimes necessary to wade through the stream. Later, as the flow drops, it's possible to use rocks as stepping stones.

The gorge is wide and open for the first 6km, until you reach the abandoned settlement of **Samaria**. The inhabitants were relocated when the gorge became a national park. Just south of the village is a small church dedicated to **Saint Maria of Egypt**, after whom the gorge is named. Every 1 May, numerous locals attend the *panigyri* (saint's day) of St Mary. This is the only night during which anyone can stay inside in the old village of Samaria – a few old houses are opened for the purpose, and camping is allowed. (For further details, check with the EOS in Hania, p43).

The gorge then narrows and becomes more dramatic until, at the 11km mark, the walls are only 3.5m apart – the famous **Iron Gates** (Sidiroportes). Here, a rickety wooden pathway leads hikers the 20m or so over the water and through to the other side.

The gorge ends at the 12.5km mark just north of the almost abandoned village of Old Agia Roumeli. From here it's a further uninteresting 2km hike to the welcoming seaside resort of Agia Roumeli, with its much-appreciated fine pebble beach and sparkling sea, where most hikers can be seen taking a refreshing dip or at least bathing sore and aching feet after finishing the hike. Be warned: falling rocks in the gorge can be a hazard and people have been injured, including two fatal incidents in 2006. On extremely hot days (generally, over 40°C) the gorge is closed for safety reasons.

There are excursions to Samaria Gorge from every sizeable town and resort in Crete, but you can get there easily enough from Hania by bus (see p53), then catch a ferry from Agia Roumeli (see p56) back to Hora Sfakion or other south-coast towns. Most travel agents have two excursions: 'Samaria Gorge Long Way' and 'Samaria Gorge Easy Way'. The first comprises the regular hike from Omalos; the second starts at Agia Roumeli and takes you up as far as the Iron Gates.

Askyfou Ασκύφου

POP 450

The road to Hora Sfakion takes you across the war-torn plain of Askyfou, which was the scene of one of the most furious battles of the Cretan revolt of 1821. The Sfakiot forces triumphed over the Turks in a bloody battle here, which is still recounted in local songs. More than a century later the plain was the scene of more strife as Allied troops retreated towards their evacuation point in Hora Sfakion. The central town of the region is Askyfou, which stretches out on either side of a hill. The post office is at the top of the hill with a minimarket and several tavernas with inexpensive rooms to rent.

As you enter Askyfou from Hania, signs direct you to the **military museum** (☑28250 95289; admission free; ☑8am-7pm Mon-Sat), which displays the gun and military odds-and-ends collection of Georgios Hatzidakis, who is eager to show you around.

For a glimpse of traditional Sfakian village life, it is worth veering right off the main road to arrive at a small square flanked by four *kafeneia* (coffee houses) and statues of local resistance heroes. Just above the small square you'll probably see local black-clad gents under the mulberry tree of the old-style **kafeneio**. Here, as well as the local *Sfakiani pita* (a thin, flat cheese pie dribbled with honey), you can normally get a basic meal such as local sausage, or at weekends traditional wild goat or lamb *tsigariasto* (sautéed) or *vrasto* (boiled), charged by the kilo – and lots of *raki*.

Imbros Gorge Φαράγγι Ιμπρου

Though less hiked than its illustrious sister at Samaria, **Imbros Gorge** (admission €2; ☺year-round), 57km southeast of Hania, is just as beautiful. Cypresses, holm oaks, fig and almond trees gradually thin to just cypresses and Jerusalem sage deep within the gorge. The walls of rock reach 300m high, while the narrowest point of the ravine is only 2m wide. At only 8km the Imbros walk is also much easier on the feet. Most people begin the walk in the mountain village of **Imbros** but you can also do it from the southern village of **Komitades**. Both places are used by gorge hikers and have

plenty of minimarkets and tavernas to fuel up at. There's nowhere to stay in Imbros village.

You'll find the well-marked entrance to the gorge next to Porofarango taverna on the road to Hora Sfakion. The track is easy to follow as it traces the stream bed past rockslides and caves. The gorge path ends at Komitades, from where you can walk 5km or take a taxi to Hora Sfakion (€22).

At the start of the gorge, the friendly family taverna **Porofarango** (mains €7-9.50) has a big balcony with great panoramic views of the gorge and serves good-value Cretan cuisine and generous *raki*. The meat is usually the taverna's own and it often has wild goat. Try the special pork *tsigariasto*.

There are three daily buses from Hania to Hora Sfakion (€7.60, one hour 40 minutes), which stop at Imbros. Buses from Hora Sfakion to Hania stop at Komitades. Check first at the Hania EOS (p43) for more information on gorge hikes here.

SOUTHERN COAST

The most eternally unchanging place in Crete – thanks to the massive cliffs running into the sea – the rocky southern coast is dotted with laid-back beach communities such as Paleohora, Sougia, Frangokastello and Loutro. These are some of the best places in Crete to relax. Many of the beaches are inaccessible by road because of the mountains and gorges that slice through and spill out to the beaches. Samaria Gorge ends at the beach village of Agia Roumeli. This region has some stunning walks and is the only place in Crete where you can boat hop along the coast to isolated beaches and settlements. Along with the impenetrable geography, the strong summer winds that blast up and down the gorges and across the Libyan Sea keep the area happily safe from mass tourism. The winds also mean there is often good windsurfing to be had, especially at Paleohora.

Agia Roumeli Αγία Ρουμελή

POP 130

The coastal village of Agia Roumeli is not spectacular on its objective merits but it is undoubtedly a divine sight for tired hikers stumbling out of Samaria Gorge. After six hours of marching down the mountain,

GORGING YOURSELF

Samaria Gorge is not western Crete's only canyon worth conquering. Along with Imbros Gorge, little-visited **Trypiti Gorge** near Mt Gingilos is one of Crete's most strenuous and longest, starting from Omalos and ending at Sougia on the south coast. You will have blissfully little company on the 10-hour jaunt, making Trypiti great for those seeking unspoilt nature and solitude. A mountain hut along the way means you can sleep over and break up the hike into a more humane two-day adventure (bring extra food and water).

Klados Gorge, marked by its sheer and unforgiving rock face, runs between and parallel to Samaria and Trypiti Gorges. This is the place to go for serious rock climbers; it offers great abseiling (rappelling) too. For something in between, try the pretty **Agia Irini Gorge**, which starts 12 kilometres north of Sougia. The 7km hike brings you through redolent and varied verdure, plus a few caves hidden in the gorge walls. The hike can be organised independently (take the Omalos bus from Paleohora or the Hania bus from Sougia, and get off at Agia Irini).

For all of these gorges, it's a wise idea not to go it alone or without prior arrangement. Check in first with Hania's EOS (p43) for advice on local conditions and lodgings, and pick up the Anavasi hiking maps, marked with GPS coordinates, trails and other key details, available in Hania bookshops.

stopping for a swim and lunch at this tiny beach settlement is just the thing to do before catching a boat, which is the only way out. Agia Roumeli is a pleasant enough stopover, though the surrounding mountains can make it very hot and stifling. The pebble beach gets exceptionally hot and thus impossible to sit on for long unless you hire a beach umbrella and sun lounger (€5).

If you're in no hurry to leave, there are quite a few places to stay and decent places to eat. There are no tourist facilities or banks, and not much to see, other than to walk up to the well-preserved ruins of a **Venetian castle** above the village (about 1km, or 30 minutes, one-way), or check out the **Panagia church** in the village, which has some surviving remnants of a Roman mosaic floor. Staying here for a day or two is a good compromise for families with small children eager to peer into Samaria Gorge, who could not survive the whole hike.

On Easter Saturday, the tavernas of Agia Roumeli put on a **post-resurrection feast**, which anyone in the village is free to join.

ⓘ Getting There & Away

The boat **ticket office** (☑ 28250 91251) is a small concrete structure near the beach.

There are two afternoon boats daily (3.45pm and 6pm) from Agia Roumeli to Hora Sfakion (€7.50, one hour) via Loutro (€5, 45 minutes) that connect with the bus back to Hania, as well as the morning boat from Paleohora to Hora Sfakion. You can also head west catching a

boat from Agia Roumeli to Paleohora (€11, 1½ hours) at 4.45pm, calling in at Sougia (€6.30, 45 minutes).

Hora Sfakion Χώρα Σφακίων
POP 310

The more bullet holes you see in the passing road signs, the closer you are to Hora Sfakion (*ho*-ra sfa-*kee*-on), long renowned in Cretan history for its rebellious streak against foreign occupiers. However, the small coastal port is an amiable if eccentric place that caters well enough to today's foreign visitors, many of whom tend to be returning hikers stumbling off the Agia Roumeli boat after walking Samaria Gorge on their way back to Hania. While most such people pause only long enough to catch the next bus out, the settlement can be a relaxing stay for a few days and there are several beaches accessible by boat or road, including the isolated **Sweetwater** and **Ilingas Beaches** to the west. It's also a convenient spot for heading westward to other resorts or taking a ferry to Gavdos Island.

Under Venetian and Turkish rule Hora Sfakion was an important maritime centre and (with the upland regional capital of Anopoli) the nucleus of the Cretan struggle for independence. The Turks inflicted severe reprisals on the town's inhabitants for their rebelliousness in the 19th century, after which the town fell into an economic slump that lasted until the arrival of tourism a couple of decades ago. Hora Sfakion played

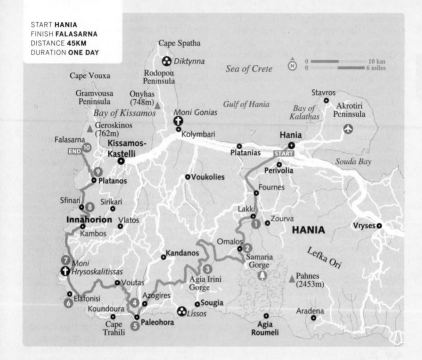

START **HANIA**
FINISH **FALASARNA**
DISTANCE **45KM**
DURATION **ONE DAY**

Driving Tour
Hania

❯ This southwestern driving tour, starting in Hania and finishing at Falasarna beach, is a steep and swerving mountain adventure into the wildest stretches of Crete – a do-it-yourself dream through bucolic, good-natured villages, past stunning ravines where olive trees cling precipitously to cliffs, and onto the island's most serene beaches. You'll hear legends and myths, look for olive oil and other natural goods in local shops, and get a glimpse of living Orthodox spirituality. It's a full-day trip, so start early.

From Hania, head south for Fournes, where the road gets interesting at the unspoilt mountain hamlet of ① **Lakki**. At the end of the road, after Omalos, peek into awe-inspiring ② **Samaria Gorge** at Xyloskalo, where the air is cool and fresh. Next, turn back a few kilometres and head west across the Omalos Plateau to the connection with the jagged north–south road; turn south by the top of ③ **Agia Irini Gorge**, less visited but equally stupendous as Samaria. The zigzagging road

south requires concentration (though you will be dying to stop everywhere for photos) and passes through several rustic villages where life continues pretty much as it always has.

Turning west at Rodovani, you will soon hit a junction at Temenia; if in need of cool refreshment, stop in at this tiny place, known for its bottled bitter lemon and orange juices. Keep heading west and then south to ④ **Azogires**, a curious village full of unusual local legends. Then continue to colourful, laid-back ⑤ **Paleohora** for a fish-taverna lunch. Take the B-road up through Agia Triada, turning left at Voutas and again at Sklavopoula. The road worsens, but you'll be rewarded by the pink sands of ⑥ **Elafonisi**, Crete's most sublime beach. After luxuriating here, head north to visit ethereal ⑦ **Moni Hrysos-kalitissas**. Continue along the coast through the ⑧ **Innahorion villages**, with traditional architecture and healthy, inexpensive local foodstuffs. After leafy ⑨ **Platanos**, you'll reach ⑩ **Falasarna**, a lovely sandy beach with accommodation (or free camping).

a prominent role during WWII when thousands of Allied troops were evacuated by sea from the town after the Battle of Crete. Today, a memorial to the last British, Australian and New Zealand soldiers evacuated after the battle stands on the eastern bluff over the town.

Hora Sfakion has a number of small gift shops, where those keen on understanding more about local traditions and history can find books on subjects ranging from linguistics to local cookery. Peter Trudgill's *In Sfakia: Passing Time in the Wilds of Crete* (Lycabbetus Press, 2008), sold in local shops, is an easygoing and often amusing memoir documenting the life, legends and values of the Sfakiots.

🏃 Activities

You can go **bungee jumping** off the Aradena bridge (see p26).

Notos Mare Diving Centre   DIVING
(☑28250 91333; www.notosmare.com; dives from €42) Offers a range of experiences for beginners and experienced divers, as well as snorkelling and boat excursions along the south coast.

🍴 Eating

When in Hora Sfakion, be sure to try the local *Sfakiani pita* (Sfakian cheese pie) – this thin, circular pie filled with sweet *myzithra* (sheep's-milk cheese) and flecked with honey makes a great breakfast when served with a bit of Greek yoghurt on the side.

Delfini   SEAFOOD €€
(fish per kg €40-55) Among the row of identical seafront tavernas, Delfini is the best for fresh fish dishes.

Thalassa Café   CAFE €
If you don't mind the stroll, you can enjoy a lovely sunset and stunning views as far as Loutro from the Thalassa, about 1.5km along the road out of town. It's good for a relaxing drink or snack.

Lefka Ori   GREEK €
This taverna at the western end of the port does some solid trade; try the goat *stifadho* and wild greens.

❶ Information

The ferry quay is at the eastern side of the harbour. Buses leave from the square up the hill on the northeastern side. There is one ATM. The post office is on the square, opposite the police station.

Sfakia Tours (☑28250 91130), next to the post office, has hire cars and can help with accommodation. There is parking near the bus stop and the ferry terminal. Check email at **Kenzo Club** (per hr €3; ⊘8am-late).

❶ Getting There & Away

Boat

Hora Sfakion is the western terminus for the south-coast ferry route to Paleohora, and like that town also offers boats to Gavdos Island. Boat tickets are sold in the **ticket booth** (☑28250 91221) in the car park. From June through August there is a daily boat from Hora Sfakion to Paleohora (€16, three hours) via Loutro, Agia Roumeli and Sougia. The boat leaves Hora Sfakion at 1pm and stops for two hours at Agia Roumeli to catch the gorge walkers heading west. There are four additional boats between Hora Sfakion and Agia Roumeli (€12, one hour) via Loutro (€5, 15 minutes). From 1 June there are boats (€15, 1½ hours) to Gavdos Island on Friday, Saturday and Sunday.

Bus

There are four buses per day from Hora Sfakion to Hania (€7.60, two hours) – the afternoon buses at 5.30pm and 7pm wait for the boats from Agia Roumeli. In summer there are three daily buses to Rethymno via Vryses (€7.30, one hour). There are two buses daily to Frangokastello (€2, 25 minutes).

Around Hora Sfakion

The forbidding. rocky moonscape of **Inner Sfakia** rises up from the sea behind Hora Sfakion. Although now almost unpopulated due to past clan vendettas and emigration, it was in fact once a powerful provincial area teeming with life. A scenic, hair-raisingly steep, 12km winding road west from Hora Sfakion takes you to **Anopoli**, a quiet village in a fertile plateau at the base of the Lefka Ori, with a memorial to resistance fighters in the main square. It was one of the few areas that did not fall to the Venetians or Turks. In earlier centuries, Anopoli was the Sfakian capital, presiding over the regional port of Loutro (still accessible, albeit on an extremely steep path, by hikers).

Hearty lunches are served at **Platanos**, a restaurant on the square known for its roast lamb and other local delicacies. The friendly English-speaking owner, Eva Kopasis, can also advise about hikes to Loutro and local beaches, as well as local rooms for rent.

The virtually abandoned stone hamlet of **Aradena**, about 2km west of Anopoli, is famous for the **Vardinogiannis bridge**, named for the wealthy local businessman who endowed it, which crosses over the Aradena gorge. Look down into the depths in fascinated horror as the chipped and rusted wood-and-steel structure buckles under your wheels. At weekends you may see people jumping into the gorge from this bridge – at 138m, the highest **bungee jumping** (☑6937615191; www.bungy.gr) bridge in Greece.

At the *kantina* (mobile kiosk) next to the bridge you can get directions for the remote **Church of Agios Ioannis**, a whitewashed early-Byzantine structure. Although only about a 15-minute walk (roughly 800m), the church is unfortunately rarely open. From it, however, begins a forking path down to the sea: the western fork leads to Agia Roumeli via the Byzantine Church of Agios Pavlos, the eastern, to **Marmara Beach**.

The more-often-used hiking route to these places through the gorge is a 1½-hour (3.5km) stroll of moderate difficulty. The trailhead is signposted before the bridge (when coming from Anopoli). Alternatively, you can start in Anopoli and walk (3.5km) to this point. From the beach, you can walk to the glittering nearby port of **Loutro**, with its creature comforts, and jump on the Hora Sfakion–Paleohora boat to get out.

Frangokastello
Φραγγοκαστέλλο
POP 60

Frangokastello (Frankish Castle) is a striking 14th-century Venetian fortress on a fine stretch of beach along the south coast, 15km east of Hora Sfakion. Constructed soon after the Fourth Crusade (1204) by the Venetians, who sought a stronghold against Sfakiot warriors, it is popular with day trippers, but the scattered beach settlement around the castle, also referred to as Frangokastello, is a peaceful retreat. The wide, white-sand beach beneath the fortress slopes gradually into shallow warm water, making it ideal for kids. Development has been kept to a minimum with most accommodation set back from the shore, leaving the natural beauty largely untouched. In summer, occasional concerts and folk dance performances are held.

Frangokastello has an eventful history. The sand-coloured fortress was built by the Venetians as a defence against pirates and rebellious Sfakiots. The legendary Ioannis Daskalogiannis, who led a disastrous rebellion against Ottoman oppression in 1770, was persuaded to surrender at the Frangokastello Fortress but was subsequently and perfidiously flayed alive by the Turks. On 17 May 1828, 385 Cretan rebels made a heroic last stand at the fortress in one of the bloodiest battles of the Cretan struggle for independence. About 800 Turks were killed along with the rebels.

Legend has it that at dawn each anniversary their ghosts, the *drosoulites,* can be seen marching along the beach. Others theorise that the 'ghosts' are an optical illusion created by peculiar atmospheric conditions and that the figures may be a reflection of camels or soldiers in the Libyan Desert. The name comes from the Greek word *drosia* meaning 'moisture', which in itself could refer to the dawn moisture that is around when the ghosts are said to appear.

There's no actual village in Frangokastello, just a series of scattered domatia (cheap accommodation rooms, usually in a private home), tavernas and residences that stretch either side of the main road from Hora Sfakion to the fortress, as well as a couple of minimarkets. The bus stops at several spots along the main road.

Exactly adjoining the castle is the stunning **Orthi Ammos beach**, a long stretch of fine sand with shallow, warm waters. It is blissful and child-friendly, unless (as is frequently the case) the wind whips up the sand and forces you to retreat into the nearby cafe.

✖ Eating

Oasis Taverna   CRETAN €
(mains €6-8) Part of an excellent family-run studio and apartment complex at the western end of the beach, this is the best place to eat. The taverna's well-executed Cretan specials include a delicious *kreatopita* (meat and cheese pie). The spacious rooms have full-sized kitchens, are set in a lovely garden and you can walk to a quiet stretch of beach.

Taverna Babis & Popi   GREEK €
(specials €3-6) This taverna serves decent, good-value meals under a shady vine canopy tucked behind the family's rooms and minimarket.

❶ Getting There & Away

In summer, two daily buses from Hora Sfakion to Plakias stop at Frangokastello (€2, 25 minutes). From Hania there's a daily afternoon bus (€8.40, 2½ hours). From Rethymno, you need to change at Vryses.

❶ Getting There & Away

Loutro is on the main Paleohora–Hora Sfakion boat route. From April to October there are four boats per day from Hora Sfakion (€5, 15 minutes), two from Agia Roumeli (€5, 45 minutes) and one boat per day from Paleohora (€14, 2½ hours). Taxi boats go to Sweetwater Beach and Hora Sfakion.

Loutro Λουτρό

POP 90

The small but densely built-up fishing village of Loutro (loo-*tro*) lies between Agia Roumeli and Hora Sfakion. The town's crescent of white-and-blue domatia, set around a narrow beach, positively sparkles on sunny days. It's a pleasant, lazy resort that is never overwhelmed with visitors, though it can get busy and rather claustrophobic in July and August. It is a popular base for walkers too.

Loutro is the only natural harbour on the south coast of Crete, an advantage that made it strategically vital in centuries past, and is accessible only by boat or on foot. The absence of cars and bikes makes it quiet and peaceful.

Its advantageous geographical position was appreciated in ancient times when it was the port for Phoenix and Anopoli. St Paul is said to have been heading to Phoenix from here when he encountered a storm that blew him off course past Gavdos Island; the journey ended with him being shipwrecked in Malta.

Loutro is a good base for boat excursions along the southern coast. You can hire canoes (per hr/day €2/7) and a small ferry goes to nearby Sweetwater beach (€3.50, 15 minutes).

✖ Eating

Given the captive market, the tavernas that line the waterfront in Loutro are surprisingly good. Most prominently display a wide range of *mayirefta* and you can't miss the dazzling range of cakes and sweets. Recommended are Notos (☑28250 91501; mezedhes €2.50-7) for excellent mezedhes, Pavlos (grills €6-8) for grills and Ilios for fish.

❶ Information

There's no bank or post office, but there are places to change money at the western end of the beach. Boats dock in front of the Sifis Hotel. The ticket stall opens an hour before departures. There is **internet access** (per hr €4) at the Daskalogiannis Hotel.

Sougia Σούγια

POP 100

Sougia is one of the most laid-back and refreshingly undeveloped beach resorts along the south coast, with a lovely wide curve of sand-and-pebble beach and a few tavernas and rooms along a shady tree-lined coastal road. It was once a popular remote hippie hang-out and many nostalgic ex-hippies return religiously each year. It retains its chilled-out atmosphere and there is little to do other than relax and recharge depleted batteries for a few days. However, while the beach is good and the waters clear, the dropoff is quick, making it not the best swimming spot for families with small children (the shallower waters at Frangokastello, Paleohora and Elafonisi are better southern beaches for kids in this respect).

Sougia's tranquillity has been preserved largely because archaeological remains at the eastern end of the beach prohibit development. It lies at the foot of a narrow, twisting road that also deters most tour buses and passing traffic. There are a few small complexes of rooms, a few tavernas, a couple of lazy beach bars, two open-air clubs and a small settlement of campers and nudists at the eastern end of the beach. It is also great hiking territory, close to Samaria and Agia Irini Gorges.

The ancient town was on the western side of the existing village. It flourished under the Romans and Byzantines when it was the port for Elyros, an important inland city (now disappeared). A 6th-century basilica that stood at the western end of the village contained a fine mosaic floor that is now in Hania's Archaeological Museum.

There is one road into Sougia and the bus drops you on the coastal road in front of the Santa Irene hotel, where there is a ticket booth. There is an ATM next to Taverna Galini. Check out www.sougia.info for information about the town.

Roxana's snack store sells boat tickets to Elafonisi. Internet Lotos (☑28230 51191; per hr €3; ⊙7am-late) can get you online.

Eating

Polyfimos
GREEK €

(mains €5-8; ☺dinner; 🖉) Tucked away off the Hania road behind the police station, ex-hippie Yianni makes his own oil, wine and *raki* and even makes dolmadhes (vine leaves stuffed with rice) from the vines that cover the shady courtyard. All Greek cuisine is strong on vegetables, but this is perhaps Sougia's most vegetarian-friendly place.

Kyma
GREEK €

(meat dishes €5.50-7) On the waterfront as you enter town, with the fish tank in the front, Kyma has a good selection of *mayirefta*. The restaurant uses its own meat, and fresh local fish is supplied by the owner's brother. Try the goat *tsigariasto* (sautéed) in wine sauce or the rabbit *stifadho*. Fried *kalamari* or the langoustine spaghetti (€70 per kg) are good seafood picks.

Taverna Rembetiko
CRETAN €

(mezedhes €2-5) On the road to Hania, this popular taverna serving mezedhes is a great place for a quick snack or varied lunch at good prices. It has an extensive menu of Cretan dishes such as *bourekia* (Turkish-influenced filo pies shaped into thin long rolls, batons and pin-wheels) and stuffed zucchini flowers, and is known for its good Greek music.

☆ Entertainment

Sougia has two open-air clubs that can get surprisingly lively for such a small resort. Alabama on the eastern side of the beach is the perennial favourite, while Fortuna, on your left before the entrance to the town, has had an impressive makeover and is a great place for a late-night drink. Both kick off after midnight.

❶ Getting There & Away

There are two buses daily from Hania to Sougia (€7.10, one hour 50 minutes). Sougia is also on the Paleohora–Hora Sfakion boat route. Boats leave in the morning for Agia Roumeli (€6.30, 45 minutes), Loutro (€12, 1½ hours) and Hora Sfakion (€13, 1¾ hours). For Paleohora (€8.50, 50 minutes) there is a departure at 5.15pm.

Lissos Λισσός

The ruins of ancient Lissos are a 3.5km walk from Sougia on the coastal path to Paleohora, which starts at the far end of Sougia's small port.

Lissos arose under the Dorians, flourished under the Byzantines and was destroyed by the Saracens in the 9th century. It was part of a league of city-states, led by ancient Gortyna, which minted its own gold coins inscribed with the word 'Lission'. At one time there was a reservoir, a theatre and hot springs, but these have not yet been excavated. Most of what you see dates from the 1st through 3rd centuries BC, when Lissos was known for its curative springs. The 3rd-century-BC Temple of Asklepion was built next to one of the springs and named after the Greek god of healing, Asclepius.

Excavations here uncovered a headless statue of Asclepius along with 20 other statue fragments now in Hania's Archaeological Museum. You can still see the marble altar base that supported the statue next to the pit in which sacrifices were placed. The other notable feature is the mosaic floor of multicoloured stones intricately arranged in beautiful geometric shapes and images of birds. On the way down to the sea there are traces of Roman ruins, and on the western slopes of the valley are unusual barrel-vaulted tombs.

Nearby are the ruins of two early Christian basilicas – Agios Kyriakos and the Panagia – dating from the 13th century.

Lissos has a lovely beach to cool off after the walk, and if you come on 15 July you will stumble on the annual festival, held in honour of Agios Kyriakos.

Paleohora Παλαιόχωρα

POP 2210

There is still a vaguely 1972 feel about Paleohora (pal-ee-*oh*-hor-a), originally 'discovered' by hippies. The place is still appealing, full of colour, and retains a laid-back feel. Popular with older tourists on package tours, it also attracts many walkers in spring and autumn, and people who come back year after year. The long sandy beach with shallow waters and general quietude also make it a good choice for families with small children, though it gets much livelier in the peak of summer. It is also the only beach resort in Crete that does not go into total hibernation in winter.

The oddly shaped town lies on a narrow peninsula with a long, curving tamarisk-shaded sandy beach (Pahia Ammos), exposed

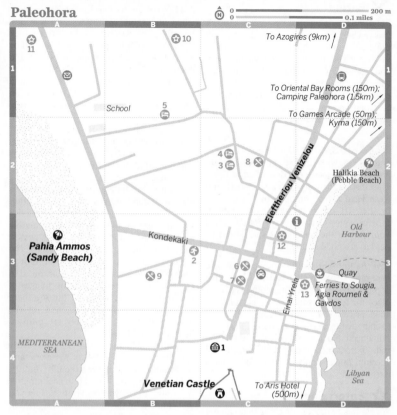

to the wind, on one side and a sheltered pebbly beach (Halikia Beach) on the other. The most picturesque part of Paleohora is the maze of narrow streets around the castle.

On summer evenings the main street and pebble beach road are closed to traffic. With the main-street tavernas moved out onto the pavement, the town garners a lively summer ambience complemented by occasional cultural happenings and Cretan and international music.

⊙ Sights

FREE Venetian Castle   CASTLE

It's worth clambering up the ruins of the 13th-century Venetian castle for the splendid view of the sea and mountains. The castle was built so the Venetians could keep an eye on the southwestern coast from this commanding position on the hill top. There's not much left of the fortress, however, as it was destroyed by the Vene-

tians, the Turks, the pirate Barbarossa in the 16th century, and the Germans during WWII.

FREE Museum of the Acritans
of Europe   MUSEUM

(☎28230 42265; ◷10am-1pm & 6.30-9pm Wed-Sun) This obscure museum next to the town's ornate church is dedicated to the border fighters and heroes of Europe's medieval and Byzantine times. It has a well-displayed historical exhibition along with musical instruments, weapons and other items from the period. The Paleohora connection remains a mystery.

🏃 Activities

There are several great beaches and walking trails nearby. From Paleohora, a six-hour walk along a scenic **coastal path** leads to Sougia, passing ancient Lissos. You can also do an easier walk around Anydri; see p65.

Paleohora

When a stiff summer breeze is blowing, **windsurfing** off sandy Pahia Ammos is excellent. This is a good and shallow beach with soft sand (though mind the erratically-juxtaposed thin rock ledges and outcroppings). If you are willing to sacrifice the sand in order to feel less wind, the 'pebble' (actually, large stones) beach on the protected side of the waterfront also offers swimming and sunbathing.

Aqua Creta Diving & Adventures DIVING
(☑28230 41393; www.aquacreta.gr; Kondekaki 4) Runs a range of diving courses from beginner dives (€50) to seven- to 10-day master courses (€580). It also runs one-day beach-hopping and snorkelling excursions to remote beaches along the southern coast and as far as Gavdos (€50 to €60).

☞ Tours

You can hike Samaria and Agia Irini Gorges from Paleohora, either through organised tours or the local KTEL bus service, returning by ferry.

In summer, you can take a day trip to Elafonisi by ferry (see p65). **Dolphin-watching trips** (3hr trip €18) leave at 5pm, but out of high season not daily and the trip depends on the weather. Tour operators claim you have a 70% chance of spotting a dolphin or two when it's not windy. Try one of the following:

Tsiskakis Travel (☑28230 42110; www.notoscar.com; Eleftheriou Venizelou 53)

Selino Travel (☑28230 42272; selino2@otenet.gr)

✖ Eating

Paleohora has some good local restaurants and the olive oil produced in this region is among the best in Greece. In summer, the little tavernas spilling out onto the closed-off central street makes for great ambience. As sometimes encountered elsewhere in Crete, almost all restaurants here will give you a complimentary *raki* and dessert just as soon as you've put your fork down. In this area, *myzithra* is generally unsweetened, unlike the sweetened *myzithra* usually served elsewhere.

PALEOHORA–SOUGIA COASTAL WALK

From the town centre of Paleohora, follow signs to the campsites to the northeast. Turn right at the intersection with the road to Anydri and soon you'll be following the coastal path marked as the E4 European Footpath. After a couple of kilometres, the path climbs steeply for a beautiful view back to Paleohora. You'll pass **Anydri Beach** and several inviting **coves** where people may be getting an all-over tan. Take a dip because the path soon turns inland to pass over **Cape Flomes**. You'll walk along a plateau carpeted with brush that leads towards the coast and some breathtaking views over the Libyan Sea. Soon you'll reach the Minoan site of **Lissos**. After Lissos the path takes you through a pine forest. The road ends at Sougia Harbour. The 14.5km walk (allow about six hours) is nearly shadeless, so take several litres of water and sunscreen. From June through August, it's best to start at sunrise in order to get to Sougia before the heat of the day.

TOP CHOICE Kyma SEAFOOD €€

(fish per kg €40-55) This very old-school eatery (established in 1960), with a patio overlooking the protected pebble beach, is famous for serving fish caught by its owner – you are invited to see what's on ice and weigh up what you want before ordering to verify the price. Offerings vary by the day, but the red mullet, red snapper and scorpion fish are all excellent seafood choices usually available, while the grills section (try the excellent *soutsoukakia,* meatballs in red sauce) will appease doubtful landlubbers.

Inochoos CRETAN €

(mains €6-10) Run by the hospitable Tsatsaronaki brothers, this popular outdoor taverna on the main street (the last on the right, when heading towards the church and museum) has a marvellous selection of well-done Cretan dishes, mixing meats with appetisers and fresh fish offerings. Even Greek staples such as tzatziki (sauce of grated cucumber, yoghurt and garlic) are extra pungent here. Try Cretan *dakos* (rusks with tomatoes and cheese) accompanied by a selection of small fish you can put together yourself (around €10 to €14 per serving).

Samaria GREEK €€

(mains €8-10) Housed in a roofless old stone building with ambient courtyard seating over tiny pebbles, this welcom-ing place does great Cretan fare delivered with gracious service. Specialities include lamb *tsigariasto* and rooster *kokkinisto* (rooster in wine sauce), as well as Cretan *myzithropites* (small pies made from a sweet cheese).

Third Eye VEGETARIAN €

(mains €5-8; 🖋) A local institution, the Third Eye, Crete's only vegetarian restaurant, has an eclectic menu of curries, salads, pastas and Greek and Asian dishes. There's live music weekly in summer. The restaurant is just in from sandy Pahia Ammos.

Karakatsanis Zaharoplasteion DESSERTS €

Just above the Inochoos restaurant, Karakatsanis is the place to go to indulge in a variety of cakes, chocolate profiteroles, and fresh-baked waffles with a dollop of ice cream. There's nice outdoor seating and service is friendly and attentive.

☆ Entertainment

La Jettee, right on the beach, has a lovely garden, while **Skala** is a portside classic bar with a nice terrace and free wi-fi internet. By night, it transforms into a more rockin' joint in the peak of summer.

Nostos Club (⊙6pm-2am) has an outdoor terrace bar and a small indoor club playing Greek and Western music. **Paleohora Club** (⊙11pm-late), next to the campsite, used to be popular for all-night, full-moon parties but

MILIA

One of Crete's ecotourism trailblazers is the isolated mountain settlement of **Milia** (📞28220 51569; www.milia.gr; cottages incl breakfast €50-70 🅿). Inspired by a back-to-nature philosophy, 16 abandoned stone farmhouses were transformed into ecocottages with only solar energy for basic needs (leave the laptop and hairdryer at home). The cottages have antique beds and rustic furnishings.

Milia is one of the most atmospheric and peaceful places to stay on the island, but it is also worth a visit just to dine at the superb taverna, which has a frequently changing seasonal menu depending on what is available from the organic produce cultivated on its farm, including its own oil, wine, milk, cheese and free-range chickens, goats and sheep. Try the *boureki* (Turkish-influenced filo pies shaped into thin long rolls, batons and pinwheels), stuffed rabbit with *myzithra* (sheep's-milk cheese) or yoghurt, or pork with lemon leaves baked slowly overnight. We loved the winter favourite – potatoes, chestnuts and baby onions in red-wine sauce. There is nothing processed.

There is a signposted turn-off on the right after the village of Vlatos. The rather narrow access road becomes a drivable 3km dirt road. Milia makes a great base for those wishing to see the Innahorion region (p72).

is now a less-appealing swanky indoor club. There's a shuttle bus from the port.

For something different, you can also see a film at the outdoor **Cinema Attikon** (tickets €7; ⊙screenings start 10pm).

For children, a small **games arcade** featuring air hockey, mini-basketball and similar diversions can be found on the road hugging the pebble beach, on the way to Kyma restaurant.

❶ Information

Paleohora has an attractive seafront promenade, along with the main road (Venizelou) which is cut off to traffic – they are the centres of activity in the early evening. Boats leave from the old harbour at the southern end of the pebble beach. There are ATMs on the main drag.

Erato Internet (Eleftheriou Venizelou; per hr €3)

Municipal tourist office (⎙28230 41507; ⊙10am-1pm & 6-9pm Wed-Mon May-Oct) On the beach road near the harbour.

Notos Internet (Eleftheriou Venizelou 53; per hr €2; ⊙8am-10pm)

Post office At the northern end of Pahia Ammos.

❶ Getting There & Away

Boat

Boat schedules change year to year, so check with travel agents in town. In summer there is a daily morning ferry from Paleohora to Hora Sfakion (€16, three hours), via Sougia (€8.50, 50 minutes), Agia Roumeli (€12.50, 1½ hours) and Loutro (€14, 2½ hours). The same boat also continues three times per week in summer to Gavdos (€15.50, 2½ hours).

From mid-April M/B *Elafonisos* ferries people to the west-coast beach of Elafonisi (€8, one hour). The service increases from three times per week to daily in mid-May through September. It departs at 10am and returns at 4pm.

Tickets can be bought at **Selino Travel** (⎙28230 42272; selino2@otenet.gr).

Bus

In summer there are four to six buses per day from the **bus station** (⎙28230 41914) to Hania (€7.60, one hour 50 minutes). There is also one daily service, departing 6.15am, to Omalos (€5.50, two hours), for Samaria Gorge, which also stops at the entrance to Agia Irini Gorge (€4.50).

❶ Getting Around

Notos Rentals (⎙28230 42110; notosgr@ yahoo.gr; Eleftheriou Venizelou) hires cars, motorcycles and mountain bikes.

The **taxi stand** is near the port. Sample fares are Kissamos-Kastelli (€40), Hania (€60; airport €70) and Elafonisi (€60).

Around Paleohora

The village of **Anydri**, 5km northeast of Paleohora, is a popular destination for walkers and is reached via a picturesque drive through a gorge. The founding fathers of the village were two brothers from Hora Sfakion fleeing a murderous vendetta, which is why most villagers have the same surname.

Many people walk a circuit route from Paleohora to Andyri via the gorge to return along the coast. Take the road that goes past the campground and follow the paved road that forks off to the left, which is bordered by steep rocks. As you enter the village you'll see a sign directing you to the **Anydri Gorge**. After a few hundred metres on a footpath you'll see an overgrown path on the left. Red markers direct you to the gorge. Alternatively, you can have a break in the village at the excellent **Kafeneio To Scholio**, a converted school, and take another path from there past the **Church of Agios Georgios**, which has 14th-century frescoes.

After walking along the dried-out riverbed, signs direct you to wide **Gialiskari Beach** at the end of the gorge. The nicest stretch is the beach with coarse sand at the eastern end, left of the *kantina*. You can take a different path back to Paleohora following the E4 markers, which will take you along the coastal cliffs. The beach is accessible by a drivable dirt road, from where it is signposted to the right well before the gorge.

The most unique village near Paleohora, however, is **Azogires**. Some 9km north of town, this eccentric place is full of legends involving river Nereids in its waterfalls and medieval ascetics who inhabited cave dwellings. Both the waterfalls and the caves can be visited today, and a handy local map lists these and other attractions. Maps, more info and some good food and drink can be found at **Alpha Restaurant** (mains €4-7) on the main square. There, American-born local guide Lakkis 'Lucky' Koukoutsakis leads tours of the village and **Azogires Gorge**, and provides local information. The related **Alpha Hotel** (⎙28230 41620; www.alfahotel azogires.blogspot.com; r from €25; [P✳@]) caters to yoga groups but has decent digs for independent travellers too, in a relaxed wooded setting just above the village centre.

GAVDOS ΓΑΥΔΟΣ

POP 55

Gavdos (*gav*-dos) is as much a state of mind as it is an island. If you want to get away from it all, there is no better place for peace and isolation. Gavdos attracts a loyal following of campers, nudists and free spirits seeking natural beaches, long walks and laid-back holidays. This is the place for chilling out, letting your beard grow, rolling cigarettes and spending the nights looking at the starry skies.

Located in the Libyan Sea 65km from Paleohora and 45km from Hora Sfakion, Gavdos is the most southerly place in Europe. Geographically it's more akin to Africa than Europe and enjoys a very mild climate. You can swim as early as February. Gavdos is surprisingly green, with almost 65% of the island covered in low-lying pine and cedar trees and vegetation, although it has a rugged natural landscape. There are several stunning beaches, some of which are accessible only by foot or boat. Most of the beaches are on the northeastern coast, as the southern coastline is all cliffs.

Gavdos has three main 'villages', which are virtually abandoned and full of ruins, and one beach settlement that gets relatively lively in July and August. At its tourist peak, the island's permanent population of about 55 residents may swell to 1000.

Archaeological excavations indicate that the island was inhabited as far back as the neolithic period. In the Greco-Roman era Gavdos, then known as Clauda, belonged to the city of Gortyna. There was a Roman settlement on the northwestern corner. Under the Byzantines, Gavdos was the seat of a bishopric, but when the Arabs conquered Crete in the 9th century the island became a pirates' nest.

Until the late 1960s Gavdos had little water and no electricity or phones, and most residents emigrated to Paleohora or other parts of Crete, or to Athens. While water is now plentiful, there can still be electricity shortages and blackouts (particularly in summer) as only part of the island has grid power – the rest uses generators, which are often turned off at night and in the middle of the day. It is wise to take a torch. Strong winds can leave visitors stranded for days on end, but you won't find too many people complaining.

◎ Sights & Activities

The biggest beach community is at **Sarakiniko**, in the northeast, which has a wide swathe of sand and several tavernas, as well as an **amphitheatre** for occasional performances. The stunning **Agios Ioannis** beach, on the northern tip, has a scraggly summer settlement of nudists and campers, though numbers swell in high summer. There are some wonderful beaches on the northern coast such as **Potamos** and **Pyrgos**, which you can reach by foot (about an hour) from Kastri if you follow the footpath leading north to Ambelos and beyond. Three giant arches carved into the rocky headland at **Tripiti** – the southernmost tip of Europe – are the island's best-known natural feature. The beach is reached by boat or on foot (about 2.6km from Vatsiana).

The restored 1880 **lighthouse** on the road to the village of Ambelos has a museum and cafe. Before it was bombed by the Germans in 1941 it was the world's second-brightest lighthouse after Tierra del Fuego.

In **Vatsiana**, the island's priest has created a small private **museum** (☑28230 42167; ☉10am-6pm Jul-Aug, knock next door at other times) in an old stone house with items collected from the island, including agricultural and domestic tools, a loom and weavings. There is a small working traditional wood oven next door and the priest's wife, Maria, runs the quaint attached *kafeneio*, where you can try her ouzo and cake.

Despite the meagre population, there are 16 small churches dotted around the island. Most boat owners offer full- and half-day **cruises**, including trips to the remote, uninhabited island of Gavdopoula, although there are no good beaches there. Ask at the tavernas.

✗ Eating

Fresh fish, of course, is the singular highlight of dining in Gavdos.

Taverna Sarakiniko   SEAFOOD €€
Run by Manolis the fisherman and his wife Gerti, this taverna serves Manolis' fresh catch daily. Try the tangy grilled octopus or red snapper braised with lemon and olive oil.

Theophilos Taverna   GREEK €
Above Agios Ioannis beach, this place has excellent trays of *mayirefta* catering to the campers coming up from the beach.

ℹ Information

The island's port is Karabe, on the east side of the island, while the capital, Kastri, is in the centre. There is no bank but you can send mail in Sarakiniko. There are a couple of minimarkets for basic supplies, and a medical clinic at Kastri. Mobile coverage is patchy but cardphones are available. Gavdos has a short season, as most tavernas and rooms shut by early September when schools start.

Gavdos has a new port and a **police station** (☏ 28230 41109) at Karabe.

ℹ Getting There & Around

Services to Gavdos vary throughout the year and can take between 2½ to five hours depending on the boat and other stops, so it can be confusing. The most direct route to Gavdos is from Hora Sfakion, which has services to Gavdos on Friday, Saturday and Sunday (€15, 2½ hours). There are also two boats per week from Paleohora, increasing to three from mid-July to August, though they go via the southern ports and Hora Sfakion, making it a long five-hour trip. There is also a Tuesday-morning post boat from Paleohora (via Sougia).

Only some ferries takes cars, so check if you plan on taking one across.

You can hire a bike or car at the port or in Sarakiniko, but check insurance details beforehand.

WEST OF HANIA

Western Crete is less affected by tourism than the city of Hania and its satellite resorts. The northern coast is defined by the virtually uninhabited Gramvousa and Rodopou Peninsulas. Kolymbari, at the foot of the Rodopou Peninsula, is the most developed tourist town (but more famous for its nationally distributed olive oil).

The Kissamos province is a rugged region of scattered villages and towns sustained by agriculture. Its capital, Kissamos-Kastelli, is the port for boats from the Peloponnese. The west coast has two of Crete's finest beaches, both of which are surprisingly underdeveloped: Falasarna in the northern corner and Elafonisi in the southern corner. The Selino province includes the Innahorion region of small mountain villages.

Rodopou Peninsula

The barren, rocky Rodopou Peninsula has a few small villages clustered at its base but the rest is uninhabited. A paved road goes as far as Afrata, but then becomes a dirt track that meanders through the peninsula. If you are travelling by foot, 4WD or motorcycle you can reach the Diktynna sanctuary at the end of the peninsula, but make sure you have planned your journey and are well supplied; there is not a drop of petrol or water, nor a morsel of food, beyond Afrata. From Afrata a road winds down to the small, gravelly pebbly **Afrata Beach**, which also supports a small seasonal snack bar.

Kolymbari Κολυμπάρι

POP 920

Kolymbari, 23km west of Hania, is at the base of the Rodopou Peninsula, and appeals to those seeking a quiet, relaxing holiday. Development of the fishing hamlet has continued, taking advantage of the village's long pebbly beach. Kolymbari is a good base for a walk to Moni Gonias and an excellent place to sample local fish at one of the well-regarded fish tavernas.

The bus from Hania drops you off on the main road, from which it is a 500m walk down to the settlement. There is an ATM on the main street and a post office in the centre of the village.

✗ Eating

Argentina   SEAFOOD €€
(fish per kg €40-55) Considered one of the best fish tavernas in the area, the classic Argentina has tables on the main road and across the street overlooking the sea. It serves seafood dishes such as octopus with olives, quality fish and has a select wine list.

Diktina   SEAFOOD €€
(fish per kg €40-60) This place has had an upmarket facelift and looks more like a city restaurant than a fish taverna, but it has sea views and a range of reliable fish dishes.

Milos tou Tzerani   SEAFOOD €€€
This cafe-bar in a restored mill on the sea is a great place for a coffee or an evening drink and also has light snacks and mezedhes.

ℹ Getting There & Away

Buses from Hania to Kissamos-Kastelli stop at Kolymbari (€3.30, 45 minutes, half-hourly).

Moni Gonias Μονή Γονιάς

Founded in 1618, **Moni Gonias** (Kolymbari; admission free, museum €2; ☺8am-12.30pm & 4-8pm Mon-Fri, 4-8pm Sat, 7am-noon & 4-8pm Sun) was damaged by the Turks in 1645, but rebuilt in 1662 and extended in the 19th century. The monastery houses a unique collection of icons dating from the 17th and 18th centuries. Some are in the church while others are in the monastery's two-room museum. The most valuable icon is that of *Agios Nikolaos,* painted in 1637 by Palaiokapas (in the museum on your left). It perfectly exemplifies the Cretan school of icon painting that flourished in the 17th century. The monastery, which also incorporates Crete's Theological College, is easy to reach from Kolymbari. Take the beach road north from the town centre for about 500m.

Diktynna Δίκτυνα

On the tip of the Rodopou Peninsula are the remains of a temple to the Cretan goddess Diktynna, which was the most important religious sanctuary in the region under the Romans. Diktynna was the goddess of hunting and she was worshipped fervently in western Crete.

Legend has it that her name derives from the word *diktyon*, which means 'net'. It was a fisherman's net that saved her when she leapt into the sea to avoid the amorous desires of King Minos. The temple dates from the 2nd century AD but it was probably built on the site of an earlier temple.

After the collapse of the Roman Empire the temple was desecrated but you can see the temple's foundations and a sacrificial altar as well as Roman cisterns. If you are 'templed out' you can relax on a lovely sandy beach. Diktynna is accessible only by dirt road from Kolymbari, but travel agencies in Hania offer boat excursions.

Kissamos-Kastelli
Κίσσαμος-Καστέλλι

POP 3970

The largest town and capital of Kissamos province is Kissamos-Kastelli, referred to interchangeably by either name by locals (though officially the former). This north-coast port town is where the ferries arrive from the Peloponnese or Kythira. It's a quiet town of mostly elderly residents, with strong sustenance from the area's vast olive groves. Kissamos has a more Greek feel than other north-coast resorts – perhaps the distance from Hania has saved it from the extremes of package tourism – and for whatever reason, most of the visitors seem to be from Crete or other parts of Greece. And, in addition to the older, small hotels, there are some smart new places that attest to Kissamos' increasing attractiveness.

For beach lovers, Kissamos-Kastelli is a great base: along with the fine sandy beach in town, there are nearby Falasarna and the beaches around Gramvousa (usually accessed by boat trip), and it is possible to drive straight south to Elafonisi from here, too.

Indeed, having a car is a big help for anyone wishing to explore the area – the Bay of Kissamos, which features isolated settlements and other beaches, is huge and even some of the town's hotels (and especially the port, at the far west of town) can be very spread out. However, if you're without a car, buses to the port (for the boat trips to Gramvousa beaches) or Falasarna beach are conveniently timed.

From Kissamos-Kastelli's central square (where the bus arrives), it is a three-minute walk down to the central waterfront, where tavernas and bars line the seafront promenade. The town beach east of this central point is pebbly, whereas the one west of the central waterfront (about 600m, after crossing a diminutive bridge) is much nicer. You can have a free umbrella here when buying a drink from the cafes above the beach.

History

In antiquity, Kissamos was the main town of the province of the same name. When the Venetians came along and built a castle here it became known as Kastelli. The name persisted until 1966 when authorities decided that too many people were confusing it with Crete's other Kastelli, near Iraklio. The official name reverted to Kissamos, though it is still often called Kastelli or Kissamos-Kastelli.

Ancient Kissamos was a harbour for the important city state of Polyrrinia, 7km inland. Vestiges of Roman buildings have been unearthed, but most of the ancient city lies beneath the modern town of Kissamos and cannot be excavated. Kissamos gained independence in the 3rd century

AD and then became a bishopric under the Byzantines. It was occupied by the Saracens in the 9th century and flourished under the Venetians. Parts of the castle wall survive to the west of Plateia Tzanakaki.

◉ Sights

FREE **Archaeological Museum of Kissamos**   MUSEUM

(☑28220 83308; Plateia Tzanakaki; ⊙8.30am-1pm) The new museum, in an imposing two-level Venetian-Turkish building on the main square, has a well-displayed collection of artefacts unearthed during archaeological digs in the area, including statues, jewellery, coins and a large mosaic floor from a Kissamos villa. There are exhibits from Falasarna and Polyrrinia and most of the collection spans the Hellenistic-Roman eras, though there are displays from Minoan excavations and Nopigia.

✖ Eating & Drinking

Papadakis   SEAFOOD €€

(fish per kg €40-55) This classic taverna on the central waterfront is the best place in town for fresh fish (caught by the iconic owner), but also has plenty of *mayirefta* and grills. Try the roast aubergines or *keftedhakia* (meatballs).

Taverna Petra   RESTAURANT €

(souvlakia €2.30) This unassuming place cornering the main square (just up from the bus stop) serves the best souvlaki pitta in town (along with a range of other grilled meats), accompanied by pungent local olive oil – a nourishing and better-value alternative to the waterfront restaurants.

Café Bar Babel   CAFE €

(waterfront; ⊙9am-2am) Not only a good choice for a quick breakfast or snack, this waterfront cafe-bar is a great place for coffee and gets lively at night with young Greeks. It has one of the most extensive beer and cocktail lists in town.

❶ Information

The port is 3km west of town. In summer a bus meets the boats; otherwise a taxi costs around €5. The bus station is on the main square, Plateia Tzanakaki, and the main commercial street, Skalidi, runs east from Plateia Tzanakaki. The post office is on the main through road, near Plateia Venizelou. There are a number of banks with ATMs along the highway and Skalidi. It's a 200m walk to reach the foreshore promenade.

Kissamos has a reasonably informative website, www.kissamos.net. **Horeftakis Tours** (☑28220 23250; www.horeftakistours.com; Skalidi) is a good source of information. **Gamers Internet Cafe** (Skalidi 17; per hr €1.70; ⊙10am-late) has the full service.

❶ Getting There & Away

Boat

ANEN Ferries operates the F/B *Myrtidiotissa* at weekends on a route that takes in Antikythira (€9.40, two hours), Kythira (€16.40, four hours) and Gythio (€22.10, five hours). Sunday's service does serve Piraeus eventually but it's far quicker to go from Hania. You can buy tickets from **Horeftakis Tours** (☑28220 23250) and the **ANEN office** (☑28220 22009; Skalidi).

Bus

From Kissamos' **bus station**, there are 13 buses per day to Hania (€4.70, one hour), where you can change for Rethymno and Iraklio; two buses per day for Falasarna (€3.50, 20 minutes), one bus per day to Paleohora (€7.20, 1¼ hours) and one to Elafonisi (€7, 1¼ hours).

❶ Getting Around

Moto Fun (☑28220 23440; www.motofun.info; Plateia Tzanakaki) Cars, bicycles and mountain bikes for hire.

Polyrrinia Πολυρρηνία

The ancient city ruins of Polyrrinia (pol-ee-ren-*ee*-a) lie about 7km south of Kissamos-Kastelli, above the village of Ano Paleokastro (also called Polyrrinia). It's a steep climb to the ruins, but the sea and mountain views are stunning and the region is blanketed with wildflowers in spring. The city was founded by the Dorians in the 6th century BC and was constantly at war with the Kydonians from Hania. Coins from the period depict the warrior-goddess Athena, who was evidently revered by the warlike Polyrrinians.

Unlike their rivals the Kydonians, the Polyrrinians did not resist the Roman invasion and thus the city was spared destruction. It was the best-fortified town in Crete and the administrative centre of western Crete from the Roman through to the Byzantine period. The Venetians used it as a fortress. Many of the structures, including an **aqueduct** built by Hadrian, date from the Roman period.

The most impressive feature of the site is the **acropolis** built by the Byzantines and Venetians. There's also a church built on the foundations of a **Hellenistic temple** from the 4th century BC. Near the aqueduct is a **cave** dedicated to the nymphs; it still contains the niches for nymph statuettes.

It's a scenic two-hour walk from Kissamos-Kastelli to Polyrrinia. To reach the Polyrrinia road, walk east along the Kissamos-Kastelli main road and turn right after the OTE (Organismos Tilepikoinonion Ellados; Greece's major telecommunications carrier) office. You can reach the site through the village on foot, passing by the interesting olive wood **workshop** of Giorgos Tsichlakis.

If you are driving, take the perimeter road at the turn-off for the **Acropolis Taverna** (mains €4-7), which has lovely views. Behind the taverna there is a path to the left about 100m before the Agios Pateras church which leads to the acropolis. You can do a full circuit around the hill to take in the views but the path can be overgrown.

There are no buses to the site.

Gramvousa Peninsula
Χερσόνησος Γραμβούσα

Northwest of Kissamos-Kastelli is the beautifully wild and remote Gramvousa Peninsula, whose main attraction is the stunning lagoon-like sandy beach of **Balos**, on Cape Tigani on the west side of the peninsula's narrow tip. The idyllic beach with turquoise waters is overlooked by the two islets of **Agria** (wild) and **Imeri** (tame). Unless you are staying over somewhere on the peninsula, or free camping, the easiest way to get here is one of the daily boat trips departing from Kissamos-Kastelli port each day.

In summer, the crowds do come – the only way to avoid this is to go independently and wake up early or stay up late. However, though it is busy from about 11am to 4pm in summer, the beach remains undeniably gorgeous, with lapping translucent waters

dotted with tiny shellfish and darting fish. There is no shade, however, and umbrellas with sunbeds cost €5.

The very rough but drivable dirt road (best in a 4WD) to Balos begins at the end of the main street of **Kalyviani** village and follows the eastern slope of Mt Geroskinos (762m). From here, the views over the shoreline and the Rodopou Peninsula are spectacular.

The road ends at a car park (with a *kantina*) from where the path to the beach is 1.2km down the sandy cliffs.

West-bound buses from Kissamos-Kastelli will let you off at the turn-off for Kalyviani, from where it is a 2km walk to the beginning of the path at the far end of the main street. The shadeless walk to Balos is around 3km – wear a hat and take plenty of water.

A far easier way to get there is on one of the three daily **cruises** (☎28220 24344; www .gramvousa.com; adult/concession €22/12) on differently sized boats. There is plenty of food (including souvlaki, €5) and drink available on board but it is perfectly fine to bring your own lunch and save money that way. Each boat stops at different places first to avoid overcrowding, either at Balos or at the island of Imeri Gramvousa, which is crowned with a **Venetian castle** from which there are stunning views of the peninsula. It's a steep 20-minute walk to the top and there is a rocky and generally unusable beach below with a (modern and not particularly compelling) shipwreck. However, if you want to go for a swim instead of sweat it up to the castle, it is deep enough to simply dive and swim off the boat while it is moored at the island.

Tickets for boat trips from the three different companies can be bought on the day at Kissamos-Kastelli port or through some local hotels in advance for a discount. Departures are at 10.15am, 10.30am and 1pm, and they have you back in Kissamos-Kastelli by 5.45pm and 8pm respectively. If it's windy the trip can be rough – or even cancelled altogether – so check the day before you plan to go to be sure it will be happening.

History

The offshore island of Imeri Gramvousa was an important vantage point for the Venetians, who built a fortress here to protect ships on their way to and from Venice. It was considered an impregnable fort and had a large cache of armaments. The Turks did not conquer Imeri Gramvousa along with the rest of Crete in 1645; the fort remained in Venetian hands. Eventually the Venetians left and the fort fell into disuse until it was taken over in 1821 by Cretan revolutionaries. It later became a notorious base for piracy before the Turks took it and used it to blockade the coast during the War of Independence. Local legend has it that the pirates amassed a fabulous fortune that they hid in caves around the island.

The **Kalyviani shipwreck**, rusting on the west side of Kalyviani beach, is a Lebanese-registered ship that struck trouble on its way from Libya to Crete in 1981.

Eating

Gramvousa GREEK €

(☎28220 22707; wood-oven specials €5.50-8.70) In the centre of the village, Gramvousa serves fine traditional Cretan cuisine in an attractively decorated stone building set in a superb garden. Try the wood-oven specials such as the suckling pig or lamb with honey.

Falasarna Φαλάσαρνα

POP 25

Falasarna, 16km west of Kissamos-Kastelli, was a Cretan city-state in the 4th century BC but there's not much of the ancient city left to see. It attracts a mixed bunch of travellers due to its long, wide stretch of sandy beach, which is considered one of the best in Crete. It is split up into several coves by rocky spits and is known for its stunning sunsets and the pink hues reflecting from the fine coral in the sand.

Along with great water clarity, Falasarna has wonderfully big waves – long rollers coming from the open Mediterranean that are great for splashing around in. It gets busy from mid-July to mid-August, primarily with day trippers from Hania and Kissamos-Kastelli, as there is neither village nor facilities – just a scattering of widely spaced rooms, a couple of tavernas and a shop among the greenhouses that somewhat mar the approach to the beach. There is no organised 'beach scene', though there is a beach bar on the cliffs at the central point of the beach, and the omnipresent beach umbrellas and sun loungers at different locations (€2). The big beach to the south

is the livelier spot, with the middle rocky cove frequented by nudists, and there's a quieter smaller beach to the north. Free camping is tolerated and allows you to feel the beach's escapist vibe after the masses have left for the day.

History

The mysterious word 'Falasarna' is of unclear provenance – it may even pre-date the Greek language itself. The area has been occupied at least since the 6th century BC, but reached the height of its power in the 4th century BC. Although it was built next to the sea, the town's ruins are about 400m away from the water because the western coast of Crete has risen over the centuries. The town owed its wealth to the agricultural produce from the fertile valley to the south. It was the west-coast harbour for Polyrrinia but later became Polyrrinia's chief rival for dominance over western Crete. By the time of the Roman invasion of Crete in 67 BC, Falasarna had become a haven for pirates. Stone blocks excavated around the entrance to the old harbour indicate that the Romans may have tried to block off the harbour to prevent it from being used by pirates.

◉ Sights

The **ruins** of the ancient city of Falasarna are the area's main attraction, although not much is visible. Signs direct you to the ancient city from the main road, following a dirt road at the end of the asphalt.

First you'll come to a large stone throne, the purpose of which is unknown. Further on there are the remains of the wall that once fortified the town and a small harbour. Notice the holes carved into the wall, which were used to tie up boats. At the top of the hill there are the remains of the acropolis wall and a temple, as well as four clay baths.

✖ Eating

Galasia Thea GREEK €

(mayirefta €4.50-6) On the cliff overlooking the great expanse of beach, this cafe has spectacular views from its huge terrace. There's a big range of baked dishes and *mayirefta* such as the *Sfakiano* lemon lamb.

Also recommended is **Sun Set**, a taverna for fish and classic Cretan food.

❶ Getting There & Away

From June through August there are two buses daily from Kissamos-Kastelli to Falasarna (€3.50), as well as three buses from Hania (€6).

Innahorion Villages
Ινναχωριών

Some of western Crete's most scenic and unvisited mountain villages, the Innahorion (derived from 'Enneia Horia', or 'nine villages'), are spread across the far western coastal region, along the route connecting Moni Hrysoskalitissas and Elafonisi beach in the south with Falasarna and Kissamos-Kastelli in the north. This quiet area renowned for its chestnuts and olives is one of the lushest and most fertile parts of the island.

The first village of interest, idyllic **Voulgaro**, is located 9km southeast of Kissamos-Kastelli on the road towards Elafonisi. Its name (by allusion, 'Bulgarian village') is said to descend from the identity of settlers brought to the place when Byzantine Emperor Nikiforos Fokas recaptured Crete from the Arabs in the 961 expedition to Crete. Testaments to the Byzantine period remain with the ruined 15th-century **Basilica of Agia Varvara**, 2km down a southeastern side road in tiny **Latsiana**, and the **church of Agios Nikolaos**, 2km beyond that in the hamlet of **Mouri**. The former was built on an ancient Greek temple site, while the latter has distinctive surviving frescoes. There are fantastic views from both sites.

From Voulgaro, the main road towards Elafonisi leads (after 3km) to **Topolia**, a lovely village clustered with whitewashed houses overhung with plants and vines. Beyond it, the road skirts the edge of the 1.5km-long **Topolia Gorge**, bending and twisting and affording dramatic views. It ends at tiny **Koutsomatados**, from where hikers can access the gorge.

After a narrow tunnel, the **Agia Sofia cave** contains evidence of settlement from as far back as the neolithic era. The cave is often used for baptisms and celebrates the patron saint's day on 13 April. A third of the way up the 250 rock-cut steps to the cave, the taverna **Romantza** has great views over the ravine. However, for the area's best eating, as well as blissfully serene traditional lodgings, continue south a couple of kilometres through the village of Vlatos to reach the

ecotourism settlement of **Milia** (p64). Firmly in the grip of forested mountains, Milia is the best place to circle the wagons for a few days while making local excursions, and it offers plenty of good forested hikes itself.

Elos, near the south of the Innahorion, is the region's largest town and centre of the chestnut trade – hence the annual **chestnut festival**, on the third Sunday of October. The plane, eucalyptus and chestnut trees around the main square make Elos a cool and relaxing place to stop. Behind the taverna on the main square stand remains of a once-working aqueduct that used to power the old mill. Further south, atmospheric **Perivolia** leads to **Kefali**, with its 14th-century frescoed church. Kefali has a handful of tavernas taking advantage of the lovely setting and view. From here, you can choose either to continue onwards to Elafonisi beach or loop back along the coast. The latter route, one of Crete's best, winds around cliffs with magnificent coastal views unfolding after every bend.

The western Innahorion villages that line the coastal road enjoy a stunning location between mountains and ravines. First is the hamlet of **Pappadiana**, about 2km west of Kefali, from where the road rises into the mountains before manifesting superlative sea views from a bluff at **Amygdalokefali**. Good hiking, beach access and decent accommodation can be found at **Kambos**, a tiny village on the edge of a gorge further along the winding road.

The coastal road winds along, after 9km, to **Sfinari**, a languid, laid-back agricultural village with a sizeable beach. With the northern end backed by many greenhouses, the beach has a small gravelly cove, a basic campsite and a few fine beachside fish tavernas. After Sfinari you'll get more coastal views before the road drops down to **Platanos**, a quiet, tree-lined and rather scattered village of whitewashed houses. As the name would suggest, this inconspicuous village is known for its leafy square, where you can enjoy a good Greek coffee under the plane trees.

Moni Hrysoskalitissas
Μονή Χρυσοσκαλίτισσας

Five kilometres north of Elafonisi is this beautiful **monastery** (admission €2; ⊙7am-7pm) perched on a rock high above the sea. Hrysoskalitissas (hris-os-ka-*lee*-tiss-as) means 'golden staircase'. Some accounts suggest the top step of the 98 steps leading to the monastery was made of gold, but could only be seen by the faithful. Another version says one of the steps was hollow and used to hide the church's treasury. In any case, during the Turkish occupation the gold, along with much of the monastery's estate, was used to pay hefty taxes imposed by the Ottoman rulers.

The church is recent but the monastery is allegedly a thousand years old and may have been built on the site of a Minoan temple.

The monastery has created two small rudimentary **museums** on site, a folk museum with a selection of weavings and objects from rural life and an ecclesiastical museum with mostly icons and manuscripts. Buses to Elafonisi drop passengers here.

There are a handful of tavernas and accommodation options nearby, offering an alternative base for Elafonisi. **Glykeria** (☏28220 61292; www.glykeria.com; d incl breakfast €50; ❋❂❄) is a small and friendly family-run hotel with neat and simple rooms with fridges and balconies overlooking the sea, as well as an inviting pool and a taverna across the road. It's on the main road before the monastery.

Elafonisi Ελαφονήσι

POP 15

As one of the loveliest sandy beaches in Crete, it's easy to understand why people enthuse so much about Elafonisi. At the southern extremity of Crete's west coast, the beach is long, wide and is separated from the Elafonisi Islet by about 50m of knee-deep water. The clear, shallow turquoise water and fine sand create a tropical paradise. There are a few snack bars on the beach and stalls to rent umbrellas and lounge chairs. The islet is marked by low dunes and a string of semi-secluded coves that attract a sprinkling of naturists. Unfortunately this idyllic scene can be spoilt by the busloads of day trippers who arrive in summer. There is some accommodation nearby for those who want to luxuriate in the quiet that descends in late afternoon, and several more options around Hrysoskalitissas.

✖ Eating

Innahorion   CRETAN €

(mains €3-6) About 2.5km before the coast at Elafonisi, this restaurant is the best in the area, serving good Cretan food on the terrace.

❶ Getting There & Away

There is one boat daily from Paleohora to Elafonisi (€8, one hour) from mid-May through September, which leaves at 10am and returns at 4pm. There is also one bus daily from Hania (€11, 2½ hours) and Kissamos-Kastelli (€7, 1¼ hours), which return in the afternoon.

EAST OF HANIA

The northeastern corner of Hania prefecture contains some interesting sights, including the island's only natural freshwater lake, Lake Kournas, and beach resorts such as Kalyves, Almyrida and Georgioupoli, which retain more of a village feel than the resorts spread along the coast west of Hania. There are also the restored village of Vamos and the ancient site of Aptera, as well as traditional villages such as Gavalohori. Increased package tourism is changing the nature of the Apokoronas Peninsula, as is the real-estate construction frenzy for holiday homes for foreigners.

Georgioupoli Γεωργιούπολη

POP 490

No longer the quiet getaway that it once was, Georgioupoli has been swamped by coastal hotel development. Popular with families and nature lovers, it still retains some of the ambience of a languid seaside tourist town. The town's most distinctive features are the eucalyptus trees lining the streets that fan out from the main square and the picturesque small chapel of Agios Nikolaos, jutting from a narrow rocky jetty in the sea.

Located at the junction of the Almyros River and the sea, Georgioupoli is a nesting area for the endangered loggerhead sea turtle. The **marshes** surrounding the riverbed are known for their bird life, especially the egrets and kingfishers that migrate into the area in April, as well as the hordes of mosquitoes in summer. The river spills its icy water near the smaller beach to the north of the port, where another small church, Agios Kyriakos, stands at the far end of the cove.

The long narrow stretch of hard-packed sand east of town, spliced by another river leading into the sea, becomes a long sandy beach that continues for about 10km towards Rethymno.

Georgioupoli was named after Prince George, High Commissioner of Crete from 1898 to 1906, who had a hunting lodge there. During Classical times it was known as Amphimalla and was the port of ancient Lappa.

It is a handy base from which to explore Hania and Rethymno.

◎ Sights & Activities

If you don't have wheels, a **tourist train** (€6) runs trips to nearby Kournas Lake and Argiroupoli.

Yellowboat   BOAT TRIPS
(per person per hr €6) Hires pedal boats and canoes to go up the river.

Adventure Bikes   CYCLING
(☎28250 61830; www.adventurebikes.org) Hires bikes and runs bike tours around the region (€35 to €56).

✕ Eating

Poseidon Taverna   SEAFOOD €€
(fish per kg €30-50) Signposted down a narrow alley to the left as you come into the village, this well-regarded place is run by a fishing family. You can choose from the fish and seafood laid out on the counter and enjoy an excellent meal under the mulberry trees in the lovely courtyard.

Arolithos   GREEK €
(mains €5-9) Near Andy's Rooms, Arolithos has an extensive selection of appetisers, traditional Greek dishes such as *spetsofaï* (sausage and pepper stew), and some creative offerings such as grilled chicken with orange sauce.

☆ Entertainment

There's not much of a bar scene in Georgioupoli, though the new **Tropicana Club**, a massive two-level beach hut, was hoping to liven things up. **Titos** is the liveliest bar on the main square.

The sprawling **Edem** park complex on the beach has a large pool open to the public. It presents live Cretan music occasionally

in summer, as do some of the hotels and tavernas in town.

❶ Information

The main street from the highway leads to the town centre, where there are a number of travel agencies, tavernas and ATMs. **Ballos Travel** (☎28250 83088; www.ballos.gr) can organise boat tickets, excursions and accommodation, and also changes money, hires out cars and arranges money transfers; it also sells stamps – the town postbox is outside. **Planet Internet Cafe** (per hr €3; ☉9am-late) is near the square. There is accommodation and other information on www.georgioupoli.net.

❶ Getting There & Away

Buses between Hania and Rethymno stop on the highway outside Georgioupoli.

Lake Kournas Λίμνη Κουρνάς

Lake Kournas, 4km inland from Georgiou-poli, is a lovely, restful place to have lunch or to pass an afternoon. The island's only natural lake, it is about 1.5km in diameter, 45m deep and is fed by underground springs. There's a narrow sandy strip around the lake and you can walk two-thirds of the way around. The crystal-clear water is great for swimming and changes colour according to the season and time of day. You can hire **pedal boats** and **canoes** (€4 per hour) and view the turtles, crabs, fish and snakes that make the lake their home, although tourist buses can crowd the lake in the peak of summer.

There are a number of tavernas around the lake, but few of the older rent-rooms above the tavernas were operating. The shady **To Mati tis Limnis** (mains €5.50-7) on the quieter end of the lake makes good traditional Greek dishes such as rabbit *stifadho* (braised with onions) or filling *myzithropites*.

You could also try **Omorfi Limni**, which dominates the other end of the restaurant strip, or stop for a drink and enjoy the stunning views of the lake and sea from up high at the oddly American Indian–themed **Empire Cafe**.

The lake is below **Kournas village**, a steep 5km up a hill. Kournas is a traditional village of whitewashed houses, a few stone homes and a couple of *kafeneia*. You can get a delicious meal at the **Kali**

Kardia Taverna (grills €5-7) on the main street. Owner Kostas Agapinakis is known for his award-winning sausages, excellent *apaki* (smoked pork) and meats cooked on the grill outside the taverna. If you are lucky you might get to try his delicious *galakto-boureko* (custard pastry) while it is still warm.

A tourist mini-train runs from Georgiou-poli to Lake Kournas in summer, but no public transport.

Almyrida Αλμυρίδα

POP 120

The former fishing village of Almyrida, 14km east of Kalyves, is considerably less developed than its neighbour, although it's getting more so. Still, it's a reasonable spot to hang out for a few days and is probably a better option for independent travellers than Kalyves. Almyrida is popular for windsurfing because of its long, exposed beach. History buffs can check out the remains of an **early Christian basilica** at the western end of the village.

One road through the village runs along the beach. There's an ATM and you can check mail at **Internet Services** (⊙11am-9pm). **Flisvos Tours** (✆/fax 28250 31100; ⊙8am-1.30pm & 5-9.30pm), just off the main road, hires cars, scooters and mountain bikes. The French-run **UCPA Sports** (✆28250 31443; www.ucpa.com) offers windsurfing (€8 per hour) and hires catamarans and kayaks. **Dream Adventure Trips** (✆6944357383) offers speedboat swimming and snorkelling trips to nearby caves, coves and Marathi beach (€15).

✖ Eating

Psaros   GREEK €
(mains €6-10) Well located right on the far end of the beach, with classic blue-and-white-chequered island decor, Psaros has fresh fish and friendly staff.

Lagos   GREEK €
(mains €5.50-8) At the entrance to the town; serves good-value traditional cooking on a lovely shaded terrace.

Dimitri's   GREEK €
(mains €4-7) This family tavern is recommended for its friendly service and produce from its farm.

Aptera Απτερα

The ruins of the ancient city of **Aptera** (⊙8am-3pm Tue-Sun), about 3km west of Kalyves, are spread out over two hills that loom over Souda Bay. Founded in the 7th century BC, Aptera was one of the most important city-states of western Crete and was continuously inhabited until an earthquake destroyed it in the 7th century AD.

It came back to life with the Byzantine reconquest of Crete in the 10th century, and became a bishopric. In the 12th century, the monastery of St John the Theologian was established; the reconstructed monastery is the centre of the site.

The site is still being excavated. Diggers recently exposed the remains of a fortified tower, a city gate and a massive wall that surrounded the city. You can also see Roman cisterns and a 2nd-century-BC Greek temple. At the western end there's a Turkish fortress, which was built in 1872 and enjoys a panoramic view of Souda Bay. The fortress was built as part of a large Turkish fortress-building program during a period when the Cretans were in an almost constant state of insurrection. Notice the 'Wall of the Inscriptions' – this was probably part of an important public building and was excavated in 1862 by French archaeologists. The Greek Ministry of Culture is continuing to restore the site, installing signs and paths.

There's no public transport to Aptera.

Vamos Βάμος

POP 650

The 12th-century village of Vamos, 26km southeast of Hania, was the capital of the Sfakia province from 1867 to 1913 and was the scene of a revolt against Turkish rule in 1896. It is now the capital of the Apokoronas province. In 1995 a group of villagers banded together to preserve the traditional way of life of Vamos. They persuaded the EU to fund a project to showcase the crafts and products of the region and develop a new kind of tourism for Crete. They restored the old stone buildings of the village using traditional materials and crafts and turned them into guesthouses, and they opened shops and cafes where visitors could taste regional products. This operation has expanded and now dominates the village, which is nonetheless a pleasant stop or base for exploring the region. While the authentic village theme is overrated, it is one of the better examples of this style of alternative tourism.

In late March or early April, Vamos celebrates **Hohliovradia** (Snail Night) with a festival of cooked snails, washed down with wine and *raki*.

The **Vamos tourist office** (☑/fax 28250 23251; www.vamossa.gr; ☺9am-9pm Jun-Oct) hires cars, books excursions and runs regular Cretan cooking lessons in a restored olive press. It arranges accommodation in a range of **Traditional Guesthouses** (cottages €75-120). The lovely restored stone cottages have kitchens, fireplaces and TVs and are decorated in traditional style. Most accommodate up to four people, but there are larger cottages including some with a pool.

The old stone taverna **I Sterna tou Bloumosifi** (mains €5-9) has a pleasant courtyard garden and is widely known for its excellent Cretan cuisine. For starters try the *gavros* (mild anchovy) wrapped in vine leaves, or the garlic and herb mushrooms, and then move on to the *hilopites* (tagliatelle) with rooster.

The other place to hang out is the understated **Liakoto** cafe-bar-cum-art gallery, which has a lovely terrace overlooking the mountains and sea. Next door, you can buy local *raki*, herbs, organic oil and other Cretan products at the **Myrovolo Wine Store & General Store**.

There are six daily buses to Vamos from Hania (€2.80, 45 minutes).

Around Vamos

The village of **Gavalohori**, 25km southeast of Hania, makes a pleasant stop. The main attraction is the **Folklore Museum** (☑28250 23222; admission €2; ☺9am-8pm Mon-Sat, 11am-6pm Sun), which is located in a renovated building that was constructed during Venetian rule and then extended by the Turks. The exhibits are well labelled in English and include examples of pottery, weaving, woodcarving, stonecutting and other Cretan crafts, including the fine *kapaneli* (intricately worked silk lace). A historical section documents Cretan struggles for independence.

Signs direct you to the **Byzantine wells**, **Venetian arches** and **Roman tombs** about 1.5km above the village.

The **Women's Cooperative** (☺10am-10pm Apr-Oct), on the main square, sells a few rare pieces of *kapaneli* made by local women. You can normally see women hard at work on this painstakingly long process. Prices for quality lacework range from €15 to €1500, depending on the size.

Vryses Βρύσες

POP 850

Most travellers just pass through Vryses, 30km southeast of Hania, on their way to or from the south coast, but this pleasant and sizeable village makes a good lunchtime interlude. The rivers Voutakas and Vrysanos run through the centre of the village, watering the giant plane trees along the banks, where you can cool off in one of the shady tavernas. Vryses is a market centre for the region's agricultural products. Many locals stop here for yoghurt and honey, a speciality of the town. The village centre is marked by a monument commemorating Cretan independence.

You will be tempted by the lamb or other tasty meat grilling on the spit outside **Taverna Progoulis** (grills €4.50-6), which has tables under the trees.

Near the crossroads in the town centre the modest **Vryses Way** serves excellent *gyros*, *Sfakianes pites* (a thin, flat cheese pie) and yoghurt with honey.

Buses from Hania to Hora Sfakion stop at Vryses, while several daily buses going from Hania to Iraklion also pass through here.

Rethymno Ρέθυμνο

Why Go?

Rethymno is a fascinating quilt of bubbly resorts, centuries-old villages and energising towns. There's astounding geographical diversity just minutes from the hustle and bustle of the region's eponymous capital on the north coast: you'll quickly find yourself immersed in endless tranquillity and natural beauty as you drift through tiny hamlets cradled by olive groves where locals cherish traditions that have stood the test of time. Descend into the spooky darkness of grotto-like caves or explore the island's 'upper storey' atop lofty Mt Psiloritis, Crete's highest peak. The south coast is a different animal altogether – a wild beauty with steep gorges and bewitching beaches in seductive isolation. Be it soaking up the rays on a sandy beach, hot-rodding it around the countryside or sipping a cocktail at a waterfront cafe-bar, just weave your way through this spellbinding land and be prepared for the unexpected at any given turn.

Best Places to Eat

» Avli (p83)
» En Plo (p83)
» O Kipos Tis Arkoudenas (p89)
» Panorama (p102)
» Taverna Kastro (p101)

Best Places to Stay

» Enagron (p187)
» Plakias Suites (p188)
» Kavos Melissa (p189)
» Kapsaliana Village (p187)
» Hotel Veneto (p185)

When to Go

During February/March, party with the locals as they let their hair down at dances, games, masquerade balls, parades and other raucous shenanigans during Rethymno's Carnival, Greece's biggest pre-Lent celebrations.

As days get longer in April, anemones, orchids, lupins and tulips are among the many springtime wildflowers that push up from rain-drenched soil and bathe hillsides, olive groves, stony fields and roadsides in an intense glow.

September and October are great for visiting southern beaches: the big crowds are gone, the sea is at its balmiest and the wicked winds have died down.

DON'T MISS

Tucking into fresh trout, grilled over a wood fire, surrounded by rushing natural mountain springs and clear, crisp air is among the delights of **Argyroupoli**, one of Rethymno's dreamiest mountain villages.

Best Beaches

» Preveli Beach (p98) – famous palm grove at the mouth of a gorge

» Triopetra (p98) – long, sandy and remote

» Agios Pavlos (p98) – isolated, cliff-fringed cove

» Karavostasi, Bali (p101) – gorgeous, kid-friendly, sandy crescent

Best Historical Sites

» Moni Arkadiou (p89) – ultimate symbol of Cretan resistance

» Rethymno fortress (p80) – massive Venetian fortifications

» Moni Preveli (p97) – famous for its key role in WWII

» Melidoni Cave (p91) – site of a terrible massacre

» Ancient Eleftherna (p90) – active archaeological site with a Dorian, Roman and Hellenistic past

Resources

» www.rethymnon.gr

» www.rethymnoatcrete.com

Getting Around

The roads in Rethymno are generally good. The E75 highway connects Rethymno with Iraklio and Hania, while coastal communities are accessed via the parallel Old National Rd. South-coast driving, meanwhile, means negotiating a maddening warren of tiny roads off the Rethymno–Agia Galini road. The going is scenic but slow here and also in other rural areas, such as the Amari Valley and the foothills of Mt Psiloritis. From about April to October, buses link Rethymno with major towns and tourist attractions on a regular basis.

THREE PERFECT DAYS

Day One

Spend the morning exploring Rethymno's **Venetian fortress** and labyrinth-like historic quarter. Then, after lunch at **Avli**, steer your car to **Marianna's** in Maroulas to stock up on her unique herbal products. Next, find out why **Moni Arkadiou** occupies such a special place in Cretan souls before poking around the ruins of **Ancient Eleftherna**. Carry on to **Margarites** to browse for handmade pottery and sip a late-afternoon cocktail on a scenic taverna terrace. For an authentic Cretan feast, make dinner reservations at **Agreco Farm**.

Day Two

Get an early start in **Plakias** and beat the crowds to **Preveli Beach**. When the hordes arrive, head back uphill for a dose of Cretan history at **Moni Preveli**. Say goodbye to civilisation and get lost in the maze of winding coastal roads leading to the fabulously secluded beaches of **Ligres**, **Triopetra** and **Agios Pavlos**. When you're done splashing, drive back for a true Cretan country dinner with Maria at **Iliomanolis** in Kanevos.

Day Three

From Panormo or Bali, take the short drive to moody **Melidoni Cave**, site of a horrendous massacre under Turkish rule; then compare it with the more classic beauty of Zoniana's **Sfendoni Cave**. Stop in Axos for an organic Cretan lunch at **Enagron**, then continue to **Anogia** to browse for textiles and check out a couple of quirky museums. All day long, majestic **Mt Psiloritis** has stood sentinel above you and now you're getting a close-up look on a drive up to the **Nida Plateau**. Take the short walk to **Ideon Cave** before heading back to sea level.

Accommodation

For sleeping options throughout this region, please see the Accommodation chapter (p175).

Rethymno Highlights

1 Explore the charismatic maze of Rethymno's Venetian and Turkish **old quarter** (p80)

2 Find out why **Moni Arkadiou** (p89) is so important to the Cretan soul

3 Escape civilisation on the south-coast beaches of **Triopetra** (p98) and **Agios Pavlos** (p98)

4 Cool off over a trout lunch by the springs of **Argyroupoli** (p89)

5 Expand your waistline with an organic gourmet dinner at **Agreco Farm** (p89), near Adele

6 Get lost amid the sweet villages of the painterly **Amari Valley** (p95)

7 Make the pilgrimage to palm-studded **Preveli Beach** (p98)

8 Fill up on excellent spring water, then hit the trails surrounding **Spili** (p94)

9 Make an in-depth exploration of the **party strip** along Rethymno's waterfront (p85)

10 Feel your spirits soar on a drive up to the **Nida Plateau** (p93)

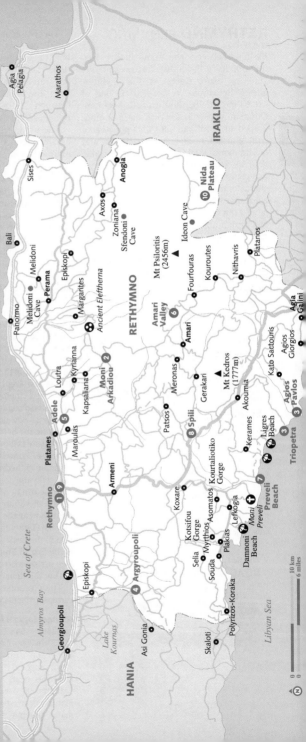

RETHYMNO ΡΕΘΥΜΝΟ

POP 28,850

Basking between the commanding bastions of its 15th-century fortress and the glittering azure waters of the Mediterranean, Rethymno (*reth*-im-no) is one of Crete's most delightful towns. Its Venetian-Ottoman quarter is a lyrical maze of lanes draped in floral canopies and punctuated with graceful wood-balconied houses and ornate monuments; minarets add an exotic flourish. While architectural similarities invite comparison to Hania, Rethymno has a character all its own, thanks in large part to a sizeable student population. Crete's third-largest town has lively nightlife, some excellent restaurants and even a decent beach right in town. The busier beaches, though, with their requisite resorts, are all outside of town along a nearly uninterrupted stretch all the way to Panormo, some 22km away.

History

Archaeological findings suggest that the site of modern Rethymno has been occupied since Late Minoan times. Around the 4th century BC, 'Rithymna' emerged as an autonomous state of sufficient stature to issue its own coinage. It waned in importance during Roman and Byzantine times but flourished again under Venetian rule (1210–1645) when it became an important commercial centre as well as a cultural and artistic hub.

The Venetians built a harbour and began fortifying the town in the 16th century against the growing threat from the Turks. Nevertheless, the massive hilltop fortress was unable to withstand the Turkish assault of 1646. Rethymno was an important seat of government under the Turks but it was also a centre of resistance to Turkish rule, resulting in severe reprisals.

The Ottomans ruled until 1897, when Russia became overseer of Rethymno during the European Great Powers' occupation. The town's reputation as an artistic and intellectual centre grew from 1923, when the mandated population exchange between Greece and Turkey brought many refugees from Constantinople.

These days, the students of the University of Crete keep the town lively outside the tourist season.

◉ Sights

Rethymno is fairly compact, with most sights, accommodation and tavernas wedged within the largely pedestrianised old quarter off the Venetian harbour. The beach is east of the harbour; one block inland, Arkadiou is the main shopping street.

TOP CHOICE **Venetian Fortress** FORTRESS
(adult/senior/family €4/3/10; ⊙8am-8pm Jun-Oct, 10am-5pm Nov-May) Built between 1573 and 1580, Rethymno's fortress cuts an imposing presence on a rocky headland above the historic quarter. Its construction was a reaction to multiple pirate raids and the mounting threat from the Turks. Despite its massive bastions and ramparts, though, it proved ineffective in staving off the Turkish invasion of 1646 and collapsed after a 22-day siege.

Inside the battlements, the most interesting feature is a meticulously restored square **mosque**, converted by the Turks from a Venetian cathedral. Its architecture is lovely, especially the dome, held up by eight arches, and the ornate mihrab (a niche that points in the direction of Mecca). The pint-sized **church** near the east gate is of more recent vintage (1899) and commemorates the eviction of the Turks. Also within the compound is the **Erofili Theatre**, a modern amphitheatre surrounded by pine trees; it gets busiest during the Renaissance Festival (p83).

The entrance to the fortress is through the eastern gate.

Archaeological Museum MUSEUM
(☏28310 54668; adult/concession €3/2; ⊙8.30am-3pm Tue-Sun) In the old Turkish prison near the fortress entrance, this small museum displays regionally excavated treasures from neolithic to Roman times. Exhibits are well labelled in English and feature bronze tools, Minoan pottery, Mycenaean figurines, Roman oil lamps and a 1st-

ROAD DISTANCES (km)

	Anogia	Plakias	Rethymno
Anogia	118		
Plakias	50	94	
Rethymno	62	56	39
Spili	26	86	24	30
	Agia Galini	Anogia	Plakias	Rethymno

century-AD sculpture of Aphrodite. Other star exhibits include fine examples of blown glass and a precious coin collection.

Venetian Harbour   HISTORICAL SITE
Rethymno's compact historic harbour is chock-a-block with tourist-geared fish tavernas and cafes. For a more atmospheric perspective, walk along the harbour walls past the fishing boats to the landmark **lighthouse**, built in the 16th century by the Turks.

Neratzes Mosque   MOSQUE
(Vernardou) This fine, triple-domed mosque was converted from a Franciscan church in 1657 and is now used as a music conservatory and concert hall. The building's minaret, the former bell tower, was built in 1890 and is undergoing lengthy restoration.

Rimondi Fountain   FOUNTAIN
(cnr Paleologou & Plateia Petihaki) Pride of place among the many vestiges of Venetian rule goes to this fountain with its spouting lion heads and Corinthian capitals, built in 1626 by city rector Alvise Rimondi. Water spouts from three lions' heads into three basins flanked by Corinthian columns. Above the central basin you can make out the Rimondi family crest.

Loggia   HISTORICAL BUILDING
(cnr Paleologou & Souliou; ☉7.30am-2.45pm Mon-Fri) This well-preserved 16th-century landmark originally served as a meeting house for Venetian nobility to discuss politics and money. Converted into a mosque, complete with minaret, during the Turkish period, it is now a gift shop selling replica classical sculptures.

Museum of
Contemporary Art   ART GALLERY
(☎28310 52530; www.cca.gr; Himaras 5; adult/concession €3/1.50 Fri-Sun, free Thu; ☉9am-1pm & 7-9pm Tue-Sun, 10am-4pm Sat & Sun) Near the fortress, this gallery organises period exhibits starring local and international artists. The permanent collection showcases the oils, drawings and watercolours of local lad Lefteris Kanakakis as well as modern Greek artists since 1950.

Porta Guora   HISTORICAL SITE
(Town Gate; cnr Ethnikis Antistaseos & Dimakopoulou) On the southern edge of the old quarter, this arched stone gate is the only remnant of the 16th-century defensive wall. Originally, it was topped with the symbol of Venice – the Lion of St Mark – now in the Archaeological Museum.

Historical & Folk Art Museum   MUSEUM
(☎28310 23398; Vernardou 26-28; adult/student €4/2; ☉9.30am-2.30pm Mon-Sat) In a lovely 17th-century mansion, this five-room exhibit provides insight into centuries of rural life with a collection spanning from clothing to baskets, weavings to farm tools. Labelling is also in English.

Paleontological Museum   MUSEUM
(☎28310 23083; www.gnhm.gr; Temple of Mastaba; adult/student/child €4/2/free; ☉9am-3pm Tue, Thu & Sat) Dwarf Cretan elephants and hippopotami may not start a ticket stampede, but it's well worth swinging by this new museum for its setting in the newly restored 17th-century Temple of Mastaba (aka Veli Pasha Mosque). Nine domes shape its silhouette, overlooked by the city's oldest minaret. The mosque grounds are being developed into a garden. The complex, which is a branch of the Goulandris Natural History Museum in Athens, is located south of the Municipal Park.

Municipal Park   PARK
(Igoumenou Gavriil) Located between Iliakaki and Dimitrakaki, this pleasant park offers a respite from the heat and crowds. Old men doze and chat in the tree-shaded *kafeneio* (coffee house), while children romp around the nearby playground.

🏃 Activities

Paradise Dive Centre   DIVING
(☎28310 26317; www.diving-center.gr; dives from €37, PADI open-water certification €350) Runs diving trips and PADI courses for all grades of divers from its base at Petres, about 15 minutes west of Rethymno by car.

Happy Walker   HIKING
(☎28310 52920; www.happywalker.com; Tombazi 56; walks from €30; ☉5-8.30pm daily, closed Sat & Sun Jul & Aug) Runs tours through gorges, along ancient shepherd trails and to traditional villages in the lush hinterland.

Mountain Club of Rethymno   HIKING
(EOS; ☎28310 57766; www.eos.rethymnon.com; Dimokratias 12; ☉8.30-10.30pm) Rethymno's chapter of the Greek Association of Mountaineers organises guided hikes for members and non-members and can also advise on independent hikes.

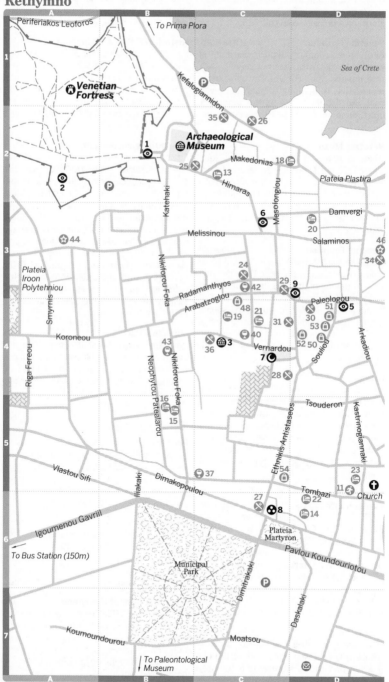

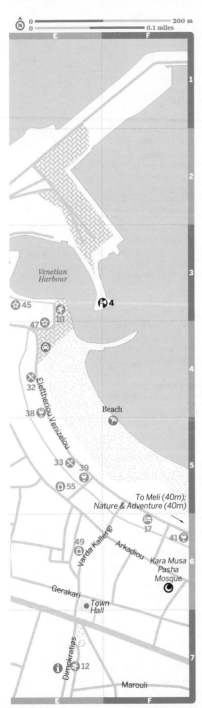

Nature & Adventure
HIKING, CYCLING

(☏28310 54135; www.nat-adv.gr; Eleftheriou Venizelou 4a) This outfit hires out bicycles and operates guided nature tours, including hikes in the nearby countryside and cycling trips around a reservoir.

☞ Tours

Dolphin Cruises
BOAT TRIPS

(☏28310 57666; www.dolphin-cruises.com; Venetian Harbour) Dolphin runs boat trips to pirate caves, day cruises to Bali, and fishing trips.

✼✼ Festivals & Events

Renaissance Festival
MUSIC

(www.rfr.gr) For two weeks in July, Rethymno celebrates its Renaissance pedigree with top-flight concerts featuring international artists, held in the fortress' Erofili Theatre and in the Neratzes Mosque.

Carnival
CARNIVAL

The annual pre-Lent celebrations bring four weeks of dancing and masquerading, games and treasure hunts, and a grand street parade. Festivities usually fall around February or March.

✕ Eating

The setting is magical but, with few exceptions, the tourist-geared tavernas in the Venetian harbour are mediocre at best. Better waterfront dining options are along Kefalogiannidon below the fortress. Eleftheriou Venizelou also has a few worthy contenders, but the best eats are to be found in the tiny side streets of the old quarter. Set menus (two or three courses, plus wine, water, *raki* and coffee) are popular.

⟨TOP CHOICE⟩ Avli
CRETAN €€€

(☏28310 58250; www.avli.com; Xanthoudidou 22, cnr Radamanthyos; mains €13.50-30) This Venetian garden villa is perfect for romantic dinners and serves some of the island's best modern Cretan food. Farm-fresh fare steers the menu, which may include lamb with wild mountain greens in lemon sauce or goat with honey and thyme, all punctiliously prepared and beautifully presented.

En Plo
GREEK €€

(Kefalogiannidon 28; mezedhes €5.50-9) Our favourite waterfront taverna, En Plo kicks Greek and Cretan comfort food into high gear. Mountain greens get a tangy twist

Rethymno

◎ **Top Sights**

with tamarind dressing, plump bacalao is paired with a feisty garlic sauce and the feta *saganaki* (fried cheese), wrapped in fluffy filo, snuggles up to caramelised figs. Sit in the arty interior or snag a table next to the waves.

Veneto   CRETAN €€
(☏28310   56634;   www.restaurantveneto.gr;
Epimenidou 4; mains €9-18; ☉May-Oct) In a 14th-century manor house that doubles as a boutique hotel (p185), Veneto oozes historic charm from every nook and cranny. The owner is a wine buff and will happily help you pick the right bottle to

complement your meal. The kitchen works with old Cretan and Greek recipes, often pushing flavour boundaries but usually with superb results.

Lemonokipos   CRETAN €€
(www.lemontreegarden.com; Ethnikis Antistaseos 100; mains €6-21) Candles, wine and a table for two in an enchanted courtyard are the hallmarks of a romantic night out. But even if your date doesn't make you swoon, the creative Cretan classics served beneath the lemon trees should still ensure an unforgettable evening.

Taverna Knossos
GREEK €€

(www.knosos-rethymno.com; Nearhou 40, Old Venetian Harbour; mains €6-12, set menus for 2 €30) Most tout-fronted tavernas in the Venetian harbour focus more on the ambience than on the quality of the food. Owned by the Stavroulaki family for half a century, Knossos is a happy exception. The fish is outstanding and the service swift and gracious.

Othonas
CRETAN €€

(☑28310 55500; Plateia Petihaki 27; mains €7-10) With its streetside 'host' and multilingual menus, Othonas may scream 'tourist trap' but it's actually a Concred member (see p244) and well respected for its regional fare. Menu stars include the lamb with artichokes and the lip-smacking 'Zeus Chicken' (with *raki*, feta, mustard and onions).

Thalassografia
GREEK €€

(☑28310 52569; Kefalogiannidon 33; mains €6.50-13.50) This casual alfresco cafe has a breathtaking cliffside setting with enviable views of the fortress and the sea. The grilled sardines are excellent, as are the stuffed mushrooms, all best washed down with the organic local Brink's beer.

Prima Plora
GREEK €€

(☑28310 56990; Akrotiriou 2, Koumbes; mains €6-16) On the beachfront west of the fortress, this stylish contender does top-notch seafood and grilled meats in a nicely subdued nautical setting near an old Venetian water pump.

Castelvecchio
GREEK €€

(☑28310 55163; Himaras 29; mains €9-19; ⊘dinner only Jul & Aug, lunch & dinner Sep-Jun) The affable Valantis will make you feel at home in the garden terrace of this family taverna located on the edge of the fortress. Try the *kleftiko* (slow oven-baked lamb).

Samaria
GREEK €

(☑28310 24681; Eleftheriou Venizelou 39-40; dishes €4-8.50; ⊘24hr) Along this busy cafe and restaurant strip, this is one of the few eateries popular with local families. The menu revolves around classic Greek feel-good food, including plenty of *mayirefta* (ready-cooked meals) and excellent soups and grills. It's also popular with night owls flocking in from the adjacent bars in need of restoring balance to the brain.

Salad Bar
INTERNATIONAL €

(☑28310 23294; Eleftheriou Venizelou 69; salads €4.50-8; ⊘8.30am-1.30am) Herbivore or meatlover, everyone can find a favourite among the carefully composed salads tossed freshly at this mod eatery. Try the chicken-avocado combo with couscous and orange slices.

Drinking

The main bar and cafe strip is along Eleftheriou Venizelou, popular with students and tourists. Another cluster is around Rimondi Fountain and on Plateia Petihaki. Wander the side streets to find quieter places. Most open around 9am or 10am, operating as cafes until the evening, when they morph into bars.

TOP CHOICE Ali Vafi's Garden
CAFE, BAR

(Tzane Bouniali 65a) This charming place is also known as Pottery Cafe thanks to its ceramic-artist owners Natasha and Giorgos. Some of their choice pieces are showcased in niches in the stone-vaulted front room, but in summer there are few locations more enchanting than the garden behind the pottery workshop.

BaRoom
LOUNGE BAR

(Eleftheriou Venizelou 63) Nicknamed 'Strawberry Bar' for the three berries affixed to the facade, this relaxed hang-out has an alternative vibe, with mismatched couches, an entire wall covered with street art, and the occasional live band.

Tholos
CAFE, BAR

(Nikiforou Foka 86) At this charismatic hang-out in a quiet part of the old quarter, you can unwind beneath the stone arches and dome of a former Venetian-Ottoman bathhouse.

Fusion Enoteca
WINE BAR

(Xanthoudidou 22, cnr Radamanthyos) Owned by the same team as Avli restaurant (p83), this handsome wine shop-cum-bar is chock-full with more than 450 hand-selected labels. If you feel like stronger stuff, hop across the street to the affiliated **Raki Baraki** bar, which often has live music.

Living Room
LOUNGE BAR, CAFE

(www.living.com.gr; Eleftheriou Venizelou 5) The sleekest and slickest on the waterfront strip, this place has eclectic decor (big mirrors, velvet chairs, stylish lamps) and is always abuzz with Rethymno's young and restless.

SWEET TREATS

One of the last traditional filo masters in all of Greece, **Yiorgos Hatziparaskos** (Vernardou 30) still makes superfine pastry by hand in his workshop. The highlight is when he whirls the dough into a giant bubble before stretching it over a huge table. His wife, Katerina, encourages passers-by to watch the spectacle and try some of the best baklava and *kataïfi* ('angel hair' pastry) they will ever eat.

At **Mona Liza** (Paleologou 36), near the Loggia, Nikos Skartsilakis is legendary for his 'crema' ice cream made from sheep's milk, as well as his excellent sweets. Try the *galaktoboureko* (custard slices), the walnut pie, or *vrahaki*, chocolate with almonds.

Loukoumadhes, doughnut-like concoctions drizzled with honey and cinnamon, have been perfected by **Kanakakis** (Plateia Martyron), just outside the Porta Guora. Locals also swear by the ice cream at **Meli**, which has a branch next to Rimondi Fountain.

Figaro
CAFE, BAR

(Vernardou 21) Housed in a handsomely restored old building, Figaro attracts a slightly older, mostly local, crowd and is great for socialising in an unpretentious setting.

Escobar
PUB

(Eleftheriou Venizelou 36) This beer bar made an instant splash among the waterfront hang-outs upon opening in late 2010. There's McFarland, Krusovice and Chimay on tap as well as over 50 bottled suds from around the world. Prices are steep by local standards.

☆ Entertainment

Nightclubs are concentrated around the Venetian harbour. Doors open around 11pm but most of the shiny, happy people don't arrive before midnight or even 1am. Some in-town clubs move to a seaside location in summer.

Fortezza
DANCE CLUB

(Nearhou 20; ☺11pm-dawn) It's a short night's journey into day at Rethymno's veteran disco, a big and flashy outpost with three bars, a laser show and international punters attempting their best Lady Gaga impressions.

Metropolis
DANCE CLUB

(www.metropolis-crete.com; Nearhou 12; ☺11pm-dawn) Hobnob with hipsters at this hot-and-heavy party palace. In summer, DJs spin mostly international chart music for the tourist crowd, while Greek pop dominates in low season.

Rock Cafe
BAR, DANCE CLUB

(www.rockcafe-rethymno.com; Petihaki 6; ☺9pm-dawn) This is one of Rethymno's classic hang-outs, with two bars and a dance floor that gets filled nightly by tourists and local students.

Asteria Cinema
CINEMA

(☑28310 22830; Melissinou 21; tickets €7; ☺9pm summer) This small open-air cinema near the fortress shows mostly new-release movies.

🔒 Shopping

Rethymno's mainstream shopping strip is along Arkadiou, while Souliou, Arabatzoglou and other side streets in the old quarter have more tourist-geared stores.

Avli Raw Materials
FOOD & DRINK

(www.avli.gr; Arabatzoglou 38-40) Foodies will love this store that's packed with a huge range of gourmet delights from around Greece, including great wines.

Frosso Bora
CERAMICS

(www.frosso-bora.com; Himaras 27) This local artist makes beautiful pots, vases, candlesticks, bowls and other vessels from local clay using the wheel or slabs. Prices are very reasonable.

Leather Studio Kanakakis
ACCESSORIES

(www.sitemaker.gr/manko; 23 Souliou) At this small store-cum-workshop you can watch the owner crank out handmade leather belts in all sorts of colours and designs. There's also a good assortment of leather handbags, wallets and shoes.

Omodamos
CERAMICS

(5 Souliou) The original ceramic designs in this shop are made by leading ceramicists from around Greece.

Zominthos
JEWELLERY

(Arkadiou 129) Come here to browse the eclectic selection of jewellery from contemporary

DESTINATION	DURATION	FARE	FREQUENCY
Agia Galini	1½hr	€6.50	up to 5 daily
Anogia	1¼hr	€5.50	2 Mon-Fri
Hania	1hr	€6.20	hourly
Hora Sfakion	2hr	€7.30	1 daily
Iraklio	1½hr	€7.60	hourly
Margarites	30min	€3.50	2 Mon, Wed & Fri
Moni Arkadiou	40min	€2.80	up to 3 daily
Omalos (Samaria Gorge)	1¾hr	€15	3 daily
Plakias	1hr	€4.50	up to 5 daily
Preveli	1¼hr	€4.50	2 daily

Greek designers, as well as some ceramics and sculptures.

En Hordais   MUSIC
(Varda Kallergi 38) This tiny store packed with handmade musical instruments is the place to get that bouzouki or Cretan *lyra* (a three-stringed instrument similar to a violin).

For English-language books, travel guides, international periodicals and maps try the following:

Ilias Spondidakis (Souliou 43)

Mediterraneo (Mavrokordatou 2)

Xenos Typos (Ethnikis Antistaseos 21)

❶ Information

There are free public wi-fi hot spots at the town hall, Plateia Iroön, the Venetian harbour and the Municipal Garden, all within the old town.

Cybernet (Kallergi 44-46; per hr €2.50; ☺9.30am-3am) Internet access.

Hospital (☑28210 27491; Triandalydou 17; ☺24hr)

Internet Cafe (Eleftheriou Venizelou 40; per hr €2, wi-fi free; ☺24hr)

National Bank (cnr Dimokratias & Gerakari) Next to the town hall. Usually has better exchange rates and lower fees than most other banks.

Post office (Moatsou 21; ☺7am-7pm Mon-Fri)

Regional tourist office (☑28310 25571; www .rethymnon.gr; Dimokratias 1; ☺8am-2.30pm Mon-Fri)

Tourist police (☑28310 28156/54340)

❶ Getting There & Away

Ellotia Tours (☑28310 24533; www.rethymnoat crete.com; Arkadiou 155; ☺9am-9pm Mar-Nov) is a helpful office that handles boat and plane tickets, changes money, hires out cars and motorcycles and books excursions.

Buses leave from the bus station at Igoumenou Gavriil. Services are reduced at weekends and outside high season.

❶ Getting Around

Auto Motor Sports (☑28310 24858; www .automotosport.com.gr; Sofoklis Venizelou 48) Hires out cars and motorbikes.

WEST OF RETHYMNO

The villages southwest of Rethymno, in the foothills of the Lefka Ori (White Mountains), make for an ideal afternoon drive. The main destination is the mountain village of Argyroupoli, built on an ancient settlement and famous for its springs and waterfalls. The road also passes through **Episkopi**, a pretty market town with winding lanes and traditional houses.

Argyroupoli Αργυρούπολη
POP 400

When the summer heat becomes too intense, you'll find a natural cooling system at Argyroupoli, 25km southwest of Rethymno. At the bottom of this village is a watery oasis formed by mountain springs that keep the temperature markedly cooler here than on the coast. Running through aqueducts, washing down walls, seeping from stones and pouring from spigots, the gushing springs supply water for the entire city of Rethymno.

Argyroupoli is built on the ruins of the ancient city of Lappa, one of the most important Roman cities in western Crete – of which, however, very few remnants survive. Being in the foothills of the Lefka Ori also

HERBAL POWER

If you're into herbs, aromatherapy, organic teas or natural beauty products, make the short drive out to **Maroulas**, a pretty, higgledy-piggledy village with panoramic sea views. Some 10km southeast of Rethymno, the protected town has a mix of nicely restored late Venetian and Turkish architecture, including 10 olive presses and a 44m tower jutting above the village.

Right on the main road, you'll find the tiny **Marianna's Workshop** (⊠28310 72432; www.mariannas-workshop.gr; ⊙10am-2pm & 4.30-8pm summer, call for winter hr). Marianna Founti-Vassi collects aromatic medicinal herbs from the mountains to make her unique range of teas and oils from natural extracts using traditional methods. There are potions for all manner of ailments, including a tea made from 40 herbs once used by midwives.

Marianna's interest in alternative therapies became a full-time obsession when she moved to Maroulas in the mid-1990s and consulted locals about identifying Crete's many herbs. 'This knowledge shouldn't be lost,' she says. 'People should recognise every plant and know what it's for.' Marianna says animals were another guide to herbs and flowers, as they don't touch toxic plants. Indeed, *kri-kri* goats have been observed using Crete's endemic *diktamo* to heal their wounds.

After stocking up on healthy herbs, report for lunch to **Katerina** (⊠28310 71627; ⊙May-Oct), a cheerful outdoor restaurant with sensational sea views and an attached animal pen. **Mylopetra**, on the teensy main square, also has coffee and snacks.

makes the town a gateway to some fine walking and hiking trails.

◉ Sights

Argyroupoli is divided into an upper town and a lower town. Most historical sights are near the main square at the top, while the springs and tavernas are at the bottom. Approaching from Rethymno, the turn-off to the lower village is on your right before the road climbs to the upper village.

Upper Town   NEIGHBOURHOOD

An ideal first stop is in the **Lappa Avocado Shop** (⊠28310 81070; www.lappa-avocado.gr; ⊙10am-7pm Mar-Nov, 11am-3pm Dec-Feb), under a stone archway just off the main square. Not only does it sell excellent avocado-based beauty products, but it doubles as an unofficial tourist office. Ask here for a free town map, which outlines a quick loop around the old quarter, starting behind the store.

Highlights include a **Roman portal**, on your left, with the inscription *Omnia Mundi Fumus et Umbra* (All things in this world are smoke and shadow). A little further on your right is the **Church of St Paraskevi**, where the lid of a baby's sarcophagus now serves as the entrance step to the courtyard. The main lane also goes past a 7000-piece **Roman mosaic floor** from the 1st century BC. The loop winds back to the main square, dominated by the stately 17th-century Venetian **Church of Agios Ioannis**.

South of here, on the main village road, the quaint **Museum of Village Life** (admission free; ⊙10am-7pm) has an eclectic collection of heirlooms and historic items amassed by the Zografakis family. If it is closed, call in at the taverna or shop and someone will probably answer to give you a tour in English.

Lower Town   NEIGHBOURHOOD

Heading downhill from the main square, then taking your first main left will get you to the tavernas clustered around the springs in the lower village. Towering chestnut and plane trees and luxuriant vegetation create a shady, restful spot for lunch among the waterfalls and fountains that have been incorporated into all the tavernas. It's especially lovely on a summer night. Aside from the tavernas, you'll find a 17th-century water-driven **fulling machine**, once used to thicken cloth by moistening and beating it, as well as the overgrown remains of a **Roman bath** and **St Mary's Church**, built atop a temple dedicated to Poseidon.

Necropolis   ANCIENT SITE

Ancient Lappa's cemetery lies north of the town and is reached via a signed 1.5km footpath from the main square. Hundreds of tombs have been cut into the rock cliffs here, especially around the Chapel of the Five Virgins. The path leads on to a **plane tree** that is supposed to be 2000 years old. Ask for directions at the Lappa Avocado Shop.

Eating

The tavernas around the springs cater to tourists but the quality is actually quite good and the shaded glen setting is spectacular. There's little difference in terms of quality, so just pick the one that looks most inviting to you. All have outdoor seating amid imaginative (and often noisy) water features. Most close around 7pm except on balmy summer nights.

Local specialities are farm-raised trout and sturgeon, which can sometimes be seen swimming around in tanks. Lamb and pork, spit-roasted over olive wood, are good non-piscine choices.

There are also some excellent eats outside the village, en route to Episkopi.

TOP CHOICE O Kipos Tis Arkoudenas CRETAN €€
(☑28310 61607; mains €5-12) One of the best tavernas around here, the 'Garden of Arkoudenas' turns superb organic produce into gorgeous dishes, many of them prepared in the wood oven.

Petrini Gonia GREEK €
(☑28310 61617; dishes €4-8) In a modern stone house, Petrini Gonia is famous for its mixed grill. It does both takeaway and sit-down service. The **cafe** opposite has a fantastic selection of mouth-watering cakes, cookies and chocolates that are like works of art.

Traditional Bakery BAKERY €
(☺8am-10pm) At the turn-off to Kato Paros, this lovely roadside bakery makes great spinach pies and cinnamon cookies.

❶ Getting There & Away

From Monday to Friday three buses ply the route from Rethymno to Argyroupoli, although only two head back to Rethymno (€3.30, 40 minutes).

THE HINTERLAND & MT PSILORITIS

Rethymno's mountainous hinterland offers a diverse range of routes and interesting detours. In a single day, you could easily combine a visit to the historic Arkadi monastery with a poke around the pottery village of Margarites while also taking in the ruins of Ancient Eleftherna. Further east, the foothills of Mt Psiloritis beckon with a couple of charismatic caves and traditional villages like Axos and Anogia; the latter is also the launch pad for the precipitous drive up to the Nida Plateau.

Moni Arkadiou Μονή Αρκαδίου

The **Arkadi Monastery** (☑28310 83136; www .arkadimonastery.gr; admission €2.50; ☺9am-8pm

---

A MODEL FARM

Embedded in the rolling hills near the village of Adele, about 13km southeast of Rethymno, **Agreco Farm** (☑28310 72129, 6947275814; www.agreco.gr; tour & lunch or dinner €30; ☺11am-10pm May-Oct) is a replica of a 17th-century estate and a showcase of centuries-old, organic and ecofriendly traditional farming methods. The brainchild of the Daskalantonakis family, owners of the Grecotel hotel chain, it uses mostly traditional machinery, including an old donkey-driven olive press, a flour watermill and winepress.

The farm is usually open May to October, but private events, such as weddings or baptisms, may keep it closed to the public at any time. Normally though, there are several ways to experience this dreamy place. **Farm tours** start at 6pm and culminate in a 30-course Cretan feast in the taverna, which was named Best Organic Restaurant by *Vanity Fair* in 2009. Most of the dishes are prepared with produce, dairy and meat grown right here on the farm. If you're more the hands-on type, swing by on Sunday at 11am when visitors are invited to participate in **traditional agricultural activities**. Depending on the time of year, you could find yourself shearing a sheep, milking a goat, making cheese or smashing grapes (see the website for the schedule). This is followed by a buffet-style **Harvest Festival Lunch**. Reservations are essential for the farm tour and the Sunday experience.

If you're just stopping by during the day, you can enjoy snacks and drinks at the *kafeneio* and stock up on farm-grown products at the shop. Do call ahead, though, to make sure they're open.

Jun-Sep, to 7pm Apr, May & Oct, to 5pm Nov, to 4pm Dec-Mar), in the hills some 23km southeast of Rethymno, has deep significance for Cretans. It's a stark and potent symbol of human resistance and considered a spark plug in the struggle towards freedom from Turkish occupation.

In November 1866, massive Ottoman forces arrived to crush islandwide revolts. Hundreds of Cretan men, women and children fled their villages to find shelter at Arkadiou. However, far from being a safe haven, the monastery was soon besieged by 2000 Turkish soldiers. Rather than surrender, the Cretans set fire to their kegs of gunpowder, killing everyone, Turks included, except for one small girl who lived to a ripe old age in a village nearby. A bust of this woman and one of the abbot who lit the gunpowder stand outside the monastery. Also here (next to the cafeteria, skip the food), in the monastery's old windmill, is the macabre **ossuary** with skulls and bones of some of the 1866 victims neatly arranged in a glass cabinet.

Arkadiou's most impressive structure, its Venetian **church** (1587), has a striking Renaissance facade marked by eight slender Corinthian columns and topped by an ornate triple-belled tower. Left of here is a cypress trunk that was scorched by the explosion and still has a bullet embedded in its bark. Behind here, the former refectory (dining room) is now a small **museum** of religious objects, icons, and weapons used in 1866. At the end of the left wing is the old wine cellar where the gunpowder was stored.

There are three buses (two on weekends) from Rethymno to the monastery (€2.80, 40 minutes).

Eleftherna Ελεύθερνα

Continuing east from Moni Arkadiou takes you to the archaeological site of **Ancient Eleftherna**. This Dorian-built settlement was among the most important in the 8th and 7th centuries BC and also experienced heydays in Hellenistic and Roman times. Excavations have been ongoing since 1985 and archaeologists make new and exciting findings all the time. The 2010 discovery, for instance, of the gold-adorned remains of a woman in a 2700-year-old double tomb made international news. And the excavation of the tomb of a high priestess and

three acolytes a year earlier even prompted the Archaeological Institute of America to include Eleftherna in its 'Top 10 Discoveries of 2009'.

Alas, most of the site is fenced off for now and thus none too visitor-friendly, although a museum is being planned. The most easily accessible section is the **Acropolis** atop a long narrow ridge behind the Akropolis taverna and the remains of a tower. From here, a path leads down to vast **Roman cisterns** carved into the hills and, further along, to a **Hellenistic bridge**.

Down in the valleys flanking the ridge, active digs include the huge 2800-year-old **necropolis of Orthi Petra** to the west, where findings have produced evidence of human sacrifice. For a closer look, follow the dirt road down a steep hill from the village of Eleftherna.

On the eastern slope, the remains of residential and public buildings from the Roman and Byzantine periods are being dug up. You can peek through the fence by following the main road east towards Margarites, turning off at the sign to the Church of the Sotiros and catching the dirt road just past this lovely Byzantine chapel.

Margarites Μαργαρίτες

POP 330

Known for its fine pottery, tiny Margarites is invaded by tour buses in the morning but by the afternoon all is calm. Then you can enjoy wonderful valley views from the eucalyptus-lined taverna terraces on the main square.

Margarites has only one road and no bank or post office but it does have more than 20 ceramics stores and studios. The pottery is of mixed quality and taste. Most shops along the main street sell fairly tacky pieces, but a happy exception is **Kerameion**, where Yiorgos Dalamvelas never tires of explaining his techniques and the history of the town. Many of his pieces are based on Minoan designs.

Like other traditional potters, Dalamvelas uses local black clay that turns red when fired. It's of such fine quality that it needs only one firing and no glazing – the outside having been smoothed with a pebble.

Also worth a closer look is **Ceramic Art**, in a lane near the main square, where Konstantinos Gallios makes some beautiful pieces. The undisputed master, though, is still the octogenarian **Manolis Syragopoulos**, who is the only one left in town to work without electricity – using only manual wheels and a wood-fired kiln – to make pottery the way his great-grandfather did. His workshop is about 1km outside the town on your left.

On the shady main square, **Mandolos** is a well-regarded taverna where you can dig into big portions of local standards while drinking in wine and views.

Two buses make the trip from Rethymno on Monday, Wednesday and Friday (€3.50, 30 minutes).

Perama to Anogia Πέραμα Προς Ανώγεια

The roads linking the small commercial hub of Perama and Anogia pass through some of the most dramatic scenery in northern Crete. Stop to explore fabulous caves or enjoy lunch in a timeless village along the foothills of Mt Psiloritis.

MELIDONI ΜΕΛΙΔΟΝΙ

About 2km outside the village of Melidoni, and also known as Gerontospilios, **Melidoni Cave** (☑28340 22650; admission €3; ◐9am-6pm Mar-Apr, 9am-7pm Jun–mid-Oct, to 5pm mid–end Oct) is famous not so much for its natural beauty but rather for its role in history. A place of worship since neolithic times, it became the site of a nasty massacre in 1824 under the Turkish occupation. More than 400 villagers sought refuge here from the Ottoman army in October 1823. When they refused to emerge even after a three-month siege, the Turkish commander ordered his soldiers to throw burning materials into the cave, thereby asphyxiating everyone inside.

The bones of the martyrs are buried in the white sarcophagus in the cave's lofty 65m-long main chamber, called the 'Hall of Heroes'. Pay your respects before exploring this marvellous underworld of evocatively shaped stalactites and stalagmites. Mind your step, though, as the cave is poorly lit and the ground uneven and slippery in places.

EPISKOPI ΕΠΙΣΚΟΠΗ

This charming village served as a bishopric under Venetian rule and is a maze of lanes lined with well-preserved stone mansions. Stop to admire the faded frescoesgracing the ruins of the 15th-century **Church of Episkopi** and the

Venetian **water fountain** next to the bridge at the end of the town.

ZONIANA ΖΩΝΙΑΝΑ

Modern and not particularly attractive, Zoniana is home to the region's other famous hole in the ground, **Sfendoni Cave** (☑28340 61734; www.zoniana.gr; adult/child incl tour €4/2; ◐10am-5pm Apr-Oct, 10am-3pm weekends Nov-Mar). Guided tours take you through seven chambers with such fanciful names as 'Sanctuary of the Fairy' and 'Zeus' Palace'. All teem with illuminated stalagmites and stalactites shaped into drapery, organ pipes, domes, curtains, waves and other strange formations. Cave-dwelling animals include bats, birds and millipedes. Tours run roughly every 40 minutes and take about 40 minutes. A new 270m-long walkway means that even the mobility-impaired can join in the experience.

From Monday to Friday, two buses make the trip out from Rethymno (€5.50).

AXOS ΑΞΟΣ

The village of Axos has the kind of lazy Cretan ambience that has made it a popular stop for tour buses. During the day, the village is quiet, but at night the tavernas with their open-air terraces host 'Cretan folklore evenings' for tourists.

Axos is home to the enchanting Enagron farm (p187), one of the nicest places to stay in this part of the island, as well as the new **Museum of Wooden Sculptures** (☑6937691387; www.woodenmuseum.gr; adult/student €5/3; ◐9am-8pm), fronted by a massive sculpture of Hercules killing the lion. The private museum is essentially a showcase of the work of self-taught artist Georgios Koutantos. An enthusiastic and voluble man, he'll happily show visitors around his workshop and explain the stories behind each of his sculptures. The large-scale works, including an eagle with a 6m wing span, are the most impressive. Others depict family members, often in a highly personal fashion. None of the pieces are for sale.

Anogia Ανώγεια

POP 2130

Anogia presides over the so-called 'Devil's Triangle' of macho mountain villages that occasionally get involved in armed stand-offs with the police (usually, over illicit cannabis cultivation, but also because of perceived affronts to local honour), much to the excitement of the Athenian media. The village is the centre of a prosperous sheep husbandry industry and a popular stopover for day trippers and those headed for the Nida Plateau. It has also spawned several of Crete's best-known musicians (see below).

During WWII Anogia was a centre of resistance and suffered heavily for it. The Nazis burned down the town and massacred all the men in retaliation for their role in sheltering Allied troops and aiding in the kidnapping of German commander General Heinrich Kreipe.

Hence, most of the buildings you see today are actually of relatively recent vintage, yet Anogia has a reputation for clinging to time-honoured traditions. Black-shirted moustachioed men lounge in the *kafeneia*, their traditional baggy pants tucked into black boots, while elderly women hunch over their canes, aggressively flogging woven blankets and embroidered textiles displayed in their shops.

◉ Sights

Anogia clings to a hillside, with the tourist shops in the lower half and most accommodation and businesses above.

Museum of Grylios MUSEUM
(☏28340 31593; donation welcome; ☺unpredictable) A short walk uphill from the lower village square, this humble museum presents the endearing paintings and sculptures of Anogia-born folk artist Alkiviadis Skoulas (1900–1997), aka Grylios. It is now run by his son Yiorgos, who is known to hold impromptu *lyra* concerts. If Yiorgos doesn't find you first, knock next door or ask at the square if the museum's not open.

FREE **Nikos Xylouris Home** MUSEUM
Nikos Xylouris was born in this little house on the lower village square that is now a *kafeneio* run by his sister. The tiny room is completely plastered in posters, letters and other memorabilia related to the singer/musician, attesting to the extent of the adulation he still receives some 30 years after his death.

✕ Eating

Ta Skalomata CRETAN €
(☏28340 31316; mains €4-9) In the upper village, Skalomata has fed locals and travellers for about 40 years, making it the oldest restaurant in town, with an open kitchen, traditional decor and panoramic windows. It does great grills (the roast lamb is especially good), homemade wine and bread, and tasty meat-free options, including zucchini with cheese and eggplant.

Arodamos CRETAN €
(☏28340 31100; www.arodamos.gr; grills €5-8.50) This big restaurant in a new stone house in the upper village is held in high regard by villagers and visitors for its perky Cretan fare and gracious hospitality. Anything with

---

ANOGIA: MUSICAL TALENT FACTORY

Anogia is known for its stirring music and has spawned a disproportionate number of Crete's best-known musicians. The main instrument is the *lyra*, a three-sided, pear-shaped string instrument played sitting down and often accompanied by lutes and guitars. One man to achieve world fame with this instrument was Nikos Xylouris (1936–80), still considered Crete's best singer and lyra player more than 30 years after his death. Nikos' idiosyncratic brother Psarantonis has since taken up the reins and is wildly popular nationwide. Brother Giannis Xylouris (Psaroyiannis) is Greece's most accomplished lute player. His heir apparent is Psarantonis' charismatic son, Giorgos Xylouris (Psarayiorgis), whose musical career has blossomed since returning to Crete after a stint living in Australia. Giorgos' sister, Niki, is one of the few female Cretan singers, and the finest, while their brother Lambis is not surprisingly also in the music game.

Other notable musicians from Anogia include the *lyra* players Manolis Manouras, Nikiforos Aerakis, Vasilis Skoulas (son of the folk painter Alkiviadis Skoulas) and Giorgos Kalomiris.

The talented but capricious Georgos Tramoundanis, alias Loudovikos ton Anogion (Ludwig from Anogia), sells his brand of folksy, ballad-style Cretan compositions to audiences all over Greece. He's also the mastermind behind the annual **Yakinthia Festival** (www.yakinthia.com), with open-air concerts held on the slopes of Mt Psiloritis the first week of July.

PEAK-BAGGING MT PSILORITIS

The classic route to the summit of Mt Psiloritis follows the east–west E4 trail from the Nida Plateau and can be done in about seven hours round trip. While you don't need to be an alpine mountaineer, it is a long slog and the views from the summit may be marred by haze or cloud cover. En route, several *mitata* (round, stone shepherd's huts) provide occasional sheltering opportunities should the weather turn inclement, while at the summit is a small, twin-domed chapel. The best map is the Anavasi 1:25,000 map of Psiloritis (Mt Ida; see p253).

lamb is tops, but so is the *saganaki* made with local *katsohiri*. Free sweet pie with ice cream caps off every meal.

Aetos　　　　　CRETAN €
(☎28340 31262; grills €5-8.50) This traditional taverna in the upper village has a giant charcoal grill out front and fantastic mountain views out the back. A regional speciality is *ofto*, a flame-cooked lamb or goat. Aetos also serves another local staple: spaghetti cooked in stock with cheese.

ℹ Information

An ATM and the post office are in the upper village. Yakinthos, across from the Hotel Aristea (p188), offers internet access.

ℹ Getting There & Away

There are up to three buses daily from Iraklio (€3.80, one hour) and two buses Monday to Friday from Rethymno (€5.50, 1¼ hours).

Mt Psiloritis Ορος Ψηλορείτης

Imposing Mt Psiloritis, also known as Mt Ida, soars skyward for 2456m, making it Crete's highest mountain. At its eastern base is the **Nida Plateau** (1400m) a wide, fertile expanse reached via a paved 21km-long road from Anogia past several *mitata* (round, stone shepherd's huts). It culminates at a huge parking lot where a simple taverna offers refreshment and spartan rooms (€25).

It gets chilly up here, even in summer, so bring a sweater or light jacket.

About 1km before the road's end, an asphalt spur veers off to the left, ending after about 3km at the **Skinakas Observatory** (www.skinakas.org.gr), Greece's most significant stargazing vantage point. The observatory opens to the public once a month during the full moon from May to September, between 5pm and 11pm (English-speaking guides in July and August only). The website has details.

The mountain's most important feature is **Ideon Cave**, also known simply as Ideon – the place where, according to legend, the god Zeus was reared (although Dikteon Cave, p162, in Lasithi claims the same). Ideon was a place of worship from the late 4th millennium BC onwards and many artefacts, including gold jewellery and a bronze shield, have been unearthed here. The cave itself is really just one huge and fairly featureless cavern about 1km from the parking lot.

Back on the plateau itself, you can make out a sprawling landscape sculpture called **Andartis – Partisan of Peace** against the hills. Created by German artist Karina Raeck in 1991, it commemorates the Cretan resistance in WWII. The monument itself is a pile of local rocks arranged in such a way that it looks like an angel when seen from above. Ask the taverna staff to point it out if you can't spot it on your own. It's a flat and easy 1.25km walk out there.

COAST TO COAST

From Rethymno, the fastest and most direct route to the south coast is via Armeni and Spili. For a more leisurely pace, travel via the almost ridiculously bucolic Amari Valley, a part of Crete that seems frozen in time.

Armeni Αρμένοι

Heading south from Rethymno, there is a turn-off to the right for the Late Minoan **cemetery of Armeni** (admission free; ⊙8am-3pm Tue-Sun), about 2km before the modern village of Armeni. Some 200 tombs were carved into the rock here between 1300 and 1150 BC, in the midst of an oak forest. Oddly, there does not seem to have been any sizeable town nearby that would have accounted for so many tombs. Excavated treasure, including pottery, weapons and jewellery, is now at the archaeological museum in Rethymno.

For sustenance, there's a good bakery and cafe with free wi-fi on the main road as you drive into town. A bit further on, **Alekos Kafeneio** serves a small but superb daily selection of traditional dishes. Alternatively, 2km south of town **Taverna Pirgos** (mains €4-9; 🛜), in a striking stone building overlooking a grand valley, does delicious salads and grilled meats.

Spili Σπήλι

POP 700

About halfway between Rethymno and Agia Galini, Spili (*spee*-lee) is a pretty mountain village with cobbled streets, flowered balconies, vine-covered rustic houses, and plane trees. Tourist buses stop here during the day, but in the evening Spili belongs to the locals. It's a good spot for lunch, and a haven for hikers. The rugged Kourtaliotiko Gorge, which culminates at the famous palm grove of Preveli Beach, starts not far south of town.

◎ Sights

Venetian fountain   FOUNTAIN
The main local attraction is this restored fountain that spurts water from 19 stone lion heads into a long trough. Fill up your own bottle with some of the island's best water. A walkway leads from the fountain uphill to the village's quiet and picturesque backstreets.

Monastery   MONASTERY
Spili is a bishop's see (seat of a bishop) based at the massive modern monastery at the west end of town. You're free to walk around and admire the arched entryways, marble-floor courtyard, stunning valley views and opulently decorated church.

🍴 Eating

TOP CHOICE **Panorama**   CRETAN €€
(☎28320 22555; mains €6-12; ⏰dinner daily, lunch Sun) Pantelis Vasilakis and his wife Calliope are the masterminds behind this fine traditional taverna on the outskirts of Spili. Enjoy memorable views from the terrace while munching on homemade bread, toothsome mezedhes or such tempting mains as succulent kid goat with *horta* (wild greens). It's an accredited Concred taverna (see p244).

Stratidakis   CRETAN €
(specials €3-6) A mother-and-son team presides over the oldest taverna in town. There's meat grilling on the spits outside and robust Cretan daily specials stewing in pots that you're free to inspect. The lovely terrace has jaw-dropping mountain views.

Kambos   CRETAN €
(mains €6-9) This no-frills family taverna is generally known only by locals. It cooks simple, traditional Cretan food from its own farm-raised meat and vegetables. It's in a lonely spot about 6km east of Spili en route to Gerakari.

Yianni's   GREEK €
(mains €4-10) Past the Venetian fountain, this friendly place has a big roadside terrace, reliably good traditional cooking and a decent house red. Try the delicious rabbit in wine or the mountain snails.

❶ Information

There are two ATMs and a post office on the main street. Some of the cafes near the fountain have wi-fi.

❶ Getting There & Away

Spili is on the Rethymno–Agia Galini bus route, which has up to five services daily.

SOUTH COAST

Rethymno's south coast is bookended by the resort towns of Plakias and Agia Galini, which are linked by a string of marvellously isolated beaches, including the famous palm beach at Preveli. Massive summertime winds have spared the area from the tourism excesses that typify the north coast.

Approaching from the north, the scenery becomes increasingly dramatic and takes in marvellous views of the Libyan Sea. From the Rethymno–Agia Galini road, it's a fabulous drive through the rugged **Kotsifou Gorge** to Plakias. The road to Preveli travels via the even more spectacular Kourtaliotiko Gorge.

Plakias Πλακιάς

POP 190

Some things in Crete never change, and Plakias is one of them. Set beside a long south-coast beach, between two immense wind tunnels – the gorges of Selia and

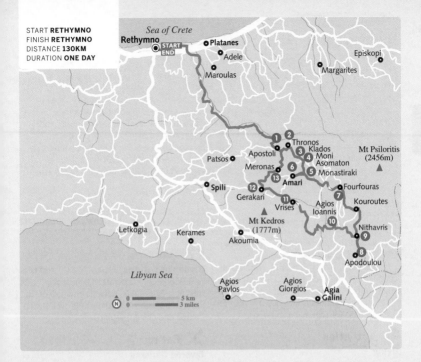

Sea of Crete

Rethymno **START END**

Platanes
Adele
Maroulas

Episkopi
Margarites

1
Apostoli **2** Thronos
Klados **3** Moni
Patsos **4** Asomaton
Meronas **6** Monastiraki
5
Spili **13** Amari
12 Fourfouras **7**
Gerakari **11** Kouroutes
Vrises Agios
Ioannis
10 Nithavris
Mt Kedros **9**
Lefkogia Kerames (1777m) **8**
Akoumia Apodoulou

Mt Psiloritis
(2456m) ▲

Libyan Sea

Agios Agios **Agia**
Pavlos Giorgios **Galini**

N 0 5 km
0 3 miles

Driving Tour
Amari Valley

❯ The Amari Valley is a quilt of unspoilt
villages punctuated by Byzantine churches
and framed by olive groves and orchards. Mt
Psiloritis looms grandly above the lyrical landscape whose charms lie less in what's there
than what isn't: traffic, billboards and mega-
resorts. You will need a good map (see p253).

Coming from Rethymno, the turn-off for
the Amari Valley is about 3km east on the
main highway. Past a reservoir, the road forks
at **1** **Apostoli**. Going left sends you on the
more scenic eastern route along the flanks of
Mt Psiloritis, while the western valley runs below Mt Kedros. The roads rejoin in Apodoulou,
making it possible to drive the entire loop.

Heading east, the first village is **2** **Thronos**,
whose Church of the Panagia has extraordinary, if faded, 14th-century frescoes (key
at next-door cafe). Continue south to arrive
at an intersection of five roads, punctuated
by the handsome **3** **Klados** country tavern.
The nearby 13th-century **4** **Moni Asomaton**
became an agricultural school in 1930 and is
now a sheep-breeding research centre.

Continue via **5** **Monastiraki**, home to a
(badly signposted) Minoan site, to **6** **Amari**,
an enchanting medley of Venetian buildings,
Byzantine churches and a climbable 19th-
century bell tower.

Next up are pretty **7** **Fourfouras**, where
trails climb up Mt Psiloritis, and **8** **Apodoulou**, with the partly ruined manor of Kalitsa
Psaraki. It is named for a girl who was
abducted by Turks and rescued (and
married) by an English traveller.

The road now winds through the western
valley, passing through several villages,
including **9** **Nithavris**, **10** **Agios Ioannis**
and **11** **Vrises**, that suffered heavily under
the German occupation in WWII. You'll see
war memorials everywhere. Next up is
12 **Gerakari**, a market town famous for its
cherries, springtime orchids and wild tulips,
and nicely frescoed 13th-century Church of
Agios Ioannis.

Complete the loop in teensy **13** **Meronas**,
where the 14th-century Church of the
Panagia and its frescoes are worth a stop.
Note the elegant Venetian south portal.

CRETAN BREW

When Dortmund-born mathematician Dr Bernd Brink moved to Crete after marrying a local girl, he did what any self-respecting German would do – he opened a brewery. In business since 2001, **Brink's Brewery** (☑28310 41243; www.brinks-beer.gr) is a sophisticated operation producing full-bodied organic blonde and dark lagers sold all over Greece. The unfiltered and unpasteurised beer is brewed in accordance with a 16th-century German law that permits only the use of water, hops, yeast and malt in beer making. Old Crete hands may know the company as Rethymnian Brewery, but it was forced to change its name in 2010 because of an obscure Greek law that does not permit beer to carry a geographical designation in its name. You'll find Brink's Brewery some 12km south of Rethymno, just past Armeni. There is a small tasting room, but hours are erratic, so call ahead or just stop by and hope for the best.

Kourtaliotiko – this unassuming resort is enlivened by Central European package tourists and the international legions quartered at the popular youth hostel.

Plakias has plenty of good restaurants, accommodation and walks through olive groves and along seaside cliffs, some leading to sparkling hidden beaches. It's also an excellent base for regional excursions.

Activities

Diving

Several diving operators run shore and boat dives to nearby rocky bays, caves and canyons, as well as all manner of courses. A two-tank boat dive, including lunch and equipment, costs about €125.

Dive 2gether   DIVING
(☑28320 32313, 6974031441; www.dive2gether
.com; ⊗8.30am-8pm Apr-Oct) A top-notch, Dutch-run operation in town with state-of-the-art equipment and super-high safety standards. Also runs a one-on-one 'Try-Out Dive' (€81) and 'Bubblemaker' sessions for kids as young as eight.

**Kalypso Rocks' Palace
Diving Centre**   DIVING
(☑28310 56861; www.kalypsodivingcenter.com) The oldest outfit around, based at the Kalypso Holidays Village, just outside Plakias.

Hiking

There are well-worn walking paths to the scenic village of Selia, Moni Finika, Lefkogia, and a lovely walk along the Kourtaliotiko Gorge to Moni Preveli. An easy 30-minute uphill path to Myrthios begins just before the youth hostel. For guided walks, including the one to Preveli Beach that gets you back by boat, contact **Anso**

Travel (☑28320 31712; www.ansotravel.com; adult/child €34/17).

Tours

Baradakis Lefteris   BOAT TRIPS
(☑6936806635; smernabar@gmail.com) In summer, Baradakis Lefteris, owner of the Smerna Bar, runs boat trips to Preveli Beach, Loutro and Gavdos Island.

Eating

Taverna Christos   CRETAN €€
(specials €5-13) This established taverna has a romantic tamarisk-shaded terrace right next to the crashing waves, and lots of interesting dishes that you won't find everywhere, including home-smoked sea bass, black spaghetti with calamari and lamb *avgolemono* (meat or vegetables cooked in an egg-lemon stock) with fresh pasta.

Tasomanolis   SEAFOOD €€
(mains €7-14; ☎) This traditional fish taverna on the western end of the beach is run by a keen fisherman. You can sample the day's catch on a nautical-themed waterfront terrace, grilled and paired with wild greens and wine.

Lisseos   GREEK €€
(dishes €6-14.50; ⊗dinner) This unfussy eatery by the bridge has excellent homestyle cooking and a fabulous chocolate cake.

Nikos Souvlaki   GREEK €
(mains €5-8; ⊗dinner) A bare-bones joint and hostel-crowd favourite for cheap souvlaki and grilled chicken.

To Xehoristo   GREEK €
(mains €5.50-10) Never mind the picture menu: locals swear by the tasty souvlaki and grills.

Drinking

Many cafes and bars line the western end of the waterfront.

Ostraco Bar CAFE, LOUNGE BAR
(⊙9am-late; ☏) This old favourite is a small upstairs bar where the gregarious gather for drinking and dancing. In the daytime, the waterfront lounge is great for chilling.

Joe's Bar BAR
(⊙9am-late) Sooner or later everyone seems to end up at Joe's, a dark, warehouse-like joint that's officially called Nufaro and is right on the central waterfront. It plays a good selection of rock and pop and service is friendly.

ⓘ Information

There are two ATMs on the central waterfront. The post office is on the first side street coming from the east. The mod cafe **Frame** (per hr €3; ⊙10am-late) above the Forum shopping centre has internet access. Several waterfront bars offer free wi-fi with purchase.

Plakias' well-stocked, multilanguage **lending library** (⊙9.30am-12.30pm Sun, Mon & Wed, 5-7.30pm Tue, Thu & Sat) is 250m beyond the youth hostel.

ⓘ Getting There & Away

There are up to five buses daily to Rethymno (€4.50, one hour) and one to Preveli (€2.30, 30 minutes).

ⓘ Getting Around

Cars Alianthos (☏28320 31851; www.alianthos .com) Reliable car-hire outlet.
Easy Ride (☏28320 20052; www.easyride.gr) Near the post office. Hires out mountain bikes, scooters and motorcycles.

Around Plakias

BEACHES AROUND PLAKIAS
Between Plakias and Preveli Beach there are several secluded coves popular with freelance campers and nudists. **Damnoni Beach** is pleasant out of high season, despite being dominated by the giant Hapimag tourist complex.

To the west is **Souda**, a quiet beach with a couple of tavernas with rooms. Continuing west are the low-key beach resorts of **Polyrizos-Koraka** (also known as Rodakino) with a handful of tavernas and a few small hotels scattered along a

pleasant stretch of beach. It's ideal if you want a quiet retreat at which to chill for a few days.

MONI PREVELI ΜΟΝΗ ΠΡΕΒΕΛΗ
The historic **Moni Preveli** (☏28320 31246; www.preveli.org; admission €2.50; ⊙8am-7pm mid-Mar–May, 9am-1.30pm & 3.30-7.30pm Jun-Oct) stands in splendid isolation high above the Libyan Sea. Like most Cretan monasteries, it was a centre of anti-Ottoman resistance and was burned by the Turks during the 1866 onslaught.

After the Battle of Crete in WWII, many Allied soldiers were sheltered here before their evacuation to Egypt. A monument featuring two bronze sculptures of a gun-toting priest and a British soldier overlooking the cliffs just before the monastery commemorates the monastery's wartime role. The small **museum** contains a candelabrum presented by grateful British soldiers after the war, alongside valuable ecclesiastical objects. The church has some fine icons, some dating back to the 17th century.

In summer, there are two daily buses from Rethymno (€4.50, 1¼ hours) and one from Plakias (€2.30, 30 minutes).

Beaches Between Plakias & Agia Galini

No amount of hyperbole can communicate the dramatically rugged beauty of Rethymno's pristine southern sandy beaches. While the palm-studded strand at Preveli gets busy in summer, remote and peaceful Ligres, Triopetra and Agios Pavlos are perfect for stress-free escapes surrounded

DON'T MISS

TAVERNA ILIOMANOLIS

Plakias has some pretty good eating options, but for a special treat, take the lovely drive through Kotsifou Gorge to this **mountain taverna** (☏28320 51053; mains €5-9; ⊙Tue-Sun, closed Nov) in Kanevos. Owner-chef Maria's hearty homestyle Cretan food is simply superb and she'll be only too happy to take you into the kitchen so you can peruse the tempting array of stews, casseroles, soups and local specialities prepared daily. Meat, wine, olive oil, cheese and *raki* all come from the family farm.

RETHYMNO AROUND PLAKIAS

DON'T MISS

MYRTHIOS ΜΥΡΘΙΟΣ

This postcard-pretty village draped across the hillside above Plakias makes for a quieter and more bucolic alternative to staying beachside. The other lures are a couple of excellent tavernas, both with bay-view terraces. Fairly swanky **Plateia** (mains €6-9) gives Greek standards a creative spin with results that should appeal to discerning palates, while **Taverna Panorama** (mains €4-11; ☉9am-late; 🛜) has a more rustic feel and gets jam-packed on Fridays, when a Greek band strikes up traditional tunes. Myrthios is a short drive (about 4km) or 30-minute walk (about 2km) from Plakias.

by photogenic splendour and popular with yoga and meditation groups. There's no megaresort to distort the idyllic ambience, only a few lone tavernas with modest rooms. Strong summer winds are common on these beaches. There is no public transport to any of them.

PREVELI BEACH ΠΑΡΑΛΙΑ ΠΡΕΒΕΛΗ

Also known as Palm Beach, Preveli Beach is one of Crete's most celebrated strands. In August 2010 a massive fire swept through the canyon, burning the proud palm trees to a black crisp and seemingly dealing another blow to the local tourism industry. But nature fought back with a vengeance and by the following summer most specimens had already sprouted new fronds.

The setting is truly stunning. It's at the mouth of the Kourtaliotiko Gorge, from where the river Megalopotamos slices across it before emptying into the Libyan Sea. The palm-lined river banks have freshwater pools good for a dip, while rugged cliffs begin where the sand ends. There's some natural shade, but umbrellas and loungers can also be hired from a couple of seasonal snack bars.

A steep path leads down to the beach (10 minutes) from a car park 1km before Moni Preveli. Alternatively, drive 5km along a signposted dirt road from a stone bridge and **Taverna Gefyra** off the Moni Preveli main road. The taverna, incidentally, makes a charming lunch stop. The road deadends at **Amoudi Beach**, where a couple of tavernas rent basic rooms for

around €25. Palm Beach is about 1km over the headland.

There's also a dirt road to Amoudi along the waterfront from points east, but this axle-busting ride should only be attempted by experienced drivers in a high-clearance vehicle.

During high season, you can also get to Preveli Beach by boat from Plakias and Agia Galini.

LIGRES ΛΙΓΡΕΣ

Serene Ligres is a long sweep of greyish sand with some good swimming. There are two tavernas with rooms here, including the enchanting **Villa Maria** (p189; mains €5-10), next to a rushing stream that culminates in the waterfall right in front of the building. Get pummelled by the chilly water, then go straight for a dip in the sea. The owners catch their own fish, best enjoyed on the outdoor deck.

Access to Ligres is via a tiny winding road. Get off the main highway at Akoumia and follow the signs.

TRIOPETRA ΤΡΙΟΠΕΤΡΑ

Triopetra is named after the three giant rocks jutting out of the sea. A headland divides the beach into 'Little Triopetra' on the eastern side and 'Big Triopetra' on the other. The former is home to **Taverna Pavlos** (mains €5-12; ☉Apr-Oct), which specialises in fresh fish caught by the owner himself. The delicious salads and vegetable sides are prepared with home-grown organic produce. Its simple but comfortable rooms (p189) are often booked by participants in monthly yoga workshops. Aside from (free) lounge chairs and umbrellas and a small harbour where you can hire boats, there's really nothing here. Because of submerged sand shelves, this section is not ideal for swimming, so head to the much longer western beach for that. There are two more tavernas with rooms along here.

Triopetra can be reached from Agios Pavlos (about 300m is drivable dirt road) or via a 12km winding asphalt road from the village of Akoumia, on the Rethymno–Agia Galini road. A new road to Ligres starts at the western end of Big Triopetra beach (the first 200m or so are dirt track).

AGIOS PAVLOS ΑΓΙΟΣ ΠΑΥΛΟΣ

Agios Pavlos is little more than a couple of small hotels and tavernas set around a picture-perfect sandy crescent cradled by rugged cliffs. In the distance you can make out the distinctive silhouette of Paximadia Island. The village claims to be the location from where Icarus and Daedalus took their historic flight in ancient mythology (although nearby Agia Galini makes the same claim).

Despite its isolation, the main cove gets busy in July and August, but you can escape the bustle by heading for the beaches behind the headland to the west, which can only be reached by scrambling down a steep sand dune. The furthest cove is the least busy and is popular with nudists. Agios Pavlos' beauty and tranquillity have made it a popular destination for yoga retreats organised by UK-based Yoga Plus (www.yogaplus.co.uk).

Agios Pavlos Hotel (p189) has rooms down in the village and super-nice apartments up on the hill, as well as a pleasant taverna and bar.

To get to Agios Pavlos, look for the turn-off to Kato Saktouria on the Rethymno–Agia Galini road and follow the winding road down to the sea.

Agia Galini Αγια Γαλήνη

POP 860

Agia Galini (a-ya ga-*lee*-nee) is an erstwhile picturesque fishing village where package tourism and overdevelopment have spoilt much of the original charm. With scores of aging hotels and apartment buildings clinging to a steep hillside and hemmed in by cliffs, small beaches and a busy harbour, the town can feel claustrophobic, especially in high season.

Compared with the north, though, it's rather sedate, attracting mostly a middle-aged crowd, families and long-term expat residents. In the shoulder seasons Agia Galini is a convenient base for visits to Phaestos, Agia Triada and the remote beaches of Agios Pavlos and Triopetra. The town all but shuts down in winter.

🏃 Activities

Agia Galini is built along a main road that plunges down to the little harbour where it terminates in a huge car park. From here, two pedestrianised lanes climb back uphill. Souvenir stores and travel agencies line the first one on the left, which is therefore nicknamed Shopping St. Paralleling it is Food St which, you guessed it, is chock-a-block with tavernas.

Acrogiali WATER SPORTS
(✆6946905781) The owner of the Acrogiali taverna on the main beach also hires out canoes and pedal boats and can arrange for waterskiing.

👉 Tours

Argonaftis BOAT TRIPS
(✆28320 91346) From late May to September, the owner of the Faros taverna (below) also runs daily cruises to Preveli Beach (€25) and the deserted offshore island of Paximadia (€30, including small lunch). Departures depend on weather conditions. For enquiries, stop by the taverna the night before or go to the port around 10am.

🍴 Eating

Faros SEAFOOD €€
(Shopping St; mains €7-15) This no-frills family-run fish taverna is usually packed to the gills, and for good reason: the owner himself drops his nets into the Med, so you know what's on the plate that night was still swimming in the sea in the morning. Squid cooked in their own ink, lobster spaghetti and fish soup are specialities.

Taverna Stohos GREEK €€
(www.stohos.gr; Main Beach; mains €7-10; ⊘late Apr–Oct) Locals swear by this beachfront taverna with attached apartments (p189). Friendly Fanourios presides over the kitchen, which churns out excellent *kleftiko* and other clay-oven dishes.

Onar GREEK €€
(Food St; mains €6-12) Even after many years in business, Onar still hasn't lost its grip on the crowd, including many regulars. There are plenty of other tavernas with romantic views over the port, but Onar's tasty mezedhes and finger-lickin' grills make it a standout option.

Taverna at Camping No Problem GREEK €€
(pizzas & pastas €4-8, mains €7-13; ⊘9am-midnight Apr-Oct; 🛜) Giorgos and Yiannis' tree-shaded and flower-filled patio is a peaceful setting for both classic and creative local fare, including spit-roasted lamb and pork fillet with honey and walnuts. In summer, there's live Cretan music on Fridays. It's about 750m from town to the eponymous campground (p190). Bring a swimsuit to cool off in the big pool.

La Strada ITALIAN €
(dishes €5-8) About 40 varieties of pizzas, pastas and risottos.

Platia CAFE €
(breakfasts €3.50-8; ⊙8am-2pm & 6pm-1am; 🛜) Excellent breakfasts plus salads, snacks and yummy homemade walnut cake.

 Drinking & Entertainment

TOP CHOICE **Blue Bar** BAR
(Shopping St) This been-there-forever pub has a reputation for playing the best music in town. Owner Heinz himself is a singer-songwriter with eclectic sound tastes, which is why turntables get a work-out with everything from R&B to rock and soul to pop.

Zanzibar CAFE, BAR
(☑28320 91142; www.kapi-crete.com; @🛜) It didn't take Kay and Pieter long to turn their newest venture into a local institu-tion. Locals, expats and tourists mingle here for coffee, drinks and communication, often until the wee hours. It's on the main road, next to the bus stop. There's live music once a month. In winter it's open for the expat crowd on Wednesdays only.

So Far So Good BAR
Drink a toast to Crete as you wiggle your toes in the sand at this beach paradise that's almost always open and draws more of a younger crowd. Tanning and chilling in the daytime, partying at night. Great cocktails and free sunbeds with lockers.

Miles Tone BAR
(Food St) Cool cats of all ages are drawn to this intimate bar that jumps with jazz and blues nightly.

ℹ️ **Information**
Buses stop in front of Zanzibar near the port, right in the commercial heart of Agia Galini. Zanzibar also has internet terminals for €1 per hour and all-day wi-fi for €1. The post office is just past the bus stop and ATMs are nearby. For web information try www.agia-galini.com.

ℹ️ **Getting There & Away**
In high season there are up to six buses daily to Iraklio (€8, two hours), up to five to Rethymno (€6.20, 1½ hours) and to Phaestos (€2.10, 30 minutes), and two to Matala (€3.30, 45 minutes).

ℹ️ **Getting Around**
Opposite the post office, **Mano's Bike** (☑28320 91551) hires out scooters and motorcycles, while **Monza Travel** (☑28320 91278) hires out cars and organises bus excursions. For a taxi call ☑6936906217 or 6942989520.

NORTHEAST COAST

Once you clear the resort strip, the coast-line east of Rethymno is indented and pockmarked with watery caves and iso-lated coves that are accessible only by boat. The chief resorts along the north coast are Bali and Panormo, both good bases for exploring the villages in the Mt Psiloritis foothills, such as Axos and Anogia.

Panormo Πάνορμο
POP 880
Panormo, about 22km east of Rethymno, is one of the few relatively unspoilt beach towns on the northern coast. Despite a couple of big hotel complexes, it retains an unhurried, authentic village feel and makes for a quieter alternative to the overcrowded scene immediately east of Rethymno and at nearby Bali. In summer, concerts and other events are held in a carob mill turned cultural centre.

⊙ **Sights & Activities**
Well-regarded Cretan cooking seminars are run by Rodialos; see p245 for details.

Basilica of Aghia Sophia ANCIENT SITE
Coins unearthed in Panormo indicate that a village flourished here between the 1st to the 9th centuries AD, but the only in situ evidence from this period are the surviving bits and pieces of this 6th-century church. It's built on the slopes above the village; look for signs directing you to the site.

Tourist train TRAIN
In summer, a cute little train chugs around Panormo (€4) and out to the pottery village of Margarites (p90) and the Melidoni Cave (p91; adult €15, child aged six to 12 years €7.50).

Atlantis Diving Center DIVING
(☑28310 71640; www.atlantis-creta.com; 2 incl equipment €102, snorkelling gear per day €15) Based at the Grecotel Club Marine Palace, this five-star PADI outfit offers both shore

DID YOU KNOW?

The name Bali has nothing to do with its Indonesian namesake; it means 'honey' in Turkish, as excellent honey was once collected and processed here. In antiquity Bali was known as Astali, but no traces of ancient Astali now remain.

and boat dives as well as the gamut of courses from beginner to instructor level.

Church of Agios Yiorgos   CHURCH
Church fans should also stop in town at Panormo's parish church, which has some stunning modern frescoes.

✖ Eating

The touristy harbour tavernas serve standard Greek and international dishes as well as fish. More traditional places can be found a block or two inland.

TOP CHOICE **Taverna Kastro**   CRETAN €€
(mains €5-10; ☺May-Oct; ☎) The flower-festooned seafront terrace is a great place to sit, but it's what's on the plates that will truly wow you. Classic Cretan recipes get a modern makeover here, which translates into such palate teasers as lentils with *apaki* (cured pork), hake with potatoes or rabbit in oregano.

To Steki tou Sifaka   GREEK €
(mains €6-8) For satisfying homestyle Cretan food, report to this no-nonsense taverna a block inland from the waterfront. Pick from the specials board out front.

Angira   SEAFOOD €€
(mains €6-20) A giant anchor at the eastern end of the harbour points you to this fish taverna, which also serves the usual grills and Greek specialities.

Stavroula   GREEK €
(meals €2-6; ☺from 6pm) Opposite the post office, this little joint makes the best souvlaki in town.

❶ Information

The bus stop is on the main road outside of town. The post office and an ATM are right in town, next to the Stavroula souvlaki joint. Further information can be found at www.panormo.gr.

❶ Getting There & Away

In high season, buses from Rethymno go to Panormo every hour (€2.20, 25 minutes). Buses stop on the main road just outside of town.

Bali Μπαλί

POP 330

Bali, 38km east of Rethymno and 51km west of Iraklio, has one of the most stunning settings on the northern coast, with a series of little coves strung along the indented shore, marked by hills, promontories and narrow sandy beaches. But helter-skelter development has significantly marred the natural beauty of this former fishing hamlet and the beaches can get crammed with sun-worshippers in summer. In low season, though, it's a fun place to come and enjoy the dramatic scenery and take advantage of lodging bargains.

🏖 Beaches

Bali has four grey-sand beaches, all of them rather kid-friendly. **Livadi** is the biggest and widest beach, with a party vibe. It's packed with chairs and umbrellas and backed along its entire length by bars, tavernas and cafes. Next is **Varkotopo**, a tiny, narrow strip of sand flanked by young palm trees. There are a couple of quite classy bars here that are nice for sunset cocktails. Further north, in the port, is **Limani**, also a rather narrow crescent but with easy access to water sports. **Karavostasi**, the last beach, is also the smallest and quietest, with just a couple of tavernas curled up beneath the rocky cliffs. A coastal footpath leads here from the port and the Bali Express goes out here as well.

🏃 Activities

Bali is rather spread out and it's a long and undulating walk from one end to the other – 25 minutes or more. A good way to get around is by the **Bali Express** (per trip €2; ☺9am-11pm), a tourist train that makes 11 stops in town and at the beaches.

Water sports

At the port, **Lefteris** (☎28340 94102, 6937200333; cat_cruises@yahoo.gr) hires out canoes (per hour €8), motorboats (per hour €35) and jet skis (€50 for 20 minutes). Waterskiing costs €35 per session, while cruises to Rethymno go for €24.

Diving

Hippocampos Dive Centre (☎28340 94193; www.hippocampos.com; single dive incl equipment €49, snorkelling gear per day €15; ⏱9am-1pm & 5-9pm, closed Mon Apr-Jun, Sep & Oct, closed Sun Jul & Aug) A few steps away from Lefteris, this well-run outfit does shore and boat dives as well as the gamut of courses, including one-week open-water certifications (€390). In high season, it's best to reserve two or three days ahead.

✗ Eating

TOP CHOICE **Taverna Nest**   CRETAN €
(mains €4-14; ⏱May-Oct) For honest-to-goodness, farm-to-table fare, report to this vine-covered terrace where home-cooked meals are served in ample portions and with big smiles. Regulars crave the barbecue and the grilled fish, nicely paired with the home-made dolmadhes and handcut fried potatoes. It's a few steps inland from the port. Satisfying breakfasts, too.

Panorama   CRETAN €€
(mains €5-16) Watch the boats bob in the port while enjoying excellent fish and homestyle Greek food high up on the terrace of this former carob warehouse. In business since 1968, it's one of the oldest and most respected eateries in town.

Taverna Karavostasi   GREEK €€
(specials €5.50-16) One of the tavernas on pint-sized Karavostasi beach, this is a nice place to unwind. The speciality is stuffed aubergines (eggplants), while the Cretan pizza (with feta) is a tasty spin on the original.

❶ Information

There is an ATM next to the Mythos restaurant and an **internet cafe** (per hr €2; ⏱9am-11pm) on your left, shortly after entering the town.

❶ Getting There & Around

Buses on their Rethymno–Iraklio run (€7.60) drop you at the main road, from where it is a 2km walk to the port of Bali (€6.30).

Best of Crete

Witnesses to History »
Life's a Beach »
Hitting the Trail »

Small church on a promontory near Loutro

Witnesses to History

At the crossroads of three continents, Crete's turbulent history has been shaped by many players. Hear the whispers of the past as you visit grand Minoan palaces, remnants of a Roman city, showcases of Venetian architecture, and monasteries with military pedigrees. If only stones could talk...

Magic Malia

1 Smaller than Knossos, and without the reconstructions and embellishments, the Palace of Malia is Crete's most accessible and easily understood Minoan site. Its sophisticated layout and infrastructure attest to this ancient society's advanced level of civilisation. Excavations are still ongoing (p145).

Glorious Gortyna

2 Get lost amid the moody ruins of Roman Crete's capital, stop to admire what's left of a beautiful early-Christian church and marvel at 2600-year-old stone tablets engraved with a surprisingly modern legal code (p135).

Fortified Monastery

3 Despite its fortifications, 15th-century Moni Toplou was sacked by pirates, looted by the Knights of Malta and finally captured by Turks in 1821. Its church shelters a precious icon by Ioannis Kornaros (p166).

Mighty Fortresses

4 The most impressive vestiges of Venetian rule are the many stalwart fortresses built to keep pirates and Turks at bay. Visit those in Rethymno (p80), Iraklio (p115) and Frangokastello (p59).

Symbol of Defiance

5 The hauntingly beautiful Moni Arkadiou is a window into the Cretan soul. During the revolt of 1866, local Cretans trapped within opted to blow up their gunpowder supplies rather than surrender to the Turks, killing nearly everyone, Turks included (p89).

Right

1. Pottery found at Malia 2. Amphitheatre, Gortyna
3. Moni Toplou 4. Frangokastello Fortress

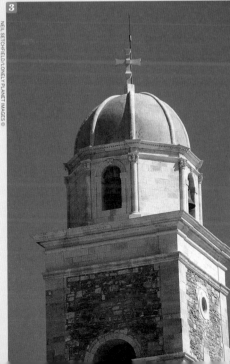

Life's a Beach

Crete has been blessed with many off-the-chart splendours, including bewitching beaches lapped by clear waters shimmering in myriad shades of blue. From bar-backed busy strips to romantic palm-fringed strands and footprint-free crescents where solitude reigns, there's a beach with your name on it.

Secluded Splendour

1 Escaping the crowds means pointing the compass to Agios Pavlos (p98) and Triopetra (p98), two hauntingly beautiful and tranquil beaches tucked into the jagged southern coastline of Rethymno. At nearby Preveli Beach (p98) you can seek shade beneath a grove of swaying palm trees.

Caribbean Crete

2 If you like nothing better than wriggling your toes in white shimmering sand and splashing in turquoise waters, make a beeline to beautiful Balos beach (p70) on the untamed Gramvousa Peninsula.

Wave Action

3 Find your favourite among the tiara of coves separated by rocky spits on Falasarna beach (p71). Work on your tan while relaxing in the pinkish sand, then cool off by jumping headlong into the big and long waves rolling in from the open sea.

Triple Treats

4 Each of Iraklio's southern beaches has its own personality. Matala (p140) is a lovely but busy crescent, while Kommos (p141) beckons with its long, undeveloped strand and Agiofarango (p142) is so remote that it can only be reached by boat or on foot.

Tropical Paradise

5 A sweeping crescent of powdery white sand, Elafonisi (p73) is one of Crete's most stunning beaches. Only a shallow lagoon with dazzlingly clear turquoise waters separates it from a little islet where dunes rise above secluded coves.

Right

1. Preveli Beach 2. Gramvousa Peninsula
3. Falasarna beach 4. Matala beach

Hitting the Trail

Like a fine wine, Crete's landscape wants to be sipped not downed in one big gulp. So get out of the car and onto the trail for a slow-mo close-up at gorges chiselled by time and the elements, a mountain where Zeus was born and a valley haunted by the ghosts of the Minoans.

Samaria's Little Sister

1 Samaria may hog the spotlight, but the Imbros Gorge is no slouch in the beauty department either. Easier, shorter and quieter, it's tailor-made for families with kids. Cypress, oak, fig and almond trees accompany you on your journey (p55).

Lovely Loutro

2 The secluded natural harbour of Loutro (p60) is the gateway to a tangle of trails accessing the spectacular and blissfully tranquil Aradena Gorge, as well as little-visited beaches otherwise only reachable by boat.

Epic Meander

3 Hats off to those who've walked the entire 10,000-plus kilometres of the E4 European long-distance path. But even tackling just a short stretch in Crete, where it culminates on the pebbly shore of Kato Zakros, has its rewards (p22).

Ghost Canyon

4 A hike through the dramatic Valley of the Dead, also known as Zakros Gorge, takes you past towering walls pockmarked with caves used by Minoans as burial sites and spills out at the cute beach town of Kato Zakros (p168).

Crete's Rooftop

5 Like a friendly giant, Mt Psiloritis (p93) serenades a green quilt of valleys and villages and often wears a monk's tonsure of snow well into spring. Climbing up Crete's tallest mountain is no walk in the park, but it doesn't require technical skills either.

Right
1. Imbros Gorge 2. Hiking above Loutro

Iraklio Ηράκλειο

Best Places to Eat

» Elia & Diosmos (p132)
» Prassein Aloga (p118)
» Brillant/Herb's Garden (p118)
» Kritamon (p130)
» Roussos Taverna (p132)

Best Places to Stay

» Lato Hotel (p191)
» Balsamico Suites (p194)
» Eleonas (p192)
» Capsis Astoria (p191)
» Villa Kerasia (p192)

Why Go?

Iraklio is Crete's most dynamic region, home to almost half the island's population and its top-rated tourist site, the Minoan Palace of Knossos. Priceless treasures unearthed here and at the many other Minoan sites around Crete have catapulted the archaeological museum in the capital city of Iraklio onto the world stage.

Even if the coastal stretch east of Iraklio is one continuous band of hotels and resorts, just a little bit inland villages sweetly lost in time provide pleasing contrast. Taste the increasingly sophisticated tipple produced in the Iraklio Wine Country, walk in the footsteps of El Greco and Nikos Kazantzakis, and revel in the rustic grandeur of such remote mountain villages as Zaros.

On the quieter southern coast, the ex-hippie hang-out of Matala is the only developed resort, while in the charming villages the laid-back life unfolds much the way it has since time immemorial.

When to Go

April and May are the perfect time for culture vultures as Knossos and other archaeological blockbusters are still mercifully crowd-free and there's minimal risk of sunstroke. Bonus: carpets of wildflowers in the countryside.

All summer long, the city of Iraklio embarks on a high-class cultural orgy of dance, music, theatre and cinema performances in enchanting outdoor venues, during the Iraklio Summer Festival.

After a long hot summer, Crete's grapes are plump and ready for harvesting. Arhanes rings in the season with a five-day wine festival in August.

DON'T MISS

The mountain village of Zaros (p133) is the gateway to some wonderful hikes, most famously the spectacular Rouvas Gorge with its ancient oak forest and chapel Moni Agios Nikolaos.

Best Ancient Sites

» Knossos (p123) – the mother of all Minoan sites

» Malia (p145) – Knossos without the reconstructions

» Gortyna (p135) – relic of Roman Crete

» Phaestos (p137) – prettiest location of all Minoan palaces

Best Rural Escapes

» Arhanes (p129) – the heart of the wine country

» Fodele (p127) – pretty village that claims to be El Greco's birthplace

» Kamilari (p141) – charismatic hillside village with a Minoan tomb

» Zaros (p133) – mountain village with famous natural spring

Resources

» www.heraklion-city.gr

» http://history.heraklion.gr

» www.historical-museum.gr

Getting Around

Iraklio has the best transport infrastructure among the Cretan prefectures. The E75 highway runs along the north coast with individual communities accessed via the parallel Old National Rd. A major road links Iraklio with the Messara Plain and the beach resorts around Matala; another travels through Knossos and the Iraklio Wine Country as far as Arkalohori. Smaller roads, too, are mostly in good condition. In summer especially, the bus service is extensive, with all major communities served regularly.

THREE PERFECT DAYS

Day One

Kick off early and make a beeline for **Knossos** to get a head start on the tour-bus crowd. Explore the site's main features in relative peace, then move on to the less popular corners when it gets busy. Enjoy a gourmet Cretan lunch at **Elia & Diosmos** in Skalani on the edge of the **Iraklio Wine Country**, followed by sampling the vintages at the nearby **Boutari** winery and paying your respects to Crete's most revered 20th-century writer, Nikos Kazantzakis, in **Myrtia**. Spend the rest of the day touring more wineries and checking out **Arhanes'** copious Minoan sites before returning to Iraklio for a rooftop dinner at **Herb's Garden**.

Day Two

Spend the morning being mesmerised by the flitting, darting and plodding submarine denizens of the state-of-the-art **Cretaquarium** in Gournes. Afterwards, grab your torch and Indiana Jones hat and descend into the belly of **Skotino Cave**, a spooky underground world with bizarre formations and a resident population of bats and other dark-loving critters. Cope with the heat by spending the rest of the day chilling and riding the slides at **Water City**, Crete's biggest water park.

Day Three

Today you're off to a site inspection of the **Palace of Phaestos**, followed by lunch at **Taverna Agios Ioannis**. Hungry for more Minoan culture? Take a spin around **Agia Triada**. Otherwise head straight to **Agiofarango Gorge** for the short hike to a lovely, secluded beach with crystal-clear water. For dinner find your favourite among the tavernas on the main square in **Sivas**.

Accommodation

For sleeping options throughout this region, please see the Accommodation chapter (p175).

IRAKLIO ΗΡΑΚΛΕΙΟ

POP 137,400

The birthplace of El Greco and Nikos Kazantzakis, Iraklio (also called Heraklion) is perhaps Crete's most underrated destination. Sure, if you arrive with a tranquil Greek holiday in mind, Greece's bustling fifth-largest city can initially be an assault on the senses. Although it's not pretty in a conventional way, Iraklio can grow on you if you take the time to wander its backstreets and explore its nuances.

In recent times, the city has undergone a period of intense urban renewal and is riding high on energy if not money. A revitalised waterfront now invites strolling and the newly pedestrianised historic centre is punctuated with bustling squares rimmed by buildings from the time when Columbus set sail.

Iraklio has a certain urban sophistication, with a thriving cafe and restaurant scene, the island's best shopping and lively nightlife. Of course, don't miss its blockbuster sights either, like the amazing archaeological museum and the Palace of Knossos, both fascinating windows into Minoan culture.

History

Settled since neolithic times, Iraklio was conquered by the Saracens in AD 824 and reputedly evolved into the slave-trade capital of the eastern Mediterranean and the launching pad for the region's notorious pirates. Byzantine troops ousted the Arabs after a long siege in 961 and the city became known as Handakas. This was changed to Candia in 1204 when Crete was sold to the Venetians.

Under the Venetians, the city became a centre for the arts and home to painters such as Damaskinos and El Greco. The magnificent fortress and many of the great public buildings and lofty churches date to this period. The Candians fought tooth and nail to keep the Ottomans at bay, even extending the fortress walls. But the Turks overran Crete in 1645, and began besieging Candia in 1648.

Under the Turks the city became known as Megalo Kastro (Big Castle). Artistic life withered and many Cretans fled or were killed. In August 1898, a Turkish mob massacred hundreds of Cretans, 17 British soldiers and the British Consul. Within weeks, a squadron of British ships steamed into Iraklio's harbour and ended Turkish rule.

Iraklio got its current name in 1922. At the time Hania was the capital of independent Crete, but Iraklio's central location soon saw it emerge as the island's commercial centre. The city suffered badly in WWII, when bombs levelled much of the old Venetian and Turkish town. It resumed its position as Crete's capital in 1971.

⊙ Sights

Iraklio's main sights are wedged within the historic town, hemmed in by the waterfront and the old city walls. Many of the finest buildings line up along the main thoroughfare, 25 Avgoustou, which skirts the lovely central square, Plateia Venizelou (also called Lion Sq after its landmark Morosini Fountain). East of here, Koraï is the hub of Iraklio's cafe scene, which leads towards the sprawling Plateia Eleftherias with the archaeological museum nearby.

TOP CHOICE Iraklio Archaeological Museum
MUSEUM

(☑2810 279 000; http://odysseus.culture.gr; Xanthoudidou 2; adult/concession €4/2; ⊙8.30am-3pm Nov-Mar, extended hr Apr-Oct, call for details) This outstanding museum is one of the largest and most important in Greece. There are artefacts spanning 5500 years from neolithic to Roman times, but it's rightly most famous for its extensive Minoan collection. A visit here will greatly enhance your understanding and appreciation of Crete's history and culture. Don't skip it.

The main museum building has been closed for restoration since 2006, with no firm reopening date available at the time of writing. In the meantime, the key exhibits are beautifully displayed in an annex entered from Hatzidaki. While the temporary exhibition only includes 400 of the 15,000 artefacts normally on display, it is presented

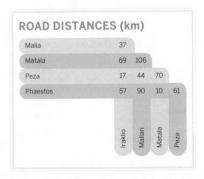

ROAD DISTANCES (km)

	Iraklio	Malian	Matala	Peza
Malia	37			
Matala	69	106		
Peza	17	44	70	
Phaestos	57	90	10	61

IRAKLIO SIGHTS

Iraklio Highlights

1 Make a date with King Minos at the **Palace of Knossos** (p123)

2 Sample the tasty local tipple in the **Iraklio Wine Country** (p131)

3 Get high on knockout views from **Phaestos** (p137)

4 Go behind the scenes of Roman Crete at **Gortyna** (p135)

5 Spend a cool day in the pools and on the slides of a **water park** (p144) at Hersonisos

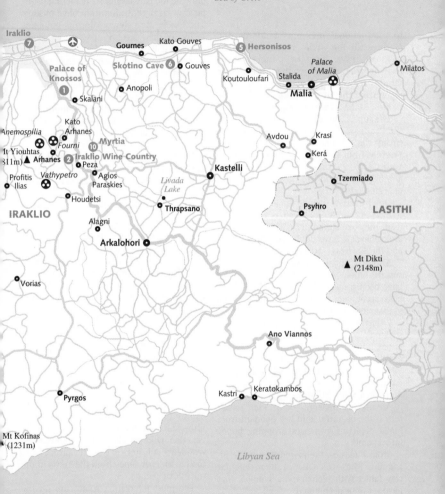

Dia

0 ——————— 10 km
0 ——————— 6 miles

Sea of Crete

Iraklio
7

Palace of
Knossos
1

Gournes

Kato Gouves

5 Hersonisos

Skotino Cave **6** ● Gouves

Koutouloufari

Stalida

*Palace
of Malia*

● Milatos

● Anopoli

● Skalani

Kato
Arhanes

Anemospilia
Fourni

It Yiouhtas
311m) ▲ **Arhanes**

Myrtia

10

Iraklio Wine Country

Peza

2

● Agios
Paraskies

Vathypetro

Profitis
Ilias

● Houdetsi

IRAKLIO

Malia

Avdou ●

Krasí ●

● Kerá

Tzermiado ●

*Livada
Lake*

Kastelli ●

Psyhro ●

LASITHI

● Alagni

Arkalohori ●

▲ Mt Dikti
(2148m)

Thrapsano ●

● Vorias

Ano Viannos
●

● **Pyrgos**

Kastri ● ● **Keratokambos**

Mt Kofinas
(1231m)

Libyan Sea

6 Descend into the earth's belly on an exploration of the mysterious **Skotino Cave** (p144)

7 Stand in awe of Minoan artistry at the **Iraklio**

Archaeological Museum (p111)

8 Marvel at nature's creativity on the scenic drive to **Zaros** (p133)

9 Swim and sun next to Minoan ruins at **Kommos** (p141)

10 Get insight into the genius of Cretan-born author Nikos Kazantzakis in **Myrtia** (p132)

WANT MORE?

Head to Lonely Planet (www.lonely planet.com/greece/crete/iraklio) for planning advice, author recommendations, traveller reviews and insider tips.

to international museum standards and features all the main masterpieces. The treasure trove includes pottery, jewellery, figurines and sarcophagi, plus some famous frescoes. The most exciting finds come from the sites of Knossos, Phaestos, Zakros, Malia and Agia Triada.

The superlative Knossos frescoes include the Procession Fresco, the Griffin Fresco (from the Throne Room), the Dolphin Fresco (from the Queen's Room) and the Bull-Leaping Fresco, which depicts an acrobat somersaulting on the back of a charging bull.

Other frescoes include the lovely restored Prince of the Lilies, as well as two frescoes from the Neopalatial period – the priestess archaeologists have dubbed La Parisienne and the Saffron Gatherer.

Also on display from the palace at Knossos are Linear A and B tablets (the latter have been translated as household or business accounts), an ivory statue of a bull vaulter and some exquisite gold seals.

From the Middle Minoan period, the most striking piece is the 20cm black stone Bull's Head, a libation vessel, with a fine head of curls, gold horns and lifelike painted crystal eyes. Other fascinating exhibits include figurines of a bare-breasted snake goddess found in a Knossos shrine.

Among the treasures of Minoan jewellery is the beautiful gold bee pendant from Malia depicting two bees dropping honey into a comb.

From Phaestos, the prized find is the intriguing Phaestos Disk, a 16cm circular clay tablet with pictographic symbols that have yet to be deciphered.

Examples of the elaborate Kamares pottery, named after the sacred cave of Kamareswhere it was first discovered, include a superbly decorated vase from Phaestos with white sculpted flowers.

Finds from Zakros include the gorgeous crystal rhyton vase discovered in over 300 fragments and painstakingly reassembled, as well as vessels decorated with floral and marine designs.

The most famous of Minoan sarcophagi, and one of Minoan art's greatest achievements, is the sarcophagus of Agia Triada, painted with floral and abstract designs and ritual scenes. Other significant Agia Triada finds include the Harvester Vase – of which only the top part remains – depicting young farm workers returning from olive picking. The Boxer Vase shows Minoans indulging in two of their favourite pastimes – wrestling and bull-grappling. The Chieftain Cup depicts a more cryptic scene: a chief holding a staff and three men carrying animal skins.

Finds from Minoan cemeteries include two small clay models of groups of figures that were found in a *tholos* tomb. One depicts four male dancers in a circle, their arms around each other's shoulders, possibly participants in a funeral ritual.

More insight into Minoan life is given in the elaborate gaming board decorated with ivory, crystal, glass, gold and silver from the Knossos new palace period.

A combined ticket with the Palace of Knossos costs €10 (€5 concession).

Historical Museum of Crete   MUSEUM
(☎2810 283 219; www.historical-museum.gr; Sofokli Venizelou; adult/concession €5/3; ◷9am-5pm Mon-Sat) If you're wondering what Crete's been up to for the past, say, 1700 years, a spin around this highly engaging museum is in order. Exhibits hopscotch from the Byzantine tothe Venetian and Turkish periods, culminating in WWII. There's excellent English labelling, multimedia and listening stations throughout.

The undisputed highlights on the 1st floor are the only two El Greco paintings in Crete – *View of Mt Sinai and the Monastery of St Catherine* (1570) and the tiny *Baptism of Christ* (1567). Other rooms contain 13th- and 14th-century frescoes, exquisite Venetian gold jewellery and embroidered vestments. A historical exhibit charts Crete's road to independence from the Turks in the early 20th century.

The most interesting rooms are on the 2nd floor. Fans of Nikos Kazantzakis can admire the famed Cretan writer's recreated study and watch snippets from *Zorba the Greek* and other films based on his books. Historically, the focus is on WWII, in particular the Battle of Crete. A state-of-the-art exhibit dramatically details the Cretan resistance, the role of Allied Secret Services, the destruction of Iraklio, the abduction of German General Kreipe and other wartime moments. A highlight is the original office of Cretan-born Emmanouil Tsouderos, who served as Greek prime minister from 1941 to 1944. It was donated by his family.

The top (3rd) floor features an outstanding folklore collection.

Koules Fortress
FORTRESS

(Harbour; adult/concession €2/1; ⊘8.30am-7pm Tue-Sun May-Oct, to 3pm Nov-Apr) Iraklio's main landmark, this squat and square 16th-century fortress at the end of an old jetty was called Rocca al Mare under the Venetians. It helped keep the Turks out for 21 years and later became a Turkish prison for Cretan rebels. On windy days, big waves add drama as the water crashes against the fortress walls and onto the jetty. Three walls still sport marble reliefs of Venice's symbol: the winged Lion of St Mark. Inside are 26 restored rooms previously used for storage and as soldiers' barracks; these days they sometimes host art exhibits and performances. The view from the top takes in the vaulted arcades of the Arsenali, built to shelter and repair the Venetian fleet, opposite the fortress.

Natural History Museum of Crete
MUSEUM

(⊘2810 282 740; www.nhmc.uoc.gr; Sofokli Venizelou; adult/concession €6/4; ⊘9am-4pm Mon-Fri, 10am-4pm Sat & Sun Jun-Sep, 8.30am-2pm Mon-Fri, 10am-4pm Sat & Sun Oct-May) In an imaginatively recycled power station, this museum uses huge dioramas and a terrarium wing to introduce you to the flora and fauna of the eastern Mediterranean, especially Crete. Star of the show, however, is the life-size representation of the elephant-like *Deinotherium gigantum,* the world's third-largest land mammal. Standing 5m tall and 7m long, it was reconstructed based on fossils found near Sitia. Another crowd-pleaser is the 3-D Earthquake Simulator. There's also a hands-on Discovery Centre where budding scientists can dig for fossils, climb into a cave or watch a movie inside a tree. More exhibits are expected to come online in the coming years. It's about a 10-minute walk west from 25 Avgoustou along the waterfront.

Morosini Fountain
FOUNTAIN

(Plateia Venizelou) Also known as Lion Fountain, this is the most beloved among the Venetian vestiges around town. On Plateia Venizelou, it spurts water from four lions into eight sinuous marble troughs. The centrepiece marble statue of Poseidon was destroyed under the Turks.

FREE | Municipal Art Gallery
ART GALLERY

(⊘2810 399 228; 25 Avgoustou; ⊘9am-1.30pm & 6-9pm Mon-Fri, 9am-1pm Sat) The three-aisled 13th-century Agios Markos Basilica was reconstructed many times and turned into a mosque by the Turks. Today it's an elaborate backdrop for art by Maria Fiorakis, Lefteris Kanakakis, Thomas Fanorakis and other Cretan creatives.

Church of Agios Titos
CHURCH

This majestic church dominates the eponymous square. It has Byzantine origins in AD 961, was converted to a Catholic church by the Venetians and turned into a mosque by the Ottomans, who also rebuilt it after the devastating 1856 earthquake. It has been an Orthodox church since 1925. Since 1966, it has once again sheltered the much-prized skull relic of St Titus, returned here after being spirited to Venice for safekeeping during the Turkish occupation.

City Walls
HISTORICAL SITE

Iraklio burst out of its walls long ago, but these massive fortifications, with seven bastions and four gates, are still very conspicuous, dwarfing the concrete 20th-century structures around them. Venetians built the defences between 1462 and 1562. You can follow the walls around the heart of the city, though it's not a particularly scenic trip.

Bembo Fountain
FOUNTAIN

The delightful fountain on Plateia Kornarou, at the southern end of Odos 1866, was cobbled together in the 1550s from antique materials, including a statue of a Roman official found near Ierapetra. The town's first fountain, it channelled fresh water to Iraklio via an aqueduct running 13km south to Mt Yiouhtas. The adjacent hexagonal building, now a cafe, was originally a pump-house added by the Turks.

Loggia
HISTORICAL BUILDING

Iraklio's town hall is housed in the attractively reconstructed 17th-century Loggia, a Venetian version of a gentleman's club, where the male aristocracy once gathered for drinks and gossip.

Tomb of Nikos Kazantzakis
HISTORICAL SITE

Crete's most acclaimed 20th-century writer, Nikos Kazantzakis (1883–1957; see p236) is buried south of the centre in the well-preserved Martinengo Bastion. The epitaph on his grave, 'I hope for nothing, I

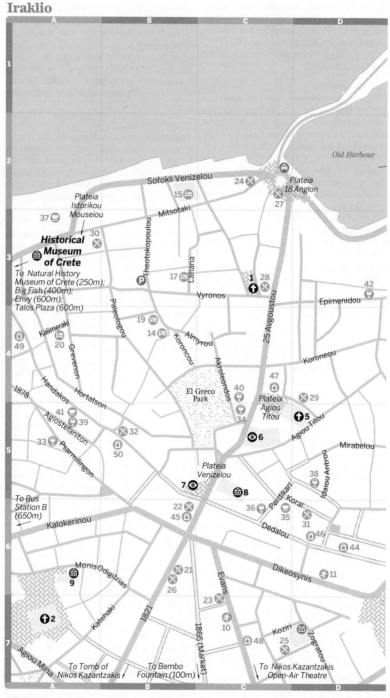

Old Harbour

Sofokli Venizelou 24

Plateia 18 Anglon 27

Plateia Istorikou Mouseiou

37 30

Historical Museum of Crete

To Natural History Museum of Crete (250m); Big Fish (400m); Envy (600m); Talos Plaza (600m)

15
Mitsotaki
Theotokopoulou
Lahana
17 Vyronos
1 28
25 Avgoustou
Epimenidou
42

49 Kalimeraki
20
Paleologou
19
14 Koroneou
Almyrou
Akroleondos
Koroneou

1878
Handakos
Grevenon
Hortatson
Agiostefaniton
41 39
33 Psarmingon
32
50
El Greco Park
40 34
47
Plateia Agiou Titou
29
5 Agiou Titou
Mirabelou

To Bus Station B (650m)
Kalokerinou
Plateia Venizelou
7 8
22 45
Idaiou Antrou
38
36 35 31
Perdikari Koral
Dedalou
46
44

Monis Odigitrias
9
Katehaki
1821
21
26
23
Evans
10
1866 (Market)
Dikeosynis 11
48 25
Koziri
Zografou

2
Agiou Mina
To Tomb of Nikos Kazantzakis
To Bembo Fountain (100m)
To Nikos Kazantzakis Open-Air Theatre

fear nothing, I am free', is taken from one of his works. To get there, pick up Moussourou at the south end of Odos 1821, follow it to the end and turn right on Plastira. The bastion will loom on your left.

FREE **Battle of Crete Museum**   MUSEUM
(☎2810 346 554; cnr Doukos Beaufort & Hatzidaki; ☺9am-1pm) This museum chronicles this epic WWII battle through photographs, letters, uniforms, weapons and other military artefacts.

Museum of Religious Art   MUSEUM
(☎2810 288 825; Moni Odigitrias) The former Church of Agia Ekaterini, in the square next to the **Agios Minas cathedral**, now houses a superb collection of Cretan icons, including six masterpieces by Michael Damaskinos, a key representative of the Cretan School of painting that flourished under the Venetians in the 16th and 17th centuries. Closed for renovation at the time of our visit, the museum was not expected to reopen until 2012.

🏃 Activities

Ammoudara, about 4km west of Iraklio, and **Amnisos**, 2km to east, are the closest **beaches**; the latter is just past the airport and gets quite a bit of noise. The strands in Agia Pelagia, some 20km west of town, are nicer.

Cretan Adventures   OUTDOOR ACTIVITIES
(☎2810 332 772; www.cretanadventures.gr; Evans 10, upstairs) This well-regarded local company organises hiking tours, mountain biking and specialist and extreme outdoor explorations.

Mountaineering Club of Iraklio   HIKING
(☎2810 227 609; Dikeosynis 53) The local chapter arranges hiking trips across the island most weekends. Anyone is welcome to join.

🎊 Festivals & Events

Iraklio Summer Festival   ARTS
Iraklio celebrates summer with two months of top-notch dance, music, theatre and cinema performances held primarily at the Nikos Kazantzakis Open-Air Theatre and the Manos Hatzidakis Open-Air Theatre from July to mid-September.

🍴 Eating

Iraklio has restaurants to suit all tastes and budgets, from excellent fish tavernas to international cuisine and fine dining. You'll find the all-night souvlaki joints around Morosini Fountain and a few atmospheric tavernas around the market, as well as on the waterfront. Note that many restaurants close on Sundays. There's a supermarket on the north side of El Greco Park.

TOP CHOICE Brillant/Herb's Garden CRETAN €€€
(☑2810 228 103; www.brillantrestaurant.gr; Epimenidou 15; mains €10-23; ☎) The avant-garde decor at Brillant, the hip culinary outpost at the Lato boutique hotel (p191) might almost distract you from the creatively composed, feistily flavoured Cretan cuisine. Orange-marinated chicken cooked with vine-leaf juice, walnuts and tomato is a typical palate tantaliser. From May to October, the restaurant renames itself Herb's Garden and moves to the hotel's rooftop for alfresco dining with harbour views.

Prassein Aloga MEDITERRANEAN €€
(☑2810 283 429; Kydonias 21, cnr Handakos; mains €7-23) This neighbourhood-adored rustic restaurant does sharp and innovative Mediterranean cuisine from an ever-changing menu. Heaping salads, pasta loaded with shrimp and mussels, and dishes based on ancient Greek recipes are menu stars. At the time of writing, there were plans to move into a bigger location by 2012.

Kouzina tis Popis   INTERNATIONAL €€
(Smyrnis 19; mains €7-11) With its big wooden tables, fireplace and photographs, this place feels as warm and welcoming as a friend's kitchen. The menu draws influences from Greek, Arabic and Mediterranean cuisines. Be sure to try the smoked mackerel fillet, the mustard chicken or the zucchini-stuffed pastry rolls.

Parasies   GREEK €€€
(Plateia Istorikou Mouseiou; mains €6-24) One of four tavernas on the little square next to the Historical Museum, Parasies is a warm and woodsy nook. It's usually packed with locals lusting after its fresh meats and seafood merrily cooking away on a wood-fired grill in the open kitchen.

Istioploikos   SEAFOOD €€
(☑2810 228 118; Harbour; mains €6-14) Watching the bobbing boats on a balmy evening is a special treat at this harbour restaurant, which is affiliated with the local yacht club. Whatever is caught that day ends up on the plates, expertly cooked over a lusty wood fire. The meatless *lachanodomadhes* (stuffed cabbage) are a highly recommended side dish.

Ippokambos   SEAFOOD €€
(Sofokli Venizelou; mezedhes €4.50-11) Locals give this unpretentious *ouzerie* an enthusiastic thumbs up and we are only too happy to follow suit. Fish's the thing here, freshly caught, simply but expertly prepared and sold at fair prices. In summer, park yourself on the covered waterfront terrace.

Pagopoieion   INTERNATIONAL €€
(www.pagopoieion.gr; Plateia Agiou Titou; mains €7-18; ⊙10am-late) In a former ice factory, this arty cafe-bar has eclectic decorations (check out the toilets and the Nazi graffiti) and is one of the hippest places in town. Regulars swear by the creative food, but it's also fine to drop in for just coffee and nibbles. At night the attached bar kicks into high gear. The upstairs performance venue occasionally hosts concerts, art and readings.

O Vrakas   SEAFOOD €
(Marineli 1; mezedhes €5-12) This small streetside *ouzerie* (serving ouzo and snacks) grills fresh fish alfresco right before you. It's a humble place but don't let that dissuade you.

SWEET STUFF   119

Satisfy your sugar cravings at any of these well-established places:

Bitzarakis Bakery (7 Odos 1821) Sells excellent freshly baked *kalitsounia* (lightly fried filled pastries) along with other traditional sweets made by a women's cooperative.

Fyllo...Sofies (Plateia Venizelou 33; bougatsa €2.50; ⊙5am-late) With tables sprawling out towards the Morosini Fountain, this is a great place to sample a breakfast *bougatsa* (creamy semolina pudding wrapped in a pastry envelope and sprinkled with cinnamon and sugar). The less-sweet version is made with *myzithra* (sheep's-milk cheese).

Loukoumades (9 Odos 1821; 6 pieces €2.50; ⊙5am-10pm Mon-Sat) Come here for delicious fluffy *loukoumadhes*, ball-shaped doughnuts drizzled with honey, sesame seeds and cinnamon.

Ouzeri tou Terzaki   GREEK €€
(Marineli 17; mezedhes €6-12) Next to the teensy Agios Dimitrios church, this place may look trendy but actually feeds friends, families and lovebirds with a richly nuanced mix of classic Greek and international plates.

Giakoumis   GREEK €€
(Theodosaki 5-8; mains €6-13) The oldest among the row of tavernas vying for business in a quiet passageway off Odos 1866, Giakoumis offers a myriad *mayirefta* (ready-cooked meals) along with grilled meats that you can inspect before they're prepared. A nice spot for a shopping-spree respite.

Peri Orexeos   GREEK €€
(Koraï 10; mains €7-13) Be careful not to spoil your appetite with the free bread, black-olive paté and zucchini pie that arrive as soon as you sit down. The kitchen turns out creative modern Greek food such as creamy chicken-filled *kataïfi* ('angel hair' pastry). The spectrum of salads is impressive as well.

 Drinking

Being a student town, nightlife in Iraklio is among the best on the island. The see-and-be-seen scene sprawls in oversized sofas along Koraï, Perdikari and Mílatou (sometimes called the Koraï quarter) and around

El Greco Park. West of here, Handakos, Agiostefaniton and Psaromiligkon are more alternative-flavoured hang-outs. Most places open mid-morning or at noon and close in the wee hours, changing stripes and clientele as the hands on the clock move on.

TOP CHOICE **Bar Blow Up** BAR, DANCE CLUB
(http://barblowup.blogspot.com; Psarmilingon 1; ☺1.30pm-late; ☎) This cool party lair has a funky underground vibe that seems more Berlin than Iraklio and draws an all-ages, unpretentious crowd for good music and cold beers. After 11pm owner Vaggelis or his international DJ friends shower punters with an alchemy of electro, goth, funk and new wave. Greek indie bands like Abbie Gale and The Callas also stop by occasionally for live concerts.

Fix CAFE, BAR
(Perdikari 4) If the trendy cafes along this pedestrian strip don't do it for you, grab a table in this down-to-earth joint that's sought out by an older crowd of chatty conversationalists.

Mayo Lounge & Harem Oriental Club CAFE, LOUNGE BAR
(Milátou) This high-octane hot spot has dramatic design and is a good place to sample the buzz. Sink into comfy wicker sofas on terraced platforms lidded by a wooden roof that's held up by giant funnel-shaped lamps, or heed the call of the kasbah upstairs where there's an overstuffed cushion with your name on it in one of the sultry tented nooks. The venue is near Idaiou Androu.

Rolling Stone BAR, LIVE MUSIC
(Agiostefaniton 19) If you're into rock and roll, this funky place scores high on the groovemeter. Regular themed nights include Greek Rock, and there's also a local talent showcase called the Local Tribute Bands Festival.

Jailhouse Bar BAR
(Agiostefaniton 19a) Next to Rolling Stone, this is another place drowning in rock tunes from Johnny Cash to Johnny Rotten. Bonus: the trashy-sophisticated decor in a barrel-vaulted Venetian-era building. Happy hour runs from 7pm to 11pm.

Fashion Cafe CAFE, LOUNGE BAR
(cnr Koraï & Perdikari) Expect loud music and plenty of eye candy both in the decor and among the 20-somethings that populate the sleek lounge chairs at the brashest and busiest of the cafes in the Koraï quarter.

Veneto CAFE, LOUNGE BAR
(Epimenidou 9) For a swanky night out, steer towards this stylish outpost above the Venetian harbour for coffee, cocktails or a light meal. It's a lofty space with exposed wooden rafters and clubby leather chairs hemmed in by a long bar, panoramic windows and a naive mural of Venice. Charming staff.

Utopia CAFE
(Handakos 51) This hushed and formal old-style cafe has the best hot chocolate in town (also a decadent chocolate fondue), although the prices are utopian indeed. Other temptations include great ice cream and homemade cookies.

Mare CAFE, BAR
(www.mare-cafe.gr; Sofokli Venizelou) In an enviable location on the beautified waterfront promenade opposite the Historical Museum, contempo Mare is great for post-cultural java and sunset drinks, but skip the food.

Central Park CAFE, LOUNGE BAR
(Akroleondos) Grab an outdoor table, guzzle a cold one and watch the world on parade at this buzzy cafe.

Draft CAFE, BAR
(Akroleondos) This always-busy drinking and people-watching den has more than 40 international varieties of beer on tap and in the bottle.

Take Five CAFE, BAR
(Akroleondos) This long-time favourite on El Greco Park draws an older crowd mostly.

☆ Entertainment

Cinemas
Catch nondubbed Hollywood blockbusters at these multiplexes: **Astoria** (☎2810 226 191; Plateia Eleftherias) in the heart of the city and **Odeon** (☎801 116 0000; www.odeon.gr) in the Talos Plaza mall on the waterfront west of the centre. In summer, the **Nikos Kazantzakis Open-Air Theatre** (☎2810 242 977; Jesus Bastion) also screens movies. It's behind the Jesus Bastion. Follow Evans south for about 700m, turn right on Papandreou and right on Georgiadou. The theatre will be on your right.

Nightclubs

Clubs line Epimenidou and Beaufort near the harbour and the western waterfront near the Talos Plaza. Cover starts at around €5; double that if there's a big international DJ at the deck. The action usually doesn't kick into high gear until 1am.

Big Fish   DANCE CLUB
(cnr Sofokli Venizelou & Makariou 17; ☉from 10.30pm) At this fun-for-all party pen in a beautifully restored old stone building on the waterfront, local and international spinmeisters feed the young and flirty with high-energy dance music.

Privilege   DANCE CLUB
(Doukos Beaufort 7; ☉from 10pm) This massive, mainstream club lures up to 1000 revellers with a high-octane mix of dance, rock, electro and Greek sounds.

Envy   DANCE CLUB
(Sofokli Venizelou & Makariou 17; ☉from 10pm) Nicknamed 'NV', this popular hot-stepping club is great for shaking your bootie alfresco on the terrace jutting over the sea. It's across from Talos Plaza.

🛍 Shopping

Iraklio has the most extensive and sophisticated shopping in Crete. Pedestrian Dedalou and Handakos are lined with mostly mainstream shops.

Aerakis Music   MUSIC
(www.aerakis.net; Dedalou 37; ☉9am-9pm) An Iraklio landmark since 1974, this little shop stocks the best range of Cretan music, from old and rare recordings to the latest releases – many on its own record label, Seistron Music.

Talos Plaza   SHOPPING MALL
(Sofokli Venizelou; ☉9am-9pm) If you need to shop when everything else is closed, report to this modern mall between Minoos and Yakinthou. It has a multiplex cinema, a dozen shops, a sports bar and international cafes, including Starbucks and Häagen Dazs. It anchors the developing area along the waterfront west of the centre.

Hondos Center   DEPARTMENT STORE
(www.hondoscenter.gr; 25 Avgoustou) Power shoppers will love this modern, multilevel mall. The huge array of cosmetics and beauty products is especially impressive and includes many Greek labels that are hard to source outside the country.

IRAKLIO MARKET

An Iraklio institution, this busy narrow market along Odos 1866 (1866 St) is one of the best in Crete and has everything you need to put together a delicious picnic. Stock up on the freshest fruit and vegetables, creamy cheeses, honey, succulent olives, fresh breads and whatever else grabs your fancy. There are also plenty of other stalls selling pungent herbs, leather goods, hats, jewellery and some souvenirs. Cap off a spree with lunch at Giakoumis (p119) or another nearby taverna (avoid those in the market itself).

Planet International   BOOKS
(☎2810 289 605; Handakos 73) Excellent selection of literature, history and travel books.

Road Editions   BOOKS
(☎2810 344 610; Handakos 29) A specialist travel bookshop with a great selection of maps and guidebooks.

Mountain Club   OUTDOOR GEAR
(Evans 15) If you haven't come prepared for hikes and adventures, you'll find outdoor clothing and footwear as well as camping, climbing and biking gear here.

Fanourakis   JEWELLERY
(Plateia Nikiforou Foka) Pick up unique baubles at this charming shop selling modern jewellery as well as beautiful copies of Minoan designs.

Folli Follie   ACCESSORIES
(Dedalou 23) The local branch of Greece's internationally successful handbag and accessories chain.

ℹ Information

Iraklio's two hospitals are far from the centre and work alternate days – call first to find out where to go. Banks with ATMs are ubiquitous, especially along 25 Avgoustou. For online information, try www.heraklion-city.gr.

Alternatively, head to **Lonely Planet** (www.lonelyplanet.com/greece/crete/iraklio) for planning advice, author recommendations, traveller reviews and insider tips.

Netc@fe (4 Odos 1878; per hr €1.50; ☉10am-2am) Has full services.

Post office (Plateia Daskalogianni; ⊙7.30am-8pm Mon-Fri, 7.30am-2pm Sat)

Tourist office (☑2810 246 299; Xanthoulidou 1; ⊙8.30am-8.30pm Apr-Oct, 8.30am-3pm Nov-Mar) Staffed by university interns with various depths of knowledge and enthusiasm. Meagre selection of brochures and maps.

Tourist police (☑2810 397 111; Halikarnassos; ⊙7am-10pm) In the Halikarnassos suburb near the airport.

University Hospital (☑2810 392 111) At Voutes, 5km south of Iraklio, this is the city's best-equipped medical facility.

Venizelio Hospital (☑2810 368 000) On the road to Knossos, 4km south of Iraklio.

ℹ️ Getting There & Away

Skoutelis Travel (☑2810 280 808; www .skoutelistravel.gr; 25 Avgoustou 24) A one-stop shop for airline and ferry bookings, excursions around Crete and to Santorini, accommodation help and car hire.

Air

Nikos Kazantzakis International Airport (www.heraklion-airport.info) About 5km east of the city centre, the airport has a bank, an ATM, a duty-free shop and a cafe-bar.

Boat

The ferry port is 500m to the east of the Koules Fortress and old harbour. Minoan, Anek and Blue Star all operate daily ferries from Iraklio to Piraeus. Anek also has a weekly service to Karpathos, Kasos, Milos, Rhodes and Santorini. Hellenic Seaways goes to Mykonos, Paros and Santorini daily. The fastest boat to Santorini is operated by Sea Jets. For contact information and more details, see p259.

Bus

Iraklio has two major bus stations. **Bus Station A**, near the waterfront east of Koules Fortress, serves eastern and western Crete (including Knossos). Local buses also stop here.

Most buses use the main coastal highway, but at least one or two each day use the scenic but

IRAKLIO BUS SERVICES

From Bus Station A

DESTINATION	DURATION	FARE	FREQUENCY
Agia Pelagia	45min	€2.50	2 daily
Agios Nikolaos	1½hr	€7.10	hourly
Arhanes	30min	€1.70	hourly
Hania	3hr	€10.50	up to 17 daily
Hersonisos	40min	€3	at least half-hourly
Ierapetra	2½hr	€11	up to 6 daily
Kastelli	1hr	€3.70	up to 5 daily
Knossos	20min	€1.50	3 hourly
Lasithi Plateau	2hr	€6.50	1 daily
Malia	1hr	€3.80	at least half-hourly
Milatos	40min	€5	2 daily
Rethymno	1½hr	€7.60	up to 17 daily
Sitia	3¼hr	€14.70	4 daily

From Bus Station B

DESTINATION	DURATION	FARE	FREQUENCY
Agia Galini	2hr	€8	up to 6 daily
Anogia	1hr	€3.80	up to 3 daily
Mires	1¼hr	€5.50	up to 11 daily
Matala	2hr	€7.80	up to 5 daily
Phaestos	1½hr	€6.30	up to 8 daily

slower Old National Rd, so double-check before boarding.

Bus Station B, just beyond Hania Gate west of the centre, serves Anogia, Phaestos, Agia Galini and Matala. Service is greatly reduced on weekends. For details, see www.bus-service -crete-ktel.com.

Long-Distance Taxi

For destinations around Crete, you can order a cab from **Crete Taxi Services** (☑6970021970; www.crete-taxi.gr) or **Heraklion Taxi** (www .heraklion-taxi.com). There are also long-distance cabs waiting at the airport, at Plateia Eleftherias (outside the Capsis Astoria hotel) and at Bus Station A. Sample fares for up to four people:

DESTINATION	FARE
Agios Nikolaos	€69
Elounda	€79
Malia	€45
Matala	€75
Rethymno	€80

❶ Getting Around

To/from the Airport

The airport is just off the E75 motorway. Bus 1 connects it with the city centre every 10 minutes between 6.15am and 10.45pm; tickets cost €1.10. Buses stop on the far side of the car park fronting the terminal building. In town, buses terminate at Plateia Eleftherias, near the Astoria Capsis hotel. A taxi into town costs around €10.

Car & Motorcycle

Iraklio's streets are narrow and chaotic, so it's best to head straight to one of the car parks dotted around the city centre. Rates depend on location but expect to pay between €3 and €5 per day.

All the international car-hire companies have branches at the airport. Local outlets line the northern end of 25 Avgoustou and include the following:

Loggetta Cars (☑2810 289 462; www.loggetta .gr; 25 Avgoustou 20)

Motor Club (☑2810 222 408; www.motorclub .gr; Plateia Anglon 18) Extensive fleet of motorcycles in addition to cars.

Sun Rise (☑2810 221 609; www.sunrise-cars -bikes.gr; 25 Avgoustou 46) In a side lane off Avgoustou.

Taxi

There are small taxi stands all over town but the main ones are at Bus Station A, on Plateia Eleftherias and at the north end of 25 Avgoustou. You can also phone for one on ☑2810 210 102/146/168.

AROUND IRAKLIO

Knossos Κνωσσός

Crete's must-see historical attraction is the **Palace of Knossos** (☑2810 231 940; adult/ concession €6/3; ☉8am-7.30pm Apr-Oct, 8am-3pm Nov-Mar), a mere 5km south of Iraklio, and the capital of Minoan Crete. To beat the crowds and avoid the heat, get there before 10am. Budget several hours to explore Knossos (k-nos-*os*) thoroughly. There is little signage, so unless you have a travel guide, or join a guided tour, it may be hard to appreciate what you are looking at. Guided tours (€10) last about 90 minutes and leave from the little kiosk near the ticket booth. Most tours are in English, although other languages are available too. For a preview, take a virtual tour at www .bsa.ac.uk/knossos/vrtour.

The on-site cafe and touristy tavernas across the street are mediocre at best, so bring a picnic or save your appetite for a meal in the nearby Iraklio Wine Country, for instance at the excellent Elia & Diosmos (p132).

A combined ticket with the Iraklio Archaeological Museum costs €10 (concession €5).

History

Knossos' first palace (1900 BC) was destroyed by an earthquake around 1700 BC and rebuilt to a grander and more sophisticated design. It was partially destroyed again between 1500 and 1450 BC, and inhabited for another 50 years before finally burning down.

The new palace was carefully designed to meet the needs of a complex society. There were domestic quarters for the king or queen, residences for officials and priests, homes for common folk, and burial grounds. Public reception rooms, shrines, workshops, treasuries and storerooms flanked a paved

Palace of Knossos

THE HIGHLIGHTS IN TWO HOURS

The Palace of Knossos is Crete's busiest tourist attraction, and for good reason. A spin around the partially reconstructed complex delivers an eye-opening peek into the remarkably sophisticated society of the Minoans, who dominated southern Europe some 4000 years ago.

From the ticket booth, follow the marked trail to the **North Entrance 1** where the Charging Bull fresco gives you a first taste of Minoan artistry. Continue to the Central Court and join the queue waiting to glimpse the mystical **Throne Room 2**, which probably hosted religious rituals. Turn right as you exit and follow the stairs up to the so-called Piano Nobile, where replicas of the palace's most famous artworks conveniently cluster in the **Fresco Room 3**. Walk the length of the Piano Nobile, pausing to look at the clay storage vessels in the West Magazines, to a staircase descending to the **South Portico 4**, beautifully decorated with the Cup Bearer fresco. Make your way back to the Central Court and head to the palace's eastern wing to admire the architecture of the **Grand Staircase 5** that led to the royal family's private quarters. For a closer look at some rooms, walk to the south end of the courtyard, stopping for a peek at the **Prince of the Lilies fresco 6**, and head down to the lower floor. A highlight here is the **Queen's Megaron 7** (bedroom), playfully adorned with a fresco of frolicking dolphins. Stay on the lower level and make your way to the **Giant Pithoi 8**, huge clay jars used for storage.

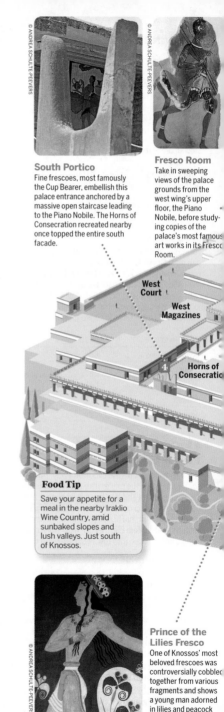

South Portico
Fine frescoes, most famously the Cup Bearer, embellish this palace entrance anchored by a massive open staircase leading to the Piano Nobile. The Horns of Consecration recreated nearby once topped the entire south facade.

Fresco Room
Take in sweeping views of the palace grounds from the west wing's upper floor, the Piano Nobile, before studying copies of the palace's most famous art works in its Fresco Room.

West Court

West Magazines

Horns of Consecration

Food Tip
Save your appetite for a meal in the nearby Iraklio Wine Country, amid sunbaked slopes and lush valleys. Just south of Knossos.

Prince of the Lilies Fresco
One of Knossos' most beloved frescoes was controversially cobbled together from various fragments and shows a young man adorned in lilies and peacock feathers.

Planning

To beat the crowds and avoid the heat, arrive before 10am. Budget several hours to explore the site thoroughly.

Throne Room

Evans imagined the mythical King Minos himself holding court seated on the alabaster throne of this beautifully proportioned room. However, the lustral basin and griffin frescoes suggest a religious purpose, possibly under a priestess.

North Entrance

Bulls held a special status in Minoan society as evidenced by the famous relief fresco of a charging beast gracing the columned west bastion of the north palace, which harboured workshops and storage rooms.

Grand Staircase

The royal apartments in the eastern wing were accessed via this monumental staircase sporting four flights of gypsum steps supported by columns. The lower two flights are original. It's closed to the public.

Piano Nobile

Central Court

Royal Apartments

3

2

1

5

8

7

Queen's Megaron

The queen's bedroom is among the prettiest in the residential eastern wing thanks to the playful Dolphin Fresco. The adjacent bathroom (with clay tub) and toilet are evidence of a sophisticated drainage system.

Giant Pithoi

These massive clay jars are rare remnants from the Old Palace period and were used to store wine, oil and grain. The jars were transported by slinging ropes through a series of handles.

N 0 ———————— 50 m

IRAKLIO KNOSSOS

Theatral Area

Royal Road

North Entrance

Lustral Basin

Charging Bull Fresco

Giant Pithoi

Fresco Gallery

Throne Room

Kouloures

West Magazines

East Entrance

Grand Staircase

Hall of the Double Axes

West Court (main entrance)

Central Court

Queen's Megaron

Water Closet

South Propylaon

Priest King Fresco

South Entrance

South House

Southeast House

central courtyard in a design so intricate that it may have been behind the legend of the labyrinth and the Minotaur (see p129).

The ruins of Knossos were unearthed in 1900 by the British archaeologist Sir Arthur Evans (1851–1941). Evans was so enthralled by his discovery that he spent 35 years and £250,000 of his own money excavating and – controversially – reconstructing sections of the palace. For more on the man and this amazing feat of modern archaeology, see p128.

Exploring the Site

Evans' reconstruction brings to life the palace's most significant parts, including the reconstructed columns; painted deep brown-red with gold-trimmed black capitals, they taper gracefully at the bottom. Vibrant recreations of frescoes add another dramatic dimension to the palace ruins. The Minoans' highly sophisticated society is further revealed by details like the advanced drainage system and the clever placement of rooms to passages, light wells, porches and verandahs that kept rooms cool in summer and warm in winter.

The first section of the palace you come across is the **West Court**, which may have been a marketplace or the site of public

gatherings. On your left is a trio of circular pits, called **kouloures**, that were used for grain storage.

Walk north along the palace's western wall to the **theatral area**, a series of shallow steps whose function remains unknown. It could have been a theatre where spectators watched acrobatic and dance performances, or the place where people gathered to welcome important visitors arriving by the **Royal Road**, which leads off to the west. Europe's first road was flanked by workshops and the houses of ordinary people. Also here, on your right, is a **lustral basin** where, so Evans speculated, Minoans performed a ritual water cleansing before religious ceremonies.

Visitors enter the palace via the north entrance. Stop to admire the **Charging Bull Fresco** before continuing to the heart of the palace, the massive **Central Court**, which in Minoan times was hemmed in by high walls. As is typical of a Minoan palace, rooms facing the western side of the courtyard had official and religious purposes, while the residential quarters were on the opposite side.

The central court gives way to the palace's most important rooms, including the **Throne Room**. Peering through security

WANT MORE?

Head to **Lonely Planet** (www.lonelyplanet.com/greece/crete/knossos) for planning advice, author recommendations, traveller reviews and insider tips.

glass, you can make out a simple, beautifully proportioned alabaster throne and walls decorated with frescoes of griffins, mythical beasts regarded as sacred by the Minoans. The room exudes an aura of mysticism and reverence and is thought to have been a shrine. The Minoans did not worship their deities in great temples but in small shrines, and each palace had several.

A **lustral basin** is in a separate room to the left of the Throne Room, but you'll get a better look at it from above in a moment. Walk past the Throne Room and up a staircase to the first floor. Inspired by Italian Renaissance palazzos, Evans called this the **Piano Nobile**, for this is where he believed the reception and staterooms were located. From up here you also have a great perspective on the **west magazines**, or storage rooms, where giant *pithoi* (clay jars) once held oil, wine and other staples.

The restored room at the northern end of the Piano Nobile looks down on the aforementioned lustral basin and also houses replicas of the most famous frescoes found at Knossos, including the **Bull-Leaper**, the **Ladies in Blue** and the **Blue Bird**. The originals are now in the Iraklio Archaeological Museum. At the far south end of the Piano Nobile, a staircase leads down to the **South Propylaion**, where you can admire the Cup Bearer fresco.

Backtrack to the Central Court and cross it to get to the impressive grand staircase, which leads down to the royal apartments. Study their layout from above, then walk to the lower level past the **Prince of the Lilies** fresco on the south side of the central court.

Much of the royal apartments is inaccessible but you can still catch glimpses of the king's quarters (megaron) in the **Hall of the Double Axes**, a spacious double room in which the ruler both slept and carried out court duties. The room had a light well at one end and a balcony at the other to ensure air circulation. It takes its name from the double axe marks *(labrys)* on its light well, a sacred symbol to the Minoans and the origin of our word 'labyrinth'.

A passage leads from the Hall of the Double Axes to the **queen's megaron**. Above the door is a copy of the **Dolphin Fresco**, one of the most exquisite Minoan artworks. A blue floral design decorates the portal. Next to this room is the queen's bathroom, complete with terracotta bathtub and a **water closet**, touted as the first ever to work on the flush principle; water was poured down by hand.

❶ Getting There & Away

Bus 2 leaves Bus Station A in Iraklio every 20 minutes for Knossos (€1.50). From the coastal road there are signs directing you to Knossos. There is free parking across from the souvenir shops but the spaces fill quickly.

WEST OF IRAKLIO

West of Iraklio the E75 highway cuts through a particularly scenic stretch with muscular hills plunging down to a couple of small beach resorts.

Agia Pelagia Αγία Πελαγία

Despite being rather built-up, this beach resort some 20km west of Iraklio hugs a lovely, sandy beach with clear water and excellent swimming. Seafront tavernas are great for people-watching even if they don't offer any culinary flights of fancy. For a glimpse of underwater life, check with **Diver's Club** (☑2810 811 755, 6944565462; www.diversclub-crete.gr), which offers the gamut of PADI courses and dives to caves, reefs and even a WWII plane wreck.

Fodele Φόδελε

POP 530

The pretty village of Fodele, 25km west of Iraklio, is famous as the birthplace of El Greco (p234). Experts dispute this, but the controversy did not stop the local government from dedicating a small **Museum of El Greco** (☑2810 521 500; www.el-greco-museum-birthplace-fodele.gr; admission €2; ⊙9am-7pm May-Oct & Easter week) in a stone building they claim he lived in as a child. Inside are reproductions of El Greco's most famous paintings as well as a 15-minute documentary about his life and work. Opposite the museum, the domed Byzantine **Church of the Panayia** (⊙Jun-Oct), built on the ruins of an 8th-century basilica, has some evocatively faded frescoes. To get to either, cross the village creek, turn right and go for about 1km past a citrus grove.

Fodele itself snuggles into a fertile valley fed by the little Pantomantris River and dotted with more Byzantine chapels. The narrow main street is lined with tourist-oriented shops and a few tavernas, of which **Domenico**, run by the charismatic George and his mother, is recommended. Rustic and homey, **Stousgioustous** (⊘closed Mon) along the road to the El Greco museum, is another good choice for hearty Cretan dishes.

Arolithos Αρόλιθος

Built in the mid-1980s, Arolithos (a-*ro*-li-thos), 11km southwest of Iraklio, is a reasonably authentic-looking recreation of a traditional Cretan village. It's a cluster of buildings containing workshops, a *kafeneio* and stores selling local products. Most visitors arrive on tour buses for a quick wander and peek inside the **Museum of Rural History & Folks Crafts** (☑2810 821 050; www.arolithosvillage.gr; adult/child €3/1.50; ⊘9am-9pm Mon-Fri, 9am-5pm Sat & Sun May-Sep, 9am-5pm Mon-Fri, 10am-6pm Sat Oct-Apr), where household and agricultural items illustrate various facets of country life. Some of the buildings have hotel rooms (from €60).

On your way here from Iraklio, keep an eye out for the double-domed **Koumbedes Taverna**, in a restored Ottoman structure that might have been a mosque, *hammam* (Turkish baths) or simply an inn. It has good food and pleasant valley views.

Tylisos Τύλισος

Once a major Minoan settlement, today's Tylisos (*til*-is-os), 13km southwest of Iraklio, is a sleepy village where you still see the sparse remains of a trio of large **mansions** (☑2810 831 498; admission €2; ⊘8.30am-3pm Tue-Sun) from the Neopalatial period (1600–1450 BC, being the period during which the mansions were built). Archaeologists found big bronze cauldrons, *pithoi*, seal stones, clay vases and frescoes on the site (storage jars), which is now hemmed in by modern houses. If the gate is closed, you can pick up a free pamphlet at the adjacent souvenir shop and take a peek over the fence, although you may find it hard to resist the aggressively charming sales efforts of the lady who owns it. Buses from Iraklio to Anogia go through Tylisos. They also go past another Minoan site at **Sklavokambos**, 8km closer to Anogia. The ruins date from 1500 BC

SIR ARTHUR EVANS – THE EXCAVATOR OF KNOSSOS

British archaeologist Sir Arthur Evans was an avid amateur journalist and adventurer, as well as curator of the Ashmolean Museum in Oxford from 1884 to 1908. His special interest in ancient coins and the writing on stone seals from Crete brought him to the island for the first time in 1894. He had a hunch that the mainland Mycenaean civilisation derived originally from Crete. With the help of the newly formed Cretan Archaeological Society, he began negotiating the purchase of the land, eventually securing it in 1900 after Greek laws changed in his favour. Digging began and the palace quickly revealed itself.

The first treasure to be unearthed in the flat-topped mound called Kefala was a fresco of a Minoan man, followed by the discovery of the Throne Room. The archaeological world was stunned that a civilisation of this maturity and sophistication had existed in Europe at the same time as the great pharaohs of Egypt.

Over the course of 35 years of excavations, Evans unearthed remains of a neolithic civilisation beneath the remains of the Bronze Age Minoan palace. He also discovered some 3000 clay tablets containing Linear A and Linear B script and wrote his own definitive description of his work at Knossos in a four-volume opus called *The Palace of Minos*. Evans received many honours for his work and was knighted in 1911.

Evans' reconstruction methods continue to be controversial – with many archaeologists believing that he sacrificed accuracy to his overly vivid imagination. For the casual visitor, though, the reconstructions are more than sufficient for visualising what the palace might have looked like at the peak of its glory.

Legend has it that after King Minos failed to sacrifice a magnificent white bull in honour of Poseidon, the god took his revenge by making the king's wife, Pasiphae, fall in love with the beast. To help her lure the bull, Daedalus, chief architect at Knossos and all-round handyman, made her a hollow wooden cow structure in which she could conceal herself. The bull apparently found her irresistible and their bizarre union produced the Minotaur: a hideous half-man, half-bull monster.

King Minos had Daedalus build a labyrinth in which to confine the Minotaur. He enraged the Athenians by demanding that Athens pay an annual tribute of seven youths and seven maidens to feed the monster, to compensate for the Athenians killing Minos' son Androgeos. The Athenian hero Theseus vowed to kill the Minotaur and sailed to Crete posing as one of the sacrificial youths. He fell in love with Ariadne, King Minos' daughter, who promised to help him if he would take her away with him. Ariadne gave him the ball of twine that he unwound on his way into the labyrinth and then used to retrace his steps after slaying the monster. The lovers eventually fled Crete together.

and were probably the villa of a district governor.

CENTRAL IRAKLIO

South of Iraklio, past Knossos, the urban sprawl segues into an unhurried landscape of undulating hills, olive groves and rows of vineyards clambering up hillsides. It's all lorded over by the proud silhouette of **Mt Yiouhtas** (811m). Several Minoan sites are scattered on and around the mountain, including a cemetery, a villa and a sanctuary. These were once affiliated with ancient Arhanes, the main town in the area and the gateway to the Iraklio Wine Country, where you can sample the local product at several estates. Also of interest is the Nikos Kazantzakis Museum in Myrtia and the pottery town of Thrapsano.

Wine also grows near **Dafnes** and **Venerato** southwest of Iraklio, along the main road to Matala and the south coast. A wonderful detour takes you west to the southern slopes of Mt Psiloritis, where Zaros is a charismatic mountain village known for its spring water and trout.

You'll need your own wheels to explore this region properly.

Arhanes & Around Αρχάνες
POP 3830

Arhanes, 14km south of Iraklio, is an agricultural town with a long history, important archaeological sites, interesting museums and excellent cafes and tavernas. Considered a model of rural town redevelopment, it's a joy to stroll along its maze of narrow, flower-filled lanes, flanked by meticulously restored houses spilling out into tree-shaded squares. Wine has been produced in Arhanes since Minoan times and today the local cooperative upholds the tradition. In August, the town celebrates its Bacchanalian heritage with a five-day wine festival.

The modern town sits atop a **Minoan palace**, of which only a tiny section has been excavated. During WWII, Arhanes was the hub of the German military command under General Heinrich Kreipe. Coming from Iraklio, at the turn-off to Kato Arhanes, a modern **monument** by local artist Manolis Tsompanakis commemorates Kreipe's famed 1944 kidnapping.

◉ Sights

Arhanes is divided into an upper and lower section, with most sights of interest clustered in the latter. Getting around the one-way streets and narrow alleys can be confusing, so it's best to park your car and explore on foot. Fans of Minoan ruins can indulge their passion by visiting several sites within a short drive of Arhanes.

FREE **Archaeological Museum of Arhanes**   MUSEUM
(☑2810 752 712; ⊗8.30am-2.30pm Wed-Mon) This small museum displays many important finds from regional excavations, especially from Minoan times. Among the highlights are clay *larnakes* (coffins) and musical instruments from Fourni, and a copy of the dagger presumably used for human sacrifice from the Anemospilia temple (p130). The

MURDER IN THE TEMPLE

Human sacrifice is not commonly associated with the Minoans, but the evidence found at Anemospilia suggests otherwise. In the western room, scientists discovered three skeletons, most notably a male placed on an altar with a bronze dagger lying on top of the trussed body. The two other skeletons are probably those of a priest and an assistant and are believed to indicate that the man's death was part of a sacrificial rite. Perhaps the sacrifice was made just as the 1700 BC earthquake began, in a desperate attempt to appease the gods.

museum is in a side street just north of the main square.

Folk Museum of Arhanes　　　MUSEUM
(☎2810 752 891; admission €1; ☺9am-1pm Mon & Wed-Fri) This restored stone building is set up like a traditional home, with a worthy collection of furniture, embroideries and handicrafts and the tools of rural life, including bloomers and kids' toys. It's signposted from the Archaeological Museum.

**Cretan Historical and
Folk Museum**　　　MUSEUM
(☎2810 751 853; admission €3; ☺9.30am-3pm Wed-Mon) In Kato Arhanes, not far past the turn-off to Arhanes from the Iraklio road, this museum has an interesting private collection from various periods of Crete's history, including personal belongings of General Kreipe.

Anemospilia　　　ANCIENT SITE
Anemospilia (Wind Caves) packs major importance into its small frame. Excavation of this middle-Minoan three-room temple yielded evidence that human sacrifice played at least some role in Minoan society. The site is closed to the public but you can peek through the fence and enjoy the sweeping views over Arhanes and surrounds. Anemospilia is about 1.5km northwest of Arhanes but not signposted; ask for directions in town.

FREE **Fourni**　　　ANCIENT SITE
(☺8.30am-2.30pm Tue-Sun) On a hill west of town and reached via a steep footpath, Fourni is the most extensive Minoan

necropolis on the island. Burials took place here over a period of 1000 years, the oldest going back to 2500 BC. One of the tombs contained the remains of a Minoan noble woman whose jewellery is on display in the Iraklio Archaeological Museum.

Mt Yiouhtas Peak Sanctuary　　　ANCIENT SITE
Driving south from Arhanes, you'll soon see the sign for the dirt track leading to the top of Mt Yiouhtas. After a bone-rattling 4km ride, you'll be rewarded with scenic views over to Mt Psiloritis and Iraklio. On the north side of the hill, near a radar station, are the fenced-in ruins of a Minoan peak sanctuary dating from around 2100 BC, which is believed to have served the inhabitants of Knossos. An altar and several rooms are among the unearthed sections.

FREE **Vathypetro**　　　ANCIENT SITE
(☺8.30am-3pm Tue-Sun) About 5km south of Arhanes, and well signposted, Vathypetro was built around 1600 BC, probably as the villa of a prosperous Minoan noble. Archaeologists discovered wine- and oil presses, a weaving loom and a kiln in storerooms. The winepress can still be seen.

🍴 Eating & Drinking

Practically all the tavernas in town have a good reputation. About a dozen of them frame the main square along with a handful of trendy lounge bars, such as Nobu opposite the more alt-flavoured Diahroniko.

TOP
CHOICE **Kritamon**　　　CRETAN €€
(☎2810 753 092; www.kritamon.gr; mains €9-14; ☺dinner daily, lunch Sat & Sun) Send your taste buds on a wild ride at this foodie outpost tucked into a narrow lane behind the Pancretan Co-Op bank off the main square. Ancient Cretan recipes result in soulful salads, rustic mains and to-die-for-desserts. Ingredients come either from the family garden or local suppliers.

Fabrika Eleni　　　GREEK €€
(☎2810 751 331) This charming restaurant-bar is in a restored olive-oil mill built around 1870 into a Minoan wall. Aside from the original press, it contains a mini-museum showcasing the owner's father's ingenious inventions. There's craft beer on tap and the occasional Cretan *lyra* (lyre) concert for entertainment. It's near the

ruins of the Minoan palace; follow the signs through the maze of backstreets.

Ampelos   GREEK €
(2810 751 039; www.iampelos.gr; mains €4-9) With its stone arches, open-beam ceiling and exposed air ducts, this large dining room exudes rustic-industrial flair. The menu has few surprises, but you can't go wrong with such classics as fried rabbit chops or chicken with orange-cream sauce.

To Spitiko   GREEK €€
(2810 751 591; mains €6-12) This one-room taverna overlooking the main square gets contemporary flair from whitewashed stone walls, burgundy table cloths and big picture windows. In fine weather, the outdoor tables are the place to be.

❶ Information

A couple of ATMs are found around the main square. A useful website is www.archanes.gr.

❶ Getting There & Away

Drivers coming from Iraklio should take the scenic Knossos road. Of several roads into town, the second turn-off takes you close to the main square. On weekdays, there's an hourly bus service from Iraklio (€1.70, 30 minutes); weekend service is sparse. Buses stop at the top of the village and close to the main square.

Iraklio Wine Country

About 70% of wine produced in Crete comes from the Iraklio Wine Country, which starts just south of Knossos. Almost two dozen wineries are embedded in a harmonious landscape of shapely hills, sunbaked slopes and lush valleys. Winemakers cultivate many indigenous Cretan grape varieties, such as Kotsifali, Mandilari and Malvasia.

There are essentially two clusters of wineries, one around Peza and Arhanes, south of Iraklio via the Knossos road, and another further west around Dafnes, along the main road towards Phaestos and Matala.

Almost all wineries are members of the **Winemakers' Network of Heraklion Prefecture** (www.winesofcrete.gr), an association founded in 2006 and dedicated to promoting Cretan wines by creating a web presence, organising wine fairs and festivals and producing informative brochures. The association's excellent *Wine Roads of Heraklion* map is available at the Iraklio tourist office and at the wine estates themselves.

◉ Sights & Activities

Here's a selection of wineries where you can sample the local product, sometimes for a small fee. Aside from tasting rooms, some estates also have mini-museums showcasing historic tools and machinery and showing videos about the winemaking process. All sell their wine below retail prices. Some wineries are stops on cruise-ship shore excursions, so if you don't like crowds come after 11am.

Boutari   WINERY
(2810 731 617; www.boutari.gr; Skalani; 1hr tour & tasting €5, tasting only €4; ☉9am-5pm Mon-Fri year-round, plus 10am-6pm Sat & Sun summer). Near Skalani, about 8km from Iraklio, Boutari is a sleek, modern operation. Take the tour to learn about local grapes and winemaking or just stick around to sample the product in the vast and modern tasting room overlooking the vineyard.

Minos-Miliarakis   WINERY
(2810 741 213; www.minoswines.gr; Peza; tasting free, video & tour €2; ☉9am-4pm Mon-Fri, 10am-3pm Sat) Right on the Peza main street, Minos is a massive winery that, in 1952, was the first to bottle wine in Crete. It makes very respectable vintages, especially under its Miliarakis label, including a full-bodied single-vineyard organic red and a fragrant Blanc de Noirs. Tastings are also held at the winery's **Vineyard House** (☉11am-6pm Mon-Sat), right next to the grapes in Sambas, about 10km east of Peza towards Kastelli.

Peza Union   WINERY
(2810 741 945; www.pezaunion.gr; Peza; ☉9am-5pm Mon-Sat) In business since 1933, this huge cooperative makes popular and inexpensive table wine sold as a 'bag in the box' in supermarkets around the island. Stopping here gives you an opportunity to taste their more sophisticated output.

Arhanes Coop   WINERY
(2810 753 208; synar@otelnet.gr; Arhanes; ☉9am-5pm Mon-Fri) Wine has been produced in Arhanes since Minoan times and the town is still one of the most important producers in Crete today. Tiered vineyards are sheltered by Mt Yiouhtas and make some outstanding wines, including the well-known Arhanes Rozaki.

Domaine Gavalas   WINERY
(28940 51060; www.domainegavalas.gr; Vorias; ☉9am-3pm Mon-Fri) Founded in 2004, this is

About 4km south of Peza, **Houdetsi** is home to a few Byzantine churches but really got put on the map by **Labyrinth** (☎2810 741 027; www.labyrinthmusic.gr; admission €3; ☺10am-4pm Mar-Oct). This beautiful stone manor is both a **Museum of Traditional Musical Instruments** and a highly reputable renowned summer-long **musical workshop** that draws top talent from around the world.

Established in 1982, Labyrinth is the brainchild of renowned musician Ross Daly, an Irishman who's one of the leading exponents of the Cretan *lyra* (lyre). He's also a master of the modal nonharmonic music of Greece, the Balkans, Turkey, the Middle East, North Africa and North India and has released more than 25 albums. Check him out at www .rossdaly.gr.

Daly is also an avid collector of traditional musical instruments, some 250 of which are displayed in the manor. These are mostly string and percussion instruments from around the world; many of them are rare. An interactive audio system allows you to hear the sound of each one.

In summer, the lovely grounds make an atmospheric backdrop for concerts. Call or check the website for the schedule.

the largest organic winery in Crete. Try its award-winning Efivos reds and whites. It's in Vorias, about 20km south of Peza.

Tamiolakis WINERY
(☎2810 742 083; tamwines@otenet.gr; Houdetsi; ☺by appointment) This organic winery is in a dazzling hilltop location above the village of Houdetsi, 4km south of Peza. It's one of Crete's excellent new-generation wineries, with Bordeaux-trained winemakers, state-of-the-art equipment and visitor-friendly facilities.

Lyrarakis WINERY
(☎2810 284 614; www.lyrarakis.gr; Alagni; ☺10am-1pm) This progressive winery some 6km south of Peza has been raking in the awards in recent years. It's known for reviving two nearly extinct white varietals called Dafni and Plyto. Call to confirm opening times.

✖ Eating

For additional eating recommendations in the wine country, see p130.

[TOP CHOICE] **Elia & Diosmos** CRETAN €€
(☎2810 731 283; www.olive-mint.com; Skalani; mains €8-17) At this foodie playground on the edge of the Iraklio Wine Country, Argiro Barda turns market-fresh ingredients into progressive Cretan dishes that are a feast of flavours. The menu chases the seasons, but classic choices include succulent lamb chops with honey, fluffy fennel pie and feisty pork with figs, plums and pistachios. It's only

a short drive from Iraklio and just a few minutes south of Knossos.

Roussos Taverna CRETAN €€
(☎2810 742 189; Houdetsi; mains €5-10; ☺lunch & dinner Jun-Oct, dinner only Tue-Sun Nov-May) Clued-in gourmets make the trip out to Houdetsi from afar to dine on Roussos' toothsome original Cretan cooking, including fantastic lamb chops and local *horta* (wild greens). It's on the main square across from Ross Daly's Labyrinth (above), whose musicians sometimes give concerts here.

Taverna Onisimos GREEK €€
(☎2810 741 754; Peza; mains €8-10; ☺dinner daily, lunch Tue-Sun) On the main road in Peza, near the Milatos winery, this handsomely decorated taverna is a good place to rebalance your brain if you've overindulged at a wine tasting. Drop by for tasty fried pumpkin balls, grilled meats or such specials as lamb in lemon sauce.

Myrtia Μυρτιά

Myrtia, some 15km southeast of Iraklio, is the ancestral village of Crete's most famous writer (see p236) and home to the excellent **Nikos Kazantzakis Museum** (☎2810 741 689; www.kazantzakis-museum.gr; adult/child €3/1; ☺9am-5pm Mar-Oct, 10am-3pm Sun Nov-Feb). In a modern building overlooking the *kafeneia*-flanked central plaza, the aesthetically lit presentation zeroes in on the life, philosophy and accomplishments of the man. Watch a short documentary, then nose around personal effects, movie posters, letters, photographs and other paraphernalia. Rooms upstairs present an overview of Kazantzakis' most famous works including, of course, *Zorba the Greek*.

Thrapsano Θραψανό

POP 1400

All those huge Minoan-style *pithoi* that grace hotel lobbies, restaurants and homes across the island most likely hail from Thrapsano, 32km southeast of Iraklio. Pottery workshops scattered around the town normally welcome visitors. Watch the giant clay pots being churned out at the traditional **Nikos Doxastakis workshop** (☑2891 041 160) up towards the municipal offices. **Vasilakis Pottery** (☑2891 041 666), just past the lake turn-off, has smaller pieces you can take home, as has **Koutrakis Art** (☑2891 041 000; www.cretan-pottery.gr) on the road into town. An annual **pottery festival** takes place in mid-July.

If you're tired of the shops, stop by the twin-aisled 15th-century **Timios Stavros church** in the middle of the village to check out its well-preserved frescoes.

Just outside the town on the road north to Apostoli is **Livada Lake**, a preserved wetland with a birdwatching lookout and a picnic area. The local bird population includes little egrets, wood sandpipers, red-rumped swallows and whiskered terns. The lake has doubled in size over time as potters have extracted clay from the lakebed.

From Iraklio, Thrapsano is best reached via the Knossos road, turning off at the village of Agios Paraskies, near Peza.

Zaros Ζαρός

POP 3370

The rustic mountain village of Zaros is famous for its natural spring water, which is bottled and sold all over Crete. It has a fabulous location at the foot of Mt Psiloritis and even just getting here via the scenic road from Agia Varvara (on the main Iraklio–Mires road) is a highly enjoyable ride. Zaros has some fine Byzantine monasteries, excellent walking in the stunning Rouvas Gorge and delicious trout in the local tavernas. Nearby excavations suggest that the steady supply of fresh water

lured Minoans, and later Romans, to settle here. If you look carefully, you can still spot bits and pieces of the water channels that supplied water to the great Roman capital of Gortyna, about 12km south.

◉ Sights & Activities

Lake Votomos LAKE
Emerald-green and tree-fringed, this small reservoir just northeast of Zaros was created in 1987 to store the town's natural spring water. It attracts scores of birds and is great for chilling in the shady park or munching away in the excellent taverna-cafe. A path accesses both Moni Agios Nikolaos (1km) and Rouvas Gorge (2.5km).

Moni Agios Nikolaos MONASTERY
Just west of Zaros, a sign directs you to this monastery at the mouth of the Rouvas Gorge, about 2km up the valley. The church has some fine 14th-century frescoes.

Moni Vrondisi MONASTERY
A few kilometres beyond Moni Agios Nikolaos, this monastery is noted for its 15th-century Venetian fountain with a relief of Adam and Eve, and early 14th-century frescoes from the Cretan School, including one depicting the Last Supper.

Domaine Zacharioudakis WINERY
(☑2892 024 733; www.zacharioudakis.com; Plouti; ☺10am-6pm Tue-Sun) Striking architecture and steeply terraced vineyards on the slopes of the Orthi Petra hill characterise this state-of-the-art boutique winery in Plouti, about 7km south of Zaros. The tasting room with views out to sea is a nice spot for sampling its fine wines, including the award-winning white Vidiano and red Orthi Petra Syrah-Kotsifali. Guided tours are also available.

[TOP CHOICE] **Rouvas Gorge** HIKING
Part of the E4 European Path, this gorge leads to the protected Rouvas Forest, home to some of the oldest oak trees in Crete. It's an especially lovely walk in springtime when orchids, poppies, irises and other wildflowers give the landscape the vibrancy of an Impressionist painting.

✖ Eating

I Limni CRETAN €€
(trout per kg €22; ☺9am-late) This lakefront taverna is a peaceful oasis serving fresh grilled trout and Cretan specialities. The

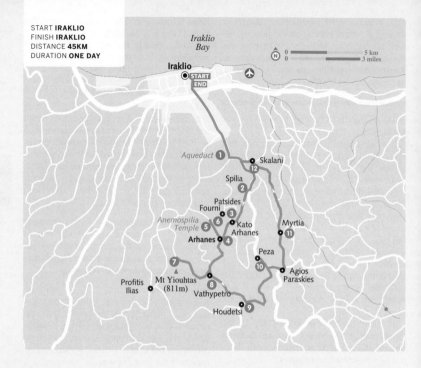

START **IRAKLIO**
FINISH **IRAKLIO**
DISTANCE **45KM**
DURATION **ONE DAY**

Iraklio Bay

Iraklio
START
END

Aqueduct 1 • Skalani
12

Spilia
2

Patsides
Fourni
Patsides 3
Anemospilia 6
Temple 5 • Kato
Arhanes • Arhanes • Myrtia
Arhanes 4 11

Peza
10

7 • Agios
Paraskies

Profitis • Mt Yiouhtas 8
Ilias (811m) Vathypetro
Houdetsi 9

Driving Tour
Iraklio Wine Country

❯ There's something undeniably painterly in the way Iraklio's suburban sprawl rolls itself into luscious wine country with snug villages awash in flowers, sun-dappled vineyards clinging to gentle hillsides and Mt Yiouhtas (811m) looming in the distance. A visit here is especially pretty during the spring bloom and the late-summer harvest. For locations of wineries, see the main section on the Iraklio Wine Country (p131).

Coming from Iraklio, follow the Knossos road south. A couple of kilometres beyond the palace ruins, the road skirts an impressive double-arched 1 **aqueduct** from the early 1800s that once supplied Iraklio with water from Arhanes. Continue through Spilia to Patsides, where a brutalist 2 **monument** at the turn-off to Kato Arhanes marks the spot where General Heinrich Kreipe was kidnapped in 1944. The nearby 3 **Cretan Historical & Folk Museum** presents some of his personal belongings. 4 **Arhanes** itself is a wine-country hub with Minoan roots, which you can

trace by visiting the 5 **Anemospilia Temple** and the necropolis at 6 **Fourni**. If your car is up to it, make a detour up Mt Yiouhtas for spellbinding wine-country views and a look at a 7 **Minoan peak sanctuary**.

Back in Arhanes, head south towards Houdetsi, stopping at 8 **Vathypetro** to see what a Minoan winepress looked like. A pretty hamlet wedged into a valley, Houdetsi's main attraction is the wonderful 9 **Museum of Traditional Musical Instruments**. From here it's a quick drive north to 10 **Peza**, the centre of wine production in Crete, with several wineries offering tastings and tours. From here, follow signs to 11 **Myrtia** to pay your respects to Nikos Kazantzakis, the Cretan-born author of *Zorba the Greek*, at the excellent museum right on the town square. Conclude the day by indulging in a gourmet Cretan dinner paired with excellent local wines at the delightful 12 **Elia & Diosmos** in Skalani.

starters that come out with the bread add a nice touch.

Votomos
SEAFOOD, GREEK €€

(trout per kg €27) Even though you're in the mountains, you can be certain that the fish is fresh at this family-run taverna, where you can see trout and salmon splashing in large tanks before they end up on your dinner plate. It's just outside town past the Idi hotel.

Vengera
GREEK €

(mains €4-6) On the main street, this excellent taverna is run by vivacious Vivi and her mother Irini, who cook five or six traditional dishes daily. They also do special €25 meal-and-lodging deals in nearby studios.

ℹ️ Information

Most businesses are clumped together at the south end of town. The post office and a supermarket are across the street from the police station. There's an ATM on the main street.

ℹ️ Getting There & Away

Travelling on the main road from Iraklio, turn west at Agia Varvara. Coming from the south, there's a smaller road heading north from Gortyna. There are two buses daily (one on Sundays) from Iraklio (€4.30, one hour).

SOUTHERN IRAKLIO

The south-central region of Crete is blessed with a trifecta of archaeological treasures – Phaestos, Agia Triada and Gortyna – and a cluster of minor sites spanning Cretan history from the Minoans to the Romans. Touring them you'll be weaving your way right through the Messara Plain, one of Crete's most fertile regions, framed by Mt Psiloritis to the north, the Dhiktean mountains to the east and the Asterousia hills to the south. A major highway links the busy commercial centres of Tymbaki, Mires, Agii Deka and Pyrgos, although they hold little interest for visitors. The same cannot be said about the coastal towns around Matala and Lendas that beckon with long stretches of sandy beach and make excellent bases for exploring the region's ample charms. Earmark time for plenty of fun diversions, be it hiking through gorges, visiting ancient monasteries, poking around flower-festooned villages, chilling with locals on the village square or simply getting lost on the winding country roads.

Gortyna Γόρτυνα

The archaeological site of Gortyna, 46km southwest of Iraklio, is the largest in Crete and one of the most fascinating. Also called Gortyn or Gortys, Gortyna (gor-tih-nah) doesn't have much from the Minoan period because it was little more than a subject town of powerful Phaestos until it began accumulating riches (mostly from piracy) under the Dorians. By the 5th century BC, however, it was as influential as Knossos. When the island was under threat from the Romans, the Gortynians cleverly made a pact with them and, after the Roman conquest in 67 BC, Gortyna became the island's capital. The city blossomed under the Roman administrators, who endowed it with lavish public buildings, including a Praetorium, amphitheatre, baths, a music school and temples. At its peak as many as 100,000 people are believed to have lived here. Except for the 7th-century-BC Temple of Apollo and the Byzantine Church of Agios Titos, most of what you see in Gortyna dates from the Roman period. Gortyna's splendour came to an end in AD 824 when the Saracens raided the island and destroyed the city.

The city sprawls over a square kilometre of plains, foothills and the summit of plains, hills and fields. An aqueduct used to bring in natural spring water from Zaros, 15km away, to feed fountains and public baths. There also must have been streets and a town square, but these have not been excavated.

There are two main sections to Gortyna, bisected by the main road. Most people only stop long enough to investigate the **fenced area** (☏2892 031 144; adult/concession/under 18yr & EC students €4/2/free; ☉8.30am-3pm Nov-Apr, to 5pm May, Jun, Sep & Oct, to 8pm Jul & Aug) on the north side of the road past the parking lot and entrance gate. However, the most important Roman temples, baths and other buildings are actually on the other side of the street, albeit scattered around a sprawling open area and thus not as easily explored. Admission to this section is free and there are no closing times. A combined ticket with Agia Triada (p138) costs €6 (concession €3).

Fenced Area

The first major monument visible within the fenced area is the 6th-century Byzantine **Church of Agios Titos**, the finest early-Christian church in Crete. Probably built

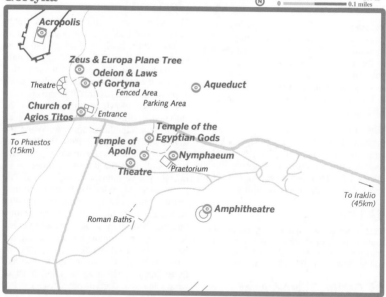

atop an even older church, its only major surviving feature is the soaring apse flanked by two side chapels, the left of which is still used as a shrine.

A few steps away is the **Odeion**, a Roman theatre from the 1st century BC, which was levelled by an earthquake and rebuilt by Trajan in the 2nd century AD. The covered, arched structure on the far side of the theatre shelters Gortyna's star attraction: the stone tablets engraved with the 6th-century-BC **Laws of Gortyna**. The 600 lines written in a Dorian dialect were the earliest law code in the Greek world and provide fascinating insight into the social structure of pre-Roman Crete. Interestingly, ancient Cretans were preoccupied with the same issues that drive people into court today – marriage, divorce, property transfers, inheritance and adoption, as well as criminal offences. It was an extremely hierarchical society, divided into slaves and several categories of free citizens, each of whom had strictly delineated rights and obligations.

South of the Highway

Monuments here are much larger but stretch out over a vast area and are therefore not as easy to locate. It's fun to wander

PLANE-LY MODEST

In Gortyna, near the Odeion, a short walkway leads to an ancient, evergreen plane tree that, according to legend, served as a love nest for Zeus and Europa. As the story goes, Zeus first spotted Europa, the daughter of the King of Phoenicia, playing on a beach in Sidon (today's Lebanon) and was immediately smitten. He disguised himself as a bull, kidnapped her, swam ashore in Matala and then whisked her off to Gortyna, where he revealed his true identity. Hanky-panky followed and Europa soon gave birth to triplets, the mythical kings named Minos, Rhadamanthys and Sarpedon. The plane tree, though, which had to witness the lovemaking, apparently felt compromised in its modesty and refused to shed its leaves from thereon. Nice story, but sorry, there's no magic to it. Although rare, there is actually a subspecies of plane tree that is evergreen. Only about 50 of these specimen have been found in Crete. Still, myths die hard: you can still see people picking its leaves in the hope of bearing plenty of sons.

around aimlessly and just stumble upon the ruins, but if you want to explore the site in a more organised fashion, locate the sign pointing to the Temple of Apollo on the main road and follow the stone path. You'll first pass the remains of the **Temple of the Egyptian Gods**, dedicated primarily to Isis, Serapis and Anubis, before arriving at the **Temple of Apollo**, which was the main sanctuary of pre-Roman Gortyna. Built in the 7th century BC, the temple was expanded in the 3rd century BC and converted into a Christian basilica in the 2nd century AD. Its rectangular outline and much of the altar are still in situ. Behind it you can spot the well-preserved **theatre**.

Turn left in front of the Temple of Apollo to reach the huge **Praetorium**. The palace of the Roman governor of Crete, it served both as an administrative building, a church and a private residence. Most of the ruins date from the 2nd century AD and were repaired in the 4th century. To the north is the 2nd-century **Nymphaeum**, a public bath supplied by an aqueduct bringing water from Zaros. It was originally adorned with statues of nymphs. South of the Nymphaeum is the **amphitheatre**, which dates from the late 2nd century AD.

Acropolis

It's a 20- to 30-minute hike, but for a bird's-eye view of Gortyna, the hilltop Acropolis is hard to beat. It also features impressive sections of the pre-Roman ramparts. To get there, walk along the stream near the Odeion to a gate that gives way to the path to the top. It's also possible to drive reasonably close to the site. Ask for directions at the ticket counter.

❶ Getting There & Away

Buses to Phaestos from Iraklio also stop at Gortyna.

Phaestos Φαιστός

The site of **Phaestos** (☎2892 042 315; adult/concession/under 18yr & EC students €4/2/free; ⏰8am-8pm Jun-Oct, 8am-5pm Nov-Apr), 63km from Iraklio, was the second-most important Minoan palatial city after Knossos and also enjoys the most awe-inspiring location, with panoramic views of the Messara Plain and Mt Psiloritis. The palace layout is similar to that of Knossos, with rooms arranged around a central court. Also like Knossos, most of Phaestos (fes-*tos*) was built over an older palace destroyed in the late Middle Minoan period. But the site also has its own

Phaestos

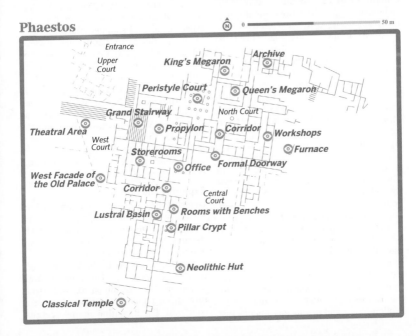

distinctive attractiveness. There's an air of mystery about the desolate, unreconstructed ruins altogether lacking at Knossos. Also in contrast to Knossos, Phaestos has yielded few frescoes; palace walls were apparently covered with white gypsum.

A combined ticket with Agia Triada cost €6 (concession €3).

History

The first palace was built around 2000 BC and destroyed by the same earthquake that devastated other Minoan palaces. The ruins formed the base of a new palace that was begun around 1700 BC and destroyed in another catastrophe in 1450 BC. In the intervening centuries Phaestos was the political and administrative centre of the Messara Plain. Ancient texts refer to the palace's importance and note that it even minted its own coins. Although Phaestos continued to be inhabited, it fell into decline as Gortyna rose in importance. Under the Dorians, Phaestos headed a battling league of cities that included Matala and Polyrrinia in western Crete. Phaestos was defeated by Gortyna in the 2nd century BC.

Exploring the Site

Past the ticket booth, the Upper Court that was used in both the old and new palaces contains the remains of buildings from the Hellenistic era. A stairway leads down to the West Court with the Theatral Area, so-called because it may have been the staging ground for performances. The seats are at the northern end, while across to the south you can see the west facade of the Old Palace. The 15m-wide Grand Stairway leads to the Propylon, which was a porch. Below the Propylon are the storerooms that still contain *pithoi* (storage urns). The square hall next to the storerooms is thought to have been an office, where tablets containing Linear A script were found beneath the floor in 1955. South of the storeroom a corridor led to the west side of the Central Court. South of the corridor is a lustral basin, rooms with benches and a pillar crypt.

The Central Court, which was once framed by columned porticos, is the centrepiece of the palace. It is well preserved and gives a sense of the size and magnificence of the palace. Note the neolithic hut in the court's southwestern corner. North of the court are the palace's best-preserved sections, the reception rooms and private apartments. Past

a column-flanked Formal Doorway a corridor leads to the north court; the Peristyle Court, which once had a paved verandah, is to the left. The royal apartments (Queen's Megaron and King's Megaron) are northeast of the Peristyle Court. The celebrated Phaestos Disk, now in the Iraklio Archaeological Museum, was found in a building to the north of the palace.

There's a decent on-site cafe but, for better food, head a few kilometres south to Agios Ioannis where Taverna Agios Ioannis (mains €4-8; ☺noon-midnight) is known for its succulent roast lamb and grilled rabbit. The tiny 10th-century Church of Agios Pavlos nearby has some moodily faded frescoes.

ⓘ Getting There & Away

Eight buses a day head to Phaestos from Iraklio (€6.30, 1½ hours), stopping at Gortyna. There are also buses from Agia Galini (€3.30, 45 minutes, two Monday to Saturday) and Matala (€1.70, 30 minutes, four Monday to Saturday).

Agia Triada Αγία Τριάδα

Pronounced ah-*yee*-ah trih-*ah*-dha, Agia Triada (☎2892 091 564; adult/concession/under 18yr & EC student €3/1.50/free; ☺10am-4.30pm summer, 8.30am-3pm winter), 3km west of Phaestos, was most likely a smaller palace or a royal summer villa and enjoys an enchanting setting on the tree-covered hillside looking out to the Gulf of Messara. Although it succumbed to fire around 1400 BC, the site was never looted, which accounts for the extraordinary number of masterpieces of Minoan art found here. These include a famous trio of vases (the Harvesters Vase, the Boxer Vase and the Chieftain Cup) now on display in the Iraklio Archaeological Museum.

A combined ticket with Phaestos (p137) costs €6 (concession €3).

Exploring the Site

Unfortunately, the site is not very visitor-friendly, as there is no labelling and not even a simple map accompanying your ticket. On the plus side, it drips with historic ambience and is rarely the scene of crowds.

Past the ticket booth, linger a moment to get your bearings. The ruins in front of you are those of the palace, with structures arranged along two sides of a central courtyard. The Byzantine chapel of Agios

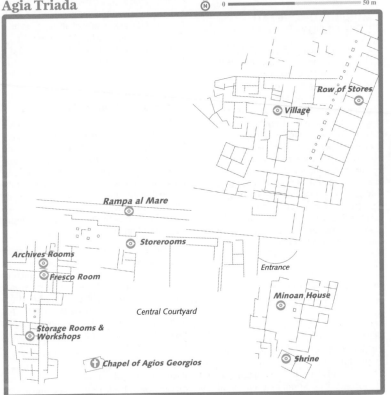
IRAKLIO AGIA TRIADA

Georgios, on the left, has some beautiful frescoes (ask for the key at the ticket office). To the right of the palace is the village area, with the cemetery (closed to visitors) beyond the fence.

To your left, as you go down the stairs, are the ruins of a **Minoan house** with a **shrine** dating from the early 14th century BC just behind it. It once featured a frescoed floor painted with octopuses and dolphins, also now at the museum in Iraklio. Beyond here is the paved **central courtyard** with the residential wing on the right beneath a protective canopy. The west wing, at the far end of the courtyard, is a maze of **storage rooms and workshops**; the 'Chieftain Cup' was found in one of them. One of the most beautiful rooms is in the northwest corner: called the **Fresco Room**, and lidded with a modern cement ceiling, it sports fitted benches, alabaster walls and gypsum floors.

A ramp running along the north side of the palace is thought to have led all the way to the sea, which was at a much higher level then; hence the name given to it by archaeologists – **Rampa al Mare**. It leads up to the **village** area with the marketplace and common residential buildings. Of special interest here is the row of **stores** that were once fronted by a portico.

On the other side of the fence, beyond the stores, is the **cemetery** that dates from around 2000 BC with two tholos tombs. The famous sarcophagus decorated with funereal scenes was found here; it too is in Iraklio.

ⓘ Getting There & Away

There is no public transport to the site, which is about a 5km walk from any major village. If you're driving, the turn-off to Agia Triada is about 500m from Phaestos on the road to Matala.

DON'T MISS

MUSEUM OF CRETAN ETHNOLOGY

This outstanding **museum** (☎2892 091 112/0; admission €3; ☺10am-6pm Apr-Oct, by appointment in winter) in the village of **Vori**, 4km east of Tymbaki, provides fascinating insights into traditional Cretan culture. The English-labelled exhibits are organised around themes such as rural life, food production, war, customs, architecture, music and food production. Most of the items are rather ordinary – hoes, olive presses, baskets, clothing, instruments etc – but they're all engagingly and intimately displayed in darkened rooms accented with spotlights. This is the best museum of its kind on the island and absolutely worth a detour. It's well signposted from the main road.

Matala Μάταλα

POP 110

Matala (*ma*-ta-la), on the coast 11km southwest of Phaestos, first made it into the history books as the place where Zeus, in the form of a bull, swam ashore with Europa on his back before dragging her off to Gortyna. The Minoans used Matala as their harbour for Phaestos and under the Romans it became the port for Gortyna. Ruins of these ancient settlements are still visible on the seabed.

Despite such an ancient pedigree, Matala to most means only one thing: hippies. Back in the late 1960s and early 1970s, long before Mykonos was hip and Ios was hot, this little town played host to a colony of flower children, some of them (like Joni Mitchell and Cat Stevens) famous. Part of the lure was rent-free living in the caves hewn into the cliffs in neolithic times. A gorgeous beach, cheap tavernas, free love and copious pot didn't hurt either. Joni Mitchell, famously immortalised the era in her song 'Carey'.

A Matala Hippie Reunion Festival in 2011 drew scores of people, but overall little of the 'peace and love' spirit is left, especially during summer when scores of day trippers flood the village to enjoy the seaside tavernas and shop at the plethora of souvenir stands.

Visit in low season, though, and it's still possible to discern the Matala magic. The setting along a crescent-shaped bay flanked by headlands is simply spectacular. The water is clear and sunset views of offshore Paximadia Island are often achingly beautiful.

Matala and the area around it is also a popular nesting ground for *Caretta caretta* sea turtles. The Sea Turtle Protection Society has a booth near the car park.

◎ Sights & Activities

Matala Caves   HISTORICAL SITE
(admission €2; ☺10am-7pm Apr-Sep) It's clearly these caves that make Matala unique and not just because of the hippie connection. Hewn into the porous sandstone cliffs in prehistoric times, they were used as tombs by the Romans under whom Matala was the port town for Gortyna. You're free to poke around the caves in the daytime but they're off-limits at night.

Red Beach   BEACH
Matala's main beach below the caves is a lovely crescent but often gets uncomfortably crammed. To escape the crowds, follow signs to Red Beach, reached in a 30-minute scramble over the rocks. It's hardly a secret but it does get fewer people, including a smattering of nudists. Bring water and snacks.

Church of Our Lady   CHURCH
Easily overlooked, this pint-sized chapel was carved straight out from a cliff, apparently during Venetian times. Inside are two marble altars, capitals from the early Byzantine period and precious icons. It's just a few steps from the central market square – follow the signs.

✗ Eating & Drinking

Eating in Matala is hardly an experience in haute cuisine, and there is little to distinguish any of the tourist joints on the bay. Self-caterers can stock up at the good-sized **supermarket** (☺7.30am-10pm) next to the big parking lot. Most bars are along the south side of the beach and stay open until dawn.

Gianni's   GREEK **€€**
(mains €7-13.50) A refreshing change from the run-of-the-mill waterfront tavernas, this been-there-forever family place just past the central square makes no-nonsense Greek food, including an excellent mixed grill with salad and potatoes.

Scala Fish Tavern
SEAFOOD, GREEK €€

(mains €7-14, fish per kg €35; ☺8am-late) Past all the bars on the easternmost end of the beach, this modern-looking place is the best restaurant in town and gets top marks for its fresh fish and superior service. The cave views are especially nice at sunset.

Mystical View
GREEK €€

(mains €6-13) Head out of town 1.2km towards Pitsidia, then turn left at the roundabout to get to this tavern with million-dollar sunset views over Kommos Beach. Fish and meat are recommended.

Lions
GREEK €

(mains €6-9) Overlooking the beach, Lions has been popular for many years and the food is better than average. It gets buzzy in the evening, making it a good place to wind down the day with a drink.

ⓘ Information

The main drag has a couple of ATMs and there's an excellent bookshop with lots of English-language novels and periodicals right on the central square.

Zafiria Internet (per hr €4; ☺8am-midnight)

ⓘ Getting There & Away

There are four buses Monday to Friday, five buses Saturday and one bus Sunday to Iraklio (€7.80, two hours), Phaestos (€1.70, 30 minutes) and Mires (€2.80, 45 minutes). There is free parking along the street as you drive into town, and a pay lot (per entry €2) on the beach.

Around Matala

If you find Matala too busy, there are several quieter and more authentic bases nearby from which to explore this south-western pocket of Iraklio. Fine beaches beckon in Kommos and Kalamaki, while inland villages like Pitsidia, Sivas and Kamilari still preserve an unhurried, traditional flair along their impossibly narrow streets. Archaeology fiends can get their fix in Kommos and Kamilari.

KOMMOS ΚΟΜΜΟΣ

The **Minoan site** of Kommos, 3km north of Matala along a fantastic wide and sandy **beach**, is believed to have been the port for Phaestos. Although fenced off, it's still possible to discern the ancient town's streets and courtyards as well as the remains of

workshops, dwellings and temples. Find the limestone-paved road leading towards Phaestos; look closely and you can make out the ruts from Minoan carts and a sewer running from the north side.

The turn-off for Kommos from the main road is at the top of the hill just before Pitsidia; look for the tiny sign 'Kommos Beach'.

PITSIDIA ΠΙΤΣΙΔΙΑ

Quiet and unspoiled, Pitsidia is only 5km northeast of Matala, but could not be more different in look and feel. Its unhurried vibe, nicely restored stone buildings and maze of narrow lanes decorated with potted flowers give it charm and artistic flair. At night, locals mix with visitors for chat and sustenance in one of the low-key tavernas or *kafeneia* around the village square. Buses en route to Matala stop on the main road.

Melanouri Horse Farm (☏2892 045 040; www.melanouri.com; rides from €20) organises horserides along the beach or into the mountains, including a day trip to the Agiofarango Gorge (p142) for €80.

For nosh, there's some excellent wood-fired pizza at **Bodikos** (pizzas & mains €5-11) on the main road. Gobble them up amid lots of knick-knacks or on the vine-covered terrace. Grilled meats and fish are also served and the owners also rent rooms from €35.

Near the village's main square, low-key **Mike's** (mains €5-8) is a great place to hang out in the evening and reflect on the events of the day over wine and simple but delicious local fare.

SIVAS ΣΙΒΑΣ

North of Pitsidia, about 2km inland from the main road, the pretty village of Sivas has a homey feel, many heritage-protected stone buildings and a pretty taverna-lined main square. The best of them is **Taverna Sactouris** (www.sactouris-sivas.com; mains €5.50-10), which makes terrific salads and vegetable dishes, usually featuring wild herbs gathered by owner-chef Jannis himself. With advance notice he also makes a fragrant fish soup.

Steps away, **Sigelakis** (mains €6-9; ☺from 5pm) has more traditional food, including a delicious goat in tomato sauce. Owner George also operates eight lovely apartments nearby (p193).

MONI ODIGITRIAS & AGIOFARANGO GORGE

This detour delivers a trifecta of treats: a visit to a monastery, an easy walk through the picturesque gorge and a nice swimming cove.

About 6km south of Sivas, **Moni Odigitrias** (admission free; ⊘9am-8pm) is a historic monastery with a tower from which the monks fought off the Turks, Germans and the odd pirate. A rickety ladder leads to the top for superb views. Afterwards, take a quick spin around the small museum with its wine- and olive presses and check out the 15th-century frescoes and icons in the church up the hill.

From the parking lot opposite the monastery it's about 3km to the beach via the **Agiofarango Gorge**. Since the first section is not especially scenic, most people continue to drive down a dirt road to another parking area from where it's roughly 1km to the sea. The gorge itself is awash in oleander and popular with rock climbers. There are caves, makeshift chapels and hermitages in the cliffs as well as a Byzantine chapel near the halfway point. The gorge emerges at a lovely pebble beach with crystal-clear water. Despite its remoteness, it gets busy on Sundays and almost daily in summer when tourist boats arrive from Matala.

On the drive back, reward yourself with a glass of homemade lemonade at the arty **Kafeneio Ksasou** (www.listarossa.gr; mezedhes €3.50-8.50; ⊘Tue-Sat 4-11pm, Sun 10am-11pm, Fri-Sun only Nov-Easter) near the village of Listaros. The owners are active environmentalists and put much emphasis on a sustainable lifestyle. Sylla is also a mean cook: try her special Ksasou pie bulging with feta and a spicy sausage called *soutzouki*. If you want to spend the night, ask if there's a vacancy in her two traditional guesthouses (€100 to €120).

KAMILARI ΚΑΜΗΛΑΡΙ

Straddling three hills about 8km from Matala, Kamilari is home to an extraordinarily well-preserved circular **Minoan tomb** with stone walls standing 2m high. Side rooms were used for ritual purposes. The tomb is in the middle of fields outside the village. Look for signs in town or at the junction before you get to the village. Park your car by the side of the road and walk for a good half-hour to reach the tomb. If unsure, ask for directions at **Kentriko** (www .kafenio-kentriko.gr; mains €5-7; ⑳), a congenial stone *kafeneio* on the narrow main drag. Decorated with old photos of village families, it's great for breakfast, a nightcap or anything in between.

For a full meal, steer towards **Taverna Mylonas** (www.milonaskamilari.gr; mains €6.50-12), which makes tasty traditional Cretan mezedhes and a daily-changing selection of *mayirefta* with ingredients trucked in from the nearby family farm. Score a terrace table to soak up the stunning views.

KALAMAKI ΚΑΛΑΜΑΚΙ

With its long sandy beach and attractive setting Kalamaki has all the trappings of an alluring resort town. Alas, at least for now, its looks are marred by dozens of skeletal half-finished buildings dotted around town. On the plus side, the town rarely gets crowded, you'll find plenty of good-value lodging here and the taverna and lounge-lined beach promenade makes for fine strolling. Ambitious types can walk all the way to Kommos Beach along the waterfront.

Of the many tavernas along the beach, **Delfinia** (fish per kg €40-50) is highly regarded for its fresh fish. For a more local flair, head one block inland to **Yiannis** (mezedhes €2.50-4.50; ⊘8am-11pm), a bare-bones eatery that enjoys cult status with locals and loyal visitors for its scrumptious mezedhes and lovably eccentric proprietor.

Lendas Λέντας

POP 80

Lendas appeals to those in search of a remote and laid-back beach retreat. Reached via a long and winding road culminating in a dramatic plunge down to the village, it clings to the cliff overlooking the beach. It attracts mostly independent travellers, including many who've been coming for 20 years. Aside from a few beach bars, there's not much going on to divert your attention from nature.

◉ Sights & Activities

Under the Romans, Lebena was a health spa cherished for its therapeutic springs. The ancient settlement stood right above the beach, but only two granite columns of a 4th-century-BC temple remain. Next to the temple was a treasury with a mosaic floor that is still visible. Very little else is decipherable and the springs have been closed since the 1960s.

The beach in town is narrow and pebbly and not particularly attractive. About 1km to the west though, over the headland, there's a nice, long stretch of sand called Diskos (or Dytikos), although it is mostly nudist and used by campers in summer. Heading east along the coastal dirt road are more small beaches, some with tavernas. After about 5km you reach Loutro Beach, which is also the launching pad for the scenic 6km-hike to Kronos via the Trakhoula Gorge.

✗ Eating

 El Greco   GREEK €€
(www.lentas-elgreco.com; specials €5-11) This friendly taverna run by the Delakis family has an excellent selection of *mayirefta* and traditional Greek dishes in a garden setting

---

WORTH A TRIP

KAPETANIANA
ΚΑΠΕΤΑΝΙΑΝΑ

In the heart of the Asteroussia mountain range that runs along the entire southern coast of Iraklio, Kapetaniana is a remote, car-free mountain hamlet that's a mecca for rock climbers and hikers. Divided into an upper and a lower village, it clings to the slopes of the Asteroussia's highest peak, Mt Kofinas (1231m). Although only 60km south of Iraklio, it's a long and arduous drive out here, partly along narrow roads corkscrewing up into the mountains. If you think that's bad, remember that as late as 2005, only a gravel road led up to the village.

The best place to say is the delightful Pension Kofinas (p194) in the upper village. Owner Gunnar is also a gourmet chef who rustles up divine dinners (€12-15 incl wine) on the terrace, which has superb views of Kofinas and out to sea.

---

overlooking the sea. Its rooms and studios rent for around €40.

Akti   GREEK €€
(mains €6-10) Also recommended is the taverna next door to El Greco, both for its food and its wine selection.

❶ Information

Entering the village, take the left fork to the car park or the right fork to the main square. The bus stops outside the car park. There are a couple of small markets but no petrol station.

❶ Getting There & Away

One bus from Iraklio makes the trip out here every Monday to Friday (€8.20, 2½ hours).

NORTHEASTERN COAST

Ever since the national road along the northern coast opened in 1972, the coast between Iraklio and Malia has seen a frenzy of unbridled development, particularly in the seaside towns of Hersonisos and Malia. Hotels deal almost exclusively with package-tour operators who block-book hotel rooms months in advance. For independent travellers, the village of Koutouloufari, above Hersonisos, is the most appealing place to stay in this area.

While Hersonisos has some family-friendly attractions, including fun water parks, Malia is primarily a party town. A bit incongruously, it's also home to the area's only significant historical site, the wonderful Minoan palace near Malia.

Buses link all the coastal towns along the Old National Rd at least every 30 minutes. If you want to avoid this area altogether, whoosh right past it on the E75 highway.

Gournes & Around

Gournes, about 15km east of Iraklio, was dominated by a huge US air force base until it closed in 1994.

TOP CHOICE Cretaquarium (☑2810 337 788; www.cretaquarium.gr; adult/senior/child 5-17yr €8/6/6; ☺9.30am-9pm May-Sep, to 5pm Oct-Apr; ☎), a vast high-tech indoor sea, now uses part of the former military grounds. Inhabited by some 2500 Mediterranean and tropical aquatic critters, this huge aquarium will likely bring smiles to even the most

SKOTINO CAVE ΣΠΗΛΑΙΟ ΣΚΟΤΕΙΝΟ

Also known as Agia Paraskevi Cave, after the chapel built above it, Skotino is one of the largest caves in Crete and deliciously spooky to boot. A gaping arch gives way to a dark chamber as lofty as a Gothic cathedral and teeming with stalactites, stalagmites and massive limestone formations. Let your mind wander and you'll make out all sorts of shapes (a bear, a dragon, a head) in the dim light. Unless you have some spelunking experience and a flashlight, you probably should not venture beyond here, because the chamber drops another 15m and it gets eerily dark.

Skotino was first explored by Arthur Evans in 1933. Later excavations have unearthed vases, bone needles and figurines dating as far back as Minoan times, suggesting that the cave has had religious significance. To this day, pilgrims leave votives and offerings.

There is no admission fee, no guard and few visitors. Wear sturdy shoes and mind your footing at all times.

The cave is near the village of Skotino, some 8km inland from Kato Gouves. About 1km past Skotino, look for the turn-off to the 'Cave of Agia Paskevi' sign and drive another 2.3km to the cave entrance.

Playstation-jaded youngster. It's a wondrous world where you can watch jellyfish dance, sharks dart, skates fly and corals sway. There are multimedia features, multilingual displays and a cool remote-controlled underwater camera, but for a more in-depth experience it's well worth investing €3 in an audio guide or joining a behind-the-scenes tour (summer only). It's affiliated with the Hellenic Center for Maritime Research next door.

Not only kids will get their jollies on a hot summer day in **Water City** (☑2810 781 316; www.watercity.gr; adult/child under 140cm/ child under 90cm €22/16/free; ☉10am-6.30pm May-Sep), Crete's largest water park, in Anopoli, about 3km inland. Plunge down wicked high-speed slides, brave wave pools or simply chill in the pool. Note that some of the 34 attractions have height and weight restrictions.

Hersonisos Χερσόνησος

Hersonisos, about 25km east of Iraklio, has grown from a small fishing village into one of Crete's largest and most popular tourist towns and gets deluged in summer. The beachfront is lined with sprawling hotels and apartment buildings and paralleled by the main thoroughfare, Odos Elefteriou Venizelos, an uninterrupted and cacophonous strip of bars, cafes, tourist shops, discos, fast-food eateries, travel agencies and quad-hire places.

Peaceful and quiet it ain't, but if you're travelling with the kids in tow, you'll actually find a slew of family-friendly

attractions here, including some temper-cooling water parks. Boat trips launch from the little harbour and there's also plenty of opportunity for watersports along the beaches.

An easy way to escape the bustle is by heading uphill to the village of **Koutoulou-fari** which, although touristy, retains some semblance of charm and has some good tavernas along the main street.

◉ Sights & Activities

TOP
CHOICE **Lychnostatis Museum** MUSEUM

(☑2897 023 660; www.lychnostatis.gr; adult/ student/4-12yr €5/3/2; ☉9am-2pm Sun-Fri) In a lovely seaside setting on the town's eastern edge, this family-operated open-air folklore museum recreates a traditional Cretan village with commendable authenticity. The various buildings include a windmill and a farmer's house. Elsewhere, there are weaving workshops, ceramics and plant-dying demonstrations, orchards and herb gardens and a theatre that hosts music and dance performances. Guided tours and audio guides (€1) are available and a *kafeneio* provides refreshments.

Acqua Plus WATER PARK

(☑2897 024 950; www.acquaplus.gr; adult/5-13yr/ under 5yr €22/14/free; ☉10am-6pm May-Sep) Wet fun awaits at Greece's oldest water park, in a lovely hillside garden setting 5km inland on the road to Kastelli. Kamikazee and 2 Black Holes are among the slides tailored to adrenaline junkies, while nervous nellies might prefer the gentle float down the 270m-long Lazy River or a soak in the jacuzzi.

Star Beach
WATER PARK

(www.starbeach.gr; admission free; ⊙10am-6pm Apr-May, to 7pm Jun-Sep) Not far from the Lychnostatis Museum and part of the eponymous hotel complex, this water park is smaller and more low-key than the competition, making it perhaps less overwhelming for small children. Admission is free but most activities – jet skiing to parasailing – are fee-based.

Aqua World
AQUARIUM

(☑2897 029 125; adult/child €6/4; ⊙10am-6pm Apr-Oct, last admission 5.15pm) Right in town, behind the big Spar supermarket, this small, private aquarium is run by a friendly Brit. It showcases mostly local fish, including such crowd-pleasers as the venomous scorpion fish and the brightly hued peacock wrasse, as well as turtles, geckos, a python and other reptiles. All animals are rescues.

Finika Stables
HORSE RIDING

(☑6945924112; www.hersonissos-horseriding.com) This outfit on the main road near the Star Beach water park organises horseriding tours into the local mountains for €60, including hotel transfer and lunch.

Crete Golf Club
GOLF

(☑2897 026 000; www.crete-golf.gr; 9/18 holes €50/80) Next to Acqua Plus, this is Crete's only 18-hole golf course. It's a tough desert-style course that makes challenging use of the hillside setting and is definitely not for hackers. Also see p26.

✗ Eating

For a more authentic experience, skip the identikit tourist tavernas and check out what's cooking uphill in Koutouloufari.

Mythos
GREEK €€

(Giampoudaki 10; mains €5-10) Honest-to-goodness Greek food is a rare commodity in Hersonisos proper, which is what makes Gianna and Manos' taverna such a find. It's tucked into a side street off the main strip.

Emmanuel Taverna
GREEK €€

(Koutouloufari; mains €6-12) Managed by a Greek-Australian family, this homely taverna specialises in spit-roasted meats and dishes cooked in the wood oven in front. The lamb in rosé wine with bay leaves is recommended.

Nikos the Fisherman
SEAFOOD, GREEK €€€

(Koutouloufari; meals €10-20) Every night, owner-chef Kleopatra prepares the fresh catch brought in by hubbie Nikos in her tiny kitchen. The food is universally excellent, but since there is no menu, you might want to clarify the cost of your meal when ordering.

❶ Getting There & Away

Buses from Iraklio run at least every 30 minutes (€3, 40 minutes).

Malia Μάλια

You won't need this guidebook to find the party in Malia, some 10km further east. The party will find you. The main strip, Dimokratias, is chock-a-block with boisterous bars, pubs and high-energy clubs filled with carousing hormone-crazed 20-somethings about to do something embarrassing they can't remember the next morning. Beaches too are packed, although crowds thin out a bit towards the eastern end, near the harbour. The best sandy strip is still further east, near the Minoan palace, which is a civilised antidote to the madness and a must-see, bar none. Another pocket of charm is tiny Old Town Malia, a classic maze of narrow lanes with a handful of above-average tavernas.

◉ Sights

[TOP CHOICE] Palace of Malia
ANCIENT SITE

(☑2897 031 597; adult/senior & EU student/under 18yr €4/2/free; ⊙8.30am-3pm Tue-Sun) About 3km east of the town of Malia, this grand palace was built at about the same time as the two other great Minoan palaces of Phaestos and Knossos. The First Palace dates back to around 1900 BC and was rebuilt after the earthquake of 1700 BC, only to be levelled again by another temblor around 1450 BC. Most of what you see today are the remains of the Second Palace where many exquisite Minoan artefacts, including the famous gold bee pendant, were found. Most are now in the archaeological museums in Iraklio or Agios Nikolaos.

Malia is a relatively easy site to comprehend, especially if you've already visited Knossos, which follows a similar ground plan. A free map and labelling throughout also help, as does the exhibition hall just past the entrance, where photographs and

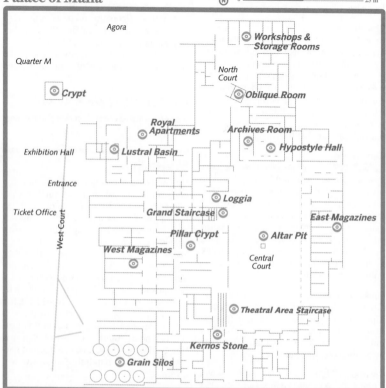

scale models of the ruined and reconstructed complex help you visualise the main palace and surrounding sites.

Access to the ruins is from the West Court. Instead of entering, though, turn right and walk south along the West Magazines to eight circular pits believed to have been grain silos. Continue east past the pits to the palace's south entrance and turn left to reach the southern end of the Central Court. On your left, in the ground, is the Kernos Stone, a disk with 24 holes around its edge. Archaeologists have yet to ascertain its function, but it probably had a religious purpose. Immediately adjacent are the four surviving steps of a large staircase that may have been used as a Theatral Area.

Walk to the sunken altar pit in the centre of the courtyard and take in its impressive dimensions: 48m long and 22m wide. Beneath a canopy on your right are the East Magazines, where liquids were stored

in giant *pithoi*. Opposite, the west wing harboured the most important rooms of the palace. These include the Pillar Crypt behind a stone-paved vestibule; the 11 remaining steps of the Grand Staircase, which might have led to a shrine; and the elevated Loggia, which was probably used for ceremonial purposes. Walk to the northern end of the courtyard and look down to see the stumps of the pillars that once held up the portico of the Hypostyle Hall. Fitted benches indicate that it may have served as a kind of council chamber. Also here is the archives room, where tablets containing Linear A script were found.

Continue along the paved walkway west of the Hypostyle Hall to the North Court, which was once lined with workshops and storage rooms. En route you'll pass by an oddly oblique room that dates to the Postpalatial period. West of the north court you can spot the royal apartments anchored by the cordoned-off Reception Hall (labelled Polymyron), a rectangular structure on a raised platform. Behind it is the lustral basin.

Malia Palace was surrounded by an entire city whose excavation is still ongoing. The canopied structure just west of the compound is described as the Crypt, while north of here the Agora was essentially one large building wrapped around a central courtyard. The most impressive section is Quarter M, a residential area a bit further west. Though fenced off, it's still possible to appreciate its size and complexity. These outer buildings date back to the First Palace period.

Buses from Iraklio stop at the palace.

✕ Eating

Avoid the main strip and head to Old Town Malia for better quality and more authentic flair.

San Giorgio   GREEK €€
(www.sangiorgiotaverna.gr; mains €6-20) There's really nothing terribly special about the menu at San Giorgio but the warm decor, congenial service and nicely prepared home-cooked food will still ensure a memorable dining experience. Sit in the flowery courtyard or upstairs in the woodsy restaurant.

Stablos & Elisabeth   GREEK €€
(www.crete-web.gr/restaurants/elisabeth; mains €6-15) The best taverna on Old Malia's main square goes for the Crete-meets-English-B&B look with plenty of knick-knacks and lace curtains. The nicely prepared Greek and international foods are best enjoyed on the roof garden.

Drossia   INTERNATIONAL €€
(cnr Dimokratias & Grammatikaki; mains €8.50-17) This all-white outdoor restaurant is an island of class and relative quiet along boom-boom Dimokratias. The kitchen churns out light, inventive and fresh fare, including innovative salads and quality meats and fish.

ⓘ Getting There & Away

There are buses to Malia from Iraklio at least every 30 minutes (€3.80, one hour).

Towards the Lasithi Plateau

From Malia, the road climbs quickly to the Lasithi Plateau, passing through the charming village of Krasí and the monastery of Kerá along the way. Krasí's main claim to fame is a 2000-year-old plane tree with a mind-boggling 16m girth. It is fed by the adjacent spring spurting from an arcaded stone basin and provides shade for the taverna tables set up beneath its massive canopy.

Continuing on takes you to Kerá, home to one of Crete's most cherished monasteries, the Panagia Kardiotissa (admission €2; ☉7am-7.30pm). Its teensy chapel is embellished with 14th-century frescoes depictingscenes from the life of Christ and the Virgin, but locals especially venerate an 18th-century icon of the Virgin and Child. Legend has it that the Turks spirited it thrice to Constantinople but it miraculously returned each time, despite being chained to a marble pillar. You'll find it on the left of the iconostatis (the wall that separates the nave from the sanctuary), next to the chains; the marble pillar is outside. There's also a small museum with religious paraphernalia.

Lasithi Λασίθι

Why Go?

Head east from Iraklio past the resorts of Malia and Hersonisos and you enter a more relaxed Cretan world that is never short of surprises.

Looking for a charming resort town with cool after-dark ambience? None better than Lasithi's main tourist draw of Agios Nikolaos. Ancient sites and culture? Lasithi has Minoan and Mycenaean sites aplenty, while local museums are crammed with enthralling artefacts. For outdoor action and spectacular landscapes head inland to the Lasithi Plateau or tackle one of the region's more accessible gorge walks, such as the dramatic Valley of the Dead at Kato Zakros.

Added value comes with such unique attractions as the historic monastery of Toplou and Vaï's famous palm-lined beach, while scores of towns and villages maintain a rich undertow of Cretan history and spirit. All of this is underpinned by a choice of accommodation and some of Crete's finest tavernas and restaurants.

Best Places to Eat

When to Go

Travel to Lasithi in the springtime to catch the colour burst of wildflowers in the mountains (and to enjoy the calm before the crowds of summer).

From June to August the beaches are at their best, and high summer is the time to come for glorious days, warm nights and a dose of Cretan culture at Agios Nikolaos' Lato Cultural Festival.

September and October bring slightly cooler weather – perfect for exploring mountain tops or hiking the region's gorges.

Best Places to Stay

Getting Around

Roads between main centres and larger resorts throughout Lasithi are good. Minor surfaced roads are adequate, but always watch out for potholes. Driving on unsurfaced roads is not advised unless with off-road vehicles and full insurance.

Most larger villages and resorts can be reached by bus from Agios Nikolaos, Sitia and Ierapetra. The best way of finding up-to-date information is from the bus stations themselves. Many villages only have early morning and midday services during school terms. Popular tourist destinations have a summer service only.

You can rent cars, bikes and scooters from main centres and from most resorts in summer.

THREE PERFECT DAYS

Day One

From Agios Nikolaos it's a short drive along the Kritsa road to the **Church of the Panagia Kera** where there's a feast of fabulous 13th-century frescoes. Then drop back two thousand years at the nearby Hellenistic-Dorian site of **Lato**. Head back to **Kritsa**, weave your way past the needlework sellers, and wander the old town. Then reflect on a day of astonishing island history and culture while dining at one of Agios Nikolaos' archetypal **Cretan restaurants**.

Day Two

A reading of the romantic novel *To Nisi* (The Island; see boxed text, p158) will lead you to the compelling island of **Spinalonga**, the one-time leper colony where the novel and its television series are set. You can get there by boat from Agios Nikolaos, Elounda or Plaka. Before you go, a visit to Agios Nikolaos' delightful **Folk Museum** conjures up a sense of time and place regarding the older Crete portrayed in the book. Finish the day at Elounda's **Oceanis** restaurant for Cretan cuisine.

Day Three

From Sitia head for **Moni Toplou**, one of Crete's outstanding monasteries. Continue to Palekastro and on to **Kato Zakros** for some Minoan magic at the remains of an ancient palace. Take a stroll into the awesome **Valley of the Dead**, and then drive back through rugged mountains to Sitia for a gourmet evening at the colourful **Balcony** restaurant.

Accommodation

For sleeping options throughout this region, please see the Accommodation chapter (p175).

DON'T MISS

Lasithi's ancient sites include the haunting Minoan settlements of Gournia (p162) and Kato Zakros (p168) and the smaller ruins of Pyrgos (p174) and Itanos (p167). Lato (p157), a Dorian foundation, is equally compelling.

Best Beaches

» Almyros (p153)
» Vaï (p166)
» Xerokambos (p169)
» Itanos (p167)
» Hiona (p167)

Best Small Resorts

» Mohlos (p163)
» Myrtos (p173)
» Kato Zakros (p168)
» Koutsouras (p173)
» Palekastro (p167)

Resources

» www.lasithitourism.com
» www.agiosnikolaos.gr
» www.sitia.gr
» www.ierapetra.gr

Lasithi Highlights

① Wander among the fascinating ruins on **Spinalonga Island** (p160)

② Visit the **Church of Panagia Kera** (p157) for the finest wall paintings in Crete

③ Walk or cycle around the **Lasithi Plateau** (p161)

④ Explore the Minoan ruins at **Gournia** (p162)

⑤ Discover the chequered history of **Moni Toplou** (p166)

⑥ Explore the Valley of the Dead at **Kato Zakros** (p168)

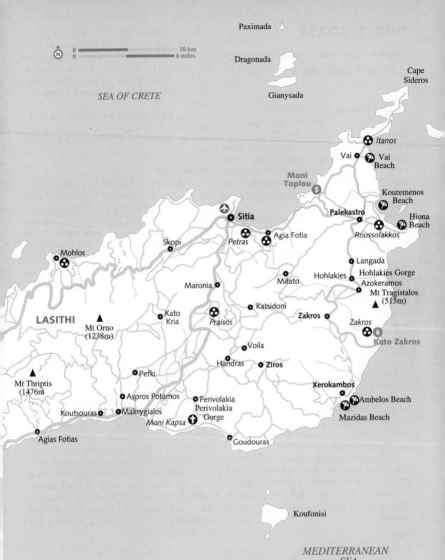

Paximada

Dragonada

Cape
Sideros

SEA OF CRETE

Gianysada

Itanos

Vai Vai
Beach

Moni
Toplou
5

Kouremenos
Beach

Sitia

Palekastro

Hiona
Beach

Skopi

Petras

Agia Fotia

Roussolakkos

Mohlos

Maronia

Mitato

Langada

Hohlakies

Hohlakies Gorge

Azokeramos

LASITHI

Mt Orno
(1238m)

Kato
Kria

Praisos

Katsidoni

Zakros

Zakros

Mt Tragistalos
(515m)

Kato Zakros
6

Voila

Mt Thriptis
(1476m)

Pefki

Handras

Ziros

Aspros Potamos

Xerokambos

Koutsouras

Makrygialos

Perivolakia
Perivolakia
Gorge

Ambelos Beach

Moni Kapsa

Mazidas Beach

Agias Fotias

Goudouras

Koufonisi

MEDITERRANEAN
SEA

7 Enjoy great Cretan
cuisine at one of **Agios
Nikolaos'** (p153)
recommended eateries

NORTH COAST

Agios Nikolaos Αγιος Νικόλαος

POP 11,286

Lasithi's capital, Agios Nikolaos (*ah*-yee-os nih-*ko*-laos) stands on the shores of the beautiful Mirabello Bay. It seems less Cretan in character than the island's other main centres, partly because of its resort style and its generally modern architecture, but there's a strong local character to Agios Nikolaos that makes it a charming and friendly place.

The town's harbour is linked by a narrow channel to the circular Voulismeni Lake. The main harbour-front road crosses the channel by a bridge and the pedestrianised lakeside is lined with cafes and restaurants. In recent years pedestrianisation has been extended to the adjacent main streets, increasing the overall relaxed atmosphere.

Agios Nikolaos' archaeological museum has a compelling Minoan collection, although, at the time of writing, the museum was closed temporarily for refurbishment. The little harbour-side Folk Museum offers a charming step into the past. By day there's a cheerful buzz around the harbour and by night a decidedly chic ambience descends on the cafes and bars, where stylish young Greeks strut the harbour-side catwalk and holidaymakers come into town from the neighbouring resorts.

A range of accommodation should suit all tastes and pockets while tavernas and restaurants offer affordable Cretan specialities to wider Mediterranean-influenced cuisine. There's free wi-fi in the harbour area and its surrounds.

History

Agios Nikolaos emerged as a port for the city-state of Lato in the early Hellenic years, when it was known as Lato-by-Kamara. The harbour was important in the Greco-Roman period after the Romans put an end to the piracy that had plagued the northern coast.

The town continued to flourish in the early Christian years and, in the 8th or 9th century, the Byzantine Church of Agios Nikolaos was built.

When the Venetians bought Crete in the 13th century, the Castel Mirabello was built on a hill overlooking the sea and a settlement arose below. The castle was damaged in the earthquake of 1303 and was burned by pirates in 1537. It was then rebuilt, but when the Venetians were forced to abandon the castle to the Turks in 1645 they blew it up, leaving it in ruins. It was the Venetians who named the bay Mirabello ('beautiful view').

Agios Nikolaos was resettled in the mid-19th century by fleeing rebels from Sfakia and was later named capital of the Lasithi region.

Orientation

The bus station is located just under a kilometre to the northwest of Voulismeni Lake. Most banks, travel agencies and shops are on Koundourou and the parallel pedestrian street 28 Oktovriou. The main roads have a one-way traffic system so, if you are driving, follow the signs to the port area or to one of the car parks near the harbour.

⊙ Sights

Archaeological Museum   MUSEUM
(☑28410 24943, 28410 22462; Paleologou Konstantinou 74; admission €4; ⊙8.30am-3pm Tue-Sun) At the time of writing the museum was closed for an unspecified period for refurbishment and expansion. Visitors are advised to phone the museum for updated information. When open, the extensive and well-displayed collection has no major showpiece, but it is probably the second-most significant Minoan collection in existence, and includes clay coffins, ceramic musical instruments and gold from the island of Mohlos. The chronological exhibits have some brief information in English and begin with neolithic finds from Mt Traóstalos, north of Kato Zakros, and early Minoan finds from Agia Fotia, then finds from Malia and Mohlos. The highlight is the odd-looking Goddess of Myrtos, a clay jug from 2500 BC.

ROAD DISTANCES (km)

	Ierapetra	Agios Nikolaos	Elounda	Sitia
Agios Nikolaos	36			
Elounda	45	10		
Sitia	62	73	70	
Kato Zakros	98	106	116	36

Folk Museum
MUSEUM

(☎28410 25093; Paleologou Konstantinou 4; admission €3; ⊙10am-2pm Tue-Sun) Next to the tourist office, this museum has a small, well-curated collection of traditional handicrafts and costumes.

🏃 Activities

Beaches

The town beaches of **Ammos** and **Kytroplatia** are small and can get busy. Kytroplatia is nearest the centre and is crowded round with cafes and restaurants. Ammos is small and busy, but has a pleasant, lively ambience. The sandy beach at **Almyros**, about 1km south of town, is the best of the lot and tends to be quieter. It can be reached on foot via a coastal path. This path starts at the seaward end of the first road that leads left from just past the municipal stadium. There's not much shade but you can hire umbrellas.

You can venture further towards Sitia to the pleasant coves with long stretches of sandy beach and turquoise waters at the signposted **Golden Beach** (Voulisma Beach) and around **Istron Bay**.

There is a **children's playground**, **swimming pool** and **mini golf** at the municipal beach on the south side of Agios Nikolaos.

Other Activities

M/S Manolis
BOAT TRIPS

(☎6974143150) The wooden sailboat M/S *Manolis* runs fishing trips that include a barbecue and swim at Kolokytha Island, adjoining Elounda, as well as private charters. Boats leave from the south side of the harbour.

Zaharias
BOAT TRIPS

(☎6937374954; www.sailcrete.com) Runs sailing trips and private charters around the Bay of Mirabello.

Creta Underwater Center
DIVING

(☎28410 22406; www.cretaunderwatercenter.com; Mirabello Hotel, Agios Nikolaos) Offers boat dives and PADI-certification courses.

Creta Semi-Submarine
BOAT TRIPS

(☎28410 24822, 6936051186) The *Nautilus* has a submerged viewing cabin that is popular with youngsters and adults alike.

Pelagos
DIVING

(☎28410 24376; www.divecrete.com) In the Minos Beach Art Hotel. Also offers dives and PADI courses.

Nostos Tours
BOAT TRIPS

(☎28410 22819; 30 Rousou Koundourou) Runs boat trips to Spinalonga (€15), including a swim at Kolokytha. Also offers trips to Spinalonga including a barbecue (€25), and fishing trips with food, including anything you catch (€30).

☞ Tours

Travel agencies offer bus tours to Crete's top attractions and the boats along the harbour advertise their various excursions.

Little Train Tours
TRAIN TOURS

(☎28140 25420; Akti Themistokleous) Youngsters love these trips that vary from a half-hour ride round town (adult/child €8/5) to a 3½-hour trip that takes in an olive farm and a visit to the village of Kritsa (adult/child €20/10). Tours start from the eastern harbourfront.

Minotours Hellas
BUS TOURS

(☎28410 23222; www.minotours.gr; 28 Oktovriou 6) Organises guided coach tours of Phaestos, Gortyna and Matala (€35), the Samaria Gorge (€50), the Lasithi Plateau (€40), Knossos (€40) and other destinations.

🎊 Festivals & Events

Lato Cultural Festival
CULTURAL FESTIVAL

In July and August Agios Nikolaos hosts the Lato Cultural Festival, with concerts by local and international musicians, folk dancing, *mantinadhes* (rhyming couplets) contests, theatre, and art exhibitions. Ask at the tourist office for details.

Marine Week
WATER SPORTS

Held during the last week of June in even-numbered years, this celebration has swimming, windsurfing and boat races.

✗ Eating

Like any resort, Agios Nikolaos has its fair share of tavernas and restaurants pushing bland and sometimes overpriced 'Greek' food. However, the back streets around town have some great options. For self catering there are small supermarkets halfway up Paleologou Konstantinou and at the bottom of Koundourou.

Migomis
INTERNATIONAL €€€

(☎28410 24353; www.migomis.com; Nikolaou Plastira 20; mains €25-35) With an inventive cuisine that draws on international themes and ingredients, Migomis has maintained the highest standards for many years. The

Agios Nikolaos

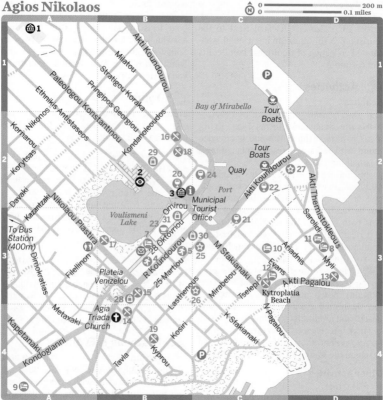

restaurant has unrivalled views from high above Voulismeni Lake and in summer you eat to the soothing sounds of a well-played baby grand piano. Bookings advised.

Chrysofillis   MEZEDHES €
(☎28410 22705; Akti Pagalou; mezedhes €4-8) Well-priced food makes this *mezedhopoleio* a classic small-plate place with several varieties of ouzo to enhance things, as well as some Greek wines. Specials include cheese pies, fresh mussels and chicken with saffron. Bookings advised.

Itanos   GREEK €
(Kyprou 1; mains €5-10) The focus is on terrific Cretan home-style cooking at this friendly restaurant. You can select from trays of fresh *mayirefta* (casseroles and oven-baked dishes) such as goat with artichokes. Owner Yiannis makes his own pastry for

delicious leek pies and there's a selection of vegetarian options.

Mare & Monte   MEDITERRANEAN €€
(Akti Koundourou; www.maremonte-restaurant.com; mains €9-22) There's a subtle Italian influence on the Cretan cuisine at this stylish seafront restaurant. A range of Greek, Italian and fish starters lead on to main dishes such as grilled chicken with feta, olives and fennel or fillet of sea bass with lemon and thyme sauce.

Pelagos   SEAFOOD €€€
(☎28410 25737; Stratigou Koraka 11; mains €9-28) A longstanding top eatery, Pelagos is housed in a restored neoclassical building and has a garden terrace. It's noted for its fish and seafood, such as sea-urchin salad in season and mullet in a herb dressing, but also offers tasty meat and pasta dishes with Cretan flair. Bookings advised.

Barko MEDITERRANEAN €€
(Kytroplatia Beach; mains €5.50-12.40) Smart decor enhances a good menu at this restaurant opposite the town beach. A decent wine list includes some fine Cretan vintages.

Sarri's GREEK €
(Kyprou 15; mains €6-8) Down-to-earth Sarri's offers tasty mezedhes, standard Greek dishes and home-baked bread. Across the road the tree-shaded garden terrace is ideal for breakfast, lunch or dinner. There's a choice of daily specials.

Jane's Fishmarket MARKET
(Plateia Venizelou; ⊙7.30am-2.30pm Mon-Sat) Has a selection of locally caught fish.

♚ Drinking & Entertainment

The waterfront cafe-bars lining Akti Koundourou above the harbour, get going mid-morning and later morph into lively bars. There are other options around town.

Top spots along Akti Koundourou that are popular with young locals include **Dioliko** and the bigger and bouncier **Caramello**, while the **Rock Music Bar** is a long-established late-night haunt, opening at 10pm

and spinning classic rock, blues, punk and heavy metal.

Visitors often head to the opposite side of the harbour to the popular **Sorrento** bar and around the corner to **Alexandros Roof Garden** for classic sounds amidst hanging plants, shrubs and funky decor.

Revved-up dance clubs, such as **Ellinadiko**, **Lotus**, **Passion** and **Cube Bar**, cluster on 25 Martiou.

A couple of entertainment options include **Peripou Café** (28 Oktovriou 13), a charming period piece, with the added bonus of having a bookstore and book exchange. The narrow balcony overlooking the lake is a delight. The **Rex Cinema** (Lasthenous; admission €7) screens the latest releases as well as art-house movies.

MOVING ON?

For tips, recommendations and reviews, head to shop.lonelyplanet.com to purchase a downloadable PDF of the Dodecanese chapter from Lonely Planet's *Greece* guide.

KRITSOTOPOULA, THE CRETAN HERO

The rousing tale of the beautiful and heroic Cretan girl Kritsotopoula (child of Kritsa) may have gained in the telling over the years, but there's a novel and a film in there somewhere. Kritsotopoula's real name was Rhodanthe and she lived in Kritsa in the early years of the 19th century during the Ottoman occupation of Crete. She was said to have a beautiful singing voice and it was her singing that one day caught the attention of a drunken Turkish officer who attempted to push his way into her house. Rhodanthe's mother resisted his attempts and was stabbed to death. The soldier then abducted Rhodanthe, but later that night, while he slept, Rhodanthe slit his throat with the knife that had killed her mother. She then cut off her long hair, dressed in male clothes and took off for the mountains to join the Cretan freedom fighters, who assumed that she was a young man from Kritsa. In 1823, Rhodanthe distinguished herself in a fierce battle with the Turks near Ancient Lato. She was shot in the chest and carried to the safety of a church where she died. Initial efforts to staunch the wounds revealed her sex and there-after she became the revered Kritsotopoula, a classic symbol of Cretan resistance. As well as a bust in Kritsa's Plateia Melinas Merkouri, there is a bas-relief on local stone by the English sculptor Nigel Ratcliffe-Springall, sited in an enclosure on the way to Lato. It depicts the dying Kritsotopoula in the arms of her father, a local priest.

Shopping

Aroma Coffee Shop   FOOD & DRINK
(Plateia Venizelou 24) Just along from Jane's Fishmarket, this aromatic shop has a selection of ground coffee, biscuits, sweets, nuts, wines and spirits, as well as beautiful handmade copper *briki* (coffee pots) for sale.

Marieli   ARTS & CRAFTS
(28 Octovriou 33) A quirky little gift store with a range of Greek handicrafts and jewellery.

Ceramica   CERAMICS
(Paleologou Konstantinou) Handmade pottery copies of museum artefacts. Can arrange postal deliveries.

Kerazoza   ARTS & CRAFTS
(Koundourou 42) Handmade masks, marionettes and figurines derived from ancient Greek theatre, along with some good-quality sculptures, ceramics and jewellery by local artisans.

ℹ Information

Anna Karteri Bookshop (Koundourou 5 & Oktovriou) Well stocked with maps, guide books and literature in English and other languages. The shop has access from both streets.

E-Net (Kapetan Kozyri 10; per hr €2; ☉9am-6am) Gaming and internet access.

General Hospital (Knossou 3) On the west side of town at the top of the steep Paleologou Konstantinou.

Municipal tourist office (www.agiosnikolaos .gr; ☉8am-9.30pm Apr-Nov) Opposite the north side of the bridge; has helpful information and maps, changes money and assists with accommodation.

National Bank of Greece (Nikolaou Plastira) Has a 24-hour exchange machine.

Peripou Café (28 Oktovriou 13; per hr €4; ☉9am-2am; 📶) Has computers and wi-fi.

Post office (28 Oktovriou 9; ☉7.30am-2pm Mon-Fri)

Tourist police (Erythrou Stavrou 47; ☉7.30am-2.30pm Mon-Fri)

ℹ Getting There & Away

Buses leave from Agios Nikolaos' **bus station** (☎28410 22234; www.crete-buses.gr) for Elounda (€1.70, 20 minutes, 16 daily), Ierapetra (€3.80, one hour, seven daily), Iraklio (€7.10, 1½ hours, 18 daily), Kritsa (€1.60, 15 minutes, 10 daily), Lasithi Plateau (Dikteon Cave; €5.80, three hours, two daily) and Sitia (€7.60, 1½ hours, seven daily). You can catch the Elounda bus at a stop opposite the tourist information centre. A local bus (every half hour) can also be boarded here for the main bus station.

ℹ Getting Around

Typical **taxi** (☎28410 24100) charges include Elounda (€13), Plaka (€18), Kritsa (€13) and Lato (€16).

Car- and motorcycle-hire outlets can be found on 28 Oktovriou and the northern waterfront.
Club Cars (☎28410 25868; www.clubcars.net; 28 Oktovriou 30) has cars for hire from about €30 per day.

Manolis Bikes (☎28410 24940; 25 Martiou 12) has a huge range of scooters, motorcycles

ordinariness to the village, and locals do a fine job of catering for visitors, regardless of their 'celebrity'. The pleasant but unremarkable town beach, to the north of the port, can get very crowded. On the south side of Elounda an artificial causeway leads to the Kolokytha Peninsula.

🏃 Activities

Ferries go regularly to Spinalonga Island from Elounda. Numerous boats offer other trips around the area. They operate through a cooperative from the harbour quay.

Blue Dolphin Diving Centre　　　DIVING
(☑28410 41802; www.dive-bluedolphin.com; dive €44) The area around Elounda offers excellent diving. Try this PADI centre at the Grecotel Elounda Village hotel.

🍴 Eating

 Oceanis　　　CRETAN €€
(☑28410 42246; mains €6.50-16) This restaurant is tucked away around the corner from Elounda's main square on the road to Plaka and between the town's two small local beaches. Enthusiastic owner Adonis Bebelakis cooks for pleasure as well as profit, refrains from overcrowding his tables, and sources his local raw materials with care. The style is slow cooking of Cretan specialities including such classics such as oven-cooked lamb with garlic and sweet wine and Bebelakis family favourites such as *melidzanes tis mamas* (slices of aubergine baked with tomatoes, hard cheese and spearmint).

Kalidon　　　CRETAN €€
(Akti Olountis; mains €5-15) Boasting a floating pontoon deck for diners, the harbour-side Kalidon turns over a decent selection of fish and meat standards. There's a mixed fish dish at €19 for one or €37 for two.

Megaro　　　GREEK €
(fish per kg up to €45, mains €5.50-8) Located on the corner of the main square, this popular place benefits from the fresh fish supplied by the owner's own boat.

Paradosiako　　　GREEK €
(☑28410 42444; mains €5.50-8.50) Catering for mainstream tastes on the way north from the centre of town, this busy place offers decent grilled and oven-baked meat dishes.

🍷 Drinking & Entertainment

There are several cheerful bars and clubs at Elounda although things are still fairly low key.

Katafygio　　　BAR
Known for its Cretan and Greek music nights and occasional belly-dancing sessions, this bar is at the southern end of the Elounda waterfront and is housed in a former carob-processing plant.

Alyggos Bar　　　BAR
A popular tourist bar on the main street opposite the harbour car park, Alyggos has an impressive display of soccer jumpers on its walls and shows top matches on its big-screen TV.

Babel　　　BAR
(Akti Vritomartidos) Attractive decor and an upbeat tone make Babel a cool venue for drinks. It's just along from the prominent clock tower on the harbour.

ℹ️ Information

The main square of Elounda is something of a large car park (parking €1 per hour, six hours €3.50), but it overlooks an attractive fishing harbour still devoted to working boats. The bus stops at the square, and the post office and a couple of ATMs are located here.

Babel Internet Café (Akti Vritomartidos, per hr €2) The Babel bar's other facility.

Municipal tourist office (☑28410 42464; ⊙8am-11pm Jun-Oct) Helps with accommodation and information, and changes money.

Olous Travel (☑28410 41324) Handles air and boat tickets and finds accommodation.

Trilogy (A Papandreou 9) An attractive craft and gift shop that offers photocopying alongside its selection of books, stationery and artefacts.

ℹ️ Getting There & Around

Boats cross to Spinalonga every half-hour (return adult/child €12/6).

There are 13 buses daily from Agios Nikolaos to Elounda (€1.70, 20 minutes).

There's a **taxi booth** (☑28410 41151) in the main square. The fare is €13 to Agios Nikolaos and €7 to Plaka.

Cars, motorcycles and scooters can be hired at **Elounda Travel** (☑28410 41800; www .eloundatravel.gr), which has several offices in town including one in the main square. High season prices for cars range from €47 to €105 per day.

Kolokytha Peninsula
Χερσόνησος Κολοκύθα

Opposite Elounda is the Kolokytha Peninsula. The narrow isthmus that once linked
it to the mainland sank as a result of
the earthquakes that have repeatedly
devastated Crete. A low causeway now
makes Kolokytha an emphatic peninsula.
Ancient Olous, which was the port of
Lato, stood on and around the original
isthmus. Olous was a Minoan settlement
that flourished from 3000 to 900 BC and
was an important trade centre. It appears
to have been destroyed by the Saracens in
the 9th century.

Most of the ruins lie beneath the water
on either side of the causeway and have
made the area a popular place for snorkelling. Many birds nest here and pass
through in spring and autumn. The
remains of an early Christian mosaic,
portraying dolphins, lies within an
enclosure near the causeway.

Coming from Agios Nikolaos the causeway and peninsula are reached as you
enter Elounda, by turning off the main road
just beyond the prominent yellow signs of
the Elounda Rent a Car offices and opposite
Mam's House snack bar. It's a tight turn.

On the eastern side of the Kolokytha
Peninsula there is a sandy beach 1km from
the causeway's end reached by a narrow
dirt track.

Plaka Πλάκα
POP 50

The small village of Plaka, 5km north of
Elounda, used to supply the leper colony
on Spinalonga Island and is now famous
internationally in the wake of the success of
the novel and television series, *To Nisi* (see
boxed text, p158).

Plaka retains some charm in spite of all
the attention. There's a reasonable stretch of
pebble beach and, perfectly framed, across
the water is *To Nisi* itself, with all its reso-
nance. The onshore focus of Plaka is a handful of busy and quite pricey tavernas. They
are located in a row of attractive stone buildings on a paved promenade that overlooks
the sea and Spinalonga.

Ask around the village or at one of the
tavernas about boats to Spinalonga Island
(about €10 return).

The popular waterfront **Taverna Giorgos**
(mains €7-16) offers decent fish dishes with
prices at about €70 per kilo as well as a
range of Cretan specialities.

Spinalonga Island
Νήσος Σπιναλόγκα

Spinalonga Island (see boxed text, p158)
and its **fortress** (admission €3; ☺10am-
6pm) lies in a picturesque setting just off
the northern tip of the Kolokytha Peninsula and opposite the onshore village of
Plaka. With the explosion of interest in
Spinalonga in the wake of the novel *The
Island*, and its television series, you're unlikely to feel lonely on the island. There's
a reconstructed section of a street from
the period featured in the novel and,
although tour group leaders stir up a fine
old babel, you can still enjoy a very pleasant
stroll round the island passing evocative
ruins of churches, turrets and other buildings. There's also a cafe and souvenir
shops.

Regular excursion boats visit Spinalonga
from Agios Nikolaos (from €15). Ferries also
run from Elounda (€12) and Plaka (€10).

Milatos Μύλατος
POP 400

Milatos, the north coast's easternmost
beach, is a fairly low-key place in contrast to
the heavily developed coastal strip between
it and Iraklio. The village of Milatos itself is
2km inland from the pebbly beach and its
straggle of tavernas and rooms.

There are two good fish tavernas,
Panorama and **To Meltemi**, at either end
of the beach.

The intriguing **Milatos Cave** is about
3km east of the village and is well signposted. It was here in 1823, during Crete's
famous bid for union with Greece, that
an estimated 2500 local people hid in the
cave as Turkish troops ravaged the area.
The cave is located high on a cliff above a
lonely gorge. The trapped Cretans held out
for over two weeks before attempting an
escape, only to be slaughtered or sold into
slavery. There is a tiny church in the mouth
of the cave. The cave is reached along a delightful walkway above the gorge. Take a
torch and be very careful of the sometimes
slippery surfaces underfoot.

LASITHI PLATEAU
ΟΡΟΠΕΔΙΟ ΛΑΣΙΘΙΟΥ

The Lasithi Plateau, 900m above sea level, is a vast expanse of green fields interspersed with pear and apple orchards and almond trees. It is more of a plain than a plateau, sitting as it does in a huge depression amid the rock-studded mountains of the Dikti range. Lasithi would have been a stunning sight in the days when it was dotted with some 20,000 metal windmills with white canvas sails. The original stone windmills were built by the Venetians in the 17th century. There are less than 5000 windmills standing today, most having been replaced by less-attractive but convenient mechanical pumps. Skeletal in winter, some of the windmills blossom in summer with petal-like sails. This is more of a tourism imperative, although increasing interest in energy saving has led to municipal grants being offered to encourage the use of wind power.

The Lasithi Plateau's rich soil has been cultivated since Minoan times. Following an uprising against Venetian rule in the 13th century, the Venetians expelled the inhabitants of Lasithi and destroyed their orchards. The plateau lay abandoned for 200 years until food shortages forced the Venetians to recolonise and cultivate the area and to build the irrigation trenches and wells that still service the region.

The plateau relies heavily on tourism and packed tour buses pass through regularly in summer, but this is essentially an agricultural area with many villages still cluttered with the down-to-earth machinery and detritus of farming.

The main approaches to the plateau are from Iraklio, via the coast road east and then by turning south, just before Hersonisos. The best approach from Agios Nikolaos is via Neapoli. The plateau is a popular **bike route**, utilising the intersecting tracks across the central plain. Enterprising cycle tour operators in Iraklio and Agios Nikolaos ferry bikes and cyclists to the plateau – there are bike trailer signs everywhere – but you can also get bikes locally.

From Iraklio there are daily buses to Tzermiado (€6.50, two hours), Agios Georgios (€6.90, two hours) and Psyhro (€6.50, 2¼ hours). There are also buses to the villages from Agios Nikolaos (p156).

Tzermiado Τζερμιάδο
POP 762

Tzermiado (dzer-mee-*ah*-do) is a likeable and down-to-earth farming town. It's the largest and most important town on the Lasithi Plateau and has a fair number of visitors from tour buses going to the Dikteon Cave. Its main hotels and eateries are remarkably well run and of good quality. A number of shops sell rugs and embroideries.

There is only one main road running through town. The general layout of Tzermiado is a touch confusing, but locals are happy to give directions. There are a couple of ATMs and a post office in the main square.

As you approach Tzermiado from the south a sign on the right indicates the **Kronios Cave**. The name Trapeza is a more authentic label. The cave is thought to have been used from the earliest human period as some form of shrine, and during the Minoan period it was used as a grave site. A rough track of about half a kilometre can be walked from the main road to where a couple of hundred steps rise to the cave's narrow entrance. A powerful torch is advised and you need to be surefooted on the uneven and occasionally muddy surfaces inside the cave.

On the outskirts of Tzermiado is well-run **Kourites** (www.kourites.eu; mains €6-12), a big taverna with a pleasant garden that offers local dishes including roast lamb and suckling pig, cooked in a wood-fired oven. They do vegetarian options also. There are clean and simple rooms above the taverna and in a nearby hotel (doubles €40, breakfast €5). Enquire about free use of bicycles. Attached to the **Argoulias Apartments** (28440 22754) is a lovely restaurant that offers traditional Lasithi cuisine at its best and it's open to non-residents. Look for signs to Argoulias on the entrance to Tzermiado coming from the east.

Agios Georgios
Αγιος Γεώργιος
POP 541

Agios Georgios (*agh*-ios ye-*or*-gios) is a tiny village on the southern side of the Lasithi Plateau and the most pleasant to stay in. If you have your own bicycle, you can base yourself here and explore the plateau at leisure.

The village also boasts a **Folklore Museum** (☏28440 31462; admission €3; ⊙10am-4pm Apr-Oct) housed in the original home belonging to the Katsapakis family. Exhibits are spread over five rooms and include some intriguing personal photos of writer Nikos Kazantzakis.

Taverna Rea (mains €5-7) is a bright little place full of local artefacts. It's on the main street and offers breakfasts and well-cooked Cretan staples, including vegetarian dishes. There are rooms for rent above the taverna (€30).

Psyhro Ψυχρό

POP 302

Psyhro (psi-*hro*) is the closest village to the Dikteon Cave. It has one main street, a sword-waving memorial statue, a few tavernas, and plenty of souvenir shops selling 'authentic' rugs and mats of largely non-Cretan origin. Buses to Psyhro stop at the northern end of the town from where it's about a kilometre's walk uphill to the cave. (The bus is known to divert to the cave car park if lots of passengers are going there, but do not bank on it.)

The long-established **Stavros** (grills €5-9) serves a range of traditional home-style Cretan dishes such as roast lamb, and they do a tasty bean soup. Ask at the **Petros Taverna** (mains €6-8.50), opposite the entrance to the Dikteon Cave, about walks in the area, including the long hike up to the summit of Mt Dikti.

Dikteon Cave
Δικταίον Αντρον

Lasithi's major sight is the **Dikteon Cave** (adult/child €4/2; ⊙8am-6pm Jun-Oct, 8am-2.30pm Nov-May) just outside the village of Psyhro. Here, according to legend, Rhea hid the newborn Zeus from Cronos, his offspring-gobbling father.

The cave, also known as the Psyhro Cave, covers 2200 sq metres and features both stalactites and stalagmites. It was excavated in 1900 by the British archaeologist David Hogarth, who found numerous votives indicating it was a place of cult worship. These finds are housed in the Archaeological Museum (p111) in Iraklio.

The cave was used for cult worship from the Middle Minoan period until the 1st century AD. Stone tablets inscribed with Linear A script were found here, along with religious bronze and clay figurines.

From the upper cave a steep staircase leads down to the more interesting lower cave. In the back on the left is a smaller chamber where legend has it that Zeus was born. There is a larger hall on the right, which has small stone basins filled with water that Zeus allegedly drank from in one section and a spectacular stalagmite that came to be known as the Mantle of Zeus in the other. The entire cave is illuminated, although not particularly well, so watch your step.

It is a steep 15-minute (800m) walk up to the cave entrance. You can take the fairly rough but shaded track on the right with views over the plateau or the less interesting, unshaded paved trail on the left of the car park. You can also let a donkey do the hard work (€10/15 one way/return).

NORTHEAST COAST

Gournia Γουρνιά

The compelling Late Minoan site of **Gournia** (☏28410 24943; admission €3; ⊙8.30am-3pm Tue-Sun), pronounced goor-*nyah*, lies just off the coast road, 19km southeast of Agios Nikolaos. The ruins, which date from 1550 to 1450 BC, are made up of a town overlooked by a palace. Gournia's palace was far less ostentatious than the ones at Knossos and Phaestos as it was the residence of an overlord rather than a king. The town is a network of streets and stairways flanked by houses with walls up to 2m high. Domestic, agricultural and trade implements found on the site indicate that Gournia was a thriving little community.

South of the palace is a large rectangular **court**, which was connected to a network of paved stone streets. Nearby is a large **stone slab** used for sacrificing bulls. The room to the west has a stone **kernos** (large earthen dish) ringed with 32 depressions and was probably used for cult activity. North of the palace was a **Shrine of the Minoan Snake Goddess**, which proved to be a rich trove of objects from the Postpalatial period. Notice the storage rooms, workrooms and dwellings to the north and east of the site. The buildings were two-storey structures with the storage and workrooms in the basement and the living quarters on the 1st floors.

Sitia and Ierapetra buses from Agios Nikolaos can drop you at the site.

Mohlos Μόχλος

POP 87

Mohlos (*moh*-los) is a fishing village reached by a 5km winding road from the Sitia–Agios Nikolaos highway. The approach is hardly scenic however, as the mountain above Mohlos has been thoroughly torn apart by a series of major quarries, leaving tiers of scarred white rock and rubble. Half-close your eyes and the quarries might almost look Minoan in their raw symmetry. Keep heading down and the delightful Mohlos makes up for it all. In antiquity, it was joined to the small island that is now 200m offshore and was once a thriving Early Minoan community from the period 3000 to 2000 BC. Excavations still continue sporadically on both Mohlos Island and at Mohlos village.

Mohlos has a small pebble and grey-sand beach, simple accommodation, and tavernas that enjoy a good reputation for fresh local fish and seafood. They are packed with locals on weekends to prove it. There's a mini-market and some gift shops, and the centre has wi-fi connection. Follow signs round left and then right towards the sea and to a final left turn to a parking area.

When swimming, beware of strong currents further out in the channel between the island and the mainland shore.

✗ Eating

Ta Kochilia   GREEK €€
(✆28430 94432; mains €4.50-16) Famed for its sea-urchin salad (available only in high summer) this great taverna is on the waterfront. Excellent fish dishes are a feature with the likes of white bream at a reasonable €16 a portion. Meat eaters can enjoy lamb with artichokes in a lemon sauce, and for vegetarians the oven-baked feta with tomatoes, peppers, oregano and olive oil takes some beating.

To Bogazi   GREEK €€
(✆28430 94200; mezedhes €2-7, mains €4.70-10.50) Another very fine taverna serving a big list of mezedhes and main dishes such as rabbit in a wine sauce and mussels with tomato sauce and feta.

There is no public transport to Mohlos. Buses between Sitia and Agios Nikolaos will drop you off at the Mohlos turn-off. You'll need to hitch or walk the 6km to the village, steeply down and steeply back.

Sitia Σητεία

POP 9257

Sitia (si-*tee*-a) is an attractive seaside town with a big open harbour backed by a wide promenade lined with tavernas and cafes. It's a friendly place where tourism is fairly low-key and where agriculture and commerce are the mainstays.

A sandy beach skirts a wide bay to the east of town. Sitia mainly attracts French and Greek tourists, but at the height of the season the town retains its relaxed atmosphere.

Above the town is the **Kazarma** (fort; admission free; ⊙8.30am-3pm), which was a garrison under the Venetians. The only remains are of fortifications that once protected the town. The site is now used as an open-air venue.

Sitia makes a good transit point for ferries to the Dodecanese islands.

History

Archaeological excavations indicate that there were neolithic settlements around Sitia and an important Minoan settlement at nearby Petras. The original settlement was

SITIA'S FRENCH CONNECTION

History is often written across the facades of old buildings. In the quiet streets of Sitia's old town, where pebbled steps amble gently uphill from the waterfront, occasional examples of Venetian architecture enliven the streetscape. On the corner of G Arkadiou and Metaxaki streets, look for a Venetian building, complete with handsome wooden balcony. Above the splendid door case is inscribed in French, '8th Regiment...Salle de Rapports'. This was the administrative base of a French garrison, part of the *Corps d'occupation de Creta* that was based in Sitia during the transition from Ottoman power in the final years of the 19th century.

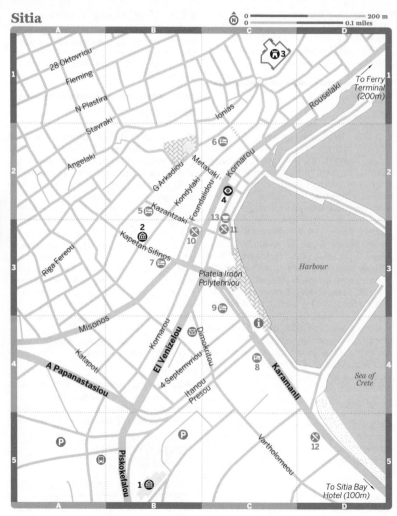

destroyed and eventually abandoned after an earthquake in 1700 BC.

In the Greco-Roman era there was a town called Iteia in or around modern Sitia, although its exact site has not yet been located. In Byzantine times Sitia became a bishopric, which was then eliminated by the Saracens in the 9th century. Under the Venetians, Sitia became the most important port in eastern Crete and their name for the port, La Sitia, is said to have given the Lasithi area its name. The town was hit by a disastrous earthquake in 1508 – a blow from which it never really recovered – and the Turkish

blockade of Sitia in 1648 marked its death knell. The remaining inhabitants fled and the town was destroyed. It was not until the late 19th century when the Turks decided to make Sitia an administrative centre that

MOVING ON?

For tips, recommendations and reviews, head to shop.lonelyplanet.com to purchase a downloadable PDF of the Dodecanese chapter from Lonely Planet's *Greece* guide.

Sitia

the town gradually came back to life. Crete's most famous poet, Vitsentzos Kornaros, writer of the epic poem the *Erotokritos*, was born in Sitia in 1614.

◎ Sights

Archaeological Museum MUSEUM
(☏28430 23917; Piskokefalou; admission €2; ◷8.30am-3pm Tue-Sun) This museum houses a well-displayed and important collection of local finds spanning neolithic to Roman times, with emphasis on the Minoan civilisation. Labelling is in English as well as Greek. One of the most significant exhibits is the *Palekastro Kouros* – a figure pieced together from fragments made of hippopotamus tusks and adorned with gold. Finds from the palace at Zakros include a wine press, a bronze saw, jars, cult objects and pots that are clearly scorched from the great fire that destroyed the palace. Among the most valuable objects are the Linear A tablets, which reflect the palace's administrative function.

Folklore Museum MUSEUM
(☏28430 28300; Kapetan Sifinos 28; admission €2; ◷10am-1pm Mon-Fri) This museum displays a collection of local weaving and other exhibits of folk life.

Petras ANCIENT SITE
About 2km southeast of town on a low hill overlooking the sea are the remains of this

Minoan palace and of later buildings. The site is always accessible. There is limited parking.

★ Festivals & Events

Kornaria Festival PERFORMING ARTS
This festival runs from mid-July to the end of August, with concerts, folk dancing and theatre productions staged in the Kazarma and other venues. Posters around town announce the events, some of which are free.

✗ Eating & Drinking

TOP CHOICE ❯ Balcony INTERNATIONAL €€€
(☏28430 25084; www.balcony-restaurant.com; Foundalidou 19; mains €11.90-18.90) The most stylish dining in Sitia is on the first floor of a neoclassical building where owner-chef, Tonya Karandinou, rules supreme with a sense of theatre. Cretan-based cuisine, with Mexican and Asian influences, ranges from grilled squid to tender goat. Fine Greek wines complement it all.

Oinodeion MEZEDHES €
(El Venizelou 157; mains €5-8) Kitted out with old-fashioned ornaments on the walls, this very local place sits quietly alongside more glitzy cafes on the main waterfront. There's a good range of mezedhes to go with meat and fish standards.

Sergiani GREEK €€
(Karamanli 38; mains €6.50-8.50) On the quiet southern end of the waterfront, this traditional place uses well-sourced local ingredients and wood-burning cooking methods. Its local fish is very good.

Nouvelle Boutique CAFE
(El Venizelou 161) Mainstream sounds range throughout the day and deep into the night at this popular waterfront cafe-bar.

❶ Information

The town's main square is Plateia Iroön Polytehniou – recognisable by its palm trees and statue of a dying soldier. There are lots of ATMs and places to change money. The bus station is inland near the museum. Ferries dock about 600m north of Iroön Polytechniou.

Akasti Travel (☏28430 29444; www.akasti. gr; Kornarou 93) Very helpful for information, accommodation, car hire enquiries and ferry tickets.

Java Internet Café (☏28430 22263; Kornarou 113; internet per hr €2; ◷9am-late)

LASITHI SITIA

National Bank of Greece (A Papanastasiou & Katapoti) Has a 24-hour exchange machine.

Post office (Dimokritou; ⊗7.30am-3pm)

Tourist office (☑28430 28300; Karamanli; ⊗9.30am-2.30pm & 5-8.30pm Mon-Fri, 9.30am-2.30pm Sat) On the promenade. Winter openings may be uncertain.

Tourist police (☑28430 24200; Therisou 31) At the main police station.

❶ Getting There & Away

Air

Sitia's **airport** (☑28430 24666) has an expanded international-size runway, but at the time of writing international flights had yet to operate.

Aegean Airlines (www.aegeanair.com) has five weekly flights to Athens (€71, one hour). **Olympic Air** (www.olympicair.com) has daily flights, except Friday, to Kassos (€48, 20 minutes) and then on to Karpathos (€54, one hour) and Rhodes (€54, two hours).

Boat

Aegeon Pelagos Sea Lines (EP; ☑28210 24000, Hania) has two ferries a week from Sitia to Iraklio (€16, three hours), Milos (€25, 11½ hours), Piraeus (€37, 17 hours), Santorini (€25, 7½ hours) and Rhodes (€29, nine hours 20 minutes). There are four ferries a week to Kassos (€11, 2½ hours) and Karpathos (€19, four hours). Several of these departures are in the early hours of the morning.

Bus

From Sitia's **bus station** (☑28430 22272) there are six buses per day to Ierapetra (€6.30, 1½ hours), seven buses to Iraklio (€14.70, three hours) via Agios Nikolaos (€7.60, 1½ hours), four to Vaï (€3.60, 30 minutes), and two to Kato Zakros (€4.80, one hour) via Palekastro (€2.80, 45 minutes) and Zakros (€5.20, one hour). The buses to Vaï and Kato Zakros only run between May and October.

❶ Getting Around

To/From the Airport

The airport (signposted) is 1.5km out of town. There is no airport bus; a taxi costs about €8.

Car & Motorcycle

Car- and motorcycle-hire outlets are mostly found on Papandreou and Itanou. Try **Club Cars** (☑28430 25104; Papandreou 4).

Moni Toplou Μονή Τοπλού

East of Sitia, the imposing **Moni Toplou** (☑28430 61226; admission €3; ⊗10am-5pm Apr-Oct, Fri only Nov-Mar) looks more like a fortress than a monastery – a necessity imposed by the dangers it faced at the time of its construction. It is one of the most historically significant and progressive monasteries in Crete. The middle of the 15th century was marked by piracy, banditry and constant rebellions. The monks defended themselves with all the means at their disposal, including a heavy gate, cannons (the name Toplou is Turkish for 'with a cannon') and small holes for pouring boiling oil onto the heads of their attackers. Nevertheless, it was sacked by pirates in 1498, looted by the Knights of Malta in 1530, pillaged by the Turks in 1646 and captured by the Turks in 1821.

Moni Toplou had always been active in the cause of Cretan independence. Under the Turkish occupation, a secret school operated in the monastery, and its reputation for hiding rebels led to severe reprisals. During WWII, Abbot Silingakis was executed after sheltering resistance leaders operating an underground radio transmitter.

The monastery's star attraction is undoubtedly the icon *Lord Thou Art Great* by celebrated Cretan artist Ioannis Kornaros. Each of the 61 scenes painted on the icon is beautifully worked out and inspired by a phrase from the Orthodox prayer that begins, 'Lord, Thou Art Great'.

A **museum** tells the monastery's history and has a collection of icons, engravings and books, as well as weapons and military souvenirs from the resistance.

The well-stocked shop sells the monastery's award-winning organic olive oil and wine.

The monastery is a 3km walk from the Sitia–Palekastro road. Buses can drop you off at the junction. A taxi from Sitia costs about €22, but depends on the length of time you stay at the monastery.

EAST COAST

Vaï Βάι

The beach at Vaï, 24km from Sitia on Crete's east coast, is famous for the large grove of *Phoenix theophrastii* palms that lies behind it. The word Vaï is a local word for palm fronds. One explanation for the presence of the palms is that they sprouted from date pits spread by either Egyptian soldiers, Roman legionaries or feasting pirates.

In July and August, you'll need to arrive early to appreciate both palms and beach. The place is packed and the beach is covered in sun-beds and umbrellas (€6). Jet skis prattle and posture offshore.

At the south end of the beach stone steps lead up to a gazebo lookout. Follow your nose about a kilometre beyond here and a rocky path descends eventually to a less crammed beach, or head over the hill to the north of Vaï Beach for a series of clothes-optional coves.

The **Restaurant-Caféteria Vai** (mains €5-7.50) is reasonable, although busy, of course.

There are buses to Vaï from Sitia (€3.70, one hour, five daily) from May to October. There is a car park where buses stop. A few hundred metres further is a beachside car park (€3).

Itanos Ἰτανος

About 3km north of Vaï is the ancient Minoan site of Itanos. It may appear fairly forlorn today, but this was an important site. Inhabited from about 1500 BC, Itanos was clearly prosperous by the 7th century BC since it was an important trading post for exports to the Near and Middle East. It was at odds with local rivals such as Praisos and later with Ierapetra (then known as Ieraptyna). Poke around and you will find remains of two early Christian basilicas and a Hellenistic wall. The basilica ruin, on high ground towards the sea, is littered with toppled columns. Look for one stone base marked with circular motifs. You can swim from coves nearby.

Palekastro Παλαίκαστρο

POP 1380

Palekastro (pah-leh-kas-tro) is an unpretentious farming village underpinned with low-key tourism. It lies in a rocky landscape interspersed with fields and is within easy distance of a beach at Kouremenos as well as the beaches of Moni Toplou and Vaï. The village has most services and facilities. If you want to explore widely your own transport is more or less essential.

About 1km from town, towards Hiona Beach, is the archaeological site of

Roussolakkos, where archaeologists believe a major Minoan palace is buried. This is where the *Palekastro Kouros* – now residing in the Archaeological Museum in Sitia – was found.

Tucked away in a back street and sign-posted from the main road, the well-presented **Folk Museum of Palekastro** (admission €2; ☉10am-1pm & 5-8pm Mon-Sat mid-Jun–mid-Oct) is housed in a traditional manor house with displays in the old stables and bakery.

✖ Eating

To Finistrini MEZEDHES €
(mezedhes €2.50-6) About 200m along the Vaï road, this neat little *ouzerie*-cum-*mezedhopoleio* (mezedhes restaurant) dishes up tasty mezedhes that go down well with a shot or 10 of *raki*.

Mythos GREEK €
(mains €5.50-8) This pleasant and popular taverna has a big vegetarian mezedhes selection and traditional *mayirefta,* fish and grills.

❶ Information

The main street forks at the village centre beside a big church with attendant palm trees. The **tourist office** (☑28430 61546; ☉9am-5pm Mon-Fri May-Oct) has information on rooms and transport. There's an ATM next door and further on a postal agent, a bank with ATM, and the very useful Argo Bookshop, which has internet access (€1 per half hour) and can also do photocopying. The shop has stationery, upmarket gifts, new books and a book exchange. The bus stop is in the centre of town.

❶ Getting There & Away

There are five buses per day from Sitia that stop at Palekastro on the way to Vaï. There are also two buses daily from Sitia to Palekastro (€2.80, 45 minutes) that continue to Kato Zakros (€5.20, one hour).

Around Palekastro

Kouremenos, north of Palekastro, is a pebble beach with good shallow-water swimming and excellent windsurfing. You can hire boards from **Freak Surf Station** (☑6979253861; www.freak-surf.com; board hire per week €240, 2hr lesson €60) on the beach.

Hiona Beach is another quiet choice to the east, with some great fish tavernas.

Zakros & Kato Zakros

Ζάκρος & Κάτω Ζάκρος

POP 912 & 22

The village of Zakros (*zah*-kros), 45km southeast of Sitia, seems a mere prelude to the compelling Kato Zakros 7km below on the coast, but the village is an important agricultural centre in its own right and it's a lively place where the *kafeneia* and *ouzeries* are always animated. Zakros is the starting point for the trail through the Zakros Gorge, known as the **Valley of the Dead**, which takes its name from the ancient burial sites in the numerous caves dotting the canyon walls.

The setting of **Kato Zakros** (*kah*-to *zah*-kros) is simply awesome. A long winding road snakes downhill from Zakros through rugged terrain. Halfway down it takes a big loop to the left and reveals a vast curtain wall of mountains ahead; the highest, Traóstalos (515m) and Lakómata (378m) dominate the skyline and the red jaws of the **Zakros Gorge** breach the foreground cliffs. On the low ground behind the pebbly beach and its huddle of tavernas, the remarkable ruins of the Minoan **Zakros Palace** are clearly defined. Add to all of this the constraints on development and the general tranquillity of the area and this is the place for escapism. Don't expect a dizzying nightlife scene, but who's complaining?

✖ Eating

A clutch of beachside tavernas compete for custom with some vigour.

Akrogiali Taverna　　　　　GREEK €€
(mains €5.50-10) Enjoy the seaside ambience while you tuck into fish dishes and decent house wine with other classic Cretan options available.

Zakros Palace

(mains €4.50-9) Local vegetables and other produce form the basis of this popular eatery's Greek staples that include rabbit *stifadho*, a rabbit stew that includes tomatoes and red wine. It's also noted for its fish dishes and vegetarian options.

ℹ️ Getting There & Away

There are buses to Zakros from Sitia via Palekastro (€4.50, one hour, two daily). From June to August, the buses continue to Kato Zakros (€5.20, one hour 20 minutes). Buses to Kato Zakros only run between May and October.

Zakros Palace

Although **Zakros Palace** (Kato Zakros; admission €3; ☺8am-7.30pm Jul-Oct, 8.30am-3pm Nov-Jun) was the last Minoan palace to have been discovered (1962), the excavations proved remarkably fruitful.

The exquisite rock-crystal vase and stone bull's head now in Iraklio's Archaeological Museum were found at Zakros, along with a treasure trove of Minoan antiquities. Ancient Zakros, the smallest of Crete's four palatial complexes, was a major port in Minoan times, trading with Egypt, Syria, Anatolia and Cyprus. Some parts of the palace complex are submerged.

If you enter the palace complex on the southern side you will first come to the **workshops** for the palace. The **King's Apartment** and **Queen's Apartment** are to the right of the entrance. Next to the King's Apartment is the **Cistern Hall**, which once had a cistern in the centre surrounded by a colonnaded balustrade. Seven steps descended to the floor of the cistern, which may have been a swimming pool, an aquarium or a pool for a sacred boat. Nearby, the **Central Court** was the focal point of the whole palace. Notice the altar base in the northwestern corner of the court; there was also a **well** in the southeast corner of the court at the bottom of eight steps. When the site was excavated the well contained the preserved remains of olives that may have been offered to the deities.

Adjacent to the central court is the **Hall of Ceremonies** in which two rhytons (ceremonial drinking vessels) were found. To the south is the **Banquet Hall**, so named for the quantity of wine vases found there. To the north of the central court is the **kitchen**. The column bases probably supported the dining room above. To the northwest of the central court is another **light well** and to the left of the banquet hall is the **Lustral Basin**, which once contained a magnificent marble amphora. The Lustral Basin served as a washroom for those entering the nearby **Central Shrine**. You can still see a ledge and a niche in the south wall for the ceremonial idols.

Below the Lustral Basin is the **Treasury**, which yielded nearly a hundred jars and rhytons. Next to the treasury is the **Archive Room**, which once contained Linear A record tablets. Close to the northwest corner of the North East Court is the **bathroom** with a cesspit.

Xerokambos Ξερόκαμπος

POP 28

Xerokambos (kse-*ro*-kam-bos) is a quiet resort and farming settlement on the far southeastern flank of Crete. Its isolation means that tourism is pretty much low-key, and it's at its busiest in July and August. The attractions for visitors are the two splendid beaches. There are a few scattered tavernas and some studio accommodation.

There are no buses to Xerokambos. From Zakros there's a signposted turn-off to the resort via 8km of winding surfaced road. The continuation to Ziros is through some very wild country and some very wild bends.

SOUTH COAST

Ierapetra Ιεράπετρα

POP 15,323

Ierapetra (yeh-*rah*-pet-rah) is a cheerful, down-to-earth seafront town and is the commercial centre of southeastern Crete's substantial greenhouse-based agri-industry. The town's approach is through a fairly discouraging countryside crammed full of greenhouses interspersed with storage depots and other buildings. Persevere, however, as Ierapetra has a lot to offer and an impressive history.

This was an important city for the Dorians and the last major outpost to fall to the Romans, who made it a major port of call in their conquest of Egypt. The city languished under the Venetians, who built the fortress at the western end of the harbour.

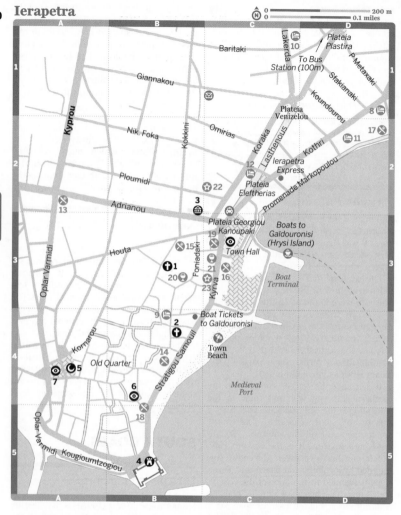

Even Napoleon is said to have stopped off on his progress towards Egypt.

There are tavernas, restaurants and chic cafes along the waterfront, an archaeological collection, a Venetian fort at the harbour and the odd remnant of a Turkish quarter. The town beach and surrounding beaches are reasonable, the nightlife lively and the overall ambience is satisfyingly Cretan.

From Ierapetra you can visit the low-lying sandy island of Gaïdouronisi (also known as Hrysi).

Every Saturday there is a street **market** on Psilinaki from 7am to 2pm.

○ Sights

Archaeological Collection MUSEUM
(☎28420 28721; Adrianou 2; admission €2; ⊗8.30am-3pm Tue-Sun) Ierapetra's small, but worthwhile, archaeological collection is located in a former school of the Ottoman period. A highlight among a collection of headless classical statuary is an intact statue of the goddess Persephone that dates from the 2nd century AD. Another splendid piece is a big larnax (clay coffin), dated around 1300 BC that is decorated with 12 painted panels showing hunting scenes, an octopus and a chariot procession.

Medieval Fortress   FORTRESS
(admission free; ⊙8.30am-3pm Tue-Sun) South along the waterfront is the medieval fortress, built in the early years of Venetian rule and strengthened by Francesco Morosini in 1626. Climb to the upper walls (watch your footing) for grand views to the eastern mountains.

Old Quarter   NEIGHBOURHOOD
Inland from the fortress is the labyrinthine old quarter, where you will see a **Turkish fountain**, the restored **mosque** with its minaret, and the old churches of **Agios Ioannis** and **Agios Georgios**.

Napoleon's House   NOTABLE BUILDING
This is where the man himself is said to have stayed incognito with a local family when his ship anchored in Crete for one night in 1798 on the way to Egypt. He apparently left a note revealing his identity. To find the building, go down the alleyway to the right of Babis Taverna. The two-storeyed corner building, in exposed stone, has wooden shutters and the number 9 on its door. There is no entry.

Town Beaches   BEACH
The main beach is near the harbour, while a second beach stretches east from the bottom of Patriarhou Metaxaki. Both have coarse, grey sand, but the main beach offers better shade.

🎆 Festivals & Events

Kyrvia Festival   CULTURAL FESTIVAL
Ierapetra's annual Kyrvia Festival runs from July to August and features a program of cultural activities including singing and dancing nights by local folk and popular groups, special concerts by famous artists, film screenings, theatre performances and much singing and dancing in the streets of the old town.

🍴 Eating

Ierapetra has a tradition of *rakadika*, relaxed evening hang-outs where a carafe of *raki* or wine comes with half a dozen or more tasty mezedhes, making it a good value slow-dining experience. You could try **To Kafeneio** opposite the town hall, the popular **Ntoukiani** in Ethnikis Antistaseos, or the modern reincarnation **Pavlis** near the port, where for €3 per carafe you get six or seven plates of mezedhes.

Napoleon   GREEK €€
(Stratigou Samouil 26; mains €4.50-8) This is one of the oldest and most popular establishments in town. It's at the southern end of the waterfront. A mixed fish plate is a good choice, as is the cuttlefish in wine. There's a good selection for vegetarians also.

Porfyra Restaurant   ITALIAN €€
(Promenade Markopoulou 8; mains €5-12) Dine in cool surroundings at the El Greco Hotel's stylish restaurant. They do a nice line in pastas and risottos and good fish dishes also. The cafe section offers bruschetta snacks and pizzas by day.

Taverna Babis   GREEK €€
(Stratigou Samouil 68; mains €6-14) Entertaining decor, including old artefacts, photographs

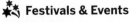
LASITHI IERAPETRA

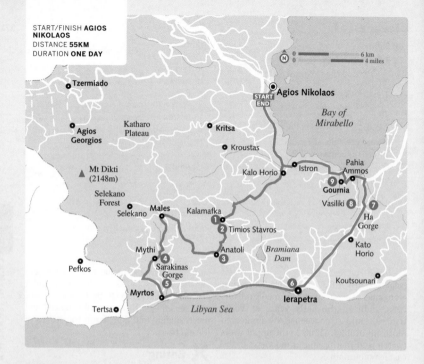

Driving Tour

Mountain Meander

A network of winding roads links tiny villages on the southeastern edge of the Dikteon Mountains within a landscape of rocky pinnacles and escarpments clothed in dense woodland and scrub.

The route from Agios Nikolaos takes you south on the E75 Sitia road. In 7km, at Istron, turn off right through Kalo Horio from where the road climbs steadily into the mountains. Follow signs for the village of ➊ **Kalamafka**. Take time here to climb the steep steps, over 220 of them, to the cave chapel of ➋ **Timios Stavros** on the summit of the rocky pinnacle of Kastelos for spectacular views.

Continue south from Kalamafka for a stroll around the village of ➌ **Anatoli** where a slow decline has been stemmed and where original shopfronts are being preserved and old houses renovated as second homes. Northwest from Anatoli you pass through wild and rocky countryside until the great valley of Sarakinas opens out.

Follow the road south through the valley to Mythi where signs direct you to the ➍ **Sarakinas Gorge**, if you fancy stretching your legs even for a short stroll. Further south you reach the coast at Myrtos. Just east of Myrtos is the ruin of ➎ **Pyrgos**, a Minoan hilltop villa reached by a path.

Continue east from here along the coast road to ➏ **Ierapetra**, through less-than-scenic plastic-greenhouse country. Stop for a short exploration of Ierapetra's pleasant seafront and town centre and then continue north alongside the escarpment of the Thripti Mountains, where views of the dramatic gash of the ➐ **Ha Gorge** dominate the last few kilometres. Turn left after about 10km to visit the small Minoan ruin of ➑ **Vasiliki**. Reach the E75 at Pahia Ammos where a left turn leads back towards Agios Nikolaos past the splendid Minoan site of ➒ **Gournia**.

and a bamboo roof, add colour to this cheerful eatery. There's an impressive list of mezedhes, such as zucchini croquettes and vegetarian pie, and the fish soup is a meal in itself.

I Kalitexnes MIDDLE EASTERN €
(28420 28547; Kyprou 26; mains €4-7) A quirky little place tucked in a side street among everyday shops, Kalitexnes has classic dishes prepared using organic ingredients. There are also spicier dishes such as falafel and kebabs introduced by the Egyptian owner. Closed on Sundays.

Ristorante Pizzeria PIZZA €€
(Promendade Markopoulou 1; mains €5-15) A good choice of classic Greek starters is followed by wood-fired pizzas as well as grilled meat dishes, crepes and local wines.

Drinking & Entertainment

Kyrva is Ierapetra's main nightlife strip, with clubs such as **Privilege** and others catering to locals with non-stop Greek club music. You'll find more nightclubs around the corner on Foniadaki. **Portego** is a classy place for a drink, while **Parados**, behind the museum, is known for jazz. **Prive** is a very laid-back cafe-bar where easy-listening sounds lull the mood even further.

ℹ Information

The bus station is inland at the eastern side of town and there are ATMs around the main square.

Ierapetra Express (☑28420 28673; express@ ier.forthnet.gr; Kothri 2) Central tourist office with friendly service and good information.

Post office (Giannakou 1; ☉7.30am-2pm)

Street Café (Markopoulou 73) There's wi-fi access for customers at this trendy and popular bar-cafe.

ℹ Getting There & Away

There are nine buses per day from Ierapetra's **bus station** (☑28420 28237; Lasthenous) to Iraklio (€11, 2½ hours) via Agios Nikolaos (€3.80, one hour) and Gournia (€1.90, 40 minutes), seven to Sitia (€6.30, 1½ hours) via Koutsounari (for camp sites; €1.60), and seven to Myrtos (€2.20, 30 minutes).

Taxis (☑28420 26600) can take you anywhere for a fixed fare. Fares are posted outside the town-hall rank for destinations including Iraklio (€120), Agios Nikolaos (€48), Sitia (€70) and Myrtos (€24). There is another rank at Plateia Venizelou.

Auto Tours (☑28420 22571; Plateia Plastira) is reliable for car hire.

Gaïdouronisi (Hrysi Island) Γαϊδαρουνήσι (Χρυσή)

Just off the coast of Ierapetra, you will find greater tranquillity at Gaïdouronisi – marketed in Ierapetra as Hrysi or Hrissi (Golden Island) – where there are good sandy beaches, a taverna, and a stand of Lebanon cedars, the only one in Europe. It can get very crowded when the tour boats are in, but you can generally still find a quiet spot.

In summer, **excursion boats** for Gaïdouronisi leave from Ierapetra's quay every morning and return in the afternoon. Most travel agents around the quay sell tickets (about €20).

East of Ierapetra

The decent beaches to the east of Ierapetra tend to be crowded in peak season and you really need a car to explore the area. About 13km east is the lovely beach of **Agias Fotias**.

Much of this coastline has been enveloped by plastic-covered greenhouses and haphazard tourism development, but there are still appealing places. A new stretch of road bypasses **Koutsouras**, but turn off the main road for **Robinsona's** (☑28430 51026; mezedhes €5-7.50; ☉3pm till late), housed in an attractively renovated Venetian-style building. The smart but welcoming interior has some quirky details including a collection of hanging light bulbs. The food is excellent and includes wood-oven pies with savoury fillings.

The fine white sandy beach at the eastern end of **Makrygialos**, 24km from Ierapetra, is one of the best on the southeastern coast. It gets very busy in summer, but the beachside promenade is a cheerful place and there are plenty of cafes and eating places.

Myrtos Μύρτος

POP 622

Myrtos (*myr*-tos) lies 14km west of Ierapetra. It has a devoted clientele who all swear by the area's easygoing ethos and creative vibe. There are no big resort-style hotels and there's a decent patch of beach. The village is framed by little-visited mountains and the coast to the west invites exploration.

There is no post office or bank. Internet access is available at **Prima Travel** (☑28420 51035; www.sunbudget.net; per hr €3.50), which can advise on a range of services and activities around the area.

Myrtos' small **museum** (☑28420 51065; admission free) houses the private collection of a former teacher who sparked the archaeological digs in the area after finding Minoan artefacts on field trips with students. The collection includes Vasiliki pottery from the nearby Minoan sites of **Fournou-Korifi** and **Pyrgos** as well as an impressive model of the Fournou-Korifi site exactly as it was found, with all the pots and items in situ.

There are a number of tavernas and cafes on the waterfront promenade. **Taverna Myrtos** (mains €4-7), attached to Hotel Myrtos, is popular with both locals and tourists for its wide range of mezedhes and *mayirefta*, which include many vegetarian options. The waterfront **Beach** (mains €5-9) is good for mezedhes and for fish dishes, while **Platanos** (mains €4.50-8), beneath its giant plane tree, is a focus of village social life and has live music on many summer evenings. It offers reliable Cretan staples. On the eastern waterfront the cheerful cafebar Korina is good for coffee and drinks.

Check out **Gallery Thea** (www.gallerythea .com), opposite Platanos, for some lovely paintings and stained glass.

There are seven buses daily from Ierapetra to Myrtos (€2.20, 20 minutes).

Accommodation

Best Places to Stay

» Enagron (p187)

» Lato Hotel (p191)

» Hotel Doma (p178)

» Villa Olga (p195)

Best Boutique Hotels

» Hotel Veneto (p185)

» Porto de Colombo (p178)

» Minos Beach Art Hotel (p195)

» El Greco (p199)

Best Inland Retreats

» Kapsaliana Village (p187)

» Eleonas (p192)

» Lefkoritis Resort (p181)

» Argoulias (p196)

Where to Stay

Crete has all types of places to unpack your suitcase – hostels, campgrounds and family hotels, rural villas and hotels (agro-tourism), apartments and luxury resorts. Good-value accommodation abounds, especially in the south and inland villages.

Where you stay is one of the most important decisions to make when planning a holiday to Crete. The island has many different regions and resort towns, each with its own character and selling points.

Broadly speaking, if you're after perfect sandy beaches, look for somewhere on the north coast; for a quiet rural retreat head for the hills or the remote villages along the southern shoreline. The Iraklio region is home to the island's most developed resorts – Malia and Hersonisos – with a 24-hour party culture. Rethymno has some quieter getaways, plus Crete's longest sandy beach; it's a good base if you want to immerse yourself in the island's culture. Hania, in the west, also has some rapidly developing beach resorts and is ideal if you want to engage in a wide range of outdoor pursuits, from scuba-diving to mountain climbing. Lasithi in the east is the island's quietest area and the exclusive resorts of Elounda and Agios Nikolaos are the strongholds of Crete's high-end tourism.

Pricing

Price indicators in this book refer to the cost of a double room in high season, including private bathroom and excluding breakfast unless noted. Budget generally covers hostels, campgrounds and simple domatia (pensions). Midrange means more creature comforts such as satellite TV, wi-fi and kitchens in small hotels, or self-catering apartments. Top-end places are usually villas and full-service resorts.

CATEGORY	COST
€ Budget	<€50
€€ Midrange	€50-100
€€€ Top end	>€100

TOP FIVE SELF-CATERING APARTMENTS

» Eliathos (p192)

» Plakias Suites (p188)

» Stella's Traditional Apartments (p198)

» Terra Minoika (p198)

» Vranas Studios (p179)

Hotels

Crete has some of the best resort hotels in Greece, including some elite spa-hotel properties, but standards vary dramatically. While most of the top hotels are world-class and have all the expected amenities, some midrange hotels are little better than domatia (rooms, usually in a private home). There's a smattering of boutique-style hotels, especially in Hania and Rethymno, which are ensconced in superbly restored Venetian mansions or historic buildings.

In this book we have tried to feature well-situated, independently owned hotels that offer good value, a warm welcome, cleanliness, at least a modicum of charm and character and a palpable sense of place.

All hotels in Greece are subject to a compulsory hotel classification system based on a rating from one to five stars. Basic criteria include the size of rooms, facilities provided, services offered and the number of bedrooms, rather than standards of cleanliness, comfort of beds and friendliness of staff – all elements that may be of greater relevance to guests. For this reason, star ratings are not quoted in reviews in this book.

Unless specified otherwise, prices quoted in this guide don't include breakfast, which is usually available for an extra €5 to €8.

All-inclusive Resorts

Almost 80% of visitors to Crete arrive on the island on a package holiday, and in many hotels there has been a shift towards all-inclusive holiday packages, only available through tour operators and perhaps less appealing to independent travellers. All-inclusive resorts are especially prevalent along the northern coast, east of Iraklio. Good-value deals often pop up at the last minute though, making this type of travel less expensive on the whole than booking flights and accommodation separately.

Studios & Apartments

If you want to slow down and get to know a place better, renting a studio or apartment for a week or two can be ideal, especially for budget-minded travellers, self-caterers, families and small groups. Studios usually consist of one room and can accommodate two persons, while apartments have separate living and sleeping quarters suitable for three or more people. Facilities include a kitchenette or full kitchen, cable or satellite TV, air-conditioning and heating units and, occasionally, washing machines. High-season rates range from €35 to €60 for a studio and €50 to €80 for an apartment for four people. During high season, owners usually insist on one-week minimum rentals, but at other times it's often possible to stay for a night or two, possibly at a small surcharge.

Domatia (Pensions)

Domatia (literally 'rooms') are the Greek equivalent of the British B&B, minus the breakfast. Simply look around for signs saying 'Rent Rooms'. Most are only open between April and October.

In former times, domatia (also called pensions) comprised little more than spare rooms in the family home that were rented out to travellers. Nowadays most are purpose-built appendages to the family home. Many have been upgraded into 'studios' and come complete with kitchenette, TV, balcony and air-con.

Domatia remain a popular option for budget travellers and are often more appealing (and sometimes better equipped) than generic midrange hotels. Expect to pay from €20 to €60 for a double, depending on whether bathrooms are shared or private, the season and the length of your stay. Family rooms sleeping three or four people are quite common. In peak season, some landlords may be reluctant to rent for a single night.

Some domatia have solar-heated water, which means that hot water is not guaranteed at all times.

BOOK YOUR STAY ONLINE

For more accommodation reviews by Lonely Planet authors, check out hotels.lonelyplanet.com/crete. You'll find independent reviews, as well as recommendations on the best places to stay. Best of all, you can book online.

Agrotourism

Agrotourism is booming in Crete, an encouraging sign that rural life and tourism don't have to be mutually exclusive. Traditional guesthouses, villas and apartments are popping up all over, usually in tranquil villages away from the coastal hubbub, where time-honoured customs and Cretan hospitality thrive.

Developments are either new and purpose-built with local materials or modernised old stone houses that have been given a 21st-century makeover while preserving such traditional features as wooden-beamed ceilings and fireplaces. Many are attached to organic farms, meaning you will be able to observe or even participate in seasonal activities, such as sheep shearing, *raki* distilling, olive harvesting, grape crushing or cheesemaking. In rooms, rustic furniture and country decor provide an atmospheric experience; balconies or terraces are common features.

On-site tavernas serve food made from home-grown, organic ingredients and use recipes based on the Cretan diet and passed down through the generations. Some owners also give cooking courses. Budget between €70 and €100 for a traditional house.

Camping

Crete's dozen or so campgrounds are privately run and range from sunbaked dirt patches to tree-shaded, resort-style grounds with pools, shops, tavernas and wi-fi. Some also rent caravans, tents and bungalows. The **Panhellenic Camping Association** (www.panhellenic-camping-union.gr) publishes information about its member sites, their facilities and opening months on its website. The core season runs from May to October, although a few sites remain open year-round.

Camping fees are a mosaic of separate charges per person. Here are some rough guidelines:

adult	€4-6
child under 12yr	€2-3
tent	€3-6
car	€3-5
caravan	from €8

Between May and mid-September it is usually warm enough to sleep out under the stars without a tent, although you will still

TOP FIVE BUDGET ABODES 177

» Arsinoi Studios (p194)
» Blue House (p182)
» Kronos Hotel (p191)
» Plakias Youth Hostel (p188)
» Hotel Arhontiko (p197)

need a lightweight sleeping bag to counter the predawn chill. It's a good idea to have a foam pad to lie on and a waterproof cover to protect your sleeping bag.

Free (wild) camping is illegal and the police are increasingly cracking down on scofflaws. Still, there are some remote beaches along the south and west coasts (such as Lendas, Sougia and Gavdos Island) that are more tolerant. Ask around before you pitch your tent and, of course, take out all of your trash. Another option is to camp on private property, such as a farm, but be sure to get the prior consent of the landowner.

Hostels

Crete does not have any Hostelling International–affiliated hostels, but there are independent contenders in Rethymno, Plakias and Iraklio, as well as a few hotels operating as unofficial hostels. The hostels in Rethymno and Plakias are well-run and sociable places, with dorm beds, basic facilities and inexpensive food. The hostel in Iraklio is extremely run-down and cannot be recommended.

Dorm beds cost about €10 or €11; discounts are usually available for longer stays.

Mountain Refuges

Crete has seven mountain shelters run by the regional mountaineering clubs: four in the Lefka Ori (White Mountains), two around Mt Psiloritis and one on Mt Dikti. Nonmembers pay around €13 per bunk bed. Facilities vary and may include basic cooking facilities, wood-burning stoves and water from a spring or a rainwater tank. Get in touch with the regional club before hitting the trail; see p25 for contacts. For an overview of shelters, check www.crete.tournet.gr/en/crete-activities/936-mountain-shelters.

ℹ️ ROOM PRIMER

Room rates in Crete fluctuate – often widely – depending on the season. Generally speaking, prices are lowest in winter (November to March), then rise a bit in the shoulder seasons (April to June and September and October) and peak in summer (July and August). Prices listed in this book reflect high-season rates. Outside the cities – and especially along the coasts – most properties close down altogether from November to March or April. In most cases, booking ahead is necessary only for the summer months. Otherwise, you can pretty much just turn up and find a place to hang your hat – look for ubiquitous 'Rent Rooms' signs.

HANIA XANIA

Hania Χανιά

Hania's Venetian quarter brims with chic boutique hotels and family-run atmospheric pensions in restored Venetian buildings. There are no hostels and the best places are definitely not budget (there is a nearby campground, though). Most hotels are open year-round. Many of the older and boutique hotels have no lift. The western end of the harbour and along Zambeliou is a good place to look, but it can be noisy and crowded at night, especially along the harbour – the price you pay for a view. There are cheaper rooms around the Splantzia quarter, but to get away from the masses head up to the Halepa neighbourhood overlooking the water (a five- to 10-minute walk). Hotel complexes with pools can be found at Nea Hora and along the beach running west to Platanes and beyond.

TOP CHOICE Hotel Doma   BOUTIQUE HOTEL €€

(off Map p44; ☏28210 51772; www.hotel-doma .gr; Venizelos 124; s/d/tr/ste incl buffet breakfast €65/90/120/150; ☉1 Apr–31 Oct; ❋🛜🛗) One could imagine Hercule Poirot peering down the curving stairway at the Doma, a quiet, century-old classic overlooking the sea in the Halepa district. Decorated with period furnishings, scattered antiquities and even an exotic Asian headdress collection, this former Austro-Hungarian and British consulate attracts couples, writers and other solitude-seekers. The rooms are well kept and classy, while the rooftop suite features an enormous balcony with amazing views. The breakfast is all natural and tasty, and the flowering back garden relaxing. But it is the extraordinarily kind service that really sets the place apart.

TOP CHOICE Casa Delfino   BOUTIQUE HOTEL €€€

(Map p44; ☏28210 87400; www.casadelfino .com; Theofanous 7; ste & apt incl buffet breakfast €180-340; ❋🛜) If you're looking for old-town opulence, this elegant 17th-century mansion is the most luxurious hotel in Hania's Venetian quarter. There are 24 individually decorated and well-appointed suites, including a palatial, split-level apartment with a jacuzzi. All have Italian marble baths. The apartment sleeps up to four people. The standard rooms don't have balconies, though. For maximum pampering, try the Ottoman-inspired spa, where you can get a variety of massage treatments. Breakfast is in the splendid pebble-mosaic courtyard, and there are great sunset views from the rooftop terrace.

Ifigenia Rooms & Studios   APARTMENTS €€

(Map p44; ☏28210 94357; www.ifigeniastudios .gr; Gamba 23, cnr Parodos Agelou; studios €45-100; ❋@) This network of refurbished houses around the Venetian harbour offers anything from simple rooms to fancy suites with kitchenettes, jacuzzis and views. There are nice touches like elaborate stone-wrought bed frames and neat archways. Some bathrooms are very basic, though. However, the patios overlooking the water are undeniably blissful (note that to get a sea view on standard rooms, expect to pay about €30 more).

Porto de Colombo   BOUTIQUE HOTEL €€

(Map p44; ☏28210 70945; www.portodel colombo.gr; Theofanous & Moshon; d/ste incl breakfast €85/110; ❋) Once the French embassy and office of Eleftherios Venizelos, this 600-year-old Venetian town house is now a charming boutique hotel with 10 lovely, well-appointed rooms; the top suites have fine harbour views. The standard rooms can fit up to three (though it's a bit snug), while the three self-catering apartments are more child-friendly and have self-catering facilities.

Splanzia Hotel

BOUTIQUE HOTEL €€€

(Map p44; ☑28210 45313; www.splanzia.com; Daskalogianni 20; d incl buffet breakfast €100; ✴@) Over in the appealing Splanzia quarter, this smart new designer hotel in an Ottoman building has eight stylish rooms, some decorated with four-poster timber beds and drapery. The back rooms overlook a lovely courtyard, which is redolent with bougainvillea and features one of Hania's only remaining Turkish wells. The local hospitality is friendly and down to earth.

Amphora Hotel

BOUTIQUE HOTEL €€€

(Map p44; ☑28210 93224; www.amphora.gr; s €95, d with view €130, ste €150; ✴) This historically evocative hotel is in an immaculately restored and kept Venetian mansion with rooms around a courtyard and in a second connected wing. The rooms are elegantly decorated and the top rooms have views of the harbour. The front rooms can be noisy in summer and there are cheaper rooms without a view. However, even not considering the breakfast (an extra €10), it seems a tad overpriced.

Hania Camping

CAMPGROUND €

(off Map p44; ☑28210 31138; www.camping-chania.gr; Agii Apostoli; camp sites per caravan/tent €7/4; ☺1 Apr–31 Oct; ✴) Hania's nearest campground is 3km west of town on the beach and has some nice features, such as a large swimming pool with separate kids' section. The site is shaded and has a restaurant, bar and minimarket. You can also rent a tent (€10), and you can do laundry and get petrol here as well. Buses heading west (every 15 minutes) from the southeast corner of Plateia 1866 can let you off at the campground.

Pension Lena

PENSION €

(Map p44; ☑28210 86860; www.lenachania.gr; Ritsou 5; s/d €35/55; ✴) Run by the friendly Lena, this pension near Nea Hora beach has tastefully done rooms with an old-world feel and a scattering of antiques, though the front rooms are the most appealing. It also now offers three separate structures, including the recently renovated **Margot's House** in the relaxed Splantzia quarter, which can sleep up to six. A second apartment, the attractive old **Stone Cottage**, should be booked in advance in summer, but out of high season can be rented for several weeks at a steep discount.

Casa Leone

BOUTIQUE HOTEL €€€

(Map p44; ☑28210 76762; www.casa-leone.com; Parodos Theotokopoulou 18; ste incl breakfast €120-150; ✴✶) This Venetian residence has been converted into a classy and romantic family-run boutique hotel. The rooms are spacious and well appointed, with balconies overlooking the harbour. There are honeymoon suites, with classic drape-canopy beds and sumptuous curtains. Discounts apply to stays of a week or more.

Pension Theresa

PENSION €

(Map p44; ☑/fax 28210 92798; www.pensiontheresa.gr; Angelou 2; r €40-50; ✴) In a building originally part of the Venetian fortifications of Hania, this creaky old house with a steep (and narrow!) spiral staircase and antique furniture has plenty of atmosphere. Some rooms have a view, but there's always the stunning vista from the rooftop terrace, where you can use the communal kitchen. The rooms are clean but fairly snug, though a good bet for the price.

Vranas Studios

STUDIOS €€

(Map p44; ☑28210 58618; www.vranas.gr; Agion Deka 10; studios €40-70; ✴) In the heart of the old town, this place is on a lively pedestrian street and has spacious, immaculately maintained studios with kitchenettes. All rooms have polished wooden floors, balconies, TVs and telephones. There's a handy internet cafe attached.

Madonna Studios & Apartments

APARTMENTS €€

(Map p44; ☑28210 94747; madonnastudios@yahoo.co.uk; Gamba 33; studios €70-110; ✴✶) This charming small hotel has five attractive and well-appointed studios around a lovely flower-filled courtyard, near the Naval Museum by the harbour, and close to the public car park. Rooms are furnished in traditional style and the front top room has a superb balcony, while the courtyard room has the original stone wash trough. The owner is kindly and hospitable, though like the other old-town places there can be street noise at night.

Nostos Hotel

BOUTIQUE HOTEL €€

(Map p44; ☑28210 94743; www.nostos-hotel.com; Zambeliou 42-46; s/d/tr incl breakfast €65/103/133; ✴) Mixing Venetian style and modern fixtures, this 600-year-old building has been remodelled into classy split-level accommodation, with kitchen, fridge, phone and TV. The 12 classy rooms have a light, airy feel and traditional Cretan decorative furnishings. It also has a roof garden. Try to get a balcony room with harbour views.

Bellmondo   BOUTIQUE HOTEL €€
(Map p44; ☑28210 36216; www.belmondohotel.com; Zambeliou 10; s/d/tr incl breakfast €65/85/103; ❋) This classy hotel has harbour views and a formal feel, with iron beds and traditional furnishings. It has Turkish and Venetian features, including part of an old *hammam* (Turkish baths) in one room. Children up to 12 years of age stay free. The nicer rooms have balconies (factor in about €20 extra to the rate).

Ionas Hotel   BOUTIQUE HOTEL €€
(Map p44; ☑28210 55090; www.ionashotel.com; cnr Sarpaki & Sorvolou; d €60-90, ste incl breakfast €120; ❋) This is one of the new breed of boutique hotels in the quiet Splantzia quarter, with an elegant wood-and-stone exterior. The historic building has a contemporary design and fit-out, nine rooms with all mod cons (including a smallish jacuzzi in one), and a terrace on the roof. The original touches include a Venetian archway in the entrance, and original walls from the mid-16th century.

Akrotiri Peninsula
Χερσόνησος Ακρωτήρι

Esplanade Apartments   APARTMENTS €€
(☑28210 64253; www.esplanade-hotel.gr; Kalathas; studios & apt €50-90; P❋❒☀⛟) Just 7km from Hania, this bright collection of apartments is centred around a swimming pool and is a good bet for families. This two-storey hotel has roomy, light and breezy studios with phone, TV and well-stocked kitchenette for self-caterers.

Georgi's Blue Apartments   APARTMENTS €€€
(☑28210 64080; www.blueapts.gr; Kalathas; apt incl continental breakfast €85-130; P❋@☀❒) Georgi's is a tasteful, rather upmarket complex of well-furnished studios and apartments with phone, satellite TV, fridge and kitchenette. There's a pleasant communal lounge area near the pool and a private little cove where you can swim off the rocks. The owner can advise about local outdoor activities and help with car hire.

Paradisio Apartments   APARTMENTS €€
(☑28210 39737; www.paradisiohotel.com; Stavros; apt €85; ❋☀⛟) Up in the olive groves in Stavros, this is a friendly family-run affair with apartments that can sleep up to five people. There's a swimming pool with a separate area for kids, and the family provide guests with their own organic fruit, olive oil and honey. The flowery courtyard with views of the nearby hills adds colour.

Blue Beach   VILLAS €
(☑28210 39404; in Hania 28210 45077; www.bluebeach.eu; Stavros; d €50; ❋☀) Right on the pretty spot on Stavros beach, Blue Beach is a low-key resort hotel that welcomes independent travellers and does a good job of looking after them. The rooms are comfortable and self-contained with fridge, kitchenette and TV, and there is a pool and bar. Friendly owner Manolis organises weekly live music at the hotel's tasty taverna. It also has an office in Hania for those arranging from there.

Sfakia & Lefka Ori
Σφακιά & Λευκά Όρι

OMALOS ΟΜΑΛΟΣ
Generally, Omalos hotels are open when the Samaria Gorge is open, although winter tourism is evolving. Most hotels have restaurants that do a bustling trade serving breakfast to hikers and are open at mealtimes the rest of the day. Most will drive you to the start of the gorge. As at other mountain locations, air-conditioning is not necessary.

Hotel Neos Omalos   HOTEL €
(☑28210 67590; www.neos-omalos.gr; s/d €20/30; P☀) Has 26 comfortable, modern, nicely decorated rooms that include phone, bathtub and satellite TV. All have balconies with nice views of the Lefka Ori. There's a pleasant lounge in the reception area. The food is fresh and local, and the owners can provide plenty of info on local hikes and other outdoor activities, and will happily transport hikers to the Samaria Gorge entrance at Xyloskalo (10 minutes away).

Hotel Exari   HOTEL €
(☑28210 67180; www.exari.gr; s/d €25/35; P) This big, traditional-style stone-built hotel has 24 well-furnished rooms with TV, bathtub and balconies. The owner Yiorgos can deliver luggage to Sougia for groups. There is also an attached restaurant with fireplace (especially nice in winter). The hotel operates year-round.

Kallergi Hut
MOUNTAIN REFUGE €

(☑28210 33199; dm without bathroom members/nonmembers €10/15) The best budget option is the bare-bones Kallergi Hut, located in the hills between Omalos and the Samaria Gorge. It has six available rooms and is maintained by the Hania EOS. It makes a good base for exploring Mt Gingilos and surrounding peaks, though it is a 2km hike to get there.

ASKYFOU ΑΣΚΥΦΟΥ

TOP CHOICE **Lefkoritis Resort**
RESORT €€

(☑28250 95455; www.lefkoritis.com; apt May-Sep €70-145; P✱🏠) This slightly swank mountain resort is a sizeable stone-built retreat that operates year-round and has a taverna and swimming pool. It has tastefully furnished rooms and apartments sleeping up to six and enjoys sweeping views of the surrounding mountains. In past years, it also catered to hunters but is now more for the unarmed. It offers child-friendly activities such as horse and pony riding, along with mountain biking.

Southern Coast

AGIA ROUMELI ΑΓΙΑ ΡΟΥΜΕΛΗ
Artemis Studios
STUDIOS €

(☑28250 91225; www.agiaroumeli.com; s/d/tr €45/55/70; ✱) Blissfully set away from the Samaria Gorge entrance, 50m from the pebble beach, the family-run Artemis has 12 self-catering studios accommodating up to five persons. It is a bit more expensive than other local options, but a good bet if you want to be near the water and away from the crowds. The owners can provide info on local hill walks too.

Oasis
PENSION €

(☑28250 91327; s/d/tr €25/30/35; ✱) The family who run these rooms live downstairs, giving this place a friendly and homely feel. The simply furnished rooms have dated but functional bathrooms, fridge and balconies.

Gigilos Taverna & Rooms
PENSION €

(☑28250 91383; gigilos@mycosmos.gr; s/d/tr €25/35/40; ✱) Right on the beach at the western end of the village, the best rooms are at the front, on the beach road. They are clean and nicely furnished, with decent new bathrooms and a communal fridge in the hall. The taverna, which serves good home-cooked Cretan fare, has a pleasant huge shady deck on the beach.

Lefka Ori
HOTEL €

(☑28250 91209; info@chora-sfakion.com; s/d €25/35; ✱) Go all the way down to the western end of the port for this friendly, long-established little hotel, which also has an excellent taverna below. It has 10 regular rooms and two apartments, all clean and well kept, though fairly basic.

Xenia
HOTEL €

(☑28250 91490; www.sfakia-xenia-hotel.gr; d €33-38; ✱🏠) The best-value, and best-located, rooms in town are to be found at this refurbished hotel well positioned at the western edge overlooking the water. The 21 rooms have mod cons such as air-con, satellite TV and a fridge.

Rooms Stavris
PENSION €

(☑28250 91220; www.hotel-stavris-chora-sfakion.com; s/d/tr €29/34/39; ✱) Up the steps at the western end of the port, this long-running place owned by the Perrakis clan has clean, basic rooms – some with kitchenettes and fridges.

FRANGOKASTELLO ΦΡΑΓΓΟΚΑΣΤΕΛΛΟ
Accommodation is reasonably good value here, especially a bit further away from the beach on the other side of the east–west road, and mostly designed for longer stays.

Stavris Studios
APARTMENTS €

(☑28250 92250; www.studios-stavris-frangokastello.com; studios €35-50; P✱🏠) This collection of 24 studios and apartments is great value, especially considering its position on the beach side of the main road, on the right as you enter from Hora Sfakion. The rooms have kitchenettes, balconies and sea views, and adjoining rooms for families. There is a leafy garden and big open area for kids to run around in, and the owners are happy to advise about local activities.

Mylos
APARTMENTS €

(☑28250 92162; www.milos-sfakia.com; studios & apt €40-60; P✱) A renovated, century-old stone windmill (*mylos* in Greek) turned into an apartment in a pretty spot on the beach is the most captivating of several atmospheric accoms available. There are also four stone cottages under the tamarisk trees, and modern well-equipped studios nearby. If you want to stay in the mill in high season book ahead. There's also a tasty taverna.

Fata Morgana & Paradisos APARTMENTS €
(☑28250 92077; www.fatamorgana-kreta.com; studios €40-60; P❋🚼) Set among an olive grove above Orthi Ammos beach, this lovely complex has a range of fully equipped but a bit old-fashioned studios and larger apartments for families, as well as two cosy mock castles (€65). There's a playground and a chook/bird pen to amuse the kids.

LOUTRO ΛΟΥΤΡΟ

Loutro has good budget accommodation options, with most places overlooking the harbour. However, note that credit cards are not accepted in Loutro.

Blue House PENSION €
(☑28250 91035; www.bluehouse.loutro.gr; d €40-50; ❋) Nestled up among the glistening white structures on the port, the Blue House has a mix of spacious, well-appointed rooms with big verandahs overlooking the water. The nicer rooms are in the refurbished top-floor section. The taverna downstairs serves excellent *mayirefta* (ready-cooked meals; €5 to €7), including delicious garlicky spinach and a great *boureki* (Turkish-influenced filo pie) baked with zucchini, potato and goat's cheese.

Hotel Porto Loutro I & II HOTEL €€
(☑28250 91433; www.hotelportoloutro.com; s/d/tr incl breakfast €50/60/65; ❋) Worth the price for those who want to be a few feet from the water, the Porto Loutro is the classiest hotel in town. Spread across two buildings, it offers rooms and studios that are simply decorated in understated island style. However, those not in the studios pay extra for a fridge. The hotel has balconies overlooking the beach. Does not accept children under the age of seven years.

Apartments Niki APARTMENTS €
(☑/fax 28250 91259; www.loutro-accommodation.com; studios & villas €50-125; ❋) These beautifully furnished studios with beamed ceilings and stone floors can accommodate two to four people, while the villa is unique in Loutro in that it can house up to six people at a time. Each has its own kitchenette for self-caterers. Niki is located just above the village and, as such, affords great views over the water from the balconies.

Rooms Sofia PENSION €
(☑28250 91354; www.sofiarooms-loutro.gr; d/tr €25/35; ❋) Above the Sofia minimarket, one street back from the beach, these are probably the cheapest rooms in town. They're plain and clean and a little cramped. Most have a fridge and air-con.

SOUGIA ΣΟΥΓΙΑ

Aretousa PENSION €
(☑28230 51178; s/d €35/40, studios €42; ❋🚼) This lovely pension on the road to Hania, 200m from the sea, has bright and comfortable refurbished rooms and studios, most with kitchenettes. There's a relaxing garden and playground for kids out back.

Rooms Ririka PENSION €
(☑28230 51167; d €45; ❋) This cosy place consists of eight double rooms with a leafy garden, just up from the eastern side of the beach.

Santa Irene Hotel HOTEL €€
(☑28230 51342; www.santa-irene.gr; d/apt €55/70; ❋@) This smart hotel on the beach has airy rooms with marble floors, TV and kitchenettes, while there are also two family rooms with baby cots available. Prices drop dramatically in low season.

Captain George PENSION €
(☑28230 51133; g-gentek@otenet.gr; s/d €37/41, studios €48; P❋) Captain George, who runs taxi-boat trips to nearby beaches in his spare time, runs these attractive, good-value rooms and studios with fridges. There is a lovely garden too. Note that in high season a minimum stay of six nights is required.

PALEOHORA ΠΑΛΑΙΟΧΩΡΑ

Homestay Anonymous PENSION €
(Map p62; ☑28230 42098; www.anonymoushomestay.com; s/d/tr €23/28/32) This simple but good-value pension with private bathrooms and shared cooking facilities in the courtyard garden is a good bet. Friendly, well-travelled owner Manolis cultivates a welcoming atmosphere and is a mine of information for local things to do and see. The rooms are clean and tastefully furnished, though a bit cramped. Rooms can connect to accommodate families. It's a two-minute walk from sandy Pahia Ammos beach.

Oriental Bay Rooms PENSION €
(off Map p62; ☑28230 41076; www.orientalbay.gr; s/d/tr €30/35/40; ❋🛜) These immaculate rooms are in the large modern building at the northern end of the stony beach. Rooms have balconies with sea or mountain views and come with kettle and fridge.

Camping Paleohora
CAMPGROUND €

(off Map p62; ☑28230 41120; camp sites per person/tent €5/3) This large campground is 1.5km northeast of the town, about 50m from the stony beach. There is a taverna but no minimarket, and facilities in general are run-down despite plans to modernise. You can hire tents (small/large €6/10).

Villa Anna
PENSION €€

(Map p62; ☑2810 346428; anna@her.forthnet .gr; apt €42-80; ❄️🎮) Set in a lovely shady garden bordered by tall poplars, these well-appointed, family-friendly apartments can sleep up to five people. There are cots, and swings and a sandpit in the garden, and the grounds are secured.

Lito Apartments
PENSION €€

(Map p62; ☑28230 64931; www.lito-paleochora .gr; d/apt €45/60; ❄️🛜) Set around a flowering courtyard, Lito has decent but somewhat dark rooms, with self-catering facilities, televisions with DVD, safes and balconies on the upper floors. The free wi-fi works around the main office area only. It's opposite Homestay Anonymous, at the corner of the road to Pahia Ammos.

Aris Hotel
HOTEL €

(off Map p62; ☑28230 41502; www.aris-hotel.gr; s/d incl breakfast €40/50) This friendly good-value hotel at the end of the road skirting the headland welcomes independent travellers. There are bright garden and sea-view rooms with some adjoining rooms and balconies for families. Rates drop in low season.

Gavdos Γαύδος

Along with the rooms, free camping is popular.

Akrogiali Taverna & Rooms
PENSION €

(☑28230 42384; d/tr €35/50) Right on Korfos beach, Akrogiali offers simple rooms with fridge and fan, and the pension overlooks the beach. The adjacent taverna is famed for its local cooking.

Sarakiniko Studios
STUDIOS €

(☑28230 42182; www.gavdostudios.gr; d/tr studios incl breakfast €50/70) Above Sarakiniko beach, these comfortable studios and new villas sleep up to five (€80 to €100). You can be picked up at the port, or it is a 20-minute (approximately 1.2km) walk north.

KOLYMBARI ΚΟΛΥΜΠΑΡΙ

Rooms Lefka
PENSION €

(☑28240 22211; s/d/tr €30/35/45; ❄️) On the way into town from the bus stop, this decent budget place is on the right. Rooms are older-style but comfortable, with fridge and rather wacky shower nozzles in the basin. They are good for families, and the taverna downstairs serves up good, honest Cretan food and a hearty breakfast (€6).

Aeolos Apartments
APARTMENTS €

(☑28240 22203; studios €45, apt €60; ❄️) Signposted to the left off the main road, this dated but well-maintained complex on the hill has big balconies with sea views and flower beds. Breezy studios and two-room apartments are spacious and comfortable, with carved timber beds, TV and kitchenettes with bar stools.

KISSAMOS-KASTELLI
ΚΙΣΣΑΜΟΣ-ΚΑΣΤΕΛΛΙ

TOP CHOICE **Stavroula Palace**
HOTEL €€

(☑28220 23260; www.varouchakis.gr/stavroula palace; s/d/tr incl breakfast €50/65/80; 🅿️❄️🛜🏊) There is great value and location to be had in this cheery new waterfront hotel offering breezy, modern rooms with balconies (some overlooking the sea). It's very well situated between Kissamos-Kastelli centre and both the town's best beach and favourite waterfront eateries and bars (all a three- to five-minute walk in different directions). There's even a pool with bar area and kids' recreation area out back. It's 30m west of Papadakis restaurant.

Camping Mithymna
CAMPGROUND €

(☑28220 31444; www.campingmithimna.com; Paralia Drapania; camp sites per person/tent €6/4; 🅿️) About 6km east of town, Camping Mithymna is an excellent shady site near the best stretch of beach with a restaurant, bar and shop. It has some games and sports for kids and is pet-friendly. Take a bus to the village of Drapanias, from where it's a pleasant 15-minute (approximately 800m) walk through olive groves to the campground (or walk 4km along the beach).

Bikakis Family
PENSION €

(☑28220 22105; www.familybikakis.gr; Iroön Polemiston 1941; s/d €20/25, studios €30; ❄️@) This good budget option is 250m inland from the beach, near the centre of town. It offers clean rooms and studios, most with garden and sea views, plus kitchenettes. It maintains a family environment and owner Giannis makes guests feel very welcome. There are bigger studios and adjoining rooms for families, and breakfast (€3 per person) is available.

Thalassa STUDIOS €
(☎28220 31231; www.thalassa-apts.gr; Paralia Drapanias; studios €35-55; ❄@☎♨) You'll need a car to get there, but the isolated Thalassa complex is ideal for a quiet beach retreat. The immaculate studios are airy and well fitted. There's a barbecue on the lawn, and a small playground. It's just across from the beach, 100m east of Camping Mithymna.

Christina Beach Hotel STUDIOS €€
(☎28220 83333; studios €60-80; P❄@) This smart studio complex on the west side of Kissamos-Kastelli represents the upper end of accommodation in town. Right on the foreshore, the modern studios are large and airy, and the best sandy beach is right nearby.

GRAMVOUSA PENINSULA
ΧΕΡΣΟΝΗΣΟΣ ΓΡΑΜΒΟΥΣΑ
A good base for touring this region is the village of Kalyviani, 7km west of Kissamos-Kastelli.

Kaliviani INN €
(☎/fax 28220 23204; www.kaliviani.com; d & tr €40-55; P❄) An attractive stone-built guesthouse with comfortable, tastefully furnished rooms with fridge and balcony. There is also an excellent and modestly priced restaurant on site to keep you nourished while out of civilisation.

Olive Tree Apartments APARTMENTS €€
(☎28220 24336; www.olivetree.gr; apt €40-70; P❄♨) This attractive complex in an olive grove at the entrance to the village has spacious, comfortable and well-presented apartments suitable for families and longer stays, as well as an inviting pool.

FALASARNA ΦΑΛΑΣΑΡΝΑ
Most accommodation is aimed at the independent traveller. The places on the beach are, unfortunately, the least attractive. There are numerous places for free camping, although like elsewhere it is officially frowned upon.

Falassarna Beach Hotel HOTEL €
(☎28220 41257; www.falassarnabeach.gr; r €25-50; ❄) This inexpensive but well-kept modern hotel (situated right where the bus from Kissamos-Kastelli stops) is a good bet for those who want to have some of the creature comforts of a hotel with quick access to the beach (a two-minute walk down the hill). There are good views from most of the sea-facing rooms and from the shady patio taverna.

Rooms Anastasia-Stathis PENSION €
(☎28220 41480; d/apt €40/50; ❄) The airy, attractively furnished rooms with fridges and large balconies are perfect for stress relief, as the friendly owner Anastasia puts it. Her enormous breakfasts (€6) are open to all comers and guests can pick vegies from the garden.

Doma APARTMENTS €
(☎28220 41726; www.domaapts.gr; studios €45, apt €50-70) This attractive complex in a garden setting has tastefully furnished studios and one- or two-room apartments that are well equipped for longer stays. There are big balconies and extras such as hairdryers and TV, while some have full-size kitchens.

Rooms for Rent Panorama PENSION €
(☎28220 41336; www.falasarna.gr; d/tr €40/50; ❄) One of the first places you will come across, signposted to the left along a gravel track, these refurbished studios are spotless and comfortable, and have a fridge or kitchenette. The well-run and friendly restaurant with a great view of the beach serves up good Cretan cooking.

INNAHORION VILLAGES ΙΝΝΑΧΩΡΙΟΝ
Kokolakis Rooms PENSION €
(☎28220 61258; Elos; d €30; P) The only accommodation in Elos is above the Kastanofolia taverna, right on the main road by the stream that runs through the village. The rooms are very basic and not good value for money, given that the bathrooms are shared.

To Metohi Tou Monahogiou FARM HOUSE €€
(☎28220 51655; Vlatos; d incl breakfast €90; P) In Vlatos you can visit this organic olive oil farm, which has tastings and attractive accommodation in a restored stone farm house in a lovely forest setting.

Sunset Rooms PENSION €
(☎28220 41128; Kambos; s/d €20/25; P) In Kambos, Sunset has great views over the valley. Rooms are basic but pleasant enough. The attached taverna serves up good value grills and salads.

Hartzoulakis Rent Rooms
PENSION €

(☎28220 41445; manolis_hartzoulakis@yahoo.gr; Kambos; s/d €20/30; P) Small and basic but very clean, with large verandahs, the rooms here make a good base for walkers. The taverna on the terrace serves up good Cretan fare and excellent *raki*.

Clara's
PENSION €

(☎28220 61537; Amygdalokefali; www.cafeclara.com; d €25-50; P) This lovely hideaway just below the coastal road in Amigdalokefali has breathtaking views. There's a lovely stone cottage with bathroom, and two rustic rooms that share an outside bathroom, including a shower in a former grape press. Ask at the *kantina* (kiosk) on the main road or call the English-speaking owner, Clara, for directions.

ELAFONISI ΕΛΑΦΟΝΗΣΙ

Rooms Panorama
PENSION €

(☎28220 61548; s/d studios €25/30; P) This place has a taverna overlooking the sea from its commanding position on a bluff. Rooms have a kitchenette and fridge, but many are rented by the month to itinerant workers.

Rooms Elafonisi
PENSION €

(☎28250 61274, s/d €30/40; P❄) The 21 spacious rooms here have fridges, and there are nicely furnished bigger rooms out the back among the olive groves, as well as apartments with kitchens. The outdoor patio has views and there's an attached restaurant.

East of Hania

GEORGIOUPOLI ΓΕΩΡΓΙΟΥΠΟΛΗ

Most of the big hotels on the beach are aimed at package tourists.

Andy's Rooms
PENSION €

(☎28250 61394; d €30, studios €25-65; P❄) To the right of the main road opposite the church are these good-value large rooms with marble floor, mosquito screens, kitchenette, TV, ceiling fan and a big balcony. There are also larger apartments for families. It's about 100m from the beach.

Porto Kalyvaki
PENSION €

(☎/fax 28250 61316; d €30-40; P❄▣) Located behind a taverna on the more isolated northern beach, Kalyvaki has a mix of rather plain studios spread across two buildings, and some quirky reconstructions of the Acropolis and other monuments scattered around the grounds.

Egeon
PENSION €

(☎28250 61161; studios €40; ❄) Near the bridge, these pleasant rooms are run by friendly Greek-American Polly and her fisherman husband, whose nets you may see laid out in the foyer. They've upgraded the furniture and installed screens on the windows, while some rooms have kitchenettes, shower curtains and TV.

RETHYMNO ΡΕΘΥΜΝΟ

Rethymno Ρέθυμνο

The old town has an ample supply of lovely restored mansions, boutique hotels and friendly pensions to cater for all budgets, and many hotels are open year-round. Along the beach east of town is an uninterrupted stretch of hotels and resorts.

TOP CHOICE Hotel Veneto
BOUTIQUE HOTEL €€€

(Map p82; ☎28310 56634; www.veneto.gr; Epimenidou 4; studios €125, ste €145; ❄🛜) This charmer personifies everything Rethymno has to offer: history, beauty, art and great food. Soak up the vibe in 10 rooms that mix traditional features such as polished wood floors and ceilings with a satisfying range of mod cons, including satellite TV and kitchenettes. Note the stunning pebble mosaic in the foyer. Optional breakfast is €8.

TOP CHOICE Vetera Suites
BOUTIQUE HOTEL €€€

(Map p82; ☎28310 23844, 6972051691; www.vetera.gr; Kastrinogiannaki 39; r €130-150; ❄🛜) A gorgeous option, this four-suite gem drips with character and attention to detail, from the lace curtains to the quality bath products. Rooms sport hand-picked antique furniture and neatly concealed kitchenettes. The bathroom tiles feature paintings by the owner's favourite artist, Degas, while DVD players and wi-fi lend a modern touch. Optional breakfast is €10.

Avli Lounge Apartments
BOUTIQUE HOTEL €€€

(Map p82; ☎28310 58250; www.avli.gr; Xanthoudidou 22, cnr Radamanthyos; r incl breakfast €189-263; ❄🛜) Luxury is taken very seriously at this discreet retreat where you'll be ensconced in warmly furnished studios sporting stone walls, beamed ceilings and jacuzzi tubs. Retire to plush beds after a first-rate dinner in Avli's romantic courtyard garden restaurant (see p83).

Atelier PENSION €

(Map p82; ✆28310 24440; http://frosso-bora
.com; Himaras 25; d €45-55; ❄️🛜) These four
clean and attractive rooms attached to a
pottery workshop near the fortress are our
top budget pick. Both are run by the local
ceramic artist Frosso Bora. They have exposed stone walls and many Venetian architectural features, as well as small flat-screen
TVs, new bathrooms and kitchenettes.

Palazzo Rimondi BOUTIQUE HOTEL €€€

(Map p82; ✆28310 51289; www.palazzorimondi
.com; Xanthoudidou 21; ste incl breakfast €145-290;
❄️🛜🏊) This scrumptious Venetian man-
sion in the heart of the old town brims with
historical ambience. Many of the 20 studios
(with kitchenettes) incorporate such architectural features as domes and stone arches.
There's a small splash pool in the courtyard
where you can load up on coffee and carbs
from the extensive breakfast buffet.

Casa dei Delfini PENSION €€

(Map p82; ✆28310 55120, 6937254857; www
.rethymnoholidays.gr; Nikiforou Foka 66-68; studios
€60-65, maisonettes €95-110; ❄️🛜) The four
rooms in this elegant guesthouse orbit a
small courtyard with a dolphin mosaic and
sport different Turkish and Venetian architectural features. Room 3, for instance, has a
hammam (Turkish baths) in the bathroom,
while Room 2 comes with a bed tucked into
an arched alcove. All have kitchenettes. For
extra room, book the two-storey maisonette
with a large private terrace.

Palazzino di Corina BOUTIQUE HOTEL €€€

(Map p82; ✆28310 21205; www.corina.gr; Damvergi
9; d €120, ste incl breakfast €160-220; ❄️🛜) This
regal Venetian mansion within a whisker
of the harbour is a classy place to unpack
your bags. Antique furniture, exposed stone
walls and timber vaulted ceilings create
an ambience of period plushness coupled
with a healthy range of mod cons, including
satellite TV and jacuzzi tubs. Note the lovely
mosaic in the courtyard.

Casa Vitae BOUTIQUE HOTEL €€

(Map p82; ✆28310 35058; www.casa-vitae.gr; Neo-
phytou Patealarou; r €80-135; ❄️🛜) This charismatic Venetian-era hotel has eight quietly
elegant rooms mixing stone and wood and
wrapped around a courtyard where breakfast is served beneath the vine-covered pergola. Romance rules in the larger suites with
iron four-poster beds, jacuzzi and private
terrace.

Hotel Civitas BOUTIQUE HOTEL €€€

(Map p82; ✆28310 58854; www.hotelcivitas
.com; Eleftheriou Venizelou 20; r incl breakfast
€245-315; ❄️🛜) Civitas is the kind of place
that dazzles with class, not glitz; a discreet
deluxe hideaway, perfect for sharp dressers
tired of anonymous big-city hotels. Old-
world charm and sophistication ooze from
every overstuffed chair, heavy silk drapes
and marble bathrooms complemented by
such 21st-century trappings as a modern
kitchen, three flat-screen TVs and a big
jacuzzi.

Rethymno Youth Hostel HOSTEL €

(Map p82; ✆28310 22848; www.yhrethymno
.com; Tombazi 41; dm without bathroom €11; 🛜)
The hostel is friendly and well run, with free
hot showers, and a patio and shaded balcony for hanging out and striking up new
friendships. Breakfast and snacks are available and there's a bar in the evening. The
reception is staffed from 8am to noon and
5pm to 9pm. If you arrive after 9pm, find a
free bed and pay in the morning.

Byzantine Hotel HOTEL €€

(Map p82; ✆28310 55609; www.byzantinehotel
.gr; Vosporou 26; d incl breakfast €60; ❄️) This
nine-room hotel in a historic building near
the Porta Guora maintains a traditional feel.
The darkish and simply decorated rooms
sport carved timber furniture and some
big bathrooms with tubs. The back rooms
overlook an old mosque and minaret.

Hotel Ideon HOTEL €€

(Map p82; ✆28310 28667; www.hotelideon.gr;
Plastira 10; s €55, d €75-107, incl breakfast; ❄️🛜🏊)
This perennial pleaser on the waterfront
has 100 rooms spread over a modern wing
and two restored old buildings with Venetian touches. The modern rooms are nicely
decorated and well appointed, and there are
balconies with sea views. Days start with a
substantial breakfast featuring a changing
roster of hot dishes.

Camping Elizabeth CAMPGROUND €

(✆28310 28694; www.camping-elizabeth.net;
camp sites per person/tent/car €7.50/5.40/4;
🕐year-round; @🛜) The closest campground
to Rethymno is about 3km east, adjacent
to beautiful Mysiria beach. Bamboo, palm
and olive trees provide plenty of shade, and
there's a taverna, snack bar and minimarket,
plus a communal fridge, free beach umbrellas and sun lounges, and a weekly beach
barbecue. It also rents out simple bungalows

and caravans from €38. An Iraklio-bound bus can drop you here.

Axos Hotel HOTEL €
(☎28310 54472; www.axos-hotel.gr; Maxis Kritis 167, Platanes; studios €44, apt €53; ✱❋✻) Never mind the busy thoroughfare: this mid-size hotel in Platanes, some 5km east of Rethymno, is a sweet retreat with modern and well-proportioned units wrapped around a sparkling pool. There's a supermarket across the street and a nice beach 200m away. Optional breakfast is €3.50.

West of Rethymno
ARGYROUPOLI ΑΡΓΥΡΟΥΠΟΛΗ

Maria's Villas APARTMENTS €€€
(☎28310 81070, 6939194767; maramanon@hotmail.com; apt €150-200; ✱❋✻) On a ridge surrounded by olive groves and vineyards and with spectacular views over Argyroupoli, these luxurious villas are the labour of love of Maria, owner of the Lappa Avocado Shop in town. Each of the units packs in a lot of design cachet with their leather sofas, gourmet kitchens, stone walls and multiple terraces.

Lappa Apartments APARTMENTS €
(☎28310 81144, 6947163362; http://lappa-apartments.com; d €30-35; ✱) Right in the village, these apartments are set around a courtyard with a lovely garden and enjoy broad mountain views. They are fully equipped with good-sized fridges, decent bathrooms and there are barbecue facilities.

Zografakis PENSION €
(☎28310 81269; d €25-30) On the main road, the Zografakis family rents decent clean and cheap rooms above their taverna.

The Hinterland & Mt Psiloritis
MONI ARKADIOU ΜΟΝΗ ΑΡΚΑΔΙΟΥ

TOP CHOICE **Kapsaliana Village** HOTEL €€€
(☎28310 83400; www.kapsalianavillage.gr; s €120, d without terrace €170, with terrace €210, incl breakfast; ✱❋✻) An entire hamlet whose olives used to supply the nearby Moni Arkadiou has taken on new life as an unrelentingly pretty and stylish hotel. There are 12 individual houses, each full of character and top-notch amenities, including ultracomfy beds, satellite TV and CD/DVD

player. The ambience is hushed and peaceful, even around the large pool and in the restaurant, which serves expertly prepared organic meals.

MARGARITES ΜΑΡΓΑΡΙΤΕΣ

TOP CHOICE **Kouriton House** BOUTIQUE HOTEL €€
(☎28340 55828; www.kouritonhouse.gr; Tzanakiana; r incl breakfast €60-108) Bunches of dried herbs and flowers dangling from the wood-beamed ceiling welcome you to this gem just outside Margarites in Tzanakiana. The beautifully restored mansion sports seven rooms, each with fridge, TV, (tiny) bathroom and lots of unique decorating touches. Owner Anastasia Friganaki is keen to show guests around the area's natural and historic attractions, and demonstrates traditional methods of making honey, picking herbs and greens, and cooking Cretan and Minoan cuisine.

PERAMA TO ANOGIA ΠΕΡΑΜΑ ΠΡΟΣ ΑΝΩΓΕΙΑ

AXOS ΑΞΟΣ

TOP CHOICE **Enagron** RESORT €€
(☎28340 61611; www.enagron.gr; studios & apt €78-130; ✱❋@✻) Enagron is a fine example of the new school of classy rural developments in Crete. It's hardly roughing it – there is a pool overlooking the mountains, comfortable stone-built studios with fireplaces, a lovely taverna serving its own organic produce, and a communal area with antiques and a country-estate feel. Guests can participate in cooking seminars and seasonal agricultural activities, including *raki* distilling and cheesemaking, or head out with the local shepherd to pick wild greens. Guided walks and horse or donkey rides are also available. Accommodation is 20% cheaper in summer. You can visit the farm and eat at the restaurant by booking ahead.

AGELIANA ΑΓΕΛΙΑΝΑ

TOP CHOICE **Dalabelos Estate** RESORT €€
(☎28340 22155; www.dalabelos.gr; d €72; ✱❋) Hemmed in by grapes, olives and herbs, these 10 traditional-style houses are a relaxing port of call. Seasonal activities include olive harvesting and *raki* distilling, as well as hands-on Cretan cooking classes. Retreat to modern rooms dressed in cheerful reds and sporting fireplaces, balconies and bathrooms with handmade sinks. It's just west of Perama, and about 10 minutes inland from Panormo.

ANOGIA ΑΝΩΓΕΙΑ

Delina Mountain Resort HOTEL €€
(📞28340 31701; www.delina.gr; d incl breakfast €80-147; 🐾🈁📶🆒) About 1km outside of Anogia, en route to the Nida Plateau, this full-service resort is a comfortable base of operation for trips up Mt Psiloritis. Posthike unwinding stations include a sauna, an indoor pool and a spa with massages, or maybe just your private in-room jacuzzi. The resort is owned by renowned local *lyra* (lyre) player Vasilis Skoulas, who also gives the occasional concert.

Hotel Aristea HOTEL €
(📞28340 31459; d incl breakfast €40, apt €50-90) In the upper village, the friendly Aristea enjoys spectacular valley views and cool breezes in straightforward but well-outfitted rooms with TV, private bathrooms and balconies. For more space and comfort, spend a little extra for one of the modern apartments next door, some sleeping up to six people.

Rooms Aris PENSION €
(📞28340 31817; www.aris.anogia.info; d €35) A good budget base with clean and cosy rooms and dreamy valley views. Optional breakfast is €6.

Coast to Coast

SPILI ΣΠΗΛΙ

Heracles PENSION €
(📞28320 22111, 6973667495; heraclespapadakis@hotmail.com; s/d €30/40; 🐾📶) The five balconied rooms here are quiet, spotless and handily furnished, but it's Heracles himself who makes the place memorable. A geologist by profession, he's intimately familiar with the area and can put you on the right hiking trail, birdwatching site or hidden beach. He also operates the Creta Natura shop on the main road nearby. Optional homemade breakfasts start at €3.85.

Green Hotel HOTEL €
(📞28320 22225; www.maravelspili.gr; s/d/tr €25/30/35; 🈁Mar-Oct; 📶) The 12 rooms here don't exactly fuel the imagination, but each has a balcony and the in-house sauna is a good spot to unwind after a long day on the road. The owner also operates the Maravel Shop, which sells organic beauty products made with ingredients grown in his huge garden nearby. Optional breakfast is €5.

South Coast

PLAKIAS ΠΛΑΚΙΑΣ

TOP CHOICE **Plakias Suites** APARTMENTS €€
(📞28320 31680, 6975811559; www.plakiassuites.com; studios €100; 🈁Apr-Oct; 🐾📶) Owners Eleni and Yiorgos have poured their hearts and money into creating this stylish outpost with a modernist yet warm aesthetic and nifty touches such as large flat-screen TVs and mini-hi-fis, rainforest showers and a chic kitchen. Staying here puts you within a whisker of the best stretch of local beach.

Plakias Youth Hostel HOSTEL €
(📞28320 32118; www.yhplakias.com; dm €10; 🈁Apr-Oct; @📶) Set around a lawn amid olive groves, about 500m from the waterfront, this purposefully lazy hostel has been run for 15 years by Chris Bilson, who fosters an atmosphere of inclusiveness and good cheer that appeals to people of all ages and nationalities. The hostel has eight-bed dorms with fans and a well-kept communal bathhouse. Inexpensive breakfast, water, wine, beer and soft drinks are available. Book ahead if possible.

Gio-Ma APARTMENTS €
(📞28320 32003; www.gioma.gr; apt €45; 🐾📶) The studios and apartments at this family-run property are pretty straightforward in terms of comfort and amenities, but it's the central location and fabulous sea views, especially from the upper units, that give it an edge. The owners also run the waterfront taverna across the street.

Morpheas APARTMENTS €
(📞28320 31583, 6974654958; www.morpheas-apartments-plakias-crete-greece.com; r €45-60, apt €67-82; 🐾📶) Modern rooms here have a generous layout, a full range of amenities (including a washing machine) and mountain or sea views. They're above a supermarket and across from the beach.

Alianthos Garden Hotel HOTEL €€
(📞28320 31280; www.alianthos.gr; d incl breakfast €60-90; 🐾📶🆒♿) Following a recent date with a paint bucket, units at this modern hotel now sparkle in breezy turquoise and come with high-end mattresses and flower-filled sea-view balconies. A children's pool, games and a playground give it an edge with families.

Camping Apollonia CAMPGROUND €
(📞28320 31318; camp sites per adult/tent/car/caravan €8/4/4/6; 🈁May-Oct; 📶🆒) There are

some olive- and eucalyptus-shaded spots here but overall the grounds are pretty cramped and the facilities could use some attention. It's on the main road into town.

AROUND PLAKIAS

BEACHES AROUND PLAKIAS

Panorama PENSION €
(☑28320 32179; Rodakino; d €30-40; ✻) At the far western end of Polyrizos-Koraka (Rodakino beach), Panorama has good-value rooms with a view built on a rise above the beach, behind the thatched-roof taverna. For more elbow room, get a self-catering studio.

MYRTHIOS ΜΥΡΘΙΟΣ

Anna Apartments APARTMENTS €
(☑6973324775; www.annaview.com; d apt €48-65; ✻) Run by a tight-knit family, this outpost has attractive and spacious units that are more comfortable and homey than the norm and thus perfect for longer stays. Balconies are a quiet kick-back zone, especially at sunset, cold beer in hand. Full kitchens, too.

Stefanos Village Hotel APARTMENTS €
(☑28320 32252; www.stephanosvillage.com; apt €33-50; ✻✻) On the outskirts of the village, this good-value option has an enticing infinity pool with panoramic views. It's a family-run three-level complex with self-catering units sporting spacious balconies and sea views. Most have small kitchens.

BEACHES BETWEEN PLAKIAS & AGIA GALINI

LIGRES ΛΙΓΡΕΣ

Villa Maria PENSION €
(☑28320 22675, 6973232793; r €45, studios €70; ⊙Apr-Oct; ✻) If you really want to be in the thick of things, don't come here. With only the waves and a rushing creek for entertainment, this friendly, family-run property on a stunning, isolated beach is great for quiet relaxation. Rooms are comfortable without being fanciful and come with balcony and kitchenette. The excellent taverna specialises in grilled meats (mains €5 to €10).

TRIOPETRA ΤΡΙΟΠΕΤΡΑ

Pension Pavlos PENSION €
(☑28310 25189; www.triopetra.com.gr; d/tr/q €36/40/45; ⊙Apr-Oct; ✻) Pavlos is the only lodging option on Little Triopetra beach and not even the most jaded can deny that the location is simply out of this world. Rooms are quite more down to earth (no TV) but each has a kitchenette and balconies that

catch the sea breeze. The attached taverna (see p98) serves mostly farm-fresh fare.

Pension Yirogiali PENSION €
(☑6974559119; d/tr €35/40; ⊙Apr-Oct; ✻) Right on Triopetra's long beach is this place run by two brothers, with their mother cooking in the kitchen. The rooms have marble floors, attractive wooden furniture, fridge, TV and balconies.

AGIOS PAVLOS ΑΓΙΟΣ ΠΑΥΛΟΣ

Agios Pavlos Hotel HOTEL €
(☑28320 71104; www.agiospavloshotel.gr; d €28-40; ⊙Apr-Oct; ✻) Most rooms, many with balconies, at this family-run place overlook the little bay. The cheapest are above the taverna, which has good Cretan food, while the adjacent cafe-bar does breakfast and drinks. The same family also runs the excellent **Kavos Melissa** (r €45-60) apartments in an attractive and sparklingly modern complex high up on the cliff.

AGIA GALINI ΑΓΙΑ ΓΑΛΗΝΗ

There is no shortage of places to stay in Agia Galini, but a large percentage of the accommodation is pre-booked by tour operators in peak season.

Palazzo Greco BOUTIQUE HOTEL €€
(☑28320 91187; www.palazzogreco.com; d with/ without sea view €80/60; ⓟ✻✺✻) A passion for design is reflected in the many stylish details at this gem overlooking the sea. Match your mood to the wall colour – green, blue or red – in fine-looking rooms with flat-screen TVs, fridges and circular marble sinks in the bathrooms. The top floor two-bedroom suite (€160) sleeps up to seven and has two bathrooms (one with jacuzzi) and a fireplace.

Irini Mare RESORT €€€
(☑28320 91488; www.irini-mare.com; d/f incl breakfast with sea view €110/148; ⊙May-Oct; ✻@✺✻✻) Great for families, this beautifully landscaped low-key resort sits a short walk from the main beach and has 98 rooms, most with sea views and terraces, in different configurations. Diversions include a gym, sauna, tennis court and table tennis, while kiddies can romp in their own pool or clamber around the playground. Half-board is an optional €15.

Stohos Rooms APARTMENTS €
(☑28320 91433; d incl breakfast €40-45; ⊙late Apr-Oct; ✻) Right on the main beach, Stohos has self-catering apartments upstairs with

big balconies and enormous studios downstairs ideal for families or groups. Excellent taverna (p99) to boot.

Adonis
HOTEL €€

(📞28320 91333; www.agia-galini.com; r €60, studios €60, apt €80-120; 🅿❄🛜🏊) It takes a healthy ego to decorate the reception with a supersized poster of oneself in strapping, hairy-chested 1970s glory. It also tells you that the proprietor is a bit of a character. Adonis still presides over this sprawling 75-room complex with the nicest being in the pool-adjacent newer building; most have sea-view balconies.

Camping No Problem
CAMPGROUND €

(📞28320 91386; camp sites per person/tent/car/caravan €6/3/3/4; ☀year-round; 🅿🛜🏊) The name is the motto at this congenial and well-maintained campground about 100m from the beach and a 10-minute walk from the town centre. There's plenty of shade for pitching your tent, plus a huge pool, an excellent taverna (p99) and small supermarket.

Northeast Coast

PANORMO ΠΑΝΟΡΜΟ

Idili
APARTMENTS €€

(📞28340 20240, 6972405863; www.idili.gr; apt €60-75; ❄🛜) If cookie-cutter rooms don't do it for you, you'll love the three traditionally furnished apartments in this protected stone house that's seen incarnations as a courthouse, a carpenter's workshop and a residence. Arches, wooden ceilings and sleeping lofts endow each unit with charm and uniqueness, while the fireplace and verandah are welcome unwinding stations.

Villa Kynthia
BOUTIQUE HOTEL €€€

(📞28340 51102; www.kynthia.gr; r €129-176; ☀Apr-Oct; ❄🛜🏊) An enterprising brother-and-sister team has converted this 19th-century merchant house in the village centre into an intimate hotel with four suites and one family-size apartment. All are decorated with iron beds, antique furnishings and trompe l'œil murals. The pool and breakfast area are in a beautiful enclosed garden. Note that the reception is closed from 2pm to 7.30pm. Breakfast is €10.

Christina
APARTMENTS €€

(📞28340 51277; www.apartments-christina.gr; studios €50, apt €60-110; ☀Apr-Oct; ❄🛜)

Meticulously kept and efficiently run by the ebullient Markella, this place has six units of varying sizes, all with seafront balcony or terrace. The snug studios are best suited for shorter stays. Unexpected bonus: the enclosed hydromassage showers.

Captain's House
APARTMENTS €

(📞2810 380 833; www.captainshouse.gr; apt €40-60; ☀Apr-Oct; ❄🛜) Updated apartments in a historic, central building above the port.

Kastro
APARTMENTS €€

(📞28340 51362, 6937097757; www.kastro.panormo.org; apt €80-93; ❄🛜) Well-equipped units, some with four-poster beds, above the namesake taverna (p101).

Lucy's Pension
PENSION €

(📞28340 51212, 6976241414; www.lucy.gr; d €45, studios €85; ❄🛜) Modern rooms with kitchenette and balconies; those on the top floor have sea views.

BALI ΠΑΛΙ

Petrino Horio
RESORT €

(📞28340 94125; d incl breakfast €42-65; ☀year-round; ❄@🛜🏊) In the quiet hills above Bali, the 'Stone Village' captures the vibe of a traditional Cretan village thanks to abundant use of natural stone and untreated wood. The dream project of its architect owner Dimitris, it features 37 carefully crafted apartments with terraces or balconies, kitchens and fireplaces set amid flowering trees and potted plants. Three pools, a petting zoo, a sauna and seasonal hands-on activities, such as grape crushing and cheesemaking, provide distractions. It's 600m from the beach and close to the Bali tourist train stop. Good restaurant, friendly service.

Sunrise Apartments
APARTMENTS €

(📞28340 94267; d/apt €40/50; ❄) Right on Karavostasi beach, the spacious studios here are a good value-for-money pick and perfect for escaping the frenzy of Bali while still staying right on the beach.

Bali Blue Bay
HOTEL €€

(📞28340 20111; www.balibluebay.gr; d incl breakfast €60; ❄🛜🏊) This sleek modern hotel has great views over Bali from the rooms and rooftop pool. The rooms are spacious and boast a tasteful, contemporary design, and are equipped with TV, fridge and hairdryers.

Iraklio Ηράκλειο

TOP CHOICE Lato Hotel
BOUTIQUE HOTEL €€

(Map p116; ☑2810 228 103; www.lato.gr; Epimenidou 15; d incl breakfast €90-120; ❄@🛜) Iraklio goes Hollywood – with all the sass but sans attitude – at this mod boutique hotel overlooking the old harbour. Rather than resting on their laurels, the owners opened an even more stylish extension in 2011 across the street, easily recognised by its jazzy facade. Rooms here sport rich woods, warm reds and vinyl floors, plus custom furniture, pillow-top mattresses, a playful lighting scheme and a kettle for making coffee or tea. Back rooms overlook a modernist metal sculpture.

Kronos Hotel
HOTEL €

(Map p116; ☑2810 282 240; www.kronoshotel.gr; Sofokli Venizelou 2; s/d €44/50; ❄@🛜) After a thorough makeover this waterfront hotel has pole-vaulted to the top of the budget hotel category. Rooms have double-glazed windows to block out the noise, as well as balconies, phone, a tiny TV and a fridge. Some doubles have sea views (€58). Optional breakfast is €6.

Capsis Astoria
HOTEL €€€

(Map p116; ☑2810 343 080; www.capsishotel.gr; Plateia Eleftherias; s/d incl breakfast €108/140; P❄@🛜≋) The hulking exterior does not impress, but past the front door the Capsis is a class act all the way to the rooftop pool from where you enjoy a delicious panorama of Iraklio. Rooms have been spiffed up and now sport soothing neutral tones, ultracomfy mattresses and dashing historic black-and-white photographs. Fabulous breakfast buffet.

Mirabello Hotel
HOTEL €€

(Map p116; ☑2810 285 052; www.mirabello-hotel.gr; Theotokopoulou 20; d with/without bathroom €60/48; ☉Apr-Nov; ❄@🛜) This friendly and relaxed hotel on a quiet street is hardly of recent vintage but it does remain a decent value-for-money standby. Rooms are immaculate if a bit cramped and sport TVs, phones and balconies; some also have fridges.

Lena Hotel
HOTEL €€

(Map p116; ☑2810 223 280; www.lena-hotel.gr; Lahana 10; d with/without €60/45; ❄🛜) Everything's a bit long in the tooth but this no-nonsense hotel is still a good budget pick. Amenities in the 16 rooms vary and not all have their own bathrooms, but communal areas are nicely maintained.

Rea Hotel
HOTEL €

(Map p116; ☑2810 223 638; www.hotelrea.gr; cnr Kalimeraki & Handakos; d with/without bathroom €45/35; ❄🛜) Popular with backpackers, the family-run Rea has an easy, friendly atmosphere. Rooms all have small TVs and balconies, but some bathrooms are shared. Family rooms are available. There's a book exchange and a communal fridge.

Kastro Hotel
HOTEL €€€

(Map p116; ☑2810 284 185; www.kastro-hotel.gr; Theotokopoulou 22; s/d/tr incl breakfast from €110/135/165; ❄@🛜) The Kastro has been subjected to a makeover but the rooms sporting floral wallpaper, marble desks and leather-padded walls are still in no danger of being featured on the pages of *House Beautiful*. At least they're large, and come with flat-screen TVs, small fridges and balconies.

Marin Dream Hotel
HOTEL €€

(Map p116; ☑2810 300 018; www.marinhotel.gr; Epimenidou 46; r incl breakfast €95-120; ❄@🛜) Although primarily a business hotel, the Marin Dream also scores with leisure travellers thanks to its great location overlooking the harbour and the fortress (be sure to get a front room with balcony). A palette of chocolate and cherry gives rooms a clean, grown-up look.

GDM Megaron
HOTEL €€€

(Map p116; ☑2810 305 300; www.gdmmegaron.gr; Doukos Beaufort 9; s/d incl breakfast from €140/168; ❄@🛜≋) Don't be put off by the towering hulk of this harbour-front hotel, for inside awaits a top designer abode with comfortable beds, jacuzzis in the VIP suites, flat-screen TVs and a fax in every room. Unwinding in the glass-sided pool and drinking in the sweeping views from the rooftop restaurant and bar are hardly run-of-the-mill features either.

West of Iraklio

AGIA PELAGIA ΑΓΙΑ ΠΕΛΑΓΙΑ

Mourtzanakis Residence
APARTMENTS €€

(☑2810 812 096, 6932467002; www.ecotourismgreece.com; Achlada; apt €80-95; ❄🛜≋) A 10-minute drive from Agia Pelagia, but seemingly a world away, this cluster of four modern loft-style guesthouses offers plenty of elbow room and thoughtfully equipped kitchens. Enjoy a dip in the smallish pool, take in the grand vistas out to sea from your balcony or stroll to the nearby historic village of Achlada.

SARHOS ΣΑΡΧΟΣ
Viglatoras
APARTMENTS €€

(2810 711 332; www.viglatoras.gr; apt €60-70; ✼🛜) On a farm in the pretty mountain village of Sarhos, some 20km southwest of Iraklio, Viglatoras is a cluster of five cosy cottages sleeping two to four. Unwind in front of the crackling fireplace before reporting for mattress duty in the sleeping loft. The eclectically decorated cafe is conducive to meeting fellow travellers, while the taverna serves delicious Cretan fare.

Central Iraklio

ARHANES ΑΡΧΑΝΕΣ
Eliathos
APARTMENTS €€€

(2810 751 818, 6951804929; www.eliathos. gr; studios €91, villas €130-182, breakfast €12; ✼🖼) Tucked into the hillside about half a kilometre south of Arhanes and with grand views of Mt Yiouhtas, this cluster of six houses is a haven of peace and quiet. The owners can help you get immersed in the local culture through cooking classes, excursions and olive oil, raki- or winemaking workshops.

Arhontiko
APARTMENTS €€

(2810 881 550; www.arhontikoarhanes.gr; apt €75-95; ✼🛜) An air of effortless sophistication pervades these four apartments in a villa with incarnations as a military barracks and an elementary school. No hint of either survives in the four bi-level apartments that combine antiques and old embroideries with full kitchens, a fireplace and the gamut of mod cons.

Kalimera Arhanes
VILLAS €€€

(2810 300 330; www.lux-hotels.com/gr /kalimera-arhanes; 1-/3-bedroom villas €176 /280; ✼) Near the Archaeological Museum, this trio of meticulously restored traditional houses built in the early 19th century sport period furniture, fireplaces, old-timey decor in a relaxed garden setting. Kitchens are big enough to whip up entire meals and come with attached balcony for alfresco dining. One-week minimum rentals preferred.

Neraidospilios
APARTMENTS €€

(2810 752 965; www.neraidospilios.gr; studios & apt €40-70; ✼🖼) On the village outskirts overlooking Mt Yiouhtas, these superbly appointed and spacious studios and apartments are run by the brothers at the Diahroniko cafe on the main square. Go there and they will direct you. The pool is an added attraction.

IRAKLIO WINE COUNTRY
Villa Kerasia
PENSION €€

(2810 791 021; www.villa-kerasia.gr; Vlahiana; r incl breakfast €75-100; ✼🛜🖼) In a gorgeous location in tiny Vlahiana, on the edge of the western section of the wine region, this converted old farm house has five rooms and two suites that are tranquil, intimate retreats with stone walls, beamed ceilings and wooden floors. Days start with an opulent breakfast entirely composed of local products that will easily tide you over to the afternoon. If dinner is offered during your stay, sign up: owner Babis is a mean cook who makes suppers veritable celebrations of Cretan cuisine.

Petronikolis
APARTMENTS €€

(2810 743 203; www.petronikolis.gr; Houdetsi; apt €60-70; ✼🛜🖼) This gem of a place in Houdetsi is composed of four spacious studios decorated in traditional style and with small kitchens. Hand-woven textiles and farming equipment from the family estate lend quaint touches, while the lovely taverna with fireplace is great for refuelling after a day on the tourist trail.

ZAROS ΖΑΡΟΣ
🏆 Eleonas
RESORT €€

(2894 031 238, 6976670002; www.eleonas.gr; r incl breakfast €60-120; ✼@🛜🖼) Cradled by olive groves, this attractive retreat is built into a terraced hillside and has smartly appointed rooms sporting the gamut of mod cons as well as fireplaces. Hang by the pool or go active by renting a mountain bike, hitting the trail or taking a cooking class. Plaudits for the sumptuous buffet breakfast.

Studios Keramos
PENSION €

(2894 031 352; www.studiokeramos-zaros.gr; s/d/tr incl breakfast €30/45/55; ✼) Close to the village centre, this little pension is run by the friendly Katerina and is decorated with Cretan crafts, weaving and family heirlooms. Many of the rooms and studios pair

ACCOMMODATION IRAKLIO

antique beds and furniture with such mod cons as TV and kitchenettes. Katerina is up early preparing a fantastic and copious traditional breakfast.

Southern Iraklio

MATALA ΜΑΤΑΛΑ

Matala Valley Village RESORT €€
(☑2892 045 776; www.valleyvillage.gr; d €48, bungalows €76; ☺May-Oct; ✴✦✵✿) Near the village entrance, this sprawling garden resort is especially popular with families. Various room types are available, the nicest of which are the 23 modernist white-washed bungalows added in 2008. Each has two bedrooms, a fridge and a spacious bathroom with jacuzzi tub and separate shower. Frolicking grounds for kids include a lawn, small playground and big pool.

Hotel Nikos HOTEL €
(☑2892 045 375; www.matala-nikos.com; r incl breakfast €40-45; ✴✦) The best property on the hotel strip, Nikos has 17 rooms on two floors along a flower-filled courtyard. The owners, Nikos and Panagiota, were born in Matala and are only too happy to share insider tips about the area with their guests.

Antonio PENSION €
(☑2892 045 123; s/d/tr €25/35/40; ☺Mar-Sep; ✴) Run by the genial Antonio and his son Manolis, this comfortable pension has 10 basic but pleasantly furnished rooms, all with fridge, set around a lovely courtyard.

Matala Camping CAMPGROUND €
(☑2892 045 720; camp sites per person/tent €4.30/3; ☺Jun-Oct) Great location near the beach but really just a shadeless dirt-patch when we visited, although there were rumours it would be fixed up.

AROUND MATALA

KOMMOS ΚΟΜΜΟΣ

Komos Camping CAMPGROUND €
(☑2892 045 596; camp sites per person/tent €4.30/3; ☺May-Oct; ✴) Right at the turn-off to Kommos Beach, this 100-site campground is clean, well kept, great for tenters and rarely gets overcrowded. Facilities include a playground, taverna and pool. The fabulous beach (partly nudist) and Minoan ruins are a 10-minute walk away. Buses stop at the junction.

PITSIDIA ΠΙΤΣΙΔΙΑ

Aretoussa PENSION €
(☑2892 045 555; www.pensionaretoussa.com; s/d/tr incl breakfast €28/36/45; ✦) This old stone house with lots of trees, flowers and herbs welcomes guests to newly spiffed-up rooms with mosquito nets over the beds. Some have access to a private garden, making them ideal for families. Light sleepers should avoid the rooms facing the main road. Breakfast is served on the cosy verandah.

Patelo PENSION €
(☑2892 045 006; http://patelo.messara.de; s/d €25/35, studios €45; ✴) Like a miniature castle, this whitewashed guesthouse crowns the highest point of Pitsidia. Views are predictably fabulous, especially from the large upstairs studio with a kitchen and huge terrace. Other guests can prepare meals in the communal kitchen. Patelo is run by the humorous and ebullient Maria.

SIVAS ΣΙΒΑΣ

Sigelakis APARTMENTS €
(☑2892 042 748; www.sigelakis-studios.gr; r €45-50; ✴✦) Maria and George Sigelakis, who also run their namesake taverna in town (see p141), are the masterminds behind these eight classily furnished and spick-and-span apartments, each with separate bedroom and a small kitchen. Stone walls and marble floors nicely complement the wood-beamed ceiling and fireplace.

KAMILARI ΚΑΜΗΛΑΡΙ

Ambeliotissa APARTMENTS €
(☑2892 042 690; www.ambeliotissa.com; apts €30-55; ✴✦✵✿) A low-key, communal spirit pervades this charmer where studios and apartments are dressed in bright colours and come with balconies overlooking the garden. With a playground, toys and a swimming pool, children will feel especially well taken care of. There's also an outdoor barbecue for socialising with fellow travellers.

Asterousia APARTMENTS €
(☑2892 042 832; www.asterousia.com; studios €35-50; ✴) Feel your stresses melt away in this enchanting place run by Monica and Jorgos, who seek to impart their love for nature and the simple things in life to their guests. They also offer various activities from guided hikes to yoga and cooking workshops.

Plaka APARTMENTS €

(☎2892 042 697; www.plakakreta.com; apt €35; ⌚Apr-Oct; ❋🛜) These four well-appointed hillside apartments just outside the village have balconies with sea views and are decorated in cool blue and white shades. There is a garden with sun loungers in the back. Ask at Taverna Mylonas (p142).

KALAMAKI ΚΑΛΑΜΑΚΙ

TOP CHOICE Arsinoi Studios APARTMENTS €

(☎2892 045 475, 6986858923; www.arsinoi-studios .gr; studios €30-35; ❋🛜) Arsinoi would be just another apartment building near the beach were it not for the fall-over-backwards friendly Papadospiridaki family. You'll instantly feel at home when big-hearted Noi ushers you to your squeaky-clean and roomy digs accented with a bowl of fruit from the family farm. She's also a killer cook and often presents her guests with homemade mezedhes and *raki* on the communal terrace in the evenings. Ask for a room with sea view.

Alexandros Beach HOTEL €

(☎2892 045 195; www.alexandros-kalamaki.com; d incl breakfast €39-55; ❋🛜) Right on the beach at the quiet end of the waterfront promenade, this 28-room peach-coloured hotel is a fine base for days on the beach or exploring the local countryside. Sea-facing rooms are the largest, while the cheaper ones out back are dark and cramped; all have balconies. If you need more space, ask about the villas (€55 to €70) on a hill top between Kalamaki and Kalamari.

KAPETANIANA ΚΑΠΕΤΑΝΙΑΝΑ

Pension Kofinas PENSION €

(☎2893 041 440; www.korifi.de; s/d €20/25) This remote haven is operated by Austrian ex-hippies Gunnar and Louisa, who organise hiking and climbing tours. There are just three double rooms and one with bunks for four; all share external facilities. Bookings are essential.

LENDAS ΛΕΝΤΑΣ

Casa Doria HOTEL €

(☎2892 095 376; www.casadoria.net; r incl breakfast €40; ❋) There's remote and then there's Casa Doria. The self-proclaimed 'slow-life hotel' has rooms exuding Zen-like simplicity and a restaurant that delivers Italian flavour explosions along with Greek and Cretan standards. Half-board is an extra €14. With easy access to the Trakhoula Gorge, this is a great base for hikers, climbers and mountain bikers. It's about 2.5km from Lendas; look for the Loutra–Trahulas turn-off.

Studios Gaitani APARTMENTS €

(☎2892 095 341; www.studios-gaitani.gr; studios €30-50; ❋) It doesn't get more beachfront than this. These modern studios and apartments are just a few steps down to the sand. They have kitchenettes, TV and fridge, and the larger ones can fit up to four.

Villa Tsapakis STUDIOS €

(☎2892 095 378, 6947571900; www.villa-tsapakis .gr; studios €35; ❋) Over the headland, on lovely sandy Diskos (or Dytikos) beach (mostly nudist), this flower-filled oasis has well-appointed, good-value studios with kitchens and balconies set around a central courtyard.

Northeastern Coast

Most hotels in this area are the purview of package-tour operators, so chances of finding a beach resort in July or August without pre-booking are practically nil. Try your luck in some of the older and smaller properties away from the coast or check in with a local travel agency.

HERSONISOS ΧΕΡΣΟΝΗΣΟΣ

If you want to stay away from the resort hubbub, pick a place up the hill in the village of Koutouloufari or in old Hersonisos.

Villa Iokasti APARTMENTS €€

(☎2897 022 607; www.iokasti.gr; Koutouloufari; 1-/2-bedroom apt €65/110; ❋@❋) Iokasti's modern and bright one- and two-bedroom apartments with cheerful colour accents are set within an attractive garden off the main drag towards the end of Koutouloufari. The taverna and cafe are regarded as among the best in town and have pleasant sea views.

Balsamico Suites STUDIOS €€

(☎2897 023 323; www.balsamico-suites.gr; Old Hersonisos; studios €85; ❋🛜) A family-run property with gracious hosts is rare in this part of the island, but Maria and Michalis deliver by the bucketful. Their stone building complex fuses old-world charm with such mod cons as flat-screen TVs and DVD players, kitchens and hairdryers. The well-proportioned traditional studios are decked out in rich, dark wood and come with balconies.

Camping Creta   CAMPGROUND €
(☏2897 041 400; www.campingcrete.de.ki; camp
sites per tent/person €5.50/4) About 7km west
of Hersonisos on a sand-and-pebble beach
in the hamlet of Gouves. There are some
nicely shaded spots catering for both tenters
and caravans, as well as a small market and
waterfront taverna.

MALIA ΜΑΛΙΑ
Matheo Hotel   HOTEL €€
(☏2897 032 980; www.hotel-matheo.com; Theodo-
ros 1; s €84-110, d €108-129; ❄🛜⛱) A winner
if you want to be in a quiet spot but close
to the action. With 70 rooms in sparkling
white villas set amid olive and lemon trees,
the hotel is small enough for staff to give
guests personal attention. All rooms are
decked out in fresh, good-mood colours,
although the standard ones are a bit
teensy. It's about 200m to the beach and
500m into town.

Villa Sonia   PENSION €€
(☏2897 032 221, 6932066776; www.villa-sonia
-kreta.info; r €75; ❄) Away from the bustling
beach road between Malia and Stalis,
German-owned Sonia has 18 clean and
utilitarian rooms in two buildings surrounded by palm trees. There is no pool,
but you can use those at nearby hotels for
free and the beach is only a short walk
away, as is the bus stop.

LASITHI ΛΑΣΙΘΙ

North Coast
AGIOS NIKOLAOS ΑΓΙΟΣ ΝΙΚΟΛΑΟΣ
⌜TOP⌝
⌞CHOICE⌟ **Villa Olga**   APARTMENTS €€
(☏28410 25913; www.villa-olga.gr; apt €80-
95; ❄🛜⛱) These delightful self-catering
places are located midway between Agios
Nikolaos and Elounda. They have terrific
views across the Bay of Mirabello from
their rising terraces, which are reached by
flights of steps. The apartments cater for
two to six people and are set in lovely leafy
gardens. They are well equipped and have
traditional furniture and artefacts scattered around. There's a small swimming
pool, and Olga, the owner, is charming and helpful. Villa Olga is reached by
following the waterfront road, Akti Koundourou, northeast from the centre of Agios
Nikolaos. At a junction above Ammoudi

Beach take the right-hand branch towards
Elounda for about 500m and look out for
the Villa Olga sign on the left.

⌜TOP⌝
⌞CHOICE⌟ **Minos Beach Art**
Hotel   BOUTIQUE HOTEL €€€
(☏28410 22345; www.bluegr.com; r incl breakfast from €200; P❄🛜⛱) This classy resort
in a superb location, just out of town, is a
veritable art gallery, with sculptures from
leading Greek and foreign artists adorning
the grounds right down to the beach. The
low-rise design and cool style maintain
the hotel's position as one of the island's
finest. The sign on the hotel reads 'Minos
Beach Hotel'. Follow the waterfront road,
Akti Koundourou, northeast from the
centre of Agios Nikolaos for about 1km.
The hotel is signposted on the seaward
side of the road.

Lato Hotel   HOTEL €€
(☏28410 24581; www.lato-hotel.com.gr; Amoudi;
s/d incl breakfast €51/68; P❄@⛱) With your
own transport, the Lato is a good choice and
offers a friendly welcome. To get there, follow the waterfront road, Akti Koundourou,
northeast from the centre of Agios Nikolaos
for just over 1km. The hotel is on the left.
There's a small pool and the beach is about
300m away. The same management runs
the charming **Karavostassi (The Stone
House) Apartments** (☏28410 24581; www
.karavostassi.gr; apt €88-116) in an old carob
warehouse on an isolated cove about 8km
east from the Lato.

Hotel Creta   APARTMENTS €
(Map p154; ☏28410 28893; www.agiosnikaloas
-hotels.gr; Sarolidi 22; s/d €45/50; ❄🛜) There's
excellent value at these well-kept and comfy
self-catering apartments, where the upper
balconies have great views. Parking is limited in the surrounding streets, but the
location is ideal for the town centre, yet in
a quiet location. There is a lift.

Hotel Doxa   HOTEL €
(Map p154; ☏28410 24214; www.doxahotel.gr;
Idomeneos 7; s/d/tr incl breakfast €45/50/65;
❄🛜) The very comfy, well-appointed rooms
and the good breakfast at this well-run hotel
make up for a rather dull location in a side
street. There is a lift. Ammos beach and car
parking are just a short stroll away.

Du Lac Hotel   HOTEL €€
(Map p154; ☏28410 22711; www.dulachotel.gr; 28
Oktovriou 17; s/d €40/60, studios €80; ❄) This

town-centre hotel has fine views over Voulismeni Lake from its decent rooms and spacious, fully fitted-out studios. Both options have stylish contemporary furnishings and nice bathrooms.

Pension Mary PENSION €
(Map p154; ☎28410 23760; Evans 13; s/d/tr €20/35/45; ❄) Old-fashioned style survives at this friendly pension in a narrow street just up from Kytroplatia Beach. Rooms are basic and clean and most have private bathrooms. There's a communal kitchen. Breakfast is €5.

Pergola Hotel HOTEL €
(Map p154; ☎/fax 28410 28152; Sarolidi 20; d with views €40-60; ❄🖥) Refurbishment a couple of years ago has perked up the pleasant rooms at this hotel. All have fridges and tea- and coffee-making facilities. There is a ver- andah under a pergola on which to relax or have breakfast. Front rooms have balconies and sea views. There is a lift.

Delta HOTEL €
(Map p154; ☎28410 28893; www.agiosnikalaos -hotels.gr; Tselepi 22; s/d €45/50; ❄) Opposite Kytroplatia beach and behind a taverna, these bright, clean rooms are run by the owners of the Hotel Creta.

KRITSA ΚΡΙΤΣΑ
Rooms Argyro PENSION €
(☎28410 51174; www.argyrorentrooms.gr; s/d/ tr €25/40/50; ❄) Well positioned at the en- trance to the village, near the car park, these immaculate and basic rooms with balconies come with a cheerful welcome. There's a little shaded area downstairs for breakfast and light meals.

Olive Press B&B €€
(☎28410 51296; www.olivepress.centerall.com; d €50-60, apt €70) This Belgian-run B&B is in a lovingly restored stone olive press in the upper part of the village, near Agios Yiorgos church. There's lots of exposed wood and stonework and one apartment incorporates the original olive press.

ELOUNDA ΕΛΟΥΝΤΑ
Many hotels in and around Elounda are booked in advance by tour operators, but the following are worth trying.

Delfinia Studios & Apartments APARTMENTS €
(☎28410 41641; www.pediaditis.gr; s/d/apt €35/ 40/55; ❄🖥❄) Pleasant rooms with some bal- conies overlooking the sea are supplemented

by options for larger groups and families in apartments. The same family also run the nearby **Milos Apartments** (prices as for Delfinia), where there is a pool. Check for details at the newspaper shop on the square.

Hotel Aristea HOTEL €
(☎28410 41300; www.aristeahotel.com; s/d/incl breakfast €30/40; ❄) A budget option beside the main square, the Aristea won't promise scenic seclusion but rooms are decent and clean, with front rooms looking out to sea and the harbour. Busy taverna traffic below is muted by double glazing.

Corali Studios APARTMENTS €€
(☎/fax 28410 41712; www.coralistudios.com; studios €75; ❄) On the northern side, these handy self-catering studios are set amid lush lawns with a shaded patio. The same family run the **Portobello Apartments** (2–4-bed apt €45-75; ❄) next door.

Elounda Island Villas APARTMENTS €€
(☎28410 41274; www.eloundaisland.gr; d €80, 4-person apt €110; P❄) A secluded option on Kolokytha Island, reached along the nar- row peninsula. The split-level apartments, with well-equipped kitchens, are set amid a pleasant garden and decorated with traditional furnishings. It's just under a kilometre walk into town.

PLAKA ΠΛΑΚΑ
Stella Mare Studios APARTMENTS €€
(☎28410 41814; studios €65-75; ❄) In a complex of very pleasant self-catering studios and apartments within a charming garden of trees and shrubs, the studios are located off the main road. Interiors are a pleasant mix of modern amenities with traditional Cretan furnishings.

Lasithi Plateau Οροπέδιο Λασιθίου

TZERMIADO ΤΖΕΡΜΙΑΔΟ
TOP CHOICE **Argoulias** APARTMENTS €€
(☎28440 22754; www.argoulias.gr; d incl breakfast €70-80; P❄) An almost alpine style makes these apartments an outstanding choice, summer or winter. Built into the hillside above the main village and constructed of exposed local stone, they have sweep- ing views across the Lasithi Plateau to the mountains. The decor and furnishings are traditional and stylish, and there are open fires to keep things cosy in winter.

The apartments are self-catering, although breakfast is delivered each morning. The owners also run an excellent restaurant across the road. Ask about use of bicycles. Look for signs to Argoulias on the entrance to Tzermiado coming from the east.

Kourites
PENSION, HOTEL €

(☑28440 22054; www.kourites.eu; s/d €35/40) There are clean and simple rooms above the taverna of the same name on the outskirts of town and also in a nearby small hotel. Breakfast is €5.

AGIOS GEORGIOS ΑΓΙΟΣ ΓΕΩΡΓΙΟΣ
Hotel Maria
HOTEL €

(☑28440 31774; d/tr/q incl breakfast €59/78/98) These pleasantly quirky rooms on the northern side of the village are in an equally quirky building that is fronted by a leafy garden. The traditional mountain beds are rather narrow and are on stone bases. Local furnishings and woven wall hangings add to the cheerful atmosphere.

Northeast Coast

MOHLOS ΜΟΧΛΟΣ
Mochlos Mare
APARTMENTS €€

(☑28430 94005; www.mochlos-mare.com; apt €50-80; ✸) Just outside the village, these spacious self-catering apartments have great sea views from the big balconies of the upper rooms. There's a communal outdoor kitchen and barbecue, and vines and vegetables flourish in the big garden, all framed by lovely rose bushes.

Hotel Sofia
HOTEL €

(☑28430 94554; sofia-mochlos@hotmail.com; r €35-45; ✸) Some of these decent rooms above the Sofia Taverna are a touch small but the front rooms have balconies with sea views. The owners have spacious apartments (€40 to €55) 200m east of the harbour, where longer stays are preferred.

Kyma Apartments
STUDIOS €

(☑28430 94177; soik@in.gr; studios €35; ✸) These well-kept self-catering studios on the west side of Mohlos are a reasonable deal. Ask at the supermarket in the village.

SITIA ΣΗΤΕΙΑ
Hotel Arhontiko
INN €

(Map p164; ☑28430 28172; Kondylaki 16; s/d €27/32, studios €34) A quiet location up-hill from the port enhances the charm of this guesthouse in a neoclassical building.

There's great period style, and everything, from entrance hall to the shared bathrooms, is spotlessly maintained. A little garden out front is shaded by jasmine and orange trees.

Sitia Bay Hotel
APARTMENTS €€€

(off Map p164; ☑28430 24800; www.sitiabay.com; Paraliaki Leoforos 8; apt & ste from €115; P✸🛜☎) Modern-style hotel with personal and friendly service of the highest order. Most of the comfortable and tasteful one- and two-room apartments have sea views, and there's a pool, hydrospa, mini-gym and sauna. Breakfast is €6.

Apostolis
PENSION €

(Map p164; ☑28430 22993/28172; Kazantzaki 27; s/d/tr €30/35/40) There are charming owners at these pleasant rooms on a quiet street. Rooms have ceiling fans, and en suite showers. There's a communal balcony and small kitchen with tea- and coffee-making facilities and a fridge.

Hotel Flisvos
HOTEL €€

(Map p164; ☑28430 27135; www.flisvos-sitia.com; Karamanli 4; s/d incl breakfast €60/70; P✸🛜) Located just out of the centre, on the southern waterfront, Flisvos is a decent modern hotel. Rooms are neat and comfortable and there is good wi-fi in each room. A larger wing behind has more spacious rooms and a lift.

Itanos Hotel
HOTEL €

(Map p164; ☑28430 22900; www.itanoshotel.com; Plateia Iroön Polytehniou; s/d incl breakfast with sea views €47/68; ✸@) The Itanos is on the front near Plateia Iroön Polytehniou. It has business-style rooms with all facilities and there's a rooftop terrace restaurant.

Hotel Krystal
HOTEL €

(Map p164; ☑28430 22284; www.ekaterinidis-hotels.com; Kapetan Sifinos 17; s/d/tr incl breakfast €35/50/60; ✸🛜) In the heart of town, this useful hotel is open year-round.

East Coast

PALEKASTRO ΠΑΛΑΙΚΑΣΤΡΟ
Hiona Holiday Hotel
HOTEL €€

(☑28430 29623; s/d incl breakfast €56/72; P✸) The rather plain, almost urban facade of this hotel belies its comfy rooms and decent facilities. There's a well-stocked bar and pleasant public areas.

Hotel Hellas
HOTEL €

(☑28430 61240; hellas_h@otenet.gr; d €45; ❉) These pleasant though basic rooms have been renovated in recent years and are convenient for the centre of the village. There's a taverna downstairs.

AROUND PALEKASTRO

Esperides
APARTMENTS €€

(☑28430 61433, 6945255243; isabel-t@otenet.gr; apt €85-105; P❉☀) In a good location, just inland from Kouremenos Bay, these lovely buildings in exposed stone have traditional furnishings and all modern self-catering facilities.

Grandes Apartments
APARTMENTS €€

(☑28430 61496; www.grandes.gr; q studios €87; P❉) Located behind Kouremenos beach, these self-catering options are surrounded by a flower-filled garden and trees. They're well equipped and decorated with style, and there's a nearby beachfront taverna run by the owners.

ZAKROS & KATO ZAKROS ΖΑΚΡΟΣ & ΚΑΤΩ ΖΑΚΡΟΣ

Rooms in Kato Zakros fill up fast in high season, so it is best to book.

TOP CHOICE / Stella's Traditional Apartments
APARTMENTS €€

(☑/fax 28430 23739; www.stelapts.com; studios €60-80; P❉) Close to the wooded mouth of Zakros Gorge, these charming self-contained studios are in a lovely garden setting. They are decorated with very distinctive wooden furniture and other artefacts made by joint owner Elias Pagianidis. There are hammocks under the trees, barbecues and an external kitchen with an honesty system for supplies. Elias has excellent knowledge and experience of hiking trails and other outdoor activities around the area. The owners also run the Terra Minoika villas on the hillside above.

Terra Minoika
VILLAS €€€

(☑28430 23739, 6976719461; www.stelapts.com; apt €120) High on the slopes above Kato Zakros a complex of stone-walled villas seems to grow naturally from the rocky ground itself. Built by Stella Ailamaki and Elias Pagianidis, who also own Stella's Traditional Apartments in the valley below, the villas were completed in 2011 and were built using the natural material of the surrounding area. Of the highest quality, the villas mix interior modernism and luxury with a sense of place. The views are, of course, exhilarating. Pagianidis has unique skills in crafting artefacts that enhance the buildings, inside and out. Sheltered courtyards and balconies add to the character. There's even a fully equipped gym, reflecting the owners' backgrounds as athletes. Both are very experienced in outdoor activities with Elias an expert on local hiking. Stella is also an accomplished dancer who can give lessons in traditional Greek dance. The Terra Minoika villas are open all year.

Kato Zakros Palace
APARTMENTS €€

(☑28430 29550; www.palaikastro.com/katozakros palace; s/d €50/60; P❉) High on the slopes above Kato Zakros beach and beside the approach road are these pleasant rooms and studios with cooking facilities and a guests' laundry room. Stunning views are inevitable and the owners are very friendly.

Athena & Coral Rooms
PENSION €

(☑28430 26893; www.katozakros.cretefamilyhotels .com; d €40-50; ❉) Above the beach and behind the Akrogiali Taverna (p168).

Katerina Apartments
APARTMENTS €

(☑28430 26893; www.katozakros.cretefamilyhotels .com; apt €70) Under the same management as Athena & Coral Rooms, these four excellent stone-built studios and maisonettes opposite Stella's can sleep up to four and enjoy a superb setting.

South Coast

ASPROS POTAMOS ΑΣΠΡΟΣ ΠΟΤΑΜΟΣ

Aspros Potamos
GUESTHOUSE €€

(☑28430 51694; www.asprospotamos.com; d/tr/q €50/65/75) These 300-year-old stone cottages have been lovingly restored by owner, Aleka Halkia, as guesthouses and are lit by oil lamps and candles. The stone floors, traditional furnishings and winter fireplaces add to the traditional ambience. Potamos is just above Makrygialos on the road to Pefki.

IERAPETRA ΙΕΡΑΠΕΤΡΑ

Cretan Villa Hotel
HOTEL €

(Map p170; ☑28420 28522; www.cretan-villa.com; Lakerda 16; s €40, d €44-50; ❉☎) This well-maintained 18th-century house manages to create a charming, almost rural, character at the heart of town. The traditionally furnished rooms cluster around a peaceful courtyard. It's only a few minutes' walk from the bus station.

TOP CHOICE El Greco
BOUTIQUE HOTEL €€

(Map p170; ☑28420 28471; www.elgreco-ierapetra .gr; Kothri 42; s incl breakfast €65-80, d €85-100; ❄️🛜) A complete refurbishment has transformed this seafront building into a boutique hotel with stylish decor. Rooms are elegant and comfortable. The sea side of the building overlooks the promenade and has fine views. There's a cafe-bar and restaurant on the ground floor.

Astron Hotel
BUSINESS HOTEL €€

(Map p170; ☑28420 25114;www.hotelastron.com .gr; Kothri 56; s/d/tr incl breakfast €70/80/95; ❄️🛜) Smooth, glossy and comfortably bland, the Astron is in a good position at the eastern end of the promenade, with the sea a few steps away. There's a downstairs cafe-bar.

Ersi Hotel
HOTEL €

(Map p170; ☑28420 23208; Plateia Eleftherias 19; s/d €30/40; ❄️) Fair-value rooms at the heart of the town, though some are a touch compact.

Coral Hotel
HOTEL €

(Map p170; ☑28420 27755; Katzonovatsi 12; s/d €30/40) Another reasonable budget option in a quiet pocket of the old town.

Koutsounari Camping
CAMPGROUND €

(☑2842061213;www.camping-koutsounari.epimlas .gr; camp sites per adult/child/tent €6.50/3.50/ 4.50; 🅿❄️) About 7km east at Koutsounari, it has a pool, restaurant, snack bar and minimarket. Ierapetra–Sitia buses pass the site.

MYRTOS ΜΥΡΤΟΣ

Villa Mertiza
APARTMENTS €€

(☑28420 51208, 6932735224; www.mertiza.com; s/d €44/55, apt €57-70; ❄️🛜) There's an excellent selection of self-catering rooms, studios and apartments at this well-run place on the outer edge of the village, where the Dutch-Greek hosts have created a friendly atmosphere. Each room has its own colourful and individual decor. The owners also have some lovely villas (€110) a little further out, and other accommodation options.

Big Blue
APARTMENTS €

(☑28420 51094; www.big-blue.gr; d €40, studios €45-75, apt €85; ❄️) On high ground at the western edge of town, this pleasant place is handy for the beach. There's a choice of large airy studios with sea views, or cheaper, ground-floor rooms. All have cooking facilities. Breakfast is €5 to €8.50.

ACCOMMODATION LASITHI

Understand
Crete

population per sq km

GREECE   ENGLAND   CRETE

≈ 75 people

Crete Today

Crete & the Fiscal Crisis

As with anywhere in Greece, Crete has certainly not been immune to the country's severe debt crisis. In April 2010, the euro-zone countries approved a €100 billion package of emergency loans to prevent the country from defaulting on its €327 billion debt (equal to 150% of its GDP). The bailout deal required the Athens government to impose strict austerity measures (public spending cuts, pension reform and across-the-board tax increases) as well as to raise €50 billion through the privatisation of state-controlled companies. However, in spring 2011 it became clear that even these measures would not go far enough. In July 2011, euro-zone leaders approved a second aid package amounting to an additional €109 billion to help Greece get its economy back on track.

Tourism on the Rebound

While the government's austerity measures were hardly popular in Crete, they did not trigger the kind of strikes and violent protests seen in Athens. Indeed, there may be reasons for quiet optimism. In 2011, after a couple of meagre years, locals breathed a collective sigh of relief when tourism was up by 15%. As a key engine of the Cretan economy, tourism generates some 40% of its output and accounts for at least one in five jobs. Though welcome, the uptick did not mean that Crete was out of the woods, especially since visitors were largely lured by lower or stagnant prices.

Meanwhile, Crete is also increasingly tapping into the potential of sustainable eco-travel. EU grants to promote green tourism and preserve cultural heritage have resulted in the restoration of historic buildings and a proliferation of traditional guesthouses, villas and apartments, especially in rural areas.

» Population: 630,000

» Area: 8336 sq km

» GDP: €9.167 billion

» GDP per capita: €23,500

» Number of visitors: 2.8 million

» Number of olive trees: 30 million

Faux Pas

» Don't dress immodestly when visiting a church or monastery. Keep your arms and legs covered.

» Although it's widely practised, don't assume you can go topless or au naturel on beaches.

» Don't call on anyone at home during the post-lunch *mesimeri* (siesta, 3pm to 5pm).

» Cretans take their hospitality seriously, so if you are treated to a drink or meal, accept graciously – rejection can cause offence.

Top Films

Zorba the Greek (1964) Boasting three Academy Awards, this is still the quintessential Crete-filmed movie.

Night Ambush (1957) Gripping retelling of the kidnapping of Nazi General Heinrich Kreipe by British forces in 1944.

belief systems
(% of population)

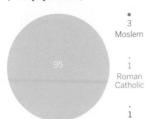

95

Greek Orthodox

• 3
Moslem

. 1
Roman Catholic

. 1
Other

if Crete were 100 people

60 would live in rural areas
40 would live in the six largest cities

Environmental Awareness

Cretans, however, are not just jumping on the green bandwagon. In fact, a growing number of locals are becoming increasingly sensitive to the long-term dangers of environmental degradation. The lack of planning and regulation is most evident in the tourist zones along the highly developed north coast. In response, local environmental groups, students and expats have of late banded together to successfully prevent several large-scale developments.

In Lasithi, for instance, activists thwarted plans by the British Minoan Group to build a 7000-bed luxury golf resort on remote Cavo Sideros. And in Timbaki, on Crete's south coast, plans to construct a massive container port by Chinese shipping giant Cosco, were also derailed due to local opposition.

Whether the country's fiscal crisis and the need to raise revenue may lead to these projects being green-lighted after all is anybody's guess for now.

Crete – the 'Greek Colombia'?

Cretans are fierce, proud and independent and they love their guns. But gun mania is not just a cultural or historic hangover. Feuding is rife in the mountain villages of Anogia, Zoniana and Livadia in remote Rethymno. Nicknamed the 'devil's triangle', they have in recent years become a notorious centre for illegal arms and drugs, the deep ravines being a haven for concealing cannabis crops. Mafia-like mayhem descended on the area in November 2007, when police staked out a gang of pot-growing shepherds and ended up walking into an ambush which left several officers critically injured. Some 40 male villagers were put on trial in Athens in 2009, with 28 of them receiving jail terms ranging from six years to life.

GAVDOS

The island of Gavdos in Hania marks the southernmost point in Europe.

Top Reads

El Greco (2007) Greek-made biopic tells the life story of the Cretan-born Renaissance painter.

Freedom or Death (Nikos Kazantzakis, 1950) Powerful account of 1889 Cretan rebellion against the Turks.

The Cretan Runner (George Psychoundakis, 1955) Cretan resistance in WWII as told by a local shepherd turned messenger.

Dark Labyrinth (Laurence Durrell, 1958) Philosophical tale of a group of English travellers determined to find and explore a dangerous labyrinth.

History

Crete's colourful history goes back 5000 years and is evident across the island, from ancient palaces and Roman cities to spectacular Byzantine churches, Venetian fortresses and Ottoman buildings. Crete's prominent place in world history dates back to the illustrious Minoans, who were lording over lavish palaces at a time when other Europeans were huddled in primitive huts. Ever since, Crete's strategic location in the middle of the Mediterranean has involved it in momentous world events. It has been the apple of discord for civilisations that have either neighboured it, such as the medieval Arabs, or that have had broader ambitions, like the Germans in WWII.

In the popular imagination, Crete's history – both real and speculative – has also left an indelible mark. It has a prominent place in ancient Greek mythology as the place where Rhea gave birth to Zeus and hid him from his child-gobbling father, and where Zeus' own son, Minos, had his legendary reign. Icarus and Daedalus launched their ill-fated flight in Crete, while Theseus made the voyage from Athens to Crete to slay the Minotaur in the famous labyrinth.

While the more mythical aspects of these tales are certainly specious, it is equally true that they could only have been created for a place boasting historical and cultural achievements on an appropriately grand scale. In short, the grandiosity of Crete's ancient legends is indicative of a real past, one rich, powerful and highly sophisticated for its time.

Crete's formative and enduring physical and cultural history has much to do with the arrival of Orthodox Christianity and its accompanying Byzantine character, which, despite occupations by Arabs, Venetians and Ottomans, managed to survive intact due to the tenacity and independence of its people. The island's formidable geography, which protected everything from holy icons, vernacular dialects and customs in Crete's mountain fastnesses, helps explain this ability to retain traditions during chaotic times.

TIMELINE

6500 BC

Crete's earliest-known inhabitants are hunter-gathers. Neolithic people live in caves or wooden houses, worship female fertility goddesses, farm, raise livestock and make primitive pottery.

3000 BC

Bronze-making North African or Levantine immigrants arrive, and the Bronze Age begins. Society changes, with these early Cretans beginning to trade. Pottery and jewellery making develops.

2000 BC

Minoan civilisation reaches its peak: architectural advances lead to the first palaces in Knossos, Phaestos, Malia and Zakros, while pottery making improves and Crete's first script emerges.

During excavations carried out in 2008 and 2009 near Plakias and Preveli, archaeologists were astonished to discover chiselled stone tools dating back at least 130,000 years. The tools came as the first evidence that humankind had engaged in sea travel so long ago. (The earliest known sea voyage previous to the Crete finds was a mere 60,000 years ago.)

The idea that the first Cretans arrived by boat much earlier than anyone had ever thought has revolutionary implications for the entire anthropological conventional wisdom, which had it that the first humans migrated to Europe from Africa by land alone. Since experts believe the Cretan tools may in fact date back up to 700,000 years, it's clear that there are more revelations ahead. The digging continues.

The intriguing blend of civilisations that have inhabited Crete over the past eight centuries has blessed it with a richly layered history, as seen in its uniquely synthetic traditional music, art, local legends and worship. Cretans have always been a proud, insular bunch, and the fact that there was even a debate about whether to become an independent state or join Greece after the Ottoman period speaks volumes about the unique character of the Cretans.

Myth & the Minoans

Crete's early history is largely shrouded in myth, making it all the more fascinating. It is clear from both legends and physical remains, however, that it was home to Europe's first advanced civilisation: the Minoans.

This enigmatic culture emerged in the Bronze Age, predating the great Mycenaean civilisation on the Greek mainland. Minoan society interacted with, and was inspired by, two great Middle Eastern civilisations: the Mesopotamians and Egyptians. Immigrants arriving from Anatolia around 3000 BC brought with them the skills necessary for making bronze, a technological quantum leap that enabled the emerging Minoans to flourish almost uninterrupted for over one-and-a-half millennia.

While many aspects of the less-attested neolithic life endured during the Early Minoan period, the advent of bronze allowed the Minoans to build better boats and thus expand their trade in the Near East. Pottery and goldsmithing became more sophisticated, foreshadowing the subsequent great achievements of Minoan art, and the island prospered from trade.

The chronology of the Minoan age is debated. But most archaeologists generally split the Minoan period into three phases: Protopalatial (3400–2100 BC), Neopalatial (2100–1450 BC) and Postpalatial (1450–1200 BC). These periods roughly correspond, with some overlap, to the older divisions of Early Minoan (some parts also called Prepalatial), Middle Minoan and Late Minoan; the terms are used interchangeably throughout.

1700 BC	1450 BC	1400 BC
The Minoan palaces are destroyed, probably by an earthquake. However, they are rebuilt bigger and better, with multiple storeys, storerooms, workshops, living quarters and advanced drainage systems.	Minoan culture comes to an abrupt and unexplained halt. The palaces (except Knossos) are destroyed by what archaeologists believe was a massive tsunami following a volcanic eruption on Santorini.	The Mycenaeans colonise Crete, building cities such as Lappa (Argyroupoli), Kydonia (Hania) and Polyrrinia. Weapons manufacture flourishes; fine arts fall into decline. Greek gods replace worship of the Mother Goddess.

NEIL SETCHFIELD/LONELY PLANET IMAGES ©

» Minoan ruins at Malia

The Minoan civilisation reached its peak during the Protopalatial period, also called the Old Palace or Middle Minoan period. Around 2000 BC, the large palace complexes of Knossos, Phaestos, Malia and Zakros were built, marking a sharp break with neolithic village life.

During this period, Crete was probably governed by local rulers, with power and wealth concentrated at Knossos. Society was organised along hierarchical lines, with a large population of slaves, and great architectural advances were made. The first Cretan script also emerged during this period. At first highly pictorial, the writing gradually changed from the representations of natural objects to more abstract figures that resembled Egyptian hieroglyphics.

In 1700 BC the palaces were suddenly destroyed by what most archaeologists believe was an earthquake. But soon after came the Minoan golden age, and the rebuilding of the palaces at Knossos, Phaestos, Malia and Zakros; their new and more complex design was remarkably advanced. There were multiple storeys, sumptuous royal apartments, grand reception halls, storerooms, workshops, living quarters for staff, and an advanced drainage system. The design later gave rise to the myth of the Cretan labyrinth and the Minotaur.

During the Neopalatial period, the Minoan state developed into a powerful *thalassocracy* (state known for prosperous maritime trade), purportedly ruled by King Minos, with the capital at Knossos. Trade with the eastern Mediterranean, Asia Minor and Egypt boomed, helped by Minoan colonies in the Aegean. Minoan pottery, textiles and agricultural produce such as olive oil and livestock subsequently found ready markets throughout the Aegean, Egypt, Syria and possibly Sicily.

Minoan civilisation came to an abrupt and mysterious halt around 1450 BC after the palaces (except for Knossos) and numerous smaller settlements were smashed to bits. New scientific evidence suggests the Minoans were weakened by a massive tsunami and ash fallout from a cataclysmic volcano that erupted on nearby Santorini. But there is much debate about both the timing and explanation for the ultimate demise of the Minoans. Some argue it was caused by a second, powerful earthquake a century later. Other archaeologists blame the invading Mycenaeans. Whether the Mycenaeans caused the catastrophe or merely profited from it, it is clear that their presence on the island closely coincided with the destruction of the palaces and Minoan civilisation.

The Rise & Fall of the Mycenaeans

The Mycenaean civilisation, which reached its peak between 1500 and 1200 BC, was the first great civilisation on the Greek mainland. Named after the ancient city of Mycenae, it is also known as the Achaean civili-

1100 BC	431–386 BC	67 BC	27 BC
The Dorians overrun the Mycenaean cities and become Crete's new masters; they reorganise the political system. A rudimentary democracy replaces monarchical government.	While Greece is embroiled in the Peloponnesian War, Crete also sees internal strife: Knossos against Lyttos, Phaestos against Gortyna, Kydonia against Apollonia, and Itanos against Ierapitna.	The Romans finally conquer Crete after invading two years earlier at Kydonia. Gortyna becomes the capital and most powerful city. The 'Pax Romana' ends internal wars.	Crete is united with eastern Libya to form the Roman province of Creta et Cyrenaica, reorganising population centres and ushering in a new era of prosperity.

sation after the Indo-European branch of migrants who had settled on mainland Greece.

Unlike Minoan society, where the lack of city walls seems to indicate relative peace under some form of central authority, Mycenaean civilisation was characterised by independent city states, the most powerful of them all being Mycenae, ruled by kings who inhabited palaces enclosed within massive walls on easily defensible hill tops.

The Mycenaeans wrote in Linear B script. Clay tablets inscribed with the script found at the Palace of Knossos is evidence of Mycenaean occupation of the island. Their colonisation of Crete lasted from 1400 to 1100 BC. Knossos probably retained its position as capital of the island, but its rulers were subject to the mainland Mycenaeans. The Minoan Cretans either left the island or hid in its interior while the Mycenaeans founded new cities such as Lappa (Argyroupoli), Kydonia (Hania) and Polyrrinia.

The economy of the island stayed more or less the same, still based upon the export of local products, but the fine arts fell into decline. Only the manufacture of weapons flourished, reflecting the new militaristic spirit that the Mycenaeans brought to Crete. The Mycenaeans also replaced worship of the Mother Goddess with new Greek gods such as Zeus, Hera and Athena.

Mycenaean influence stretched far and wide, but eventually weakened by internal strife; they were no match for the warlike Dorians.

Classical Crete

Despite fierce resistance, Dorians conquered Crete around 1100 BC, and many inhabitants fled to Asia Minor. Those who remained, known as Eteo-Cretans or 'true Cretans', retreated to the hills and thus preserved their culture.

The Dorians heralded a traumatic break with the past. The next 400 years are often referred to as Greece's 'dark age', although it would be unfair to dismiss the Dorians completely: they brought iron with them and developed a new style of pottery, decorated with striking geometrical designs. They also worshipped male gods instead of fertility goddesses and adopted the Mycenaean gods of Poseidon, Zeus and Apollo, paving the way for the later Greek religious pantheon.

The Dorians reorganised Crete's political system and divided society into three classes: free citizens who owned property and enjoyed political liberty (including land-holding peasants); merchants and seamen; and slaves. The monarchical system was replaced by a rudimentary democracy. Free citizens elected a ruling committee that was guided by a council of elders and answered to an assembly of free citizens. Unlike in Minoan times, women were subordinate.

By about 800 BC, local agriculture and animal husbandry had become

Killer Waves

Minoan civilisation was probably destroyed by a tsunami. Minoan artefacts mixed with pebbles, shells and marine life have been found at sites 7m above sea level, and dated to 1450 BC, when Santorini's volcano erupted, sending a 23m-high wave spanning 15km into Crete's north coast.

HISTORY CLASSICAL CRETE

AD 63	250	395	415
Christianity emerges after St Paul visits Crete and leaves his disciple, Titus, to convert the island. St Titus becomes Crete's first bishop.	The first Christian martyrs, the so-called Agii Deka (Ten Saints) are killed in the village of the same name, as Roman officials begin major Christian persecutions.	The Roman Empire splits and Crete is ruled by Byzantium. Crete becomes a self-governing province; Gortyna is its administrative and religious centre. Trade flourishes; many churches are built.	The second earthquake in 50 years destroys many towns, but prosperity continues as Crete remains an untroubled backwater.

sufficiently productive to trigger renewed maritime trading. As new Greek colonies were established throughout the Mediterranean basin, Crete took on a prominent trade role.

The various city-states were unified by the development of a Greek alphabet, the verses of Homer and the founding of the Olympic Games. The establishment of central sanctuaries, such as Delphi, gave Cretans a sense of national identity as Greeks.

Rethymno, Polyrrinia, Falasarna, Gortyna, Phaestos and Lato were built according to the new defensive style of Dorian city-states, with a fortified acropolis at the highest point, above an *agora* (market), a bustling commercial quarter, and beyond it residential areas.

As the rest of Greece entered its golden age from the 6th to 4th centuries BC, Crete remained a backwater. Constant warfare between large commercial centres and smaller traditional communities left the island increasingly impoverished. Although Crete did not participate in the Persian Wars or the Peloponnesian Wars, economic circumstances forced many Cretans to sign up as mercenaries in foreign armies or turn to piracy.

During this time, Crete's role as the birthplace of Greek culture drew the attention of philosophers such as Plato and Aristotle, who wrote extensively about Crete's political institutions. Knossos, Gortyna, Lyttos and Kydonia (Hania) continued to vie for supremacy, causing ongoing turmoil. Egypt, Rhodes and Sparta got involved in the Cretan squabbles and piracy flourished.

The Empire & Orthodoxy

In order to turn the Mediterranean into a 'Roman lake', the empire needed to curtail piracy and control shipping routes. As the most strategic island in the central Mediterranean, Crete had been on Rome's to-do list since the 3rd century BC. But it wasn't until the third Mithridatic War (73–63 BC) that it was able to intervene, playing the piracy card. When Mark Antony's father, Marcus Antonius, unsuccessfully attacked, the Cretans sent envoys to Rome, but were rebuffed. An army of 26,000 men was hastily established to defend the island. Roman consul Metellus launched the decisive invasion in 69 BC near Kydonia, and within two years had taken Crete, despite valiant local resistance.

Roman rule and reorganisation brought a new era of peace to Crete, and land and towns were given as favours to various Roman allies. In 27 BC, Crete was united with eastern Libya to form the Roman province of Creta et Cyrenaica. By this time, the Romans had spent decades building up their new possession, with Gortyna (established in 67 BC) becoming the capital and most powerful city. Roman amphitheatres, temples and public baths livened things up, and the population increased. Knossos fell into disuse, but Kydonia (Hania) in the west became an important

727

Cretan supporters of icon worship revolt after iconoclast Emperor Leo III bans them. The uprising is smashed and a fierce wave of retribution is unleashed.

824

Arab Saracens conquer Crete and establish a fortress called Chandax in Iraklio to store their pirated treasure. The island sinks into a century-and-a-half gloom and cultural life dwindles.

» Basilica of Agios Titus, Gortyna

centre. Roman towns were linked by roads, bridges and aqueducts, parts of which are still visible in places. Under the Romans, the Cretans continued to worship Zeus in the Dikteon and Ideon Caves, and also incorporated Roman and Egyptian deities into their rituals.

Christianity Comes to Crete

In AD 63, Christianity was brought to Crete by St Paul himself. His disciple, St Titus (who died in AD 107 at the age of 94), remained to convert the island and became its first bishop. Although the early years of Cretan Christianity seem to have been quiet, the 3rd century brought large-scale persecution, as elsewhere in the empire. The first Christian martyrs, the so-called *Agii Deka* (Ten Saints), were killed in the eponymous village in 250.

In 324, Emperor Constantine I (also known as Constantine the Great), a Christian convert, transferred the capital of the empire from Rome to Byzantium, which was renamed Constantinople (now İstanbul). By the end of the 4th century, the Roman Empire was formally divided into western and eastern sections; Crete, along with the rest of Greece, fitted naturally in the eastern half.

Although the minor doctrinal differences that would later separate Catholicism from Orthodox Christianity were centuries from realisation, the division of the empire geographically also expedited divergences in practice, custom and allegiances that would come to define the Orthodox Church, presided over by the patriarch in Constantinople.

In the early Byzantine Empire, Crete was a self-governing province, with Gortyna as its administrative and religious centre. Piracy decreased and trade flourished, leaving the island wealthy enough to build many churches.

Crete's attachment to the worship of icons provoked a revolt in 727 when Emperor Leo III banned their worship as part of the iconoclastic movement, which broke out in different periods of the 8th and 9th centuries and had complex theological, economic and political roots, but was partly influenced by questions provoked by the rise of Islam. The uprising was smashed and the Byzantine emperor unleashed a fierce wave of retribution against Crete's iconophiles. However, the policy became officially overturned for good by decree of Empress Theodora in 843, an event still celebrated as the 'Triumph of Orthodoxy' on the first Sunday of Lent.

The branches given to athletes during the 2004 Athens Olympic Games were cut from a 3250-year-old olive tree – one of the world's oldest – which grows near Kavousi in northeast Crete.

Between Pirates & the Pope

The peaceful period of Byzantine rule came to an end around 824 with the arrival of Arabs from Spain, who gradually conquered Crete and used it as a base for marauding around the Aegean. The Arabs established a

960	1204	1363	1453
Byzantine General Nikiforos Fokas launches the 'Expedition to Crete', liberating the island. Coastal defences are fortified, and Chandax becomes capital and archdiocese seat.	After Crusaders sack Constantinople, Boniface of Montferrat sells Crete to Venice. Venice rapidly colonises Crete, importing settlers and building towns and defences in Rethymno, Hania, Iraklio and elsewhere.	Venice quells a joint uprising by Crete's Venetian leaders and Greeks in the Revolt of St Titus, though fighting continues for several years against Greek nobles like the Kallergis clan.	Constantinople falls to the Turks. Byzantine scholars and intellectuals flee to Crete, sparking a renaissance of Byzantine art. The 'Cretan School' of icon painting emerges,

Remnants of St Titus
At Gortyna, the remnants of the 6th-century-AD Basilica of Agios Titus attest to this disciple of St Paul. St Titus' relics, recovered in 1966 from Venice, where they had been taken for safekeeping during the Ottoman period, are today found in the cathedral named after him in Iraklio.

fortress called Chandax in what is now Iraklio, essentially to store their pirated treasure. As the island's criminal reputation grew, its economy dwindled and its cultural life ground to a halt. There are few records for this period, considered Crete's 'dark age'. While some of the population seems to have been forcibly converted to Islam, this would not outlive the occupation.

Byzantine armies sought to rescue Crete several times, in 842 and again in 911 and 949, but were not successful until Nikiforos Fokas launched the legendary 'Expedition to Crete' in 960. After a bitter siege of Chandax, Crete was liberated in 961, and the Byzantines quickly started fortifying the Cretan coast and consolidating their power. Chandax emerged as the new capital of the theme (a Byzantine term for province) of Crete, and was the seat of the restored Cretan archdiocese. The church undertook efforts to bring errant sheep back to the Christian flock.

The following two-and-a-half centuries were relatively peaceful, save for a short-lived revolt by the governor, Karykes, in 1092. A few years later, it was brought with southern Greece and the Peloponnese under the control of the Byzantine navy's main commander.

This happy existence was shattered by the perfidious Fourth Crusade of 1204, which saw Venetian-bankrolled Western crusaders opt to attack Christian Constantinople rather than the infidels down in Egypt. While Crete was originally granted to the Crusader leader Boniface of Montferrat, he soon sold it to the Venetians. However, the latter's Genoese archrivals seized it first, and it took until 1212 for Venice to finish things; their colonial rule would last until 1669. Today, Venice's former influence is evident throughout Crete's major towns, in former mansions and massive fortresses that guarded the port towns and harbours.

Venice colonised Crete with noble and military families, many of whom settled in Iraklio (Candia). About 10,000 settlers came during the 13th century alone, to be rewarded with the island's best and most fertile land. Formerly landowners, the Cretans now worked as serfs for their Venetian masters. Cretan peasants were ruthlessly exploited, and taxes were oppressive. Further, the all-powerful influence of the papacy meant that Venetian rulers sought to impose Catholicism over Orthodoxy. Unsurprisingly, revolts were frequent.

Sophistication & Spirit

Over time, the wealth and stability that the Venetian empire could provide for Crete would pay cultural dividends; a very unique environment developed in which the cosmopolitan ideas and goods that came along with a maritime trade power combined with local creative talent and tradition. While Western Europe, the Balkans and Byzantium were being decimated by civil wars, dynastic disputes and Islamic invasions, Crete

1493	1541	1587	1645
Cretan-born scholar Markos Mousouros assists with the Aldine publications of ancient Greek classics. They become immensely popular and increase the influence of Greek thought in the Renaissance.	Dominikos Theotokopoulos, later known as 'El Greco', is born in Candia; his subsequent creations in Italy and Spain are marked by both 'Cretan School' influence and bold personal innovation.	Vitsentzos Kornaros of Sitia writes the *Erotokritos*, a voluminous verse epic that becomes Crete's greatest literary achievement – and remains one of the most important works of all Greek literature.	A huge Turkish force lands in Hania, establishing the Turks' first foothold on the island. After Rethymno is defeated, they secure the western part of the island.

remained a tranquil isle in the sun where thinkers could take refuge and where first-rate educations were available, generally through the Church. However, Venetian Crete also was known for its intellectual centres, such as the Accademia degli Stravaganti in Candia, where rhetoricians sparred and philosophers pored over the ancient texts.

This cultural flowering was greatly expedited by two factors: the renewed Western curiosity in ancient Greek and Latin thought, and the fall of Constantinople in 1453. After the captures of Trebizond and Mystras in the Peloponnese a few years later, Crete became the last major remaining bastion of Hellenism, and Byzantine scholars and intellectuals relocated to the island. They brought their manuscripts, icons and experience, and established schools, libraries and printing presses.

A MINOR CRUSADE & A SHORT-LIVED REPUBLIC

Some interesting twists in Crete's many revolts against the oppressive Venetians indicate a complex and interesting reality, revealing what life was like then – and how the Cretans and their Italian 'guests' got on.

One example was the August 1363 Revolt of St Titus, which saw oppressed Cretans join forces with Venetian settlers exasperated at a new tax. Despite attempts at an amicable settlement, top officials proved tone-deaf and the call to arms was raised. Aside from the obvious commercial grievances that motivated rebels, the event showed that after only a couple generations of living in Crete, the settlers seem to have 'gone native', looking at their Greek neighbours as fellow countrymen instead of those in far-off Italy.

The rebellion quickly resulted in the overthrow of the local government and the pronunciation of equality for the Greeks and Orthodoxy. In fact, the island's patron saint, Titus, became the official emblem for this, the new 'Commune of Crete', a place where Greeks would even be allowed to serve on governing committees. However, Venetian diplomats dissuaded other great powers, particularly the Genoese, from aiding the rebels, and by spring 1364 a military force had retaken Candia. After the leaders of the uprising were executed, Venetians celebrated in June. But it was not the end by any means.

Indeed, the mass of fighters had already escaped into Crete's rugged mountains, where Greek noble families such as the Kallergis clan in the west sought to overthrow the Latin rule completely, and reunite with Byzantium.

This was all too much for the Venetian doge, who convinced the Pope to declare a crusade against the Kallergis. But under the banner of a battle for the salvation of Orthodoxy, the whole west of Crete joined the rebellion, and it would take the Venetians almost five years to restore order.

Although Venice kept ultimate control, these rebellions were not in vain, as they forced the colonisers to make concessions. And so, by the 15th century, Cretans of both Greek and Italian background had made a sort of truce – one that allowed a remarkable and unique cultural flowering that would help shape the Italian Renaissance.

1669	1770	1821	1828
Iraklio (Candia) finally falls to the Turks, 24 years after the capture of the rest of the island. Ottoman rule sees construction of mosques and heavy taxation of Christians.	Under Ioannis Daskalogiannis, 2000 Sfakians revolt in Sfakia, but are defeated. Daskalogiannis is skinned alive in Iraklio's central square.	The Greek War of Independence is declared. The insurgency spreads to Crete but Turkish-Egyptian forces outnumber the rebellion. Continued resistance provokes massacres of Cretans.	In one of the bloodiest battles in the war for independence, 385 rebels make a heroic last stand at Frangokastello. About 800 Turks are killed along with the rebels.

Vintage Venetians

» Morosini (Lion) Fountain, Iraklio

» Harbour fortresses, Iraklio, Rethymno and Hania

» Spinalonga Island, near Elounda

» Moni Arkadiou, south of Rethymno

» Frangokastello Fortress, south coast

The cross-pollination between Byzantine traditions and the flourishing Italian Renaissance is particularly famous for its 'Cretan School' of icon painting, which became most highly developed in the 16th and 17th centuries, combining Byzantine and Venetian elements. Already, from the 13th to the early 16th centuries, churches around Crete had been adorned with frescoes – many of which can still be seen today. The 14th century's greatest icon painter was Ioannis Pagomenos, while the world's best-known such artist is Dominikos Theotokopoulos, who studied in Italy before moving to Spain, where he became known as El Greco – 'The Greek'.

At the same time, Crete enjoyed a tremendous literary flowering, in which the traditional Cretan folk verse style influenced – and was influenced by – poetic and musical trends popular in France, Italy and Constantinople. As was the case with visual art, it can be said that here too, Cretan spirit was matched with Italian sophistication.

Indeed, the island's literary masterpiece, the epic *Erotokritos,* was penned in Greek by the Venetian-descended Vitsentzos Kornaros of Sitia in the late 16th century. A vernacular epic of more than 10,000 lines, it has a verse structure based on traditional Cretan songs (*mantinadhes,* a style of traditional Cretan rhyming couplets), but in its subjects of courtly love, honour and bravery resembles 15th-century French predecessors, which themselves were influenced by earlier Byzantine Greek vernacular epics. Indeed, the poem's decapentasyllabic (15-syllable) verse structure is typical of all Byzantine vernacular literature.

Resistance & the Tourkokratia

By the 17th century, the expanding Ottoman Empire was finally able to take on Venice on the high seas, with Cyprus and Crete the two most strategic Venetian possessions sought by the sultans. Following a two-month Turkish siege, Hania fell to the Turks in 1645, followed soon by Rethymno. However, Candia's massive walls kept the besieging Ottomans out until 1669. Only the fortresses of Gramvousa, Spinalonga and Souda remained in Venetian hands, the latter two until 1715.

One of the few bright things under Ottoman rule was some measure of freedom for the Orthodox Church. As elsewhere in the empire, non-Muslim populations were given the status of a 'protected people' and their beliefs were tolerated – provided they paid the onerous taxes demanded of them. Unsurprisingly, as in other Ottoman lands, many converted to Islam for the economic and social benefits the status conferred. By the 18th century, however, living standards had slightly improved, with grain exports and a new olive-oil soap industry helping the farmers.

The more rebellious and stubborn Cretans took to the mountains, where they could enjoy freedom and attack the Turks, especially in the

1830	1840	1866	1877–78
The Great Powers give Crete to Egypt. Egyptian rule brings improvements, with Muslims and Christians treated equally, schools organised and infrastructure rebuilt, but high taxes spark protests.	The Turks defeat Egypt and the Great Powers give Crete back to the Ottomans. Crete wins important new privileges but repeated violations spark another uprising and demand for union.	About 2000 Turkish soldiers attack Moni Arkadiou, where over 900 rebels and their families shelter. Refusing to surrender, the Cretans light a store of gunpowder, killing almost everyone.	The Russo-Turkish War prompts another Cretan uprising, but despite gains the Treaty of Berlin rejects union with Greece. Crete becomes a semi-autonomous, discontented Ottoman province.

rugged, southwestern Sfakia region. In 1770, Sfakian leader Ioannis Daskalogiannis led 2000 fighters into battle, after Russia promised aid. However, help never came, and Daskalogiannis was skinned alive in Iraklio's main square.

The 1821 Greek War of Independence fuelled another fruitless uprising, and the Ottomans massacred Cretan civilians and priests, who they (quite rightly) identified as ideological agitators behind Greek nationalism. Nevertheless, the Cretan resistance, combined with the Peloponnesian and mainland Greek insurrections, forced the sultan to ask Egypt's rulers to attack the Christians, which they did with relish, massacring many thousands across the Aegean. Crete's rebels fought furiously, but lost to the numerically superior Turkish-Egyptian forces.

In 1830, Greece became independent, but the Great Powers gave Crete to Egypt, hoping that peace based on amnesty and equal rights for Muslims and Christians could be enforced. Yet Egypt was defeated by the Turks in Syria, and in 1840 Crete reverted to Ottoman rule. Although they tried to continue reforms, *Enosis i Thanatos* (Union or Death) became a slogan for new rebellions in western Crete.

The Turks and Egyptians brought more massacres to the Cretans, whose struggle attained international notoriety in 1866, when 900 resolute rebels and their families in Moni Arkadiou ignited their entire gunpowder stock, killing themselves and 2000 besieging Turkish soldiers. The event shocked the world, fuelling sympathy for the heroic Cretans. Yet Great Britain and France maintained a pro-Turkish stance, and ordered Greece against aiding the Cretan rebels.

Cretan author Nikos Psilakis' 2008 book *Byzantine Churches & Monasteries of Crete* is a very useful and well-illustrated portable guide to hundreds of Crete's spiritual sites.

Getting Things Together

However, even the Great Powers could not stop the wave of revolutionary nationalism sweeping southeastern Europe. The 1877 Russo-Turkish War, which liberated Bulgaria and almost toppled the Ottoman government, encouraged both Cretan rebels and the Greek government. Despite significant gains by the Cretan rebels, the highly controversial Treaty of Berlin in 1878 rejected the idea of Enosis; instead, Crete gained semi-autonomous status, with Greek becoming the official language and a general amnesty declared.

A new rebellion against Turkish rule in 1889 followed parliamentary infighting, prompting another Turkish crackdown. In Sfakia, Manousos Koundouros' secret fraternity, which sought to secure autonomy and eventual unification, besieged the Turkish garrison at Vamos, leading to violent reprisals and eventual intervention by the Great Powers, who forced a new constitution on the Ottomans.

When violence erupted again in 1896, the Greek government sent troops, declaring unification with Crete. However, the Great Powers

1883

Greece's most famous writer, Nikos Kazantzakis, is born in Iraklio. He becomes famous for works like *Zorba the Greek* and *The Last Temptation of Christ* in the mid-20th century.

1889

Fierce political infighting within the Cretan parliament sparks a new rebellion and the Great Powers eventually force the Turks to agree to a new constitution.

» Byzantine icon, Moni Toplou

FORGET PATRICK/SAGAPHOTO.COM/ALAMY ©

blockaded the coast, preventing both Turks and Greeks from reinforcing their positions, and Greece withdrew. The unpopular Prince George, son of King George of Greece, was appointed as high commissioner of Crete by the Great Powers.

However, murderous outrage soon accomplished what decades of high international diplomacy hadn't: the expulsion of the Turks. In 1898 a British military detachment was implementing the transfer of power in Iraklio when a group of enraged Muslim Turks stormed through the city, slaughtering hundreds of Christian civilians – along with 17 British soldiers and the British consul. The 17 main leaders were found and hanged, and a British squadron of ships arrived. Ottoman rule over Crete was finally over.

The charismatic Eleftherios Venizelos, a young politician from Hania and Prince George's minister of justice, broke with the regent, who refused to consider the idea of Enosis. Venizelos convened a revolutionary assembly in the village of Theriso near Hania, in 1905, raising the Greek flag and declaring unity with Greece.

Venizelos' upstart rival government was given teeth by armed support from local Cretans. The Great Powers asked King George to appoint a new governor. In 1908 the Cretan assembly declared unity with Greece, but even with Venizelos now prime minister, the Greek government refused to allow Cretan deputies into parliament, fearing it would antagonise both Turkey and the Great Powers. Not until the First Balkan War (1912) did Cretans finally enter parliament in Athens. The 1913 Treaty of Bucharest formally recognised Crete as part of the Greek state.

After the disastrous Greek invasion of Smyrna, the 1923 Treaty of Lausanne mandated a population exchange between Greece and Turkey. Crete's Muslim population of 30,000 people was swapped for incoming Greek refugees from Anatolia. The last signs of the Tourkokratia were no more.

WWII & the Battle of Crete

As in innumerable conflicts previous, Crete's strategic geographical position made it highly enticing to foreign invaders in WWII. Hitler sought to dominate the Mediterranean and have a base from which to challenge British Egypt. On 6 April 1941, Greece was rapidly overrun from the north, as the Royalist Yugoslav government was defeated. Greek leader Emmanouil Tsouderos set up a government in exile in his native Crete.

With all available Greek troops fighting the Italians in Albania, Greece asked Britain to help defend Crete. Churchill obliged, as he recognised the strategic significance of the island and was determined to make a stand and block Germany's advance through southeastern Europe. More than 30,000 British, Australian and New Zealand troops poured into the

1896	1898	1900	1905
Violence erupts again. Greece sends its forces, declaring unification with Crete; the Great Powers reject this. Greece recalls an army; the Great Powers appoint Prince George high commissioner of Crete.	Turks slaughter hundreds of Christian civilians, 17 British soldiers and the British consul in Iraklio. Britain orders the Turks out; Crete is placed under international administration, with Hania as capital.	Arthur Evans begins excavations at Knossos, quickly unearthing the palace and stunning the archaeological world with the discovery of the advanced Minoan civilisation.	A revolutionary assembly in Theriso declares unity with Greece. Eleftherios Venizelos sets up a rival government to administer the island. The Great Powers appoint a new governor of Crete.

last remaining part of free Greece, two-thirds of them having first been evacuated from mainland Greece.

From the start, the defenders were faced with difficult challenges. The Allies were in a poor position to defend the island, since commitments in the Middle East were already draining military resources. The island's defences had been seriously neglected. There were few fighter planes and military preparation was hampered by six changes of command in the first six months of 1941. Crete's difficult terrain also meant the only viable ports were on the exposed northern coast, while inadequate roads precluded resupplying the army from the more protected southern ports.

Hitler was determined to seize Crete and use it as an air base to attack British forces in the eastern Mediterranean. In a stunning disregard for Crete's rebellious history, Hitler actually believed that German forces would be welcomed by the native population. They were not.

After a week-long aerial bombardment, Hitler launched the world's first airborne invasion on 20 May, starting what became known as the Battle of Crete, one of the war's most significant battles. Aiming to capture the airport at Maleme 17km west of Hania, thousands of parachutists floated down over Hania, as well as Rethymno and Iraklio.

Elderly men, women and children grabbed rifles, old shotguns, sickles and whatever else they could find to defend their homeland. German

Literature and Society in Renaissance Crete, by David Holton, is a comprehensive study of the literature of the Cretan Renaissance in its historical, social and cultural context, with chapters on the poetic and dramatic genres contributed by leading experts in the field.

WAR MEMORIALS

The Battle of Crete had a monumental impact on the outcome of WWII, and the massive casualties on all sides make it a significant war memorial pilgrimage. Every May, war veterans from Great Britain, Australia, New Zealand and Greece attend commemoration celebrations held throughout Crete.

Major anniversaries include a re-enactment of the airborne invasion at Maleme, west of Hania. Participation of those who served in Crete has dwindled with time, but the anniversaries remain important memorials for Greeks and Allied ex-service personnel and there are regular battlefield tours of Crete.

More than 1500 Allied soldiers are buried at the immaculate Souda Bay War Cemetery near Hania. Ironically, one of the long-term caretakers of the German war cemetery at Maleme, where 4500 soldiers are buried, was the late George Psychoundakis, the former shepherd boy whose story about being a runner during the German occupation is told in *The Cretan Runner*.

There are also war memorials across the island, including a striking monument overlooking the cliffs at Moni Preveli and at Stravromenos on the north coast of Rethymno, as well as at the southern port of Hora Sfakion, from where Allied troops were evacuated following the battle.

1908	1913	1921	1941
The Cretan assembly declares unity with Greece, but Cretan deputies are not allowed to sit in the Greek parliament until 1912.	Turkey, angered by the parliamentary move, seeks revenge but is defeated in the Balkan Wars by Greece, Bulgaria, Serbia and Montenegro. The postwar Bucharest Treaty officially unites Greece with Crete.	Eight years after the 1913 Bucharest Treaty united Crete with Greece, the Greek-Turkish population exchange sees 30,000 Cretan Muslims replaced by Anatolian Greeks. Ottoman structures languish.	Germany invades Greece. Allied troops arrive to defend Crete. Germany launches an airborne invasion to capture the airport at Maleme, in the famous Battle of Crete. Allied soldiers are evacuated from Hora Sfakion.

A Ghastly Sight

Imagine sitting on the beach one morning and seeing phantom warriors marching into the sea. The *drosoulites* – the ghosts of 385 Cretan fighters killed by the Turks, during a heroic last stand at Frangokastello on the south coast in 1828 – appear to those who believe each year in May.

casualties were appalling, but they managed to capture the Maleme airfield on the first day and, despite the valiant defence, the Allies lost the battle within 10 days.

After the battle of Crete, the Cretans risked German reprisals by hiding thousands of Allied soldiers and helping them get to the south to escape across the Libyan Sea. Allied undercover agents supplied from North Africa coordinated the guerrilla warfare waged by the Cretan fighters, known as *andartes*. Allied soldiers and Cretans alike were under constant threat from the Nazis while they lived in caves, sheltered in monasteries such as Preveli, trekked across peaks or unloaded cargo on the southern coast. Among them was celebrated author Patrick Leigh Fermor, who lived in the mountains for two years with the Cretan Resistance and was involved in the daring kidnapping of German commander General Kreipe in 1944.

After this embarrassment, German troops responded with fierce reprisals against the civilian population. Cities were bombed, villages burnt down and men, women and children lined up and shot. When the Germans finally surrendered in 1945 they insisted on surrendering to the British, fearing that the Cretans would inflict upon them some of the same punishment they had suffered for four years.

Peace, Prosperity & Reconstruction

Although the German occupation of Greece had ended, the strife was hardly over for the country. The postwar scenario of a capitalist West trying to contain a communist East would play out violently in Greece, where the mainland resistance had been dominated by communists. When WWII ended, the communists boycotted the 1946 election that saw King George II reinstated, with the backing of Winston Churchill and other Western leaders.

Fortunately for Crete, the island was largely spared the bloodshed and bitterness during the three-year civil war. Owing to the valiant sacrifices the British had made for the Cretans, and the close cooperation they had enjoyed, the islanders were not swayed to fight for communism. To cement Greece's footing firmly in the Western camp, the country joined NATO in 1951 (together with Turkey) and the new alliance established military bases in Greece, with the Souda Bay air and sea base being the most important in Crete. Today it remains a vital strategic possession for both NATO and the Greek armed forces, and was utilised heavily in the 2011 air campaign against Libya's Colonel Gaddafi.

For Crete as for Greece, the major challenge following the wars was reconstruction and the need to rebuild a shattered economy, while also adjusting to life in a world that was modernising rapidly. Particularly in backwaters like Crete, where rural customs and tradition played a

» German troops heading for the 20 May invasion

BETTMAN/CORBIS ©

1944

The Cretan Resistance kidnaps German commander General Kreipe and, aided by the Allies, sends him to Egypt, sparking fierce German reprisals. Cities are bombed, villages annihilated and civilians shot.

1946–49

Greek civil war breaks out between communists and right-wing royalists. The communists fail to infiltrate Crete, which is largely spared the bloodshed and bitterness that engulfs Greece.

strong social role, liberal trends elsewhere in Europe were not always welcome. In the 1960s and '70s, however, changes came with the arrival of foreign tourists. Tourism became a major industry to complement the Cretans' traditional agrarian livelihood, helping make the island one of the wealthiest parts of Greece over time.

Democracy Challenged & Restored

In 1967, four Greek army colonels staged a coup, establishing a military junta that imposed martial law, abolished all political parties, banned trade unions, imposed censorship, and imprisoned, tortured and exiled thousands of citizens. In Crete, resentment intensified when the colonels muscled through major tourist development projects rife with favouritism. However, when in 1974 the junta sought to depose Cyprus' president, Archbishop Makarios, Turkey invaded the northern third of Cyprus on the pretext of safeguarding the Turkish minority there. Turkey's continued occupation of northern Cyprus remains one of the world's great unresolved geopolitical issues today.

The Cyprus debacle toppled the Athenian colonels and restored democracy to Greece. The excesses of the right-wing junta's regime, which included cases of torture and other persecution of domestic critics, resulted in a resurgence of support for left-wing parties and causes following the overthrow of the junta in 1974. A new democratic constitution was passed, as were laws preventing police from entering university campuses, (still on the books today), and the position of trade unions was also strengthened.

A 1975 referendum officially deposed the king, Konstantinos II, ending the last vestiges of Greek royalism, and previously exiled politician George Papandreou returned to Greece. A towering figure in modern Greek history, Papandreou founded the socialist PASOK party, winning elections in 1981; PASOK would remain in power for much of the next 24 years. (Andreas' son George Papandreou has continued his legacy, winning elections in 2009.) With its strong agrarian identity and historic traditional anti-Royalist tendencies, Crete has usually supported the left-wing PASOK.

However, in 1989 Cretans turned out to vote local son – and nephew of the renowned Eleftherios Venizelos – Konstantinos Mitsotakis of the centre-right New Democracy party into power. In contrast to Andreas Papandreou, Mitsotakis took a strongly-pro American, pro-NATO stance. Although his government only lasted until 1993, the Mitsotakis clan has remained politically influential, with Konstantinos' daughter Dora Bakoyiannis serving as foreign minister from 2006–09, when ND was next in power.

Thus, despite the country's post-1974 return to democracy, many Greeks remain disillusioned by the continuation of a very few family

Fly the Flag

Intrepid and dedicated shoppers will occasionally still find (especially in village shops) late-19th-century flags emblazoned with the famous Enosis i Thanatos (Union or Death) slogan under which Cretan rebels fought against the Turks.

HISTORY DEMOCRACY CHALLENGED & RESTORED

1951	**1967**	**1971**	**1974**
Greece joins NATO, together with Turkey. Both become key Western allies during the cold war. Military bases, used still (in 2011, against Libya's Colonel Gaddafi), are established at Souda Bay.	Army colonels stage a coup and impose martial law across Greece. The junta is toppled seven years later following the Turkish invasion of northern Cyprus.	Iraklio resumes its position as the island's capital, relegating Hania to secondary status. It develops as Crete's industrial and commercial base, with the island's major airport and ports.	Turkish forces invade Cyprus following a botched junta-sponsored attempt to depose President Archbishop Makarios. The junta falls; democracy returns to Crete. The monarchy is abolished.

dynasties atop the political pyramid. Charges of nepotism, cronyism and corruption have all resonated with regular Greeks, something that contributed to the popular backlash to government austerity reforms in 2010 and 2011.

Tourism & Development

Crete: The Battle and the Resistance by Antony Beevor is a short and readable analysis of the Allied defeat.

The past 30 years have seen major changes in Crete. Greece joined the EU (then known as the EEC) in 1981, and Cretan farmers have since enjoyed the benefits of EU agricultural subsidies, while the island's infrastructure has also been modernised thanks to EU largesse. Tourism boomed with direct charter flights to Crete, almost tripling tourist arrivals between 1981 and 1991, and tourism numbers doubled again with the advent of package tourism and budget airlines during the next decade.

With a climate that stays warmer for more months annually than anywhere else in Greece, and none of the social and cultural problems that afflict other parts of the country, Crete has been liberated from its traumatic past and enjoys a level of wealth envied by many other Greeks. The retention of strong family ties and traditions means that societal safety structures remain in place – things like retirement homes are almost unheard of in Crete (except, of course, for the thousands of northern Europeans who have chosen to buy a property to retire to here).

Crete takes in more than two million visitors annually, which has an impact on both the environment and the economy: the majority of tourists are sequestered in north-coast all-inclusive package hotels. In general terms, the major population centres of the north attract companies, industry and universities, whereas agriculture accounts for the bulk of economic activity in the less-populated interior and south. In specifically tourism terms, however, the overdevelopment of much of north-coast Crete has left hotel owners susceptible to larger trends in the travel world, whereas less ambitious, cosier places elsewhere on the island experience less volatile swings as the economy waxes and wanes. New EU grants have been given to promote green tourism and restore historic buildings and traditional settlements, and there is a growing awareness that sustainable, ecofriendly tourism will pay dividends as the tastes of foreign visitors change.

Challenges Ahead

Agriculture remains a major force and way of life in Crete, though fewer and fewer Cretans seem to be actively engaged in it. As with other farming areas of Greece, Cretans have relied on foreign (usually, illegal) workers to pick the olives, lemons, tomatoes and so on. But the last few years have seen a shift: whereas previously Albanians and other Balkan peoples were doing the manual labour, massive illegal immigration into

1981	1988	1990	1993
Greece becomes the 10th member of the EEC (now EU), giving Cretan farmers new access to EU funds. The islanders strongly back the first PASOK socialist government, led by Andreas Papandreou.	A shortfall of US$132 million is discovered in the Bank of Crete, causing a scandal that damages the government, though a 1992 court decision will absolve Papandreou of any wrongdoing.	Cretan Konstantinos Mitsotakis is elected prime minister of Greece when New Democracy (ND) narrowly wins. A breakaway party is formed after corruption allegations, ending ND's capacity to govern.	PASOK returns to power. Andreas Papandreou resigns in 1996 due to ill health, ending an era in Greek politics. Costas Simitis takes over, introducing austerity measures and reforms.

Greece has meant that they are being replaced by African and Southeast Asian migrants – a rather novel sight for the average Cretan villager.

The EU has become increasingly concerned about Greece's role in human trafficking; a European border policing mission, Frontex, began operations on the Greece-Turkey border and on the high seas in 2010. The flow of migrants escaping North Africa due to the 'Arab Spring' revolts in 2011 also raised concerns, and traffickers' vessels packed with migrants in inhumane conditions have in recent years been found both washed up on Cretan shores and off the island. It is clear that the issue, which has become a major political one across the country, will continue to be a challenge for Crete.

The major challenge affecting all Greece, however, has been the country's financial woes and the government's controversial austerity measures, which caused major protests, strikes and shutdowns in 2010 and 2011. Debates unthinkable only a few years ago about size of pensions, employment issues and even possibly ditching the euro have escalated as Greek society and political factions grow more divided. Significantly, the participation of Greeks from all walks of life in symbolic protests indicate that the country is becoming increasingly disenchanted with its tradition of 'hereditary' political leadership, and less faithful in the ability of their leaders to know how to handle the complex problems facing Greece today. Prognosticators both local and foreign have divined all manner of darkness and despair for Greece in the years ahead. Yet it is likely that for its part, Crete itself will weather whatever storms are coming better than elsewhere in the country. Crete's relative abundance of natural resources and geographical isolation from the more urbanised mainland shield it to a degree from problems, such as violent protests, encountered in Greece's larger cities.

In the long term, the main challenge facing Cretans will be to find a way to hang on to their culture and traditions, while also forging ahead in an increasingly globalised world. How they manage to balance the two will have an important effect not only on the health, wealth and prosperity of the islanders, but the country as a whole.

Distinguished British archaeologist John Pendlebury, who took over Arthur Evans' work at Knossos, was executed by the Germans in 1941 while fighting with the Cretan Resistance. He is buried at the Allied war cemetery in Souda.

RESISTANCE

2002	**2004**	**2007**	**2009**
Greece becomes a full member of the European Monetary Union and the drachma is replaced by the euro. Prices jump across the country.	Over a century since the modern Olympic Games were revived in Greece, the Games return to Athens. Some events are held in Crete, introducing the island to new foreign visitors.	Weeks after fires ravage Greece, Kostas Karamanlis' ND is re-elected. PASOK is routed and the minor parties gain more seats, including the communist party (KKE) and the right-wing LAOS party.	Disillusionment with ND rises, as PASOK wins 2009 elections. However, the new government is forced to deal with Greece's budget deficit; austerity measures provoke widespread unrest, including strikes.

The Cretan People

For a useful but by no means exhaustive list of books about Crete, with reviews, visit www.hellenicbook service.com.

The Cretans are a very distinctive clan of Greeks, with their own spirited music and dances, distinct cuisine and traditions. Proud, patriotic yet famously hospitable, Cretans uphold an undeniable connection to their culture. They will always identify themselves as Cretans before they say they are Greek, and even within different parts of Crete people maintain strong regional identities. This becomes particularly apparent when you leave the major tourist centres. In rural areas, many Cretans still speak a local dialect or have a distinct accent.

Centuries of battling foreign occupiers have left the island with a stubbornly independent streak, residual mistrust of authority and little respect for the state; personal freedom and democratic rights are almost sacrosanct and there is a strong aversion to the Big Brother approach of over-regulated Western nations. The inherent insubordinate streak means that national laws are routinely ignored. Guns, for example, are strictly regulated in Greece, yet the evidence suggests that Cretans are stashing an astounding arsenal. Several smoking bans (the last one was introduced in 2010) have been widely flaunted. When it comes to road rules, many visitors are surprised to learn that they even exist. Despite hefty fines, wearing a seatbelt is treated as an optional inconvenience; creative and inconsiderate parking is the norm; dangerous overtaking is rife; and you may well see people riding motorbikes, carrying their helmets as they chat on their mobile phones.

These days, though, the resilience of Cretan culture and traditions is being tested by globalisation, market forces and social change. The current generation is dealing with a massive technological divide: multilingual children playing games on their mobile phones while their illiterate grandfathers spend days chewing the fat over sweet Greek coffee in a *kafeneio* (coffee house).

Harvard anthropologist Michael Herzfeld makes interesting anthropological observations of Cretans in *The Poetics of Manhood: Contest and Manhood in a Cretan Village*, while his *A Place in History* looks at life in and around Rethymno, including issues such as the Cretan vendetta.

Cretan society is deeply influenced by the Greek Orthodox Church and its rituals and celebrations. It maintains strong family ties and a sense of family honour. Crete's infamous vendettas, while increasingly rare, have not entirely ended.

Cretan weddings and baptisms are still huge affairs, and while shooting pistols in the air is becoming more politically incorrect (not to mention dangerous – people have been accidentally hit and killed), it is still common in some areas, where bullet-riddled road signs are a characteristic part of the landscape.

Rivalries between the prefectures are strong. As the island's capital until 1971, Hania considers itself the historical heart of the island, while Rethymno claims to be its cultural centre.

Lifestyle

The Cretan lifestyle has changed dramatically in the past 30 years, the most obvious change being that life has got a lot easier. As Cretan society has become increasingly urbanised, living standards have improved significantly; Cretans are conspicuously wealthier and the towns are full of sophisticated restaurants, bars and clubs. In the shift from living a largely poor, agrarian existence to becoming increasingly sophisticated urban dwellers, Cretans are also delicately balancing cultural and religious mores. The younger generation is highly educated and most speak English and often German as well. They are also living in a wealthier and much more multicultural society than their parents and grandparents.

As with most households in Greece, the Cretans have felt the brunt of higher living costs since the introduction of the euro. Eating out has become much more expensive, although there are still many reasonably priced tavernas, particularly in the villages. Still, Cretans have a work-to-live attitude and pride themselves on their capacity to enjoy life. They are social animals and enjoy a rich communal life. You will often see them dressed up and going out on masse for their *volta* (evening walk) and filling tavernas and cafes. They socialise in packs, with family or their *parea* (group of friends). Solitude is neither valued nor sought.

Unlike many Western cultures where people avoid eye contact with strangers, Cretans are unashamed about staring and blatantly observing and commenting on the comings and goings of people around them. Few subjects are off limits, from your private life and why you don't have children to how much money you earn or how much you paid for your house or shoes. And they are likely to tell you of their woes and ailments rather than engage in polite small-talk.

Cretans turn their heads downward to indicate yes (*nai*) and upward to signal no (*ohi*). The latter is often accompanied by an upward eye roll and a tongue click.

Family Life

Cretan society is still relatively conservative and it is uncommon for Greeks to move out of home until they are married, apart from leaving temporarily to study or work. While this is slowly changing among professionals, lack of economic opportunities and low wages are also keeping young people at home.

Parents strive to provide homes for their children when they get married, with many families building apartments for each child above their

---

TRIGGER-HAPPY

Sitting in a cafe in Askyfou one afternoon, a man at the next table pulls out a semiautomatic pistol and fires a few rounds, just for fun. Late one night after a festival near Lissos, gunshots ring out every time the group of merry Cretans on the beach finishes a song. At Cretan weddings and celebrations, volleys of gunshots – and accidents from stray bullets – have become so common that many musicians refuse to play in certain areas unless they get an assurance that there won't be any guns.

A few years ago, acclaimed composer Mikis Theodorakis led a campaign trying to change the island's gun culture, but Cretans have not laid down their arms. Conservative estimates indicate that one in two Cretans owns a gun, while others suggest there could be over one million weapons on Crete – more than the island's population.

Road signs riddled with bullet holes are the first inkling that you are entering the somewhat lawless mountain country that was historically a stronghold for Crete's resistance fighters, particularly around Sfakia in Hania and Mylopotamos province in Rethymno.

The endemic, machismo gun-ownership – and the act of shooting off a few rounds – is traditionally seen as an act of independence and pride (these days it's also a reckless show of excess and an expensive habit).

own homes. Construction is often done in a haphazard fashion depending on cash flow, which accounts for the large number of unfinished houses you encounter throughout the island.

Extended families often play an important role in daily life, with parents preferring to entrust their offspring to the grandparents rather than hiring outside help.

Cretans who moved away to other parts of Greece or overseas maintain strong cultural and family links and return regularly to their ancestral land. Even the most remote mountain villages are bustling with family reunions and homecomings during national and religious holidays.

City vs Countryside

Generational and rural/city divides are other features of modern Crete. In rural areas you will see shepherds with their flocks and men congregating in the *kafeneia* after their siesta. Mountain villages are repositories of traditional culture and you'll find that many older women and many men are still clad in black *vraka* (black, baggy trousers) and leather boots.

But even pastoral life has changed. While people still live off the land – and provide for their families in the cities – subsistence farming has mostly given way to commercial production. Well-to-do farmers drive pick-up trucks and shepherds can often be seen tending to their flocks while chatting away on their mobile phones. In the fields, foreign workers do most of the grunt work.

Hospitality & Tourism

The Cretan people have a well-justified reputation for hospitality and for treating strangers as honoured guests, a gesture of pride rather than subservience. They pride themselves on their *filotimo* (dignity and sense of honour) and their *filoxenia* (hospitality, welcome, shelter). If you wander into mountain villages you may well be invited into someone's home for a coffee or even a meal. In a cafe or taverna it is customary for people to treat another group of friends or strangers to a round of drinks (however, be mindful that it is not the done thing to treat them straight back – in theory, you will do the honours another time).

Surprisingly, this hospitality and generosity seem to extinguish themselves in the public sphere, where customer service is not a widely grasped concept. The notion of the greater good often plays second fiddle to personal interests and there is little sense of collective responsibility in relation to issues such as the environment. The pride Cretans show in their homes rarely extends to public spaces.

ROADSIDE SHRINES

Buzzing around Crete's winding country roads, you'll see them everywhere: dollhouse-sized chapels plopped on metal pedestals by the roadside. Called *kandylakia*, they come in all sorts of shapes and sizes, some simple, some elaborate, some weathered, some shiny and new. A votive candle may flicker behind tiny dust-encrusted windows, faintly illuminating the picture of a saint. Since they are especially prevalent in hairpin turns, blind curves and on the edges of precipitous slopes, you'd be forgiven for assuming that they've been put there by the families of those who died in an accident in this very spot. While this is indeed often the case, some are also set up in gratitude by those who miraculously survived such accidents or to honour a particular saint. As you're driving, pull over to the side of the road (safely, of course) and pause for a moment by these symbols of both tragedy and happy endings to reflect upon all those things important to Cretans: family, faith and tradition.

THE GREAT SCHISM

Greece was one of the first places in Europe where Christianity emerged, with St Paul reputedly first preaching the gospel in AD 49 on the mainland. After Constantine the Great officially recognised Christianity in AD 313 (converted by a vision of the Cross), he transferred the capital of the Roman Empire to Byzantium (today's İstanbul) in 330.

By the 8th century, differences of opinion and increasing rivalry emerged between the pope in Rome and the patriarch of the Hellenised Eastern Roman Empire. A key dispute was over Rome's doctrine of papal supremacy, that is, the belief that the pope enjoys, by divine right, supreme and universal power over the entire church. Another important issue was over the wording of the Creed, which stated that the Holy Spirit proceeds 'from the Father', but Rome then added 'and the Son'.

Ultimately, these differences became irreconcilable, and in the Great Schism of 1054 the pope and the patriarch went their separate ways as the Orthodox Church ('orthodoxy' means 'right belief') and the Roman Catholic Church.

The Greek Orthodox Church is closely related to the Russian Orthodox Church; together they form the third-largest branch of Christianity. The Orthodox Church of Crete is independent from the Greek Orthodox Church and answers directly to the Patriarchate of Constantinople.

Cretans often deal with the seasonal invasion of foreign tourists by largely operating in a different space-time continuum to their guests. They will often tell you a particular place is 'only for tourists', and that's normally your cue to avoid it. From April to around October, many live in the hurly-burly of the coastal resorts – running shops, pensions or tavernas – and then return to their traditional life in the hills for the autumn olive and grape harvests.

While tourists eat early in the evening in restaurants along a harbour or beach, Cretans drive out to a village taverna for a dinner that begins as late as 10pm. Many of these tavernas produce their own meat and vegetables.

The New Testament was written beginning around AD 50 in Koine Greek, which was the day-to-day language in the eastern part of the Roman Empire at the time.

Multiculturalism

After the exodus of Crete's Turkish community in the population exchange of 1923, the island became essentially homogeneous and its population virtually all Greek Orthodox. In recent years, though, Crete has become an increasingly multicultural society as migrants from the Balkans and Eastern Europe, especially Albania, Bulgaria and Russia, are filling labour shortages in the field of agriculture, construction and tourism. The total foreign population is now about 10%.

Economic migrants are a relatively new phenomenon for Crete which, like most of Greece, is struggling to come to terms with the new reality and concepts of multiculturalism. While there are tensions and mistrust, migrants appear to have fared better in Crete than in many other parts of Greece.

A small group of English, German and northern European refugees have also settled and bought property on Crete, though they live on the more affluent fringes. Foreign women married to Cretan men, a particularly common occurrence in the 1980s, are another characteristic minority group in Cretan society.

Religion

The Orthodox faith is the official and prevailing religion of Crete and a key element of Greek identity, ethnicity and culture. There is a prevailing view that to be Greek is to be Orthodox. While the younger generation isn't necessarily devout, nor attends church regularly, most observe the

LANGUAGE

You see men stroking, fiddling and masterfully playing with them everywhere: the de-stressing worry beads called *komboloï*, an amalgam of the words *kombos* (knot) and *leo* (to say). Although they look like prayer beads, *komboloïa* (plural) have no religious purpose and are only used for fun and relaxation – there just seems to be something soothing about flicking and flipping those beads. Some people also use them to help them stop smoking.

Komboloïa were traditionally made from amber, but coral, handmade beads, semiprecious stones and synthetic resin are also widely used. No exact number is prescribed but most *komboloïa* have between 19 and 23 beads strung up on a loop. There's a fixed bead that is held between the fingers, a shield that separates the two sides of the loop, and a tassel.

The vast majority of what you see in souvenir shops is plastic but there are also prized rare and old *komboloïa* that can be worth thousands of euros and are considered highly collectable.

rituals and consider the faith integral to their identity. Between 94% and 97% of the Cretan population belongs at least nominally to the Greek Orthodox Church.

The Orthodox religion held Cretan culture together during the many centuries of foreign occupation and repression, despite numerous efforts by the Venetians and Turks to turn locals towards Catholicism and Islam. Under Ottoman rule, religion was the most important criterion in defining a Greek.

Despite growing secularism, the Church still exerts significant social, political and economic influence. Non-Orthodox Greeks may find it hard to join the civil service or military and religious affiliation appeared on national identity cards until recently. The year is centred on the saints' days and festivals of the church calendar. Name days (celebrating your namesake saint) are more important than birthdays, and baptisms are an important rite. Most people are named after a saint, as are boats, suburbs and train stations. If you're invited to a name-day celebration, it's a good idea to bring a present, but don't be surprised if it won't be opened until you've left.

The most common name for women in Crete is Maria. The most common names for men are Yannis (John), Giorgos (George) and Manolis.

There are hundreds of tiny churches dotted around the countryside, predominantly built by individual families, dedicated to particular saints. Regrettably, many small churches and chapels are kept locked nowadays, but it's usually easy enough to locate the caretakers, who will be happy to open them for you.

NAMES

Women in Society

The role of women in Cretan society has been complex and shifting since Greek women first gained universal suffrage in 1952. While traditional gender roles are prevalent in rural areas and among the older generation, the situation is much more relaxed for younger women in cities and large towns. Entrenched attitudes towards the 'proper role' for women are changing fast as more women are educated and entering the workforce. Still, although some 40% of Greek women are in the workforce, they struggle mightily when it comes to even finding the career ladder or earning the same as their male counterparts. Women hold only 16% of seats in parliament. There are few public programs to help them balance careers and motherhood, which is why Greece now has the second-lowest birth rate in Europe, exceeded only by Italy.

Paradoxically, despite the machismo, Cretan society is essentially matriarchal. Men love to give the impression that they rule the roost and take a front seat in public life, but it's often the women who run the show, both at home and in family businesses. As Toula's mother says so memorably in the 2002 movie *My Big Fat Greek Wedding*: 'The man is the head, but the woman is the neck, and she can turn the head any way she wants.'

In villages, men and women still tend to occupy different spheres. When not tending livestock or olive trees, Cretan men can usually be found in a *kafeneio* (coffee house) playing *tavli* (Greek backgammon), gossiping and drinking coffee or *raki*. Although exceptions are made for foreign women, the *kafeneio* is a stronghold of male chauvinism and is off limits to Cretan women.

The older generation of Cretan women is house-proud and spends much time cultivating culinary skills. Most men rarely participate in domestic duties (or certainly don't own up to it). While it's becoming rarer these days, women busy themselves in their free hours with sewing, crocheting or embroidery, often in a circle of other women. But young Cretan women are more likely to be found in a cafe than behind a loom.

Greece has compulsory nine-month military service for all males aged 19 to 45 years. Women are accepted into the Greek army, though they are not obliged to join and rarely do.

THE CRETAN PEOPLE WOMEN IN SOCIETY

Minoan Art & Culture

The rich legacy of Minoan civilisation uncovered in the palaces, settlements and tombs around Crete reflect the glory and brilliance of perhaps the most peaceful and prosperous era in the island's history. The Minoans surrounded themselves with art and their palaces were lavishly decorated. The surviving paintings, small-scale sculptures, carved seals, mosaics, pottery and jewellery at archaeological sites and museums in Crete provide insight into the Minoan world, and demonstrate the Minoans' extraordinary artistry.

In Crete, Minoan painting is virtually the only form of Greek painting to have survived, because large-scale sculptures have not survived the island's various disasters (natural or otherwise). Minoan art inspired the invading Mycenaeans, and its influence spread to Santorini and beyond. At the same time, their inscrutable written hieroglyph system, Linear A, provides another indication of a culture that was very advanced.

Minoan Society

Mystery shrouds the Minoans: we don't even know what they called themselves, 'Minoan' being the term given by archaeologist Arthur Evans, in honour of the mythical King Minos. They are thought to have been possibly related to the pre-Greek, Pelasgian people of western Anatolia and the Greek mainland, and to have spoken a unique language unrelated to the Indo-European ones.

Evidence uncovered in the island's grand palaces indicates they were a peaceful, sophisticated, well-organised and prosperous civilisation with robust international trade, splendid architecture and art, and seemingly equal status for men and women. The Minoans had highly developed agriculture, extensive irrigation systems and advanced hydraulic sewerage systems. The accounts and records left behind suggest that their society was organised as an efficient and bureaucratic commercial enterprise.

Although the evidence for a matriarchal society is scant, women apparently enjoyed a great degree of freedom and autonomy. Minoan art shows women participating in games, hunting and all public and religious festivals. They also served as priestesses, administrators and participated in trade.

Pottery

Pottery techniques advanced in the Early Minoan years. Spirals and curvilinear motifs in white were painted on dark vases and several distinct styles emerged. Pyrgos pottery was characterised by black, grey or brown colours, while the later Vasiliki pottery (made near Ierapetra) was

You can take a virtual step-by-step video tour of Knossos on the British Archaeological School at Athens website, www.bsa.ac.uk.

KNOSSOS

polychrome. In the Middle to Late Minoan period, the style shifted to a dark-on-light colour technique.

Highly advanced levels of artisanship developed in the workshops of the first palaces at Knossos and Phaestos. Kamares pottery, named after the cave where the pottery was first found, was colourful, elegant and beautifully crafted and decorated with geometric, floral, plant and animal motifs. Human forms were rarely depicted. During the entire Middle Minoan period, Kamares vases were used for barter and were exported to Cyprus, Egypt and the Levant.

With the invention of the potter's wheel, cups, spouted jars and *pithoi* (large Minoan storage jars) could be produced quickly and there was a new crispness to the designs. The most striking were the 'eggshell' vases with their extremely thin walls.

In the late Neopalatial era, marine and floral themes in darker colours reigned. After 1500 BC, vases sprouted three handles and were frequently shaped as animal heads, such as the bull's-head stone *rhyton* (libation vessel) in the Iraklio Archaeological Museum. The decline of Minoan culture saw the lively pottery of previous centuries degenerate into dull rigidity.

Jewellery & Sculpture

Jewellery making and sculpture in various media reached an exceptional degree of artisanship in the Protopalatial period. The exquisite bee pendant found at Malia displays extraordinary delicacy and imagination. Another Minoan masterpiece is a 15th-century-BC gold signet ring found in a tomb at Isopata, near Knossos, which shows women in an ecstatic ritual dance in a meadow with lilies, while a goddess descends from the sky.

Minoan sculptors created fine miniatures, including idols in faience (quartz-glazed earthenware), gold, ivory, bronze and stone. One of the most outstanding examples is the bare-breasted serpent goddess with raised arms wielding writhing snakes above an elaborately carved skirt. Another incredible piece is the small rock-crystal rhyton from the Palace of Zakros. All of the above are displayed at Iraklio's Archaeological Museum.

Minotaur: Sir Arthur Evans and the Archaeology of the Minoan Myth by Joseph Alexander MacGillivray is a fascinating portrait of the British archaeologist who revealed the Palace of Knossos to the world, and a study in relative archaeology.

KING MINOS: MAN OR MYTH?

The legend of King Minos has captured the imagination of generations of scholars intent on finding evidence for Homer's depiction in *The Odyssey: Out on the dark blue sea there lies a rich and lovely land called Crete that is densely populated and boasts 90 cities...One of the 90 cities is called Knossos and there for nine years, King Minos ruled and enjoyed the friendship of the mighty.*

The legendary ruler of Crete was the son of Zeus and Europa and attained the Cretan throne, aided by Poseidon. With Knossos as his base, Minos gained control over the whole Aegean basin, colonising many of the islands and ridding the seas of pirates. He married Pasiphae, the daughter of Helios, who bore him a number of children, including the infamous half-bull, half-human Minotaur.

How long King Minos actually reigned, however, is open to debate. The Homeric reference *enneaoros* used to describe Minos could mean 'for nine years' or 'from the age of nine years'. Was Minos able to create an empire in nine short years, or was he a long-reigning monarch who started his kingly career as a boy? Either way, he eventually came to a nasty end while chasing down Daedalus, then under the protection of King Kokalios. After Minos threatened a war if the legendary father of flight did not turn up, the Sicilian king tricked the Cretan into bathing with his daughters – who promptly killed him by pouring boiling water over his head.

The art of seal-stone carving also advanced in the palace workshops. Using semiprecious stones and clay, artisans made miniature master-pieces that sometimes contained hieroglyphic letters. Goats, lions and griffins, and dance scenes were rendered in minute detail. Arthur Evans spent much of his first trip to Crete collecting these seals.

In the Postpalatial period, the production of jewellery and seal-stones was replaced by the production of weaponry, reflecting the influence of the warlike Mycenaeans.

For photos and descriptions of more than 50 Minoan sites around Crete, see archaeology buff Ian Swindle's comprehensive website at www.uk.digiserve.com/mentor/minoan/index.htm.

MINOAN SITES

The Famous Frescoes

Minoan frescoes are renowned for their vibrant colours and the vivid naturalism in which they portray landscapes rich with animals and birds; marine scenes teeming with fish and octopuses; and banquets, games and rituals. Although fresco painting probably existed before 1700 BC, all remnants vanished in the cataclysm that destroyed Minoan palaces around that time. Knossos yielded the richest trove of frescoes from the Neopalatial period, most of which are on display in the Iraklio Archaeological Museum.

Only fragments of the frescoes survive but they have been very care-fully (and controversially) restored and the technique of using plant and mineral dyes has kept the colours relatively fresh. Minoan fresco painters borrowed heavily from certain Egyptian conventions but the figures are far less rigid than most Egyptian wall paintings.

The Knossos frescoes suggest Minoan women were white-skinned with elaborately coiffured glossy black locks. Proud, graceful and unin-hibited, these women had hourglass figures and were dressed in stylish gowns that exposed shapely breasts. The bronze-skinned men were tall, with tiny waists, narrow hips, broad shoulders and muscular thighs and biceps; the children were slim and lithe.

Many of the frescoes show action scenes, from boxing and wrestling to solemn processions, saffron gathering to bull-leaping.

Religious Symbols

The Minoans were not given to building colossal temples or religious statuary. Caves and peak sanctuaries appear to have been used for cult or religious activity. Minoan spiritual life was organised around the wor-ship of a Mother Goddess. Often represented with snakes or lions, the Mother Goddess was the deity-in-chief and the male gods were clearly subordinate.

The double-axe symbol that appears in frescoes and on the palace walls at Knossos was a sacred symbol for the Minoans. Other religious symbols that frequently appear in Minoan art include the mythi-cal griffin and figures with a human body and an animal head. The Minoans appear to have worshipped the dead and believed in some

---

NO BULL

The bull was a potent symbol in Minoan times, featuring prominently in Minoan art. The peculiar Minoan sport of bull-leaping, where acrobatic thrill-seekers seize the charging bull's horns and leap over its back, is depicted in several frescoes, pottery and sculp-tures. Scantily clad men and women are shown participating in the sport, which may have had religious significance. One of the most stunning examples is the Middle Minoan bull-leaping fresco found at the Palace of Knossos, which shows a man leaping over the back of a bull with a female figure on each side. Another prized bull is the carved stone *rhyton* (libation vessel) in the shape of a bull's head, with rock-crystal eyes and gilded wooden horns.

DECIPHERING THE MYSTERIES OF LINEAR B

The methodical decipherment of the Linear B script by English architect and part-time linguist Michael Ventris in 1952 provided the first tangible evidence that the Greek language had a recorded history longer than any scholar had previously believed. The language was an archaic form of Greek 500 years older than the Ionic Greek used by Homer.

Linear B was written on clay tablets that lay undisturbed for centuries until they were unearthed at Knossos in Crete. Further tablets were unearthed later on the mainland at Mycenae, Tiryns and Pylos in the Peloponnese and at Thebes in Boeotia in central Greece.

The clay tablets, found to be mainly inventories and records of commercial transactions, consist of about 90 different signs, and date from the 14th to the 13th centuries BC. Little of the social and political life of these times can be deduced from the tablets, although there is enough to give a glimpse of a fairly complex and well-organised commercial structure.

Importantly, what is clear is that the language is undeniably Greek, thus giving the modern-day Greek language the second-longest recorded written history, after Chinese. Read Andrew Robinson's biography, *The Man Who Deciphered Linear B*, to learn more about the fascinating life and great genius of Michael Ventris.

form of afterlife, while evidence uncovered in Anemospilia suggests that human sacrifice may also have taken place.

Minoan Writing

The Cretan hieroglyphic was the system of writing used in the Protopalatial period that later evolved into Linear A and B script. The most significant example of this writing is on the inscrutable 3600-year-old terracotta tablet known as the Phaestos Disk, which has been the object of much speculation since it was discovered at Phaestos in 1908. The disk, about 16cm in diameter, consists of an Early Minoan pictographic script made up of 242 'words' written in a continuous spiral from the outside of the disk to the inside (or the other way round). The repetition of sequences of words or sentences has led to speculation it may be a prayer. It has never been deciphered.

As far as the spoken language of the Minoans goes, this too remains unclear. While Mycenaean-era Linear B records something that is definitely an archaic form of Greek, Linear A may well be a script for something completely different. Scholars have speculated that it may have had connections with pre-Greek Mesopotamian tongues, but unless more samples are found, it will remain a mystery.

The Minoans knew how to enjoy themselves – playing board games, boxing, wrestling and performing bold acrobatic feats including the sport of bull-leaping, while Minoan dancing was famous throughout Ancient Greece.

MINOAN ART & CULTURE MINOAN WRITING

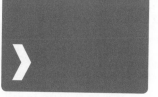

Music & Dance

Music

Cretan music is the most dynamic and enduring form of traditional music in Greece today. It remains the most popular music in Crete, staving off mainstream Greek and Western pop and accompanies weddings, births, holidays, harvesting and any other celebration.

Crete's thriving local music scene continues to spawn a new generation of folk performers who play regularly and produce new recordings of traditional songs as well as a contemporary style of music based on Cretan tradition. Cretan music also has a presence in the world-music scene as a genre in its own right.

The oldest surviving folk songs in Greece, dating from the 17th century, were found at Mt Athos and were revealed to be *rizitika* (patriotic songs) from western Crete.

Instruments & Musical Styles

Cretan music has been influenced by many musical traditions over the centuries and resembles eastern modal music. The lead instrument is the *lyra,* a three-stringed instrument similar to a violin that is played resting on the knee. It is often accompanied by the eight-stringed *laouto* (lute), which keeps the rhythm for the *lyra.* Other traditional instruments include the *mandolino* (mandolin), the *askomandoura* (bagpipe), the *habioli* (wooden flute) and the *daoulaki* (drum). The bouzouki, so associated with Greek music, is not part of Cretan music.

One of Crete's favourite forms of musical expression is the *mantinadha* (a style of traditional Cretan rhyming couplets), which expresses the timeless concerns of love, death and the vagaries of fate. Thousands of *mantinadhes* helped forge a sense of national identity during the long centuries of occupation. *Mantinadhes* rely on the decapentasyllabic (15-syllable) count of Byzantine vernacular literature going back at least to the 12th century. The best 'rhymers' at Cretan festivals would tailor their songs to the people present and try to outdo each other in skill and composition. These days, young Cretans continue the tradition, and *mantinadhes* are still part of the modern courtship ritual, albeit often via mobile-phone text messages. The best-known piece of Cretan Renaissance literature, the 17th-century *Erotokritos* by Vitsentzos Kornaros, consists of language and rhyme consistent with *mantinadhes.* It has provided ample material for performers and continues to inspire Crete's musicians today.

To learn more about Cretan music, go to www.cretan-music.com (in English and Greek).

Another popular form of music is *rizitika* (patriotic songs), which are centuries-old songs from western Crete, especially the Lefka Ori (White Mountains) region. They are thought to have derived from the songs of the border guards of the Byzantine Empire, though their roots may be even older. Many of the *rizitika* deal with historical or heroic themes. One of the most popular is the song of Daskalogiannis, the Sfakian hero who led the rebellion against the Turks in 1770; it has 1034 verses. The period of German occupation in WWII also produced a fertile crop of *rizitika.*

Traditional folk music was shunned by the Greek bourgeoisie during the period after independence when they looked to Europe – and classical music and opera – rather than their eastern or 'peasant' roots. However, a new wave of *entehni mousiki* (artistic music) that emerged in Athens in the 1960s drew on urban folk instruments such as the bouzouki and created popular hits from the works of Greek poets.

Acclaimed composer Yiannis Markopoulos (from Ierapetra) upped the ante by introducing rural folk music into the mainstream. He's best known internationally for his composition for the TV series *Who Pays the Ferryman*? Markopoulos was also responsible for bringing the icon of Cretan music, the late Nikos Xylouris, to the fore. The latter's career was tragically cut short in 1980 when he died of a brain tumour at the age of 43. With his superb voice and talent on the *lyra,* he remains the biggest-selling and most revered Cretan musician. During the junta years, Xylouris' music became a leading voice of the resistance. Xylouris was one of a swag of artists who emerged from the village of Anogia, and part of an extraordinary musical family (see the boxed text, p92).

Xylouris, Thanasis Skordalos and Kostas Mountakis are considered the great masters of Cretan music, and most current musicians follow one of their styles. The most prominent Cretan musician today is the legendary Psarantonis (Antonis Xylouris, brother of Nikos); he's known for his unique style of playing music and is instantly recognisable from his wild beard and straggly mane of hair. Psarantonis performs regularly – everywhere from the smallest Cretan village to the clubs of Athens and the international festival circuit.

One of the most respected and intriguing figures of Crete's music scene is Ross Daly (of Irish descent), a master of the *lyra* and the creator of a high-calibre world-music workshop in Houdetsi (see the boxed text, p92).

The excellent sextet Haïnides is one of the more popular acts to emerge from Crete in recent years, playing their own brand of music and giving memorable live performances around Greece. Other leading figures include Mitsos and Vasilis Stavrakakis and contemporary musicians such as the band Palaïna, Stelios Petrakis from Sitia, Papa Stefanis Nikas and Yiannis Haroulis. Other names to watch include Australian-born Sifis Tsourdalakis and Belgian-born Mihalis Tzouganakis.

Popular artists of Cretan origin playing mainstream Greek music include the talented Manos Pirovolakis with his rock-*lyra* sound. One of Greece's most famous international performers, Nana Mouskouri, was born in Hania, though her family moved to Athens when she was three years of age.

Greeks have been playing music for thousands of years. In fact, archaeologists have found ancient Greek vases decorated with depictions of an instrument very much resembling the *lyra.*

One of the oldest pieces of written music ever found is from 408 BC. The music was sung by a choir in the ancient Greek tragedy *Orestes* by Euripides.

Dance

Dancing has been part of social life in Crete since the dawn of Hellenism. Some folk dances derive from the ritual dances performed in ancient Greek temples. Dancers are also depicted on ancient Greek vases and there are references to dance in Homer's works which laud especially the ability of Cretan dancers.

Cretan dances are dynamic, fast and warlike, and many of them are danced by groups of men. Dances for women are traditionally related to wedding or courtship, and are more delicate and graceful. Like most Greek dances they are normally performed in a circle; in ancient times, dancers formed a circle to seal themselves off from evil influences. In times of occupation, dancing became an act of defiance and a way to keep fit under the noses of the enemy.

CRETAN MUSIC TOP 10

The following broad selection of recordings provides an introduction to Cretan music past and present.

» *Tis Kritis Ta Politima* (2009) – this double-CD compilation is a good overall introduction to Cretan music, featuring a broad selection of traditional songs by leading Cretan musicians and Greek artists.

» *Dimotiki Anthologia-Nikos Xylouris* – a 1976 album that shot Crete's legendary musical son, Nikos Xylouris, to stardom. It's also available in a good-value double-CD set (*I Kriti Tou Nikos Xylouris*) with another classic album, *Ta Pou Thimoume Tragoudo* (1975).

» *Ta Oraiotera Tragoudia Tou* 1974 – a fine anthology paying tribute to the postwar master of Cretan music, Kostas Mountakis, known as 'the teacher'.

» *Thanasis Skordalos* – part of the *To Elliniko Tragoudi* series (2006) documenting the greats of Greek music, this is a taste of one of Crete's *lyra* legends.

» *Anastorimata* – a landmark album from 1982 heralding the idiosyncratic Psarantonis' unique musical style. It also features *mantinadhes* by Vasilis Stavrakakis, and Ross Daly makes his first appearance.

» *Beyond the Horizon* – Ross Daly's 2002 album presents his exceptional orchestration of traditional Cretan music, continuing the Irishman's influence on Cretan music.

» *Embolo* – a 2004 double-disc set featuring Yiannis and Giorgos Xylouris, two of the greats of Cretan music, with the best Cretan lute you can hear.

» *Xatheri* – a stellar collaboration from 2003 featuring Crete's top vocalist Vasilis Stavrakakis, Giorgos Xylouris on lute, Nikos Xylouris and other leading musicians playing Cretan classics with a fresh sound.

» *Palaïna Seferia* – the excellent 1997 self-titled first album of this contemporary Cretan ensemble led by Zacharias Spyridakis, a student of the *lyra* master Mountakis.

» *Haïnides* – the 1991 self-titled first album of this popular Cretan band gives you a good feel for its unique style based on Cretan music.

The most popular Cretan dances are the graceful and slow *syrtos* and the *pentozali*. The latter was originally danced by armed warriors and has a slow version and a faster one that builds into a frenzy, with the leader doing kicks, variations and fancy moves while the others follow with more mild steps. Another popular dance is the *sousta*, a bouncy courtship dance with small precise steps that is performed by couples. The *maleviziotiko* (also known as *kastrino* or *pidikto*) is a fast triumphant dance.

Dancing well is a matter of great personal pride, and most dancers will take their turn at the front to demonstrate their prowess. Be aware that cutting in on somebody's dance is absolutely bad form, as families have usually paid for the dance (this is how Cretan musicians often make their living).

The best place to see Cretan dancing is at festivals, weddings and baptisms. Folkloric shows are also put on for tourists in many areas. Although these are more contrived, they can still be a decent show.

Fine Arts, Literature & Film

Fine Arts

The artistry of the Minoans has still not been surpassed within Greece. During a brief artistic renaissance on the island that lasted from the 8th to the 7th centuries BC, a group of sculptors called the Daedalids perfected a new technique of making sculptures in hammered bronze, working in a style that combined Eastern and Greek aesthetics. Their influence spread to mainland Greece. Cretan culture went into decline at the end of the 7th century BC, though there was a brief revival under the Romans, a period notable for richly decorated mosaic floors and marble sculptures.

Byzantine Art

Greek painting came into its own during the Byzantine period, which lasted roughly from the 4th century BC until the fall of Constantinople in 1453. It was heavily influenced by Roman art. Much Byzantine art was destroyed in popular rebellions during the 13th and 14th centuries. In the 11th century, émigrés from Constantinople brought portable icons to Crete, but the only surviving example from this period is the icon of the Virgin at Mesopantitissa, now in Venice. From the 13th to the early 16th centuries, churches around Crete were decorated with frescoes on a dark-blue background with a bust of Christ in the dome, the four Gospel writers in the corners supporting the dome, and the Virgin and Child in the apse. They also feature scenes from the life of Christ (the Nativity, baptism, the Crucifixion) and figures of saints. Many fine frescoes can still be seen today, albeit moodily faded.

Byzantine art flowered under the Palaeologan emperors who ruled from 1258 to 1453 because of a growing cultural exchange between Byzantine and Italian artists. The great icon painter of the 14th century was Ioannis Pagomenos, who worked in western Crete. Examples of his frescoes can be found in the churches of Agios Nikolaos in Maza, where he's also buried, and in Agios Georgios in Sfakia.

> The first complete English prose translation of Crete's 10,000-line epic *Erotokritos* was published by Byzantina Australiensia in 2004, with a scholarly introduction and notes, translated by Gavan Betts, Stathis Gauntlett and Thanasis Spilias.

The Cretan School

With the fall of Constantinople in 1453, Crete became the centre of Greek art as many Byzantine artists fled to the island. At the same time, the Italian Renaissance was in full bloom and many Cretan artists studied in Italy. The result was the 'Cretan School' of icon painting that combined technical brilliance and dramatic richness. Artists drew inspiration from both Western and Byzantine styles. In Iraklio alone there were more than 200 painters working from the mid-16th to mid-17th centuries.

The most famous and internationally successful of these artists was El Greco, who was heavily influenced by the great Iraklio-born Michael Damaskinos (1530–91). Damaskinos' long sojourn in Venice introduced him to new techniques of rendering perspective, which he brought to the Byzantine style of icon painting. The centrepieces of the collection of the Museum of Religious Art in Iraklio are six portable Damaskinos icons, although they're not currently on view as the museum is undergoing a lengthy renovation. The third star in the trio of Cretan top artists is Theophanes Strelitza (aka Theophanes the Cretan), who was a prominent wall painter of the day, although all of his frescoes are in mainland Greece.

Nikos Kazantzakis modelled his Zorba character on a real person, Yorgos Zorbas, a workman from Macedonia, whom he first met in 1915 and hired two years later to help him set up a lignite mine in the Peloponnese to help meet the demand for coal during WWI.

Contemporary Arts

The fine arts have a relatively low profile in Crete today, though there are many contemporary artists and artisans working and exhibiting on the island. Many Cretan-born artists live and work in Athens and abroad. Rethymno's Museum of Contemporary Art (p81) is one of the island's leading galleries for local and international artists and has a permanent collection of the work of local painter Lefteris Kanakakis. In addition to exhibitions of local artists held by municipal art galleries around Crete, new private galleries are starting to appear in Hania and Iraklio.

Literature

Crete has a rich literary tradition that sprang from the Cretan love of songs, verses and wordplay. In the late 16th and early 17th centuries, the island experienced a tremendous literary flowering under Venetian rule. The era's greatest masterpiece was undoubtedly the epic *Erotokritos,* written in Cretan dialect by Vitsentzos Kornaros of Sitia. More than 10,000 lines long, this poem of courtly love is full of nostalgia for the dying Venetian regime that was threatened by the rise in Turkish power. Revolving around the troubled love story between Erotokritos, an adviser to King Heracles, and the king's daughter, Aretousa, it is an intricate tale of love, honour, friendship and bravery. The poem was recited for centuries by illiterate peasants and professional singers alike, embodying the dreams of freedom that enabled Cretans

EL GRECO THE CRETAN

One of the geniuses of the Renaissance, El Greco ('The Greek' in Spanish), was in fact a Cretan named Dominikos Theotokopoulos. He was born in the Cretan capital of Candia (present-day Iraklio) in 1541, during a time of great artistic activity, following the arrival of painters fleeing Ottoman-held Constantinople. These painters had a formative influence upon the young El Greco, giving him early grounding in the traditions of late-Byzantine fresco painting that was to give such a powerful spiritual element to his later paintings.

El Greco went to Venice in his early twenties, joining the studio of Titian, but he came into his own as a painter after he moved to Spain in 1577, where his highly emotional style struck a chord with the Spanish. He lived in Toledo until his death in 1614. The most famous of his works, such as his masterpiece *The Burial of Count Orgaz* (1586), are in Toledo but his paintings are in museums around the world. *View of Mt Sinai and the Monastery of St Catherine* (1570), painted during his time in Venice, hangs in Iraklio's Historical Museum of Crete, next to the tiny *Baptism of Christ*. You can see *Concert of Angels* (1608) at the National Gallery in Athens.

A white marble bust of the painter stands in Iraklio's Plateia El Greco, and there are streets, taverns and hotels named after him throughout the island. A small museum dedicated to El Greco has been established in the village of Fodele, in a house he allegedly spent time in as a child. The 2007 biopic *El Greco* was partly shot in Iraklio.

to endure their many privations. Many of the verses were incorporated into Crete's beloved *mantinadhes* (a style of traditional Cretan rhyming couplets). It is considered the most important work of early modern Greek literature.

Literary Lions

Greece's best-known and most widely read author since Homer is Nikos Kazantzakis (1883–1957), born in Crete amid the last spasms of the island's struggle for independence from the Turks. His novels, all of which have been translated into English, are full of drama and larger-than-life characters such as the magnificent title character in *Zorba the Greek* (1946) and the tortured Captain Michalis in *Freedom and Death* (1950), two of his finest works. Along with Zorba, *The Last Temptation* was also made into a film, starring Willem Dafoe and Harvey Keitel. *Zorba the Greek* takes place in Crete and provides a fascinating glimpse into the harsher side of Cretan culture. Kazantzakis had a chequered, and at times troubled, literary career, clashing frequently with the Orthodox Church for his professed atheism (see p236).

Kazantzakis may be Crete's internationally most famous writer, but he never won the Nobel Prize in Literature. This honour was bestowed upon fellow Cretan Odysseus Elytis (1911–96) in 1979. The Nobel committee praised his poetry, which, 'against the background of Greek tradition, depicts with sensuous strength and intellectual clear-sightedness modern man's struggle for freedom and creativeness.' One of his main works is *Axion Esti – It is Worthy* (1959), a complicated poem that deals with existentialist questions and the identity of the main character's country and people. It was set to music by Mikis Theodorakis and to this day is one of the best-known poems and songs in Greece.

Eyltis is a major representative of the '1930s generation' who came of age shortly after WWII and the Greek Civil War. Another is Rethymno-born Pandelis Prevelakis (1909–86). Primarily known as a poet, Prevelakis also wrote plays and novels. His best-known work is *The Tale of a Town,* a nostalgic look at his home town in the early 20th century.

Contemporary Writers

Contemporary Cretan writers include Rhea Galanaki (b 1947), whose prize-winning *The Life of Ismail Ferik Pasha* (1989) has been translated into six languages; it's a story about the clash of Christianity and Ottoman Islam in Crete. It is listed in Unesco's Collection of Representative Works.

Literature and Society in Renaissance Crete by David Holton is a comprehensive study of the literature of the Cretan Renaissance in its historical, social and cultural context, with chapters on the poetic and dramatic genres contributed by leading experts in the field.

FINE ARTS, LITERATURE & FILM LITERATURE

RENAISSANCE

Ioanna Karystiani (b 1952), who wrote the screenplay for *Brides* (2004), is another important contemporary woman writer. She received the Greek National Award for Literature for her only novel *Mikra Anglia* (Little England), which describes the romances, lives and work of a sailor's family on the island of Andros in the first half of the 20th century.

One institution upholding Crete's literary tradition is the nonprofit Centre for Cretan Literature, founded in 1987 as an adjunct to the Nikos Kazantzakis Museum in Myrtia. Its goal is to record, study and promote island literature by hosting literary events honouring both living and dead Cretan writers, including Minas Dimakis, Manolis Pratikakis, Yiorgis Manoussakis and Victoria Theodorou.

The *syrtaki* dance, immortalised by Anthony Quinn in the final scene of *Zorba the Greek*, was in fact a dance he improvised, as he had injured his leg the day before the shoot and could not perform the steps and leaps originally planned. The scripted energetic dance became a slow shuttle that he falsely claimed was traditional.

Film

Crete has no local film industry but it has been the location for many films, most famously of course, the 1960s classic *Zorba the Greek,* which was shot in Stavros on the Akrotiri Peninsula and around the island and went on to win three Academy Awards. In 1956 the American director Jules Dassin *(Never On Sunday)* chose the village of Kritsa as the backdrop for *He Who Must Die,* the film version of Kazantzakis' novel *Christ Recrucified* starring Dassin's wife, Melina Mercouri.

Other movies shot in Crete include the 2000 romantic comedy *Beware of Greeks Bearing Guns,* an old-fashioned tale of mistaken identity and a Cretan vendetta. The Greek–Australian co-production was shot in Crete and Melbourne, Australia.

The 2007 epic *El Greco* about the life of the famous Crete-born painter, directed by Yiannis Smaragdis, was partly shot in Crete, as

NIKOS KAZANTZAKIS – CRETE'S PRODIGAL SON

Crete's most famous contemporary writer is Nikos Kazantzakis. Born in 1883 in Iraklio, the then Turkish-dominated capital, Kazantzakis spent his early childhood in the ferment of revolution and change that was creeping upon his homeland. In 1897 the revolution that finally broke out against Turkish rule forced him to leave Crete for studies in Naxos, Athens and later Paris. It wasn't until he was 31 that he finally turned his hand to writing by translating philosophical books into Greek. For a number of years he travelled throughout Europe, thus laying the groundwork for a series of travelogues in his later literary career.

Kazantzakis was a complex writer and his early work was heavily influenced by the prevailing philosophical ideas of the time, including the nihilistic philosophies of Nietzsche. In his writings, Kazantzakis is tormented by a tangible metaphysical and existentialist anguish. His relationship with religion was always troubling – his official stance being that of a nonbeliever, yet he always seemed to toy with the idea that perhaps God did exist. His self-professed greatest work is his *Odyssey,* a modern-day epic loosely based on the trials and travels of the ancient hero Odysseus (Ulysses). A weighty and complex opus of 33,333 iambic verses, *Odyssey* never fulfilled Kazantzakis' aspirations to be held in the same league as the works of Homer, Virgil or the Renaissance Italian Tasso.

Ironically it was only much later in his career, after Kazantzakis turned to novel writing, that his star shone the brightest. It was through works such as *Christ Recrucified* (1948), *Kapetan Mihalis* (1950; now known as *Freedom and Death*) and *The Life and Adventures of Alexis Zorbas* (1946; later renamed *Zorba the Greek*) that he became internationally known. This last work gave rise to the image of the ultimate, free-spirited Greek male, 'Zorba the Greek', immortalised by Anthony Quinn in the movie of the same name.

Kazantzakis died while travelling in Freiburg, Germany, on 26 October 1957. Despite resistance from the Orthodox Church, he was given a religious funeral and buried in the southern Martinengo Bastion of the old walls of Iraklio.

was Olga Malea's *First-Time Godfather* (2007), a humorous look at Greek culture based on an autobiographical short story by Nikos Papandreou, son of the former Greek prime minister. Also filmed in Crete was the romantic comedy *Reception Will Follow* (2007), starring Greek-Australian actor Alex Dimitriades and produced by Greek-American Christine Crokos.

Major TV productions filmed in Crete include the popular 2006–07 series *Tis Agapis Mahairia* (The Knives of Love), a drama based on a Cretan vendetta. In 2009 a huge film crew descended upon Spinalonga for the shooting of *To Nisi*, the 26-episode TV adaption of Victoria Hislop's best-selling novel *The Island*. The series premiered on Greek TV in October 2010; see p158.

Jennifer Aniston's real name is Jennifer Anastasakis and she's the daughter of Cretan-born Ioannis Anastasakis, who is also an actor.

Cretan Cuisine

Waistlines be damned: Crete is one tasty place to indulge your appetite. The local cuisine has its own distinct identity within Greek cooking. Regional specialities found across Crete and the quality and range of produce grown on the island by various small-scale producers present a diverse gourmet trail. One of the delights of travelling through Crete is coming across a family-run taverna where traditional local dishes are made from ancient recipes but with farm-fresh, home-grown produce, where the wild aromatic greens were picked in the mountains earlier that day, the oil and cheese is homemade, the tender lamb is from a local shepherd and the fish was caught by the owner.

With the advent of mass tourism, the food dished up to visitors at many of the island's all-inclusive resorts and bland tourist tavernas has hardly done Cretan cuisine justice. This is changing, however, as pride in promoting local cooking increases and more traditional homestyle dishes are appearing on restaurant menus. Some tavernas have entirely stopped pandering to foreign predilections, trading schnitzel for *stifadho* (meat, game or seafood cooked with onions in a tomato puree). Meanwhile, a new generation of professional chefs is experimenting with variations on traditional dishes, flavours and textures to create Modern Cretan cuisine.

Crete may be a potential gourmet travel destination, but the essence of its rustic cuisine remains its simple seasonal and balanced approach, which reflects the bounty of a sun-blessed fertile land and a history of resourcefulness that comes from subsistence living during hard times.

Cretan cuisine gained legendary status for its health benefits following scientific studies of the Mediterranean diet in the 1960s that showed Cretans had the lowest levels of heart disease and other chronic illnesses. This was largely attributed to a greater reliance on pulses, fresh vegetables and fruit than on meats and processed foodstuffs. Copious use of virgin olive oil also played its part.

Food and the ritual of dining together play an integral role in Cretan life, whether at home or eating out with family and friends. Cretans will travel far to get to a great restaurant or eat specific food, heading to the mountains for local meat and the sea for fresh fish. Some of the best tavernas are tucked away in unexpected places.

PRICE RANGES

Price indicators in this book refer to the average cost of a main course:

- » € Budget   <€7
- » €€ Midrange   €7-15
- » €€€ Top end   >€15

THE GOOD OIL

The Minoans were among the first to grow wealthy on the olive, and Crete remains an important olive-growing area, producing the largest quantity of extra virgin olive oil in Greece. More and more organic oil is being produced and at least nine olive regions have gained the EU's Protected Appellation of Origin status.

The best Cretan olive oil is from Kolymbari, west of Hania, and Sitia in the east. Biolea, near Hania, makes superb organic olive oil, as do monasteries – particularly the award-winning olive oil produced at Moni Agia Triada near Hania and Moni Toplou, east of Sitia.

The oil that is prized above all others is *agoureleo* (meaning unripe), a thick green oil pressed from unripe olives.

Greeks are the world's biggest per-capita consumers of olive oil; in Crete annual per-person consumption averages 31L.

The Cretan Kitchen

The Cretan diet evolved from subsistence and what could be grown or made locally.

Greek and Cretan dishes often overlap, but there are Cretan specialities as well as regional variations across the island. The cuisine has its roots in antiquity and has been influenced by various cultures over time, but it essentially relies on organically grown, farm-fresh, unadulterated seasonal produce, aromatic herbs and quality farm-grown meats. Cretan olive oil, produced in vast quantities across the island, is among the world's best and is an integral part of meals. Apart from its beneficial qualities, olive oil also adds flavour to vegetables and salads.

Crete's climate is conducive to growing produce year-round. In fact, the region is Greece's main supplier of early fruit and vegetables, including avocados and grapefruit.

Vegetables

For centuries Cretans have been gathering *horta* (wild greens) from the hills and boiling them for warm salads or cooking them in pies and stews. Cretan *paximadia* (rusks), a hangover from times of famine, are made from barley flour or whole wheat and double-baked to produce a hard, dry cracker that can keep, literally, for years. They are moistened with water and topped with tomato, olive oil and feta or *myzithra* (sheep's-milk cheese) in the popular dish called *dakos* (or *koukouvagia*). Cretan cuisine also shines in such vegetable dishes as artichokes and broad beans or tasty zucchini flowers *(anthoi)* stuffed with rice and herbs. There are more than 100 edible *horta* (wild greens) on Crete, although even the most knowledgeable would not recognise more than a dozen.

Meat & Fish

Meat features in Cretan cuisine more regularly today than it did in the past. Cretans eat a lot of locally reared lamb and goat and are also fond of rabbit, which is stewed with rosemary and *rizmarato* (vinegar). While grilled meats dominate taverna menus, Cretans have their own way of barbecuing called *ofto*, in which big chunks of meat are grilled upright around hot coals. In parts of Crete meat is cooked *tsigariasto* (sautéed), while in traditional mountain village tavernas you will find surprisingly tasty *vrasto* (mutton or goat stew). Meat is also cooked with vegetables, often lamb stewed with *stamnagathi* (a type of wild greens) or artichokes, or chicken with okra. The resourceful Cretans use almost every part of the animal – including *ameletita* ('unspeakables'; fried sheep's testicles) and *gardhoumia* (stomach and offal wrapped in intestines).

Hohlioi (snails) are collected after rainfall and prepared in dozens of interesting ways: try *hohlioi bourbouristoi,* simmered in vinegar and rosemary, or snails stewed with *hondros* (cracked wheat).

Top Resources

» www.greek-recipe.com

» www.gourmed.gr

» www.greek wine.gr

» www.greek winemakers .com

Psari (fish) has long been a staple along the coast and is cooked with minimum fuss – usually grilled whole and drizzled with *ladholemono* (a lemon-and-oil dressing). Smaller fish like red mullet and tiny whitebait are usually lightly fried.

The Glorious Foods of Greece by award-winning Greek-American food writer Diane Kochilas is a 'must-have' for any serious cook, with a regional exploration of Greek food and a 60-page chapter on Crete.

Cheese

As well as the ubiquitous feta, Crete produces wonderful cheeses from goat's and sheep's milk, or a combination. *Graviera,* a nutty, mild gruyere-like sheep's-milk cheese, is often aged in special mountain caves and stone huts called *mitata.* It is delicious eaten with thyme honey. Other local cheeses include *myzithra* (a soft, mild ricotta-like cheese that can be eaten soft or hardened for grating), the hardened sour *xino-myzithra, anthotiro* (a buttery white cheese that can be soft or dry) and *galomyzithra* (a creamy speciality of Hania). *Staka* is a rich, soft buttery cheese, often added to rice *pilafi* (pilaf) to make it creamier.

Thick, tangy sheep's-milk yoghurt is something to savour, best eaten with honey, walnuts or fruit.

Drinks

Wine

Krasi (wine) has been produced in Crete since Minoan times, and Crete's farmers have long made wine for their own consumption. Commercial production, however, did not start until the 1930s and only in 1952 did Minos in Peza become the first winery to bottle wine on Crete.

Today, Crete produces about 20% of Greek wine, most of it through huge cooperatives that aim for higher yields rather than higher quality. Much of it is blended and sold in bulk. This is usually what you get when you order 'house wine' in restaurants. Quality can be uneven but most of it is actually quite drinkable.

When it comes to finer, bottled vintages, Cretan wines have not made connoisseurs tremble with delight in the past. Fortunately, this is slowly changing thanks to a growing crop of boutique wineries helmed by a new generation of forward-thinking, internationally trained winemakers. Minos-Miliarakis, Lyrakakis and the Sitia Coop are among wineries that are now producing more distinguished wines, some of which are exported around Europe and to the USA. Wine tourism, too, is picking up as wineries build new visitor centres that double as mini-museums and wine-tasting rooms.

Crete has three wine-producing areas. The largest is the Iraklio Wine Country, which makes about 70% of Cretan wine. It produces mostly Kotsifali, Mandilaria and Vilana grapes in two centres; one around Peza/Arhanes south of Iraklio and the other around Dafnes, a bit further west. The smallest wine region is east of here in Lasithi. Vineyards cluster primarily around Sitia and are specialised in Liatiko grapes. In western Crete, the main grape-growing region is west of Hania, where the main varietal cultivated is Romeiko.

Retsina, white wine flavoured with the resin of pine trees, has taken on an almost folkloric significance with foreigners. An acquired taste, it goes well with strongly flavoured mezedhes and seafood.

Raki & Ouzo

Also known as *tsikoudia, raki* is an integral part of Cretan culture. A shot of the fiery brew is offered as a welcome, at the end of a meal and pretty much at any time and on all occasions. Distilled from grape stems and pips left over from the grapes pressed for wine, it is similar to the Middle Eastern *arak,* Italian grappa, Irish poteen or Turkish raki. Each October, the *raki* distilling season starts, with distilleries around the island (including many private stills) producing massive quantities. The season is usually accompanied by lots of drinking and feasting. If you pass a village distilling *raki*, you may well get an invitation. Good *raki* has a smooth mellow taste with no noticeable after-burn.

There are literally hundreds of family-owned distilleries around the island who bottle the potent brew in used water bottles and sell them in small shops, tavernas or by the roadside. No self-respecting Cretan would dream of buying commercially bottled *raki* in the supermarket, and neither should you. Good *raki* generally does not induce hangovers, assuming you're consuming it in sensible quantities and eat food with it.

Ouzo, the famous Greek aniseed spirit, has a more limited following in Crete, where it is drunk mostly by mainlanders or foreigners. It is served neat, with ice and a separate glass of water for dilution (which makes it turn milky white).

Beer

The major Greek brands are Mythos and Alfa, while boutique beers include the Vergina and Hillas lagers from northern Greece, organic Piraiki made in Piraeus, and Craft, which is widely available in draught form. The only beer actually produced on Crete are the organic lagers made by Brink's Brewery (see p96) near Rethymno. Greeks are not big beer drinkers however: they only consume about half the EU per capita average. Supermarkets are the cheapest place to buy beer, which is also available in kiosks.

Coffee & Tea

A legacy of Ottoman rule, Greek coffee is traditionally brewed on hot sand in a special copper *briki* (pot) and served in a small cup, where the grounds sink to the bottom (don't drink them). It is drunk *glykos* (sweet), *metrios* (medium) and *sketo* (plain; without sugar). Greek coffee is, however, struggling to maintain its place as the national drink against the ubiquitous frappé, the iced instant-coffee concoction that you see everyone drinking. Alternatives are espresso and cappuccino chilled – *freddo*. Herbal teas are popular, especially camomile or aromatic Cretan *tsai tou vounou* (mountain tea), which is both nutritious and delicious. The endemic *diktamo* (dittany) tea is known for its medicinal qualities, while Crete's reputedly medicinal warm tipple is *rakomelo* – raki, honey and cloves.

Dining Out

Eating out with family and friends is an integral part of social life, and Cretans eat out regularly, regardless of socioeconomic status. The key to picking a restaurant is to find where locals are eating, rather than 'tourist' tavernas (touts and big illuminated photos are a dead giveaway). Hotel recommendations can be tricky as some have deals with particular restaurants or may suggest one owned by a relative.

January

The *vasilopita*, a New Year's cake, comes with a hidden coin and promises its finder a year of good luck.

February

The olive harvest reaches its peak. A great time to stock up on the new freshly pressed crop.

March

The Easter feast features *mayiritsa* (lamb's offal soup), roast lamb and *kreatotourta* (meat pies). Red-dyed boiled eggs are everywhere and also used to decorate the *tsoureki*, a brioche-style bread.

April

Marvel at the number of ways to prepare slimy snails while attending Hohliovradia (Snail Night) in Vamos.

May

Pick edible wild plants and herbs and feast on fresh, young artichokes, best eaten raw and whole with a drizzle of lemon.

June

Cheesemaking kicks into high gear. Fresh *myzithra*, a fresh soft cheese and *malakos*, a sheep's-milk cheese curd, are widely available.

July

Watermelon, fresh figs, peaches, apricots, cherries and other fruit jam-pack markets; mussel season reaches its peak.

Cretans eat
more snails than
the French do.
Cretan snails are
even exported
to France.

SNAILS

Try to adapt to local eating times – a restaurant that was empty at 7pm might be heaving with locals at 11pm (for more details, see Habits & Customs, p244).

By law, every eating establishment must display a written menu including prices. Most restaurants levy a small charge for bread and nibbles served on arrival. Tipping is not mandatory but the bill is usually rounded up or around 10% is added for good service.

Mezedhes & Salads

Cretans love to share a range of mezedhes (appetisers), often making a full meal of them or adding a main or two. You can also order a *pikilia* (mixed mezedhes plate).

Common mezedhes are dips such as *taramasalata* (fish roe), tzatziki (yoghurt, cucumber and garlic), *melidzanosalata* (smoky purée of grilled eggplant or aubergine) and *fava* (split-pea puree). Hot mezedhes include *keftedhes* (small tasty rissoles, often made with minced lamb, pork or veal), *loukaniko* (pork sausages), *saganaki* (skillet-fried cheese) and *apaki* (Cretan cured pork).

Vegetarian mezedhes include rice-filled dolmadhes (vine leaves), deep-fried zucchini or aubergine slices, *gigantes* (lima beans in tomato and herb sauce). Hand-cut potatoes fried in olive oil are also a favourite.

Typical seafood mezedhes are pickled or grilled *ohtapodi* (octopus), *lakerda* (cured fish), mussel or prawn *saganaki* (usually fried with tomato sauce and cheese), crispy fried *kalamari* (calamari, squid), fried *maridha* (whitebait) and *gavros* (mild anchovy), either marinated or grilled.

Soup is not normally eaten as a starter, but can be an economical and hearty meal in itself, perhaps paired with a salad. *Psarosoupa* is a fish soup with vegetables; *kakavia* (Greek bouillabaisse) is made to order and laden with seafood. If you're into offal, don't miss *mayiritsa,* the traditional Easter tripe soup.

The ubiquitous Greek salad, *horiatiki salata,* accompanies most meals and is made with tomatoes, cucumber, onions, olives and feta cheese, sprinkled with oregano and dressed with olive oil, occasionally garnished with fresh *glistrida* (purslane or capers). In spring, you'll also find wonderful wild greens salad prepared with leaves gathered by hand in the countryside.

Mains

Tavernas normally have a selection of one-pot stews, casseroles and *mayirefta* (ready-cooked meals) in addition to food cooked to order *(tis oras)* such as grilled meats. *Mayirefta* are usually prepared early and left to cool, which enhances the flavour. They are often better served lukewarm, though many places microwave them. The most common *mayirefta* are *mousakas* (baked layers of eggplant or zucchini, minced meat and potatoes topped with cheese sauce), *boureki* (a cheese and vegetable pie), *pastitsio* (layers of buttery macaroni and seasoned minced lamb), *yemista* (stuffed vegetables), *yuvetsi* (a hearty dish of baked meat or poultry in a fresh tomato sauce with *kritharaki,* rice-shaped pasta), *stifadho, soutzoukakia* (meat rissoles in tomato sauce) and *hohlioi* (snails). *Ladhera* are largely vegetable dishes stewed or baked with plenty of olive oil. Meat is commonly baked with potatoes, with lemon and oregano, or cooked in tomato-based stews or casseroles *(kokkinisto).*

Tasty charcoal-grilled meats – most commonly lamb cutlets and pork chops – are usually cooked to order and priced by weight.

Seafood mains may include octopus with macaroni, and squid stuffed with cheese and herbs or rice. Cuttlefish *(soupies)* is excellent grilled or stewed with wild fennel. Fried salted cod served with *skordalia* (a lethal garlic and potato dip) is another tasty dish.

Fish is usually sold by weight in restaurants and it is customary to pick your victim from the selection on display or in the kitchen. Make sure it's weighed (raw) so you don't get a shock when the bill arrives, as fresh fish is not cheap.

While Crete's fishing industry ensures a lot of fresh fish, there is certainly not enough local fish to cater for the millions of tourists who descend each summer. Most places will state if the fish and seafood is frozen, though sometimes only on the Greek menu (indicated by the abbreviated 'kat' or an asterisk). Smaller fish are often a safer bet – the odder the sizes, the more chance that they are local.

The choice fish for grilling are *tsipoura* (sea bream), *lavraki* (sea bass) and *fangri* (bream), while smaller fish such as *barbounia* (red mullet) are delicious fried.

Sweet Treats

Fruit, rather than sweets, is traditionally served after a meal – but that's not to say that you won't find some delectable local sweets and cakes. Women pride themselves on their baking and confectionary skills.

As well as traditional Greek sweets such as baklava, *loukoumadhes* (ball-shaped doughnuts served with honey and cinnamon), *kataïfi* ('angel hair' pastry; chopped nuts inside shredded pastry soaked in honey), *rizogalo* (rice pudding), and *galaktoboureko* (custard-filled pastry with syrup), Cretans have their own sweet specialities.

Sfakianes pittes, from the Sfakia region of Hania, are fine pancake-like sweets with a light *myzithra* filling, served with honey. *Xerotigana* are deep-fried pastry twirls with honey and nuts.

Traditional syrupy fruit preserves (known as spoon sweets) are served on tiny plates but are also delicious as a topping on yoghurt or ice cream. Some tavernas serve *halva* (made from semolina) after a meal.

Quick Eats

Souvlaki is the favourite fast food of Crete. Skewered or kebab versions are wrapped in pitta bread, with tomato, onion and lashings of tzatziki. There are plenty of Western-style *fastfoudadika,* as fast-food joints are known, in major cities and towns. A range of *pites* (pies) – including *kalitsounia* (filled pastries) and the classic *tyropita* (cheese pie) and *spanakopita* (spinach pie) – can be found in bakeries. If you are in a hurry but want a real meal, tavernas with *mayirefta* are the best bet.

The Cretan Diet

The health benefits of the Cretan diet first gained attention after an influential international study, begun in the 1960s, found that Cretan men had the lowest rate of heart disease and cancer. Thirty years later, half the Cretan participants were still alive, compared with no survivors in Finland. The mystery is attributed to a balanced diet high in fruits, vegetables, pulses, whole grains, olive oil and wine. Another important factor may be the *horta* (wild greens) that Cretans gathered in the hills

August
A month of food festivals: Sitia pays homage to the sultana raisin, Tzermiado celebrates the lowly potato and Arhanes raises a toast to the grape during its wine festival.

September
The grape harvest begins!

October
Sample plump, juicy and sweet chestnuts in the village of Elos (near Kissamos), which ushers in autumn with the quirky Chestnut Festival.

November
The *raki* distilling season hits a peak with raucous festivals all over Crete, especially in the mountain villages.

December
Sugar-dusted *kourabiedes* (almond shortcake) and honey-dipped nutty *melomakarona* are typical Christmas cookies, while *Christopsomo* (Christ Bread) is a round loaf decorated with a cross.

and survived on during wars, which may have protective properties that are not yet fully understood. Regular fasting may also play a role, along with the use of sheep and goat's milk instead of cow's; and many will swear by the medicinal properties of *raki* and wine and their role in ensuring longevity.

Apart from the health benefits, Cretan cuisine is also finally being recognised as a key part of the cultural heritage. A resurgence of interest and pride in Cretan cuisine has started to change the island's gastronomic map. In recent years more emphasis is being placed on promoting Cretan cuisine through initiatives such as **Concred** (www.concred.gr), a restaurant certification program, which has about 35 restaurants on board. Some are in large hotels, others are classy restaurants and simple tavernas, both in cities and villages.

Cretan Cooking by Maria and Nikos Psilakis is a well-translated version of their popular guide to Cretan cooking. It contains 265 mouth-watering recipes, some fascinating asides on the history of the dishes and background to the Cretan dietary phenomenon.

Vegetarians & Vegans

Crete has few vegetarian restaurants per se, but a combination of lean times and the Orthodox faith's fasting traditions has made Cretans accidental vegans, so there are normally plenty of meatless meals available. Beans and pulses were the foundation of the winter diet, so you will find dishes such as delicious *gigantes*. Also look for *fasolakia yiahni* (green bean stew), *gemista* (stuffed tomatoes) and *bamies* (okra). Aubergines are also widely used, particularly in dishes such as *briam* (oven-baked vegetable casserole).

Horta are extremely nutritious. The *vlita* (amaranth) variety is the sweetest, while *stamnagathi*, found in the mountains, is considered a delicacy and served boiled as a salad or stewed with meat. Other common *horta* include wild radish, dandelion, nettles and sorrel.

Habits & Customs

Hospitality is a key element of Cretan culture, from the glass of water on arrival to the customary complimentary fruit and *raki* at the end of a meal. People prefer to share lots of dishes, which makes for more social and relaxed dining and allows you to taste everything. Cretans rarely eat alone.

Cretans aren't big on breakfast. Budget hotels usually provide continental-style breakfasts (rolls or bread with jam, and tea or coffee) and

CRETAN WINE VARIETALS

» Dafni – lively with subtle acidity and an aroma resembling laurel, common in Lasithi and Iraklio wine regions.

» Kotsifali – indigenous red grape with high alcohol content and rich flavour, typical of Iraklio region, often blended with Mandilaria.

» Liatiko – very old indigenous red variety with complex character found mainly around Sitia.

» Malvasia – original Cretan variety, strong flower aroma with notes of muscat, ages well if blended with Kotsifali.

» Mandilaria – dark-coloured but light-bodied red wine, prevalent around Arhanes and Peza.

» Romeiko – red grapes mostly grown around Hania and turned into robust red, white and rosé wines.

» Vidiano – white indigenous wine with intensive and complex peach and apricot aromas; often blended with Vilana.

» Vilana – main white grape of Iraklio growing area, fresh, low-alcohol wine with a delicate aroma evoking apples.

» **Estiatorio** A restaurant where you pay more for essentially the same dishes as in a taverna, but with a nicer setting and formal service. These days it also refers to an upmarket restaurant serving international cuisine.

» **Kafeneio** One of the oldest institutions, a *kafeneio* (coffee house) serves Greek coffee, spirits and little else, though those in villages may also serve food. They remain largely the domain of men.

» **Mayireio** A restaurant specialising in ready-cooked traditional homestyle one-pot stews, casseroles and baked dishes (known as *mayirefta*).

» **Mezedhopoleio** The key here is lots of different mezedhes, small dishes that are shared.

» **Ouzerie** Traditionally serves tiny plates of mezedhes with each round of ouzo.

» **Psarotaverna** Taverna or restaurant specialising in fish and seafood.

» **Psistaria** A taverna specialising in char-grilled or spit-roasted meat.

» **Rakadiko** The Cretan equivalent of an *ouzerie* serves increasingly sophisticated mezedhes with each round of *raki*. Particularly popular in Sitia, Ierapetra and Rethymno.

» **Taverna** The most common, casual, family-run (and child-friendly) place, where the server arrives with bread and cutlery in a basket. They usually have barrel wine, paper tablecloths and fairly standard menus.

» **Zaharoplasteio** A cross between a patisserie and a cafe (though some only do takeaway).

more-upmarket hotels serve full buffets including Cretan-style pastries. One traditional breakfast food is *bougatsa,* a pastry stuffed with creamy custard or cheese and sprinkled with powdered sugar. It originated in Thessaloniki but some places in Crete serve it too.

Although changes in working hours are affecting traditional meal patterns, lunch is still usually the big meal of the day and does not start until after 2pm. Most Greeks wouldn't think of eating dinner before dark, which coincides with shop closing hours (see p250), so restaurants don't fill up until after 10pm. In between, cafes do a roaring trade, particularly after the mid-afternoon siesta.

Dining is a drawn-out ritual so, if you are eating with locals, pace yourself and don't gorge on mezedhes, because there will be plenty more to come. The service can be slow by Western standards, but staff are not in a rush to get you out of there either. Once you have your meal they are likely to leave you alone and will often not clear the table until you ask for the bill. Cretans order plenty of dishes and have food left over at the end of the meal. Many places will oblige if you want to take leftovers with you, though when locals do so, it really is a doggie bag.

Ordering a Greek salad or tzatziki as a meal – a common practice among young and budget tourists – is often quietly sneered at by the restaurant staff.

Greeks don't traditionally drink coffee after a meal and many tavernas don't offer it.

With an estimated 30 million olive trees in Crete, it works out to 62 olive trees for every man, woman and child.

OLIVE TREES

Cooking Courses

Culinary tours and cooking courses are becoming more popular in Crete. General courses start at €50.

Rodialos (☎28340 51310; www.rodialos.gr) regularly hosts one- to seven-day cooking seminars in a lovely villa in Panormo near Rethymno. Mary

Frangaki takes participants through the principles of Cretan cooking and cooks several courses. Workshops cost €50 per day and include eating what you cook. Stays at the villa cost €30. Check the website for more details.

Enagron (☑28340 61611; www.enagron.gr), outside the village of Axos, runs cooking workshops and organises seasonal events around the production of cheese, wine and *raki*. The farm setting is lovely and there is accommodation on site (see p187).

Crete's Culinary Sanctuaries (www.cookingincrete.com) focuses on organic agriculture and traditional approaches to Cretan cuisine with hands-on classes and demonstrations in people's homes, visits to local farmers and producers. Headed by Greek-American chef and writer Nikki Rose, seminars usually last two days and are limited to 12 people. The cost is around €290.

Wildlife & Birdwatching

The Land

With an area of 8335 sq km, Crete is the largest island in the Greek archipelago. It's 250km long, about 60km at its widest point and 12km at its narrowest. The island has an extraordinary geographical and ecological diversity, with mountain ranges, dramatic gorges, a vast coastline and a plethora of caves. Crete's biodiversity also provides a broad range of habitats for wildlife in a relatively small geographic area, including a few interior wetlands. The island is renowned for its flora and in spring there is an abundance of wildflowers, including many endemic and rare species.

Samaria Gorge is the only national park in Crete and is on the tentative list of Unesco World Heritage sites.

Wildlife

Animals

While Crete is known for its large population of sheep and goats, the island is also home to some endemic fauna, including hares, rabbits and weasels and its own subspecies of badger. You are unlikely to catch sight of the big-eared Cretan spiny mouse, but you never know. The island also has a large population of bats, insects, snails and invertebrates.

Other local species include the tiny Cretan tree frog and the Cretan marsh frog.

The southern coastline with its steep underwater cliffs is home to the Mediterranean Sea's most significant population of sperm whales, who gather, feed and possibly mate in the area year-round. Keep your eyes open while on boat trips. Groups of striped dolphins, Risso's dolphins and Cuvier's beaked whales frequent waters off the south coast. Bottlenose dolphins are often spotted in the shallow waters off Paleohora between Gavdos and its tiny neighbouring islet of Gavdopoula.

The Cretan Sperm Whale Project, run by the Pelagos Cetacean Research Institute, monitors the whale population. Private dolphin-spotting trips are run from Paleohora.

Hard-core bird-watchers should come equipped with *A Birdwatching Guide to Crete* by Stephanie Coghlan or, for a comprehensive reference on Greece's bird life, try *The Birds of Greece* by Christopher Helm.

Bird Life

Crete flies high in the bird world. It lies on the main Africa–Europe migratory routes and well over 300 species have been recorded on the island, including both resident and migratory species. Along the coast you'll find birds of passage such as egrets and herons during spring and autumn migrations.

The mountains host a wealth of interesting birds. Look for blue rock thrushes, buzzards and the huge griffon vulture. Other birds in the mountains include alpine swifts, stonechats, blackbirds and Sardinian

ENDANGERED SPECIES

Crete's most famous animal is the *agrimi* or *kri-kri,* a distinctive wild goat with large horns often depicted in Minoan art. Only a few survive in the wild, in and around Samaria Gorge and on the islands of Agioi Theodori off Hania and Dia off Iraklio.

You may spot a lammergeier (bearded vulture) – one of the rarest raptors in Europe, with a wingspan of nearly 3m – in Samaria Gorge or hovering above the Lasithi Plateau. A few golden eagles and Bonelli's eagles are also recorded in these areas and elsewhere, including the Kato Zakros area. Much good work has been carried out by various organisations in rehabilitating raptors such as bearded vultures and eagles and releasing them into the more remote areas of the Lefka Ori (White Mountains) and other ranges.

Crete is battling to protect its population of loggerhead turtles, which have been nesting on island shores since the days of the dinosaurs. The island also has a small population of the rare and endangered Mediterranean monk seal, breeding in caves on the south coast.

The Flowers of Greece & the Aegean by William Taylor and Anthony Huxley is the most comprehensive field guide to flowers in Greece and Crete.

warblers. The fields around Malia host tawny and red-throated pipits, stone-curlews, fan-tailed warblers and short-toed larks. On the hillsides below Moni Preveli you may find subalpine and Ruppell's warblers. The Akrotiri Peninsula is good for birdwatching – around the monasteries of Agias Triadas and Gouvernetou you'll find collared and pied flycatchers, wrynecks, tawny pipits, black-eared wheatears, blue rock thrushes, stonechats, chukars and northern wheatears. Migrating species, including avocets and marsh sandpipers, can be spotted in wetland areas such as Elafonisi.

Plants

Crete blooms in every sense of the word. An estimated total of about 2000 plant species are said to make Crete their home and about 160 of those are endemic to the island. Crete's gorges are mini-botanical gardens and their isolation has helped preserve many species.

Along the coast, sea daffodils flower in August and September. In April and May knapweeds are in flower on the west coast and the purple or violet petals of stocks provide pretty splashes of colour on sandy beaches. At the same time of year in eastern Crete, especially around Sitia, watch for crimson poppies on the borders of the beach. At the edge of sandy beaches that are not yet lined with a strip of hotels you'll find delicate pink bindweeds and jujube trees that flower from May to June and bear fruit in September and October. In the same habitat is the tamarisk tree, which flowers in spring.

There are more than 200 species of wild orchid on Crete, including 14 endemic varieties and Crete's famous *Ophrys Cretica*, which uses its insect-like appearance as a disguise to attract male insects.

If you come in summer, you won't be deprived of colour, since milky white and magenta oleanders bloom from June through to August.

On the hillsides look for cistus and brooms in early summer, and yellow chrysanthemums in the fields from March to May. The rare endemic blue flowers of *Anchusa caespitosa*, a type of Bugloss, are only found in the high peaks of the Lefka Ori.

WILDLIFE & BIRDWATCHING WILDLIFE

Survival Guide

Directory A–Z

Business Hours

» In this book we give high-season hours for sights and attractions; hours are generally reduced in winter.

» *Periptera* (kiosks) open from early morning until late at night and sell everything from bus tickets and cigarettes to condoms.

» Opening times of museums and archaeological sites depend on budgeting, ie if there's enough cash to hire afternoon staff. Check if you plan to visit after 3pm. Most sites are closed on Mondays.

Customs Regulations

Goods brought in and out of countries within the EU incur no additional taxes provided duty has been paid somewhere within the EU and the goods are only for personal consumption.

Exporting antiquities is strictly forbidden unless permission has been granted by the Ministry of Culture & Sciences. It is an offence to remove even the smallest piece from an archaeological site.

If you're lucky to carry more than €10,000 in cash, you must declare it.

Duty-free allowances (for adults) are:

» 200 cigarettes or 50 cigars or 250g of tobacco
» 1L spirits
» 2L wine
» 50ml perfume
» 250ml eau de toilette
» other goods up to the value of €175 (€90 for under 15yr)

Discount Cards

Discounts are widely available for seniors, children and students, often without using a discount card. In some cases you may be asked to show ID to prove your age. If you qualify for one of the following discount cards, you can reap additional benefits, for instance on travel, shopping, attractions and entertainment.

Camping Card International (CCI; www.campingcard international.com) Gives up to 25% savings in camping fees and third-party liability insurance while on the campground.

European Youth Card (Euro<26 card; www.european youthcard.org) Wide range of discounts for anyone under 26 years of age, in some countries under 30. Sold online.

International Student Identity Card (ISIC; www .isic.org) The most popular discount card, but only for full-time students. Available at ISIC points, though there are none in Crete. See the website for locations in your country.

International Youth Travel Card (IYTC; www.istc.org) Similar benefits to ISIC for nonstudents under 26 years of age. Available at ISIC points (see website).

STANDARD HOURS

Throughout this book, we've only listed business hours where they differ from the following standards:

BUSINESS	OPENING HOURS
Banks	8am-2.30pm Mon-Thu, 8am-2pm Fri
Bars	8pm-late
Cafes	9am-midnight
Post offices	7.30am-2pm Mon-Fri
Restaurants	11am-3pm & 7pm-1am
Shops	9am-2pm Mon-Sat; 5.30-8.30pm or 9pm Tue, Thu & Fri; all day in summer in resorts
Supermarkets	8am-9pm Mon-Fri, to 6pm Sat

Climate
Crete (Iraklio)

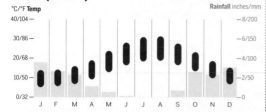

°C/°F **Temp**

Rainfall inches/mm

Electricity

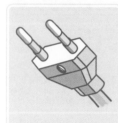

220V/50Hz

220V/50Hz

Gay & Lesbian Travellers

» Although homosexuality is legal over the age of 17, Crete does not really have much of a gay, let alone lesbian, scene. There is no overtly gay nightlife and public displays of affection are frowned upon outside the cities.

» The island's only dedicated gay bar is **Eros Bar** (www.eros barcrete.com) in Malia, while nearby Hersonisos has the gay-owned and -oriented guest house **Villa Ralfa** (www.villaralfa.com). Many venues in Iraklio are quietly gay-friendly, as are relaxed resorts such as Paleohora and most nude beaches.

» The annually updated *Spartacus International Gay Guide* (Bruno Gmunder, Berlin) is the leading gay travel guide. The best

website is www.gaygreece.gr, which has some information on cruising areas as well as gay-friendly bars, pubs and clubs.

Health

Crete is a healthy place so your main risks are likely to be sunburn, foot blisters, insect bites, minor stomach problems and hangovers.

Before You Go

» Bring your medications in their original, clearly labelled containers.

» A signed and dated letter from your doctor describing your medical conditions and medications, including generic names, is also a good idea. It is illegal to import codeine-based medication without a doctor's certificate.

» No vaccinations are required for travel to Crete but the World Health Organization (WHO) recommends that all travellers be covered for diphtheria, tetanus, measles, mumps, rubella and polio.

Availability & Cost of Health Care

» If you need an ambulance call ☑166.

» For minor illnesses, trained staff in pharmacies can provide valuable advice, sell medication and advise you

---

THE WINDS OF CRETE

No matter what time of year you visit Crete, fierce wind is a force you'll have to reckon with. There are dozens of different types: cool ones and hot ones, some blowing in from the north, others whistling in from Africa. From May to September, the most common wind is the *meltemi*, a ferocious and dry northerly wind that can blow for days on end. Usually it reaches its peak in the afternoon and dies down around sunset. While the *meltemi* brings relief from the summer heat, especially in the evening, it can also keep ferries in port and toss around beach umbrellas like joss sticks. Churning waves can be a problem on the north coast, while on the southern beaches you'll be pummelled by airborne sand. Because of their protected locations, some beaches are largely immune to winds, including Bali, Agia Pelada, Loutro and Myrtos.

EMBASSIES & CONSULATES

The UK is the only country with a consulate in Crete. Other countries are represented by their embassies in Athens. Some also have honorary consuls. Call or consult the website for details.

COUNTRY	TELEPHONE	WEBSITE
Australia	☑ 210 870 4000	www.greece.embassy.gov.au
Canada	☑ 210 727 3400	www.greece.gc.ca
France	☑ 210 339 1000	www.ambafrance-gr.org
Germany	☑ 210 728 5111	www.athen.diplo.de
Ireland	☑ 210 723 2771	www.embassyofireland.gr
Netherlands	☑ 210 725 4900	www.dutchembassy.gr
New Zealand	☑ 210 692 4136	www.nzembassy.com
UK	☑ 2810 224 012	www.ukingreece.fco.gov.uk/en
USA	☑ 210 720 2419	http://athens.usembassy.gov

on whether you need to see a doctor.

» Medical training is of a high standard in Greece, but the health service is chronically underfunded. Public hospitals are often overcrowded, hygiene can be a problem and relatives are expected to provide food for the patient. That said, Iraklio, Hania and Rethymno have modern, well-equipped hospitals.

» Condoms are widely available (eg in kiosks, supermarkets and pharmacies) but emergency contraception may not be, so take the necessary precautions.

Water

» Tap water is chlorinated and safe to drink, although it may not be to your taste.

» Bottled water is widely available and cheap, even when ordered in a restaurant.

» Coffee is usually served alongside a free glass of water or a small bottle of water.

» Filling up your own water bottle at natural springs or fountains is fine.

Insurance

» Comprehensive travel insurance to cover theft, loss

and medical problems is highly recommended.

» Some policies specifically exclude dangerous activities such as scuba-diving, motorcycling and even trekking; read the fine print.

» Check that the policy covers ambulances or an emergency flight home.

» Find out in advance if your insurance plan makes payments directly to providers or reimburses you for health expenditures.

» If you have to file a claim later, ensure you keep all documentation.

» Paying for your airline ticket with a credit card sometimes provides limited travel accident insurance – ask your credit-card company what it is prepared to cover.

Internet Access

» Numerous cafes and bars tout wi-fi hot spots that let laptop owners hook up for free. If necessary, you'll be given a password when ordering.

» Many hotels have an internet corner for their

EUROPEAN HEALTH INSURANCE CARD

Citizens of the EU, Switzerland, Iceland, Norway and Liechtenstein receive free or reduced-cost state-provided (not private) health-care coverage with the European Health Insurance Card (EHIC) for medical treatment that becomes necessary while in Crete. Each family member needs a separate card. UK residents can get application forms from post offices or download them from the Department of Health website (www.dh.gov.uk).

You will need to pay directly and fill in a treatment form; keep the form to claim any refunds. In general you can claim back around 70% of the standard treatment cost.

Citizens of other countries need to check if there is a reciprocal arrangement for free medical care between their country and Greece.

guests, often at no charge. These places are identified in this book with the internet icon @.

» The wi-fi icon 🛜is used if a place has...you guessed it....wi-fi. Note that in hotels such access is often limited to some rooms and/or public areas, so if you need in-room access be sure to specify so at the time of booking.

» Internet cafes are listed throughout the destination chapters. Unfortunately, most seem to have the lifespan of a fruit fly, so please forgive us if listings are outdated and ask staff at your hotel for a recommendation.

» There's free municipal wi-fi in Hania, Paleohora, Rethymno, Iraklio and Agios Nikolaos.

Legal Matters

» Greek drug laws are the strictest in Europe. Greek courts make no distinction between possession and pushing. Possession of even a small amount of marijuana is likely to land you in jail.

» Carry your passport with you at all times in case you're stopped by the police and questioned. Greek citizens are presumed to have identification on them and the police expect much the same from foreign visitors.

» If you're arrested insist on an interpreter (*the*-lo dhi-ermi-*nea*) and/or a lawyer (*the*-lo dhi-ki-*go*-ro).

Maps

If you're planning on doing extensive driving around Crete, especially in rural areas, a good road map is essential. Maps are widely available in bookshops and tourist shops and cost around €8. Car-hire agencies and hotels often distribute free maps but these are not always accurate.

» **Anavasi** (www.anavasi.gr) Publishes excellent road and

hiking maps, including three separate road maps covering *Hania*, *Rethymno and Iraklio*, and *Lasithi* at a scale of 1:100,000 and the comprehensive *Crete Atlas* at a scale of 1:50,000. Walking maps cover the *Lefka Ori* (Sfakia and Pahnes), *Samaria/Sougia*, *Mt Psiloritis* and *Zakros-Vai* at a scale of 1:25,000.

» **Harms** (www.harms-ic-verlag.de) This German publisher puts out 1:100,000 *Kreta Touristikkarte* maps covering the east (*Der Osten*) and the west (*Der Westen*) of Crete.

» **Michelin** (www.michelin.com) Produces a single-sheet map of the entire island at a scale of 1:140,000.

» **Petrakis Editions** (☎2810 282 630) Iraklio-based trekker Giorgos Petrakis has produced trekking and road maps for each of the four prefectures at a scale of 1:100,000. They include the E4 trail and all the mountainous routes of Crete.

» **Road Editions** (www.road.gr) Athens-based publisher of the 1:200,000 blue-covered *Crete* map, which also has handy maps of the major cities. There is also a 1:100,000 *Eastern Crete* map.

Money

The unit of currency in Crete is the euro (€). Euros come in seven notes (five, 10, 20, 50, 100, 200 and 500 euros) and eight coins (one- and two-euro coins and one-, two-, five-, 10-, 20- and 50-cent coins). Some fluctuations

notwithstanding, the euro is a stable currency with an inflation rate of around 2.8%. A guide to costs and exchange rates (at time of publication) can be found on pp12 and 13.

ATMs

» The easiest, quickest and usually cheapest way to obtain cash is by using your debit (bank) card at an ATM linked to international networks such as Cirrus, Plus, Star and Maestro.

» There are ATMs in almost every town large enough to support a bank – and certainly in all the tourist areas. In rural areas, only the larger villages and towns have ATMs, so plan ahead.

» Keep in mind that ATMs are not always refilled during the weekends, so make sure you have some cash left.

Cash

Cash is king in Crete, so always carry some with you and plan to pay in cash almost everywhere. It's also a good idea to set aside a small amount of euros as an emergency stash.

Credit Cards

» The main credit cards – MasterCard and Visa – are widely accepted. American Express and Diners Club are common in tourist areas only.

» Big resorts and hotels accept credit cards, but family-owned properties rarely do. Ask when checking in. Likewise, upmarket shops and restaurants accept plastic but village tavernas and small shops almost never do.

» Stickers in the front windows indicate which cards, if any, are accepted.

Moneychangers

» Banks will exchange all major currencies in either cash or travellers cheques. A passport is required to change travellers cheques, but not always for cash.

» Commission charged on the exchange of banknotes is less than for travellers cheques (some banks charge €2 per cheque, regardless of the amount).

» Post offices can exchange banknotes – but not travellers cheques – and charge less commission than banks.

» Travel agencies and hotels often change money and travellers cheques at bank rates, but commission charges are higher.

Tipping

There are no hard-and-fast rules for tipping in Crete, so the following should be regarded as a mere guideline. In restaurants, check if your bill includes a service charge, in which case you only leave a small amount to round off the bill. If the charge is not included, tip about 10% if you were satisfied.

WHERE/WHO	CUSTOMARY TIP
bar	round to the nearest euro
hotel cleaning staff	€1-2 per day
hotel porter	€1 per bag
taxi	round up the fare

Travellers Cheques

Travellers cheques are becoming increasingly obsolete in the age of network-linked ATMs. It doesn't help that local businesses generally don't accept them, even if denominated in euros, and banks charge exorbitant fees

for cashing them (currency exchange offices are usually better).

Photography

» Crete is a photographer's dream, with its picture-perfect beaches, gorgeous mountains, imposing fortresses, quaint mountain villages, historic cities and lively tavernas. A good general reference guide is Lonely Planet's *Travel Photography* by Richard l'Anson.

» Never photograph a military installation or anything else that has a sign forbidding photography.

» Flash photography is not allowed inside churches, and it's considered taboo to photograph the main altar.

» People generally don't seem to mind being photographed in the context of an overall scene, but if you want a close-up shot, you should ask first. The same goes for video cameras.

Post

Tahydromia (post offices) are easily identifiable by the yellow signs outside. Normal postboxes are also yellow, with red boxes for express mail.

Postal Rates

The rate for letters up to 20g to destinations anywhere in the world is €0.75. For letters up to 50g the rate is €1.15 within the EU and €1.30 outside the EU. Mail within Europe takes four to five days; to the USA, Australia and New Zealand takes five to eight days. Some tourist

shops also sell stamps, but with a 10% surcharge. Don't wrap a parcel before you send it, as post office staff may wish to inspect the contents.

Public Holidays

Banks, shops, post offices and public services as well as most museums and ancient sites close on public holidays. The following Greek national public holidays are observed in Crete:

New Year's Day 1 January
Epiphany 6 January
First Sunday in Lent February
Greek Independence Day 25 March
Good Friday March/April
(Orthodox) Easter Sunday March/April
Spring Festival/Labour Day 1 May
Feast of the Assumption 15 August
Ohi Day 28 October
Christmas Day 25 December
St Stephen's Day 26 December

Safe Travel

Crete is generally a safe, friendly and hospitable place and crime rates are much lower here than in other parts of southern Europe. Thefts, especially, are more likely to be committed by other tourists than locals. Still, as with anywhere, it pays to follow a few simple precautions to lower your risk of getting ripped off.

» Keep track of your possessions on public transport, in markets and other crowded areas. Do not leave luggage unattended in cars.

» Lock your rental car and hotel rooms. If the latter doesn't lock properly, including windows, ask for your valuables to be locked in the hotel safe.

» Avoid dark streets and parks at night, particularly in the major cities.

Telephone

The Greek telephone service is modern and reasonably well maintained. Public telephones are ubiquitous but often out of order, a result of the decline in demand that went hand in hand with the proliferation of mobile phones.

All phone numbers have 10 digits. Landline numbers start with '2' while mobile numbers start with '6'.

Mobile Phones

» Mobile (cell) phones operate on GSM900/1800. If your home country uses a different standard, you'll need a multiband GSM phone in Crete.

» Check with your service provider about roaming charges – charges for calls to a mobile phone from a landline or another mobile can be exorbitant.

» If you have an unlocked multiband phone, getting a prepaid SIM card with a local number might work out cheaper than using your own network. Cards are available from Greece's three mobile

phone service providers – Vodafone, Cosmote and Wind. These automatically revert to global roaming when you leave Greece and can be used to send and receive SMS messages. Top up cards are sold at supermarkets, kiosks and newsagents.

» The use of a mobile phone while driving is prohibited unless you're using a headset.

Phone Codes

» **Calling Crete from abroad** Dial your country's international access code, then ✆30 (Greece's country code) followed by the 10-digit local number.

» **Calling internationally from Crete** Dial ✆00 (the international access code), the country code, and the local number.

» **Reverse-charge (collect) calls** Dial the operator (domestic ✆129; international ✆139) to get the number in the country you wish to call.

Phonecards

» Public phones take phonecards (*telekarta*), not coins. These cards are sold at kiosks, corner shops and tourist shops.

» For instructions in English on how to use a public telephone, push the 'i' button. Don't remove your card before you are told to do so or you could wipe out the remaining credit. Local calls cost one unit per minute.

» You can also buy a range of prepaid international calling cards (*hronokarta*). This

involves dialling an access code and then punching in your card number. Cards come with instructions in Greek and English.

Time

Clocks in Greece are set to eastern European time (GMT/UTC plus two hours). Daylight-saving time kicks in on the last Sunday in March and ends on the last Sunday in October.

Toilets

» One peculiarity of the Greek plumbing system is that it can't handle toilet paper as the pipes are too narrow and back up easily. Toilet paper, sanitary towels, tampons, etc should be placed in the small bin provided.

» Very occasionally outside the big towns you might come across squat toilets in older houses, *kafeneia* (coffee houses) and public toilets.

» Public toilets are rare, except at airports and bus and train stations. Cafes are the best option if you get urgently caught, but you may be expected to buy something for the privilege.

Tourist Information

Local tourist offices are a mixed bag. Some are super-helpful and right on the money, while others are staffed by keen but not always very knowledgeable university interns. Expect limited opening hours outside high season and only a smattering of free maps and brochures.

Travellers with Disabilities

If mobility is a problem, visiting Crete will present some serious challenges. Most hotels, ferries, museums and

TOURIST POLICE

If you think that you've been ripped off, report it to the **tourist police** (✆171); there's always at least one English-speaking staff member. Hotels, restaurants, travel agencies, tourist shops, tourist guides, waiters, taxi drivers and bus drivers all come under their jurisdiction. If you need to report a theft or loss of a passport, the tourist police will act as interpreter between you and the regular police. Some tourist police also dispense maps, brochures and transport information.

sites are not accessible to the wheelchair-bound and narrow streets, steep curbs, no or small pavements and parked cars all get in the way of getting around. Newly built hotels are required to be more disability-friendly by having lifts and rooms with extra-wide doors and spacious bathrooms.

If you are determined, then take heart in the knowledge that wheelchair users do go to Crete for holidays. The **Eria Resort** (☑28210 62790; www.eria-resort.gr) in Maleme in western Crete is one of the few in Greece designed for travellers with disabilities. It caters for special needs and equipment and offers medical support and appropriate excursions and activities.

There is some useful English-language information on travelling in Greece on www.disabled.gr.

Visas

» EU nationals and citizens of Norway, Iceland and Switzerland only need their national identity card or passport to enter and stay in Greece, even for stays over 90 days.

» Citizens of Australia, Canada, Israel, Japan, New Zealand, Poland, Switzerland and the US are among those countries that need only a valid passport but no visa if entering Greece as tourists for up to 90 days. For longer stays, contact your nearest Greek embassy or consulate and begin your application well in advance.

» Nationals from other countries need to apply for a Schengen Visa, named after the 1995 agreement that abolished passport controls between most European countries, including Greece.

» Applications for a Schengen Visa must be filed with the embassy or consulate of the country that is your primary destination. It is valid for stays up to 90 days. Legal residency in any Schengen country makes a visa unnecessary, regardless of your nationality.

» If you're in Greece on a 90-day visa and wish to prolong your stay, you need to apply for an extension with the nearest Aliens' Bureau (*Ypiresia Allodhapon*) no later than 20 days prior to the expiration date. If approved, you will be allowed to stay for an additional six months. Many long-term travellers get around this by leaving Greece every three months and re-entering a short time later.

» For details, see the website of the Ministry of Foreign Affairs (www.mfa.gr) or contact your Greek embassy or consulate.

Women Travellers

» Crete is remarkably safe for women to explore, even for solo travellers. Going alone to cafes and restaurants is perfectly acceptable, even at night. This does not mean that you should be lulled into complacency; bag-snatching and sexual harassment do occur, although rape is very rare.

» On beaches and in bars and nightclubs, solo women are likely to attract attention from men. The Greeks even have a word for men on the hunt for foreign women, *kamaki,* which translates as 'fishing trident'. *Kamaki* are not as active today as they were two or three decades ago, but there are still men out there looking to shag as many female tourists as possible.

» In general, though, if you don't want company, most will respect a firm 'no, thank you'. If you feel threatened, protesting loudly will often make the offender slink away with embarrassment or spur others to come to your defence.

» If assaulted, call the **police** (☑100) or, if you prefer, a **women's crisis hotline** (☑302 651 078 810), whose staff members are trained to help you deal with the emotional and physical trauma surrounding an attack.

COME ON BABY, LIGHT MY FIRE

Greeks hold the record for being the most nicotine-addicted nation within the EU, with nearly half of the adult population lighting up regularly. Several smoking bans have been instituted – and flaunted – over the years, but in September 2010 the government's latest attempt went into effect. It's the toughest yet, prohibiting tobacco advertising as well as smoking in all enclosed public spaces, including cafes, restaurants, nightclubs, offices and businesses and transport stations.

As the time of writing, the law was again widely ignored, both by smokers and by local police. Ashtrays are still on the tables in restaurants and cafes, as owners argue that they simply cannot afford to lose even more business during these tough economic times. Smokers can be fined between €50 and €500 for lighting up, while business owners could have to cough up between €500 and €10,000 if they allow smoking on their premises. But even these painful fines are no deterrence unless they're enforced, which rarely happens.

According to a government estimate, smoking-related health costs amount to some €2 billion per year.

Work

Permits

EU nationals don't need a work permit, but they need a residency permit and a Greek tax file number if they intend to stay longer than three months. Nationals of other countries should obtain a work permit.

Bar & Hostel Work

The best bar and hotel jobs can pay quite well – so well that they are usually taken by young Greeks from the mainland or seasonal workers from Eastern Europe working through agencies. You can try your luck at the bigger resorts or more remote places in the south. Resorts such as Hersonisos and Malia that cater for British travellers are the best bet for Brits looking for bar work. April and May are the times to go looking.

Holiday Representatives

Crete provides terrific opportunities for working as a representative for a package tour company. British-based companies begin looking for personnel around February for the summer season. The pay is low but you can make tips and some outfits allow reps to earn a percentage of the packages they sell.

Volunteer Work

Crete for Life (www.creteforlife.com) A recuperative holiday camp for disadvantaged kids near Ierapetra.

Global Volunteers (www.globalvolunteers.org) Teach conversational English to children in Gazi west of Iraklio.

Sea Turtle Protection Society of Greece (www.archelon.gr) Includes monitoring programs.

Other Work

Jobs are often advertised in the classifieds of the English-language newspapers, or you can place an advertisement yourself. Seasonal harvest work is handled by migrant workers, mostly from Balkan nations, and is no longer a viable option for travellers.

Transport

GETTING THERE & AWAY

Flights, tours and rail tickets can be booked online at www.lonelyplanet.com/bookings.

Entering the Country

Entering Crete is usually a very straightforward procedure. If arriving from any of the 25 Schengen countries (ie the 22 EU member states plus Iceland, Norway and Switzerland), passports are not even checked, though customs may be interested in what you are carrying. EU citizens may also enter with a national identity card.

Passport

Citizens of most Western countries can enter Crete without a visa; other nationals may need a Schengen Visa; see p256 for details.

Air

Most travellers arrive in Crete by air, usually with a change in Athens. Between May and October, charter and low-cost airlines operate direct flights to Crete, mostly from UK and German airports.

Airports & Airlines

Hania (www.chania-airport.com) Convenient for travellers heading to western Crete.

Iraklio (www.heraklion-airport.info) Crete's main airport is officially known as Nikos Kazantzakis International Airport.

Sitia (☎28430 24666) Domestic flights only.

INTERNATIONAL CARRIERS

AirBerlin/Niki (www.airberlin.com) Most major airports in Germany, Austria and Switzerland.

Condor (www.condor.com) Most major German airports.

easyJet (www.easyjet.com) Berlin, Bristol, Geneva, London-Gatwick, Manchester, Milan and Rome.

Fly Thomas Cook (www.flythomascook.com) London-Gatwick, Belfast, Birmingham, Bristol, Cardiff, East Midlands, Glasgow, Manchester and Newcastle.

Germanwings (www.germanwings.com) Most major German airports plus London-Stansted (via Cologne).

Jet2 (www.jet2.com) Leeds, Manchester, East Midlands and Newcastle.

Jetairfly (www.jetairfly.com) Brussels and other Belgian cities.

Lufthansa (www.lufthansa.com) Athens.

Monarch (www.monarch.co.uk) London-Gatwick and Manchester.

Ryanair (www.ryanair.com) Frankfurt (Hahn) and Milan (Bergamo) from Hania.

Smartwings (www.smartwings.com) Prague and Ostrava.

Transaero (www.transaero.ru/en) Moscow.

CLIMATE CHANGE & TRAVEL

Every form of transport that relies on carbon-based fuel generates CO_2, the main cause of human-induced climate change. Modern travel is dependent on aeroplanes, which might use less fuel per kilometre per person than most cars but travel much greater distances. The altitude at which aircraft emit gases (including CO_2) and particles also contributes to their climate change impact. Many websites offer 'carbon calculators' that allow people to estimate the carbon emissions generated by their journey and, for those who wish to do so, to offset the impact of the greenhouse gases emitted with contributions to portfolios of climate-friendly initiatives throughout the world. Lonely Planet offsets the carbon footprint of all staff and author travel.

Transavia France (www
.transavia.com) Amsterdam,
Paris-Orly, Lille, Lyon,
Nantes.

Tuifly (www.tuifly.com) Most
major airports in Germany,
Austria and Swtizerland.

DOMESTIC CARRIERS

Aegean Airlines (www
.aegeanair.com) Athens and
Thessaloniki, with onward
connections throughout
Europe. Direct flights from
London-Heathrow, Milan,
Paris and Rome.

Olympic Air (www.olympicair
.com) Athens and Thessaloniki, with onward connections
throughout Europe.

Sky Express (www.skyexpress
.gr) About a dozen Greek
destinations, including
Athens, Rhodes, Santorini
(Thira), Kos and Ikaria.

Tickets

If you're planning to travel
between June and September,
it's wise to book well ahead.
Purchasing airline tickets
has never been easier. Most
airlines sell tickets online,
offering good deals and
eliminating the fear of losing
your precious ticket while on
holiday. If you're coming
from outside Europe, consider
a cheap flight to a European
hub and an onward ticket on
a low-cost carrier. Charter
flights are often block-
booked by tour operators
selling holiday packages.
However, tickets are sometimes so cheap it may be
worth buying a package just
for the flight and then
continuing your travels
independently.

Land

There are no bus services
to Greece from western or
northern Europe.

Car & Motorcycle

When bringing your own
vehicle to Greece, you need a
valid driving licence, your car
registration certificate and
proof of insurance. Foreign

cars must display a nationality
sticker unless they have
official Euro-plates. You
should also carry a warning
(hazard) triangle, fire extinguisher and first-aid kit. For
road rules and other driving-
related information see p263.

From most European
countries travelling to Crete
by car takes several days and
thus only makes sense for
longer stays. The fastest way
is to hop on a ferry from Italy.
There are overnight ferries
to Patra at the northwestern
tip of the Peloponnese from
Ancona (21 hours), Bari (14½
hours), Brindisi (14½ hours)
and Venice (31 hours). See
www.greekferries.gr for
schedules and prices. From
here it's about a 200km
drive south to Piraeus (near
Athens), where you can
catch another ferry to Iraklio,
Sitia or Hania (see p261 for
details).

It is still possible to drive
to Greece via Slovenia,
Croatia, Bulgaria and the
Former Yugoslav Republic of
Macedonia, but the savings
are not huge and are far
outweighed by the distance
involved and the necessity of
crossing five borders.

Train

As the time of writing, all
international train services to
Greece had been suspended
indefinitely as part of the
country's austerity measures.
As a result, Greece has also
been removed from the
Eurail and InterRail pass
system. You can still use
the pass to travel by train
to an Italian port and catch
the ferry to Patra on the
Peloponnese.

Sea

Crete is well served by ferry,
with at least one daily departure from Piraeus (near
Athens) to Iraklio and Hania
year-round and three or four
per day in summer. There are
also slower ferries once or
twice a week to Sitia in the
east and the small western
port of Kissamos (Kastelli).
Services are considerably
curtailed from November
to April. Timetables change
from season to season, and
ferries are subject to delays
and cancellations at short
notice due to bad weather,
strikes or mechanical
problems.

Tickets

As ferries are prone to delays
and cancellations, for short
trips it's often best not to
buy a ticket until it has been
confirmed that the ferry is
leaving. During high season,
of if you're bringing a car, you
should book well in advance,
especially for overnight
and high-speed catamaran
services. If a service is cancelled, you can transfer your
ticket to the next available
service with that company.
There are also ferries from
Kissamos to Gythio on the
Peloponnese and from Iraklio to other Greek islands,
including Santorini (Thira),
Rhodes and Mykonos.

Tickets are best purchased
online either from the ferry
company directly or through a
booking engine such as www
.greekferries.gr and www
.ferries.gr. Prices are government-regulated and deter-
mined by the distance and
the level of comfort, which

WANT MORE?

For in-depth information, reviews and recommendations
at your fingertips, head to the Apple App Store to purchase
Lonely Planet's Athens City Guide iPhone app.

Alternatively, head to **Lonely Planet** (www.lonelyplanet
.com/greece/crete) for planning advice, author recommendations, traveller reviews and insider tips.

ranges from deck class to double-berth outside cabins. Children, students and seniors usually qualify for discounts ranging from 10% to 50%. Children under the age of five often travel for free.

Yacht

Although yachting is a popular way to explore the Greek Islands, Crete is a long way from other islands and does not have a huge yachting industry. The sailing season lasts from April until October, however between July and September the *meltemi* winds (p251) can ground you regularly.

GETTING AROUND

Bicycle

Cycling is becoming more common in Crete, but the often-hilly terrain means you need strong leg muscles and endurance. You can hire bikes in most tourist areas. Prices range from €8 to €20 per day. Bicycles are carried free

on ferries. See the Hiking & Outdoor Activities chapter, p21, and www.cycling.gr for more details, as well as information on mountain-biking tours.

Boat

Smaller boats link the towns along Crete's south coast, some of which are only accessible by sea.

In summer there are daily boats from Paleohora to Hora Sfakion, via Agia Roumeli, Sougia and Loutro. Schedules change from year to year, but there are usually two to three boats a day between Hora Sfakion and Agia Roumeli and one boat a day from Hora Sfakion to Paleohora. Boats to Gavdos Island leave from Hora Sfakion and Paleohora.

Tourist boats run excursions to offshore islands, including Ierapetra to Gaïdouronisi (Hrysi) Island, Agios Nikolaos to Spinalonga, and Kissamos to the Gramvousa Peninsula.

Taxi Boat

A taxi-boat service operates in several southern coastal towns. These are essentially small speedboats that transport people to places that are difficult to get to by land. Some owners charge a set price for each person, and others charge a flat rate for the boat, with the cost divided by the number of passengers. Either way, prices are quite high.

Bus

Buses are the only form of public transport in Crete but a fairly extensive network makes it relatively easy to travel around the island. Fares are government-regulated and very reasonable by European standards. For schedules and prices, go to www.bus-service-crete-ktel.com.

There's hourly service along the main northern coastal road and less-frequent buses to the inland villages and towns on the south coast. Buses also go to major tourist attractions,

For current routes and timetables, consult the ferry company's website or go to www.gtp.gr, www.openseas.gr, www.ferries.gr and www.greekferries.gr. The latter two also have a ticket booking function.

ROUTE	COMPANY	DURATION	FARE	FREQUENCY
Hania-Piraeus	Anek	8½hr	€35	1-2 daily
Iraklio-Karpathos	Aigaion Pelagos (Anek)	7½hr	€18	2 weekly
Iraklio-Kasos	Aigaion Pelagos (Anek)	5¾hr	€18	2 weekly
Iraklio-Milos	Aigaion Pelagos (Anek)	7½hr	€22	2 weekly
Iraklio-Mykonos	Hellenic Seaways	4¾hr	€77	1 daily
Iraklio-Paros	Hellenic Seaways	4hr	€75.50	1 daily
Iraklio-Piraeus	Minoan	6½-7½hr	€28	1-2 daily
Iraklio-Piraeus	Anek	6½-9½hr	€36	1-2 daily
Iraklio-Rhodes	Anek	12½hr	€29	1 weekly
Iraklio-Santorini (Thira)	Anek	4¼hr	€15	2 weekly
Iraklio-Santorini (Thira)	Sea Jets	2¼hr	€51.50	1 daily
Iraklio-Santorini (Thira)	Hellenic Seaways	2hr	€48.50	1 daily
Iraklio-Sitia	Anek	2¾hr	€16	2 weekly
Kissamos-Antikythira	Lane	2hr	€9	2 weekly
Kissamos-Gythio	Lane	6½hr	€20	2 weekly
Kissamos-Kythira	Lane	3½hr	€14	1-2 daily
Kissamos-Piraeus	Lane	10½hr	€24	2 weekly
Sitia-Iraklio	Anek	2¾hr	€16	2 weekly
Sitia-Karpathos	Anek	4¼hr	€19	2 weekly
Sitia-Kassos	Anek	2½hr	€11	2 weekly
Sitia-Milos	Anek	11hr	€25	2 weekly
Sitia-Piraeus	Anek	16½hr	€35	2 weekly
Sitia-Rhodes	Aigaion Pelagos	10½hr	€28	2 weekly
Sitia-Santorini (Thira)	Anek	7½hr	€25	2 weekly

including Knossos, Phaestos, Moni Arkadiou, Moni Preveli, Omalos (for Samaria Gorge) and Hora Sfakion.

Larger towns usually have a central, covered bus station with waiting rooms, toilets and a snack bar. In small towns and villages the 'bus station' may be no more than a stop outside a *kafeneio* (coffee house) or taverna, which often doubles as a ticket office. If not, or if it's closed, you can buy your ticket on the bus.

Car & Motorcycle

Having your own vehicle is a great way to explore Crete if you can brave the roads and drivers. There are plenty of places to hire cars and motorcycles and roads have

FERRY COMPANIES

» **Anek Lines** (www.anek.gr) Older vessels to/from Piraeus; one weekly ferry to the Cyclades operated by the affiliated Aegeon Pelagos company.

» **Hellenic Seaways** (www.hellenicseaways.gr) High-speed services to the Cyclades.

» **LANE Lines** (www.lane.gr) Long-haul ferries to/from Piraeus from Kissamos.

» **Minoan Lines** (www.minoan.gr) High-speed luxury ferries to/from Piraeus.

» **Sea Jets** (www.seajets.gr) High-speed catamarans to/from Santorini (Thira).

improved enormously in recent years, but in the more remote areas (particularly the south) you'll still find unpaved roads that are only suitable for 4WDs. Also be extra careful on narrow and windy mountain roads.

Motorcycles are great for short-haul trips but bear in mind Crete is a massive island and the distances can make it hard work for bikers.

Beyond the main highways, prepare to spend a lot of time poring over maps, as country roads are generally badly signposted. Road signs, when they exist, are usually marked in Greek and English (the English phonetic sign follows a few metres after the Greek) except in remote areas. Even when written in Latin letters, the spelling of place names can vary wildly from the names on your map or in this book. Invest in a good map, but even the best maps don't cover all the side roads. Don't expect reassuring signs along the way telling you you're on track or the remaining distance to your destination. The rule of thumb is just to keep going until told otherwise and keep in mind you generally won't get much warning before a turn-off.

Automobile Associations

The Greek automobile association ELPA offers reciprocal services to members of national automobile associations with a valid membership card. If your vehicle breaks down, dial ☏10400.

Driving Licences

Drivers with an EU driving licence can drive with it in Crete. If your driving licence is from outside the EU, you need to obtain an International Driving Permit (IDP) before you leave home; check with your local automobile association.

To hire a motorcycle, you must produce a licence that shows proficiency to ride the category of bike you wish to rent; this applies to everything from 50cc up.

Fuel & Spare Parts

Fuel is widely available in Crete, but service stations may be closed on Sunday and public holidays. Self-service pumps are not the norm in Greece, nor are credit-card pumps, and out-of-the-way stations don't take plastic at all, so it is always advisable to keep the tank topped up.

Spare parts can be tricky to find, especially if you are in the more remote parts of the island. For a referral to the nearest dealer ask at a service station or call ELPA on ☏10400.

Hire
CAR
Crete has cheaper car hire than many islands due to the level of competition. All the major international companies have branches at airports and in the towns, but you may get a better deal if you hire from a local company and negotiate.

As anywhere, rates for car hire vary quite considerably by model, pick-up date and location, but you should be able to get an economy-size vehicle from about €35 per day, plus insurance and taxes. Expect surcharges for additional drivers and one-way hire. Child or infant safety seats may be hired for about €5 per day and should be reserved at the time of booking. Most hire cars are manual, so book ahead if you need an automatic car as they are rare and usually more expensive.

In order to hire your own wheels you'll need to be at least 21 or 23 years old, possess a valid driving licence and a major credit card. Some companies hire out to younger drivers for an additional charge. Most require a credit card, although some local car-hire outfits may accept cash or a travellers cheque as deposits.

Pre-booked and prepaid packages, arranged in your home country, usually work out much cheaper than on-the-spot-rentals. Check for deals with online travel agencies such as the **Auto Europe** (www.autoeurope .com) or UK-based **Holiday Autos** (www.holidayautos .co.uk).

See the Getting Around sections in the destination chapters for local car-hire outlets.

MOTORCYCLE
Mopeds and motorcycles are widely available for hire but Crete is not the best place to initiate yourself into the world of motorcycling. Caution should be exercised at all times, as roads change without warning from smooth and paved to cracked and pothole-ridden.

Experienced motorcyclists will find that a lightweight

Enduro motorcycle between 400cc and 600cc is ideal for negotiating Crete's roads. In many cases maintenance is minimal, so check the machine thoroughly before you hire it – especially the brakes: you'll need them! When you hire a moped, tell the agent where you'll be going to ensure that your vehicle has enough power to get you up Crete's steep hills.

Motorbike-hire rates range from €25 per day for a scooter or 50cc motorbike to €50 for an Enduro 650cc. Low-season prices drop considerably.

Insurance

Third-party liability insurance is compulsory for all vehicles in Greece, including cars brought in from abroad. When hiring a vehicle, make sure your contract includes adequate liability insurance. Car-hire agencies almost never include insurance that covers damage to the vehicle itself, called Collision Damage Waiver (CDW) or Loss Damage Waiver (LDW). It's optional, but driving without it is not recommended. Some credit-card companies cover CDW/LDW for a certain period if you charge the entire rental to your card. Always confirm with your card issuer ahead of time what coverage it provides in Greece.

For motorcycles, third-party insurance is usually included in the price, but this will not include medical expenses, so check that your travel insurance covers you for motorbike injuries – many don't. Helmets are compulsory for bikes of 50cc or more and rental agencies must provide them as part of the hire deal.

Road Hazards

The main danger of driving in Crete lies in the local driving culture. The laid-back Cretans are manic drivers and always in a hurry once they get behind the wheel. Expect to be tailgated, honked at and aggressively overtaken if you move too slowly. Slower drivers are expected to straddle the narrow service lane and let the traffic pass. Overtaking on bends and ignoring double lines and stop signs is prevalent. Road rules are routinely ignored and there is barely any police presence.

It is best to avoid driving at night, especially as late-night revellers are plentiful and drink-driving laws are barely enforced.

Road surfaces can change unexpectedly when a section of road has succumbed to subsidence or weathering. In the mountains, not a day will pass without being slowed down by a herd of sheep or goats wandering on the road. Many falling rock zones are not signposted nor hemmed in with tarps, so keep your eyes peeled for loose rocks on the road.

Road Rules

Driving is on the right and overtaking on the left. Outside built-up areas, traffic on a main road has right of way at intersections. In towns, vehicles coming from the right have right of way.

Major highways have four lanes, although some are still two-lane highways with large hard shoulders. These hard shoulders are used for driving in, especially when being overtaken. Move over if someone wants to pass you.

Driving in the major cities and small towns is a nightmare of erratic one-way streets, double parking and irregularly enforced parking rules. Cars are not towed away but fines can be expensive. Designated parking for disabled drivers is a rarity.

Seatbelts must be worn in the front and back seats and children under 12 years of age are not allowed in the front seat. You must, in theory, travel with a first-aid kit, fire extinguisher and warning

SMART TRAVEL

Flying has become second nature in this era of low-cost airlines and few of us stop to consider using alternative travel methods and doing our bit for the environment. Yet, getting to Crete without a plane can be an enjoyable journey and more comfortable than you might think; best of all, it also leaves a much smaller carbon footprint. Take the trip from London to Iraklio, for instance. If you're flying, you're generating 0.55 metric tons of emission. If you're driving, it's about the same or more, depending on your vehicle. However, travelling by train, you can cut that number down dramatically to just 0.05 metric tons.

Of course, travelling to Crete by train is not quick. Depending on where you started, budget two or three days. Coming from London, for instance, you'd pick up the Eurostar to Paris and then board a night train to Venice to hop on the ferry to Patra. From Patra, a bus takes you to Athens' port at Piraeus where you catch the Crete-bound ferry.

Alternatively, you could catch take the overnight train from Paris to Bologna, change to another train to Bari and catch the overnight ferry to Patra.

If and when international trains start operating again, it's also possible to travel by train all the way to Athens via Paris, Munich, Vienna, Budapest, Bucharest and Thessaloniki. The excellent website www.seat61.com monitors the situation and has comprehensive details.

triangle. Carrying cans of petrol is not permitted. The blood-alcohol limit is 0.05%; anything over 0.08% is a criminal offence.

Speed limits for cars are 120km/h on highways, 90km/h on other major roads and 50km/h in built-up areas. Speed limits for motorcycles are 70km/h (up to 100cc) and 90km/h (above 100cc). Hefty fines are levied for speeding and other traffic and parking offences.

Traffic fines are not paid on the spot – you will be told where to pay. In the case of noninjury accidents, the police are not required to write a report, but it is advisable to go to a nearby police station and explain what happened. A police report is required for insurance purposes. If an accident involves injury, a driver who does not stop and does not inform the police may face a prison sentence.

Hitching

Hitching is never entirely safe in any country and, as a rule, we don't recommend it. If you decide to hitch, remember that it's safer to travel in pairs and be sure to inform someone of your intended destination. Women should hitch with a male companion. In Crete you don't hitch with your thumb up as in northern Europe, but with an outstretched hand, palm down to the road.

Getting out of major cities tends to be hard work; hitching is much easier in remote areas. On country roads, it is not unknown for someone to stop and ask if you want a lift even if you haven't asked for one.

Local Transport
Bus

City buses operating around Iraklio, Rethymno and Hania service mostly the residential suburbs and thus are rarely useful for visitors. Tickets are normally bought at *periptera* (kiosks) or from the driver.

Taxi

Taxis are widely available except in remote villages, and are relatively cheap by European standards. Large towns have taxi stands that post a list of prices to outlying destinations, which removes any anxiety about overcharging. Otherwise you pay what's on the meter. Rural taxis often do not have meters, so you should always settle on a price before you get in.

Language

The Greek language is believed to be one of the oldest European languages, with an oral tradition of 4000 years and a written tradition of approximately 3000 years. Due to its centuries of influence, Greek constitutes the origin of a large part of the vocabulary of many Indo-European languages (including English), and many of the terms used in science.

Greek is the official language of Greece and co-official language of Cyprus, and is spoken by many emigrant communities throughout the world.

The Greek alphabet is explained on the next page, but if you read the blue pronunciation guides given with each phrase in this chapter as if they were English, you'll be understood. Note that dh is pronounced as 'th' in 'there'; gh is a softer, slightly throaty version of 'g'; and kh is a throaty sound like the 'ch' in the Scottish 'loch'. All Greek words of two or more syllables have an acute accent (´), which indicates where the stress falls. In our pronunciation guides, stressed syllables are in italics.

In Greek, all nouns, articles and adjectives are either masculine, feminine or neuter – in this chapter these forms are included where necessary, separated with a slash and indicated with 'm/f/n'.

BASICS

Hello.	Γειά σας.	ya·sas (polite)
	Γειά σου.	ya·su (informal)
Good morning.	Καλή μέρα.	ka·li me·ra
Good evening.	Καλή σπέρα.	ka·li spe·ra
Goodbye.	Αντίο.	an·di·o
Yes./No.	Ναι./Οχι.	ne/o·hi

WANT MORE?

For in-depth language information and handy phrases, check out Lonely Planet's *Greek Phrasebook*. You'll find it at **shop .lonelyplanet.com**, or you can buy Lonely Planet's iPhone phrasebooks at the Apple App Store.

Please.	Παρακαλώ.	pa·ra·ka·lo
Thank you.	Ευχαριστώ.	ef·ha·ri·sto
That's fine./ You're welcome.	Παρακαλώ.	pa·ra·ka·lo
Sorry.	Συγγνώμη.	sigh·no·mi

What's your name?
| Πώς σας λένε; | pos sas le·ne |

My name is ...
| Με λένε ... | me le·ne ... |

Do you speak English?
| Μιλάτε αγγλικά; | mi·la·te an·gli·ka |

I (don't) understand.
| (Δεν) καταλαβαίνω. | (dhen) ka·ta·la·ve·no |

ACCOMMODATION

campsite	χώρος για κάμπινγκ	kho·ros yia kam·ping
hotel	ξενοδοχείο	kse·no·dho·khi·o
youth hostel	γιουθ χόστελ	yuth kho·stel
a ... room	ένα ... δωμάτιο	e·na ... dho·ma·ti·o
single	μονόκλινο	mo·no·kli·no
double	δίκλινο	dhi·kli·no
How much is it ...?	Πόσο κάνει ...;	po·so ka·ni ...
per night	τη βραδυά	ti·vra·dhya
per person	το άτομο	to a·to·mo

GREEK ALPHABET

The Greek alphabet has 24 letters, shown below in their upper- and lower-case forms. Be aware that some letters look like English letters but are pronounced very differently, such as **B**, which is pronounced 'v'; and **P**, pronounced like an 'r'. As in English, how letters are pronounced is also influenced by how they are combined, for example the **ου** combination is pronounced 'u' as in 'put', and **οι** is pronounced 'ee' as in 'feet'.

Α α	a	as in 'father'	**Ξ ξ**	x	as in 'ox'
Β β	v	as in 'vine'	**Ο ο**	o	as in 'hot'
Γ γ	gh	a softer, throaty 'g'	**Π π**	p	as in 'pup'
	y	as in 'yes'	**Ρ ρ**	r	as in 'road',
Δ δ	dh	as in 'there'			slightly trilled
Ε ε	e	as in 'egg'	**Σ σ, ς**	s	as in 'sand'
Ζ ζ	z	as in 'zoo'	**Τ τ**	t	as in 'tap'
Η η	i	as in 'feet'	**Υ υ**	i	as in 'feet'
Θ θ	th	as in 'throw'	**Φ φ**	f	as in 'find'
Ι ι	i	as in 'feet'	**Χ χ**	kh	as the 'ch' in the
Κ κ	k	as in 'kite'			Scottish 'loch', or
Λ λ	l	as in 'leg'		h	like a rough 'h'
Μ μ	m	as in 'man'	**Ψ ψ**	ps	as in 'lapse'
Ν ν	n	as in 'net'	**Ω ω**	o	as in 'hot'

Note that the letter **Σ** has two forms for the lower case – **σ** and **ς**. The second one is used at the end of words. The Greek question mark is represented with the English equivalent of a semicolon (;).

air-con	έρκοντίσιον	er·kon·di·si·on
bathroom	μπάνιο	ba·nio
fan	ανεμιστήρας	a·ne·mi·sti·ras
TV	τηλεόραση	ti·le·o·ra·si
window	παράθυρο	pa·ra·thi·ro

DIRECTIONS

Where is ...?
Πού είναι ...; pu i·ne ...

What's the address?
Ποια είναι η διεύθυνση; pia i·ne i dhi·ef·thin·si

Can you show me (on the map)?
Μπορείς να μου δείξεις bo·ris na mu dhik·sis
(στο χάρτη); (sto khar·ti)

Turn left.
Στρίψτε αριστερά. strips·te a·ri·ste·ra

Turn right.
Στρίψτε δεξιά. strips·te dhe·ksia

at the next corner
στην επόμενη γωνία stin e·po·me·ni gho·ni·a
at the traffic lights
στα φώτα sta fo·ta

behind	πίσω	pi·so
in front of	μπροστά	bro·sta
far	μακριά	ma·kri·a
near (to)	κοντά	kon·da
next to	δίπλα	dhi·pla
opposite	απέναντι	a·pe·nan·di
straight ahead	ολο ευθεία.	o·lo ef·thi·a

EATING & DRINKING

a table for ...	Ενα τραπέζι για ...	e·na tra·pe·zi ya ...
(two) people	(δύο) άτομα	(dhi·o) a·to·ma
(eight) o'clock	τις (οχτώ)	stis (okh·to)
I don't eat ...	Δεν τρώγω ...	dhen tro·gho ...
fish	ψάρι	psa·ri
(red) meat	(κόκκινο) κρέας	(ko·ki·no) kre·as
peanuts	φυστίκια	fi·sti·kia
poultry	πουλερικά	pu·le·ri·ka

What would you recommend?
Τι θα συνιστούσες; ti tha si·ni·*stu*·ses

What's in that dish?
Τι περιέχει αυτό το ti pe·ri·e·hi af·*to* to
φαγητό; fa·ghi·*to*

That was delicious.
Ήταν νοστιμότατο! *i*·tan no·sti·*mo*·ta·to

Cheers!
Εις υγείαν! is i·*yi*·an

Please bring the bill.
Το λογαριασμό, to lo·ghar·ya·*zmo*
παρακαλώ. pa·ra·ka·*lo*

Key Words

appetisers	ορεκτικά	o·rek·ti·*ka*
bar	μπαρ	bar
beef	βοδινό	vo·dhi·*no*
bottle	μπουκάλι	bu·*ka*·li
bowl	μπωλ	bol
bread	ψωμί	pso·*mi*
breakfast	πρόγευμα	*pro*·yev·ma
cafe	καφετέρια	ka·fe·*te*·ri·a
cheese	τυρί	ti·*ri*
chicken	κοτόπουλο	ko·*to*·pu·lo
cold	κρυωμένος	kri·o·*me*·nos
cream	κρέμα	*kre*·ma
delicatessen	ντελικατέσεν	de·li·ka·*te*·sen
desserts	επιδόρπια	e·pi·*dhor*·pi·a
dinner	δείπνο	*dhip*·no
egg	αβγό	av·*gho*
fish	ψάρι	*psa*·ri
food	φαγητό	fa·yi·*to*
fork	πιρούνι	pi·*ru*·ni
fruit	φρούτα	*fru*·ta
glass	ποτήρι	po·*ti*·ri
grocery store	οπωροπωλείο	o·po·ro·po·*li*·o
herb	βότανο	*vo*·ta·no
high chair	καρέκλα	ka·*re*·kla
	για μωρά	yia mo·*ro*
hot	ζεστός	ze·*stos*
knife	μαχαίρι	ma·*he*·ri
lamb	αρνί	ar·*ni*
lunch	μεσημεριανό	me·si·me·ria·*no*
	φαγητό	fa·yi·*to*
main courses	κύρια φαγητά	*ki*·ri·a fa·yi·ta
market	αγορά	a·gho·*ra*
menu	μενού	me·*nu*
nut	καρύδι	ka·*ri*·dhi
oil	λάδι	*la*·dhi

pepper	πιπέρι	pi·*pe*·ri
plate	πιάτο	*pia*·to
pork	χοιρινό	hi·ri·*no*
restaurant	εστιατόριο	e·sti·a·*to*·ri·o
salt	αλάτι	a·*la*·ti
spoon	κουτάλι	ku·*ta*·li
sugar	ζάχαρη	za·kha·ri
vegetable	λαχανικά	la·kha·ni·*ka*
vegetarian	χορτοφάγος	khor·to·*fa*·ghos
vinegar	ξύδι	*ksi*·dhi
with/without	με/χωρίς	me/kho·*ris*

To get by in Greek, mix and match these simple patterns with words of your choice:

When's (the next bus)?
Πότε είναι *po*·te *i*·ne
(το επόμενο (to e·*po*·me·no
λεωφορείο); le·o·fo·*ri*·o)

Where's (the station)?
Πού είναι (ο σταθμός); pu *i*·ne (o stath·*mos*)

I'm looking for (Ampfilohos).
Ψάχνω για *psakh*·no yia
(το Αμφίλοχος). (to am·*fi*·lo·khos)

Do you have (a local map)?
Έχετε οδικό e·he·te o·dhi·*ko*
(τοπικό χάρτη); (to·pi·*ko* khar·ti)

Is there a (lift)?
Υπάρχει (ασανσέρ); *i·par*·hi (a·san·*ser*)

Can I (try it on)?
Μπορώ να bo·*ro* na
(το προβάρω); (to pro·*va*·ro)

I have (a reservation).
Έχω (κλείσει e·kho (*kli*·si
δωμάτιο). dho·*ma*·ti·o)

I'd like (to hire a car).
Θα ήθελα (να tha *i*·the·la (na
ενοικιάσω ένα e·ni·ki·a·so e·na
αυτοκίνητο). af·to·*ki*·ni·to)

Drinks

beer	μπύρα	*bi*·ra
coffee	καφές	ka·*fes*
juice	χυμός	hi·*mos*
milk	γάλα	*gha*·la
soft drink	αναψυκτικό	a·nap·sik·ti·*ko*
tea	τσάι	*tsa*·i
water	νερό	ne·*ro*
(red) wine	(κόκκινο) κρασί	(*ko*·ki·no) kra·*si*
(white) wine	(άσπρο) κρασί	(*a*·spro) kra·*si*

EMERGENCIES

Help!	Βοήθεια!	vo·i·thya
Go away!	Φύγε!	fi·ye
I'm lost	Έχω χαθεί.	e·kho kha·thi
There's been an accident.	Έγινε ατύχημα.	ey·i·ne a·ti·hi·ma

Call ...!	Φωνάξτε ...!	fo·nak·ste ...
a doctor	ένα γιατρό	e·na yi·a·tro
the police	την αστυνομία	tin a·sti·no·mi·a

I'm ill.
Είμαι άρρωστος. *i·me a·ro·stos*

It hurts here.
Πονάει εδώ. po·na·i e·dho

I'm allergic to (antibiotics).
Είμαι αλλεργικός/ *i·me a·ler·yi·kos/*
αλλεργική a·ler·yi·ki
(στα αντιβιωτικά) (sta an·di·vi·o·ti·ka) (m/f)

NUMBERS

1	ένας/μία	e·nas/ mi·a (m/f)
	ένα	e·na (n)
2	δύο	dhi·o
3	τρεις	tris (m&f)
	τρία	tri·a (n)
4	τέσσερεις	te·se·ris (m&f)
	τέσσερα	te·se·ra (n)
5	πέντε	pen·de
6	έξη	e·xi
7	επτά	ep·ta
8	οχτώ	oh·to
9	εννέα	e·ne·a
10	δέκα	dhe·ka
20	είκοσι	ik·o·si
30	τριάντα	tri·an·da
40	σαράντα	sa·ran·da
50	πενήντα	pe·nin·da
60	εξήντα	ek·sin·da
70	εβδομήντα	ev·dho·min·da
80	ογδόντα	ogh·dhon·da
90	ενενήντα	e·ne·nin·da
100	εκατό	e·ka·to
1000	χίλιοι/χίλιες	hi·li·i/hi·li·ez (m/f)
	χίλια	hi·li·a (n)

SHOPPING & SERVICES

I'd like to buy ...
Θέλω ν' αγοράσω ... *the·lo na·gho·ra·so ...*

I'm just looking.
Απλώς κοιτάζω. ap·los ki·ta·zo

May I see it?
Μπορώ να το δω; bo·ro na to dho

I don't like it.
Δεν μου αρέσει. dhen mu a·re·si

How much is it?
Πόσο κάνει; *po·so ka·ni*

It's too expensive.
Είναι πολύ ακριβό. *i·ne po·li a·kri·vo*

Can you lower the price?
Μπορείς να κατεβάσεις bo·ris na ka·te·va·sis
την τιμή; tin ti·mi

ATM	αυτόματη μηχανή χρημάτων	af·to·ma·ti mi·kha·ni khri·ma·ton
bank	τράπεζα	tra·pe·za
credit card	πιστωτική κάρτα	pi·sto·ti·ki kar·ta
internet cafe	καφενείο διαδικτύου	ka·fe·ni·o dhi·a·dhik·ti·u
mobile phone	κινητό	ki·ni·to
post office	ταχυδρομείο	ta·hi·dhro·mi·o
toilet	τουαλέτα	tu·a·le·ta
tourist office	τουριστικό γραφείο	tu·ri·sti·ko ghra·fi·o

TIME & DATES

What time is it? Τι ώρα είναι; ti o·ra i·ne

It's (2 o'clock). είναι (δύο η ώρα). *i·ne (dhi·o i o·ra)*

It's half past (10). (Δέκα) και μισή. (dhe·ka) ke mi·si

today	σήμερα	si·me·ra
tomorrow	αύριο	av·ri·o
yesterday	χθες	hthes
morning	πρωί	pro·i
(this) afternoon	(αυτό το) απόγευμα	(af·to to) a·po·yev·ma
evening	βράδυ	vra·dhi

Monday	Δευτέρα	dhef·te·ra
Tuesday	Τρίτη	tri·ti
Wednesday	Τετάρτη	te·tar·ti
Thursday	Πέμπτη	pemp·ti
Friday	Παρασκευή	pa·ras·ke·vi
Saturday	Σάββατο	sa·va·to
Sunday	Κυριακή	ky·ri·a·ki

January	Ιανουάριος	ia·nu·ar·i·os
February	Φεβρουάριος	fev·ru·ar·i·os
March	Μάρτιος	mar·ti·os
April	Απρίλιοςα	a·pri·li·os
May	Μάιος	mai·os
June	Ιούνιος	i·u·ni·os
July	Ιούλιος	i·u·li·os
August	Αύγουστος	av·ghus·tos
September	Σεπτέμβριος	sep·tem·vri·os
October	Οκτώβριος	ok·to·vri·os
November	Νοέμβριος	no·em·vri·os
December	Δεκέμβριος	dhe·kem·vri·os

Signs

ΕΙΣΟΔΟΣ	Entry
ΕΞΟΔΟΣ	Exit
ΠΛΗΡΟΦΟΡΙΕΣ	Information
ΑΝΟΙΧΤΟ	Open
ΚΛΕΙΣΤΟ	Closed
ΑΠΑΓΟΡΕΥΕΤΑΙ	Prohibited
ΑΣΤΥΝΟΜΙΑ	Police
ΑΣΤΥΝΟΜΙΚΟΣ ΣΤΑΘΜΟΣ	Police Station
ΓΥΝΑΙΚΩΝ	Toilets (women)
ΑΝΔΡΩΝ	Toilets (men)

cancelled	ακυρώθηκε	a·ki·ro·thi·ke
delayed	καθυστέρησε	ka·thi·ste·ri·se
platform	πλατφόρμα f	plat·for·ma
ticket office	εκδοτήριο εισιτηρίων	ek·dho·ti·ri·o i·si·ti·ri·on
timetable	δρομολόγιο	dhro·mo·lo·gio
train station	σταθμός τρένου	stath·mos tre·nu

TRANSPORT

Public Transport

boat	πλοίο	pli·o
(city) bus	αστικό	a·sti·ko
(intercity) bus	λεωφορείο	le·o·fo·ri·o
plane	αεροπλάνο	ae·ro·pla·no
train	τραίνο	tre·no

Where do I buy a ticket?
Πού αγοράζω εισιτήριο; pu a·gho·ra·zo i·si·ti·ri·o

I want to go to ...
Θέλω να πάω στο/στη ... the·lo na pao sto/sti...

What time does it leave?
Τι ώρα φεύγει; ti o·ra fev·yi

Does it stop at (Iraklio)?
Σταματάει στο (Ηράκλειο); sta·ma·ta·i sto (i·ra·kli·o)

I'd like to get off (at Iraklio).
Θα ήθελα να κατεβώ tha i·the·la na ka·te·vo
(στο Ηράκλειο). (sto i·ra·kli·o)

I'd like (a) ...	Θα ήθελα (ένα) ...	tha i·the·la (e·na) ...
one-way ticket	απλό εισιτήριο	a·plo i·si·ti·ri·o
return ticket	εισιτήριο με επιστροφή	i·si·ti·ri·o me e·pi·stro·fi
1st class	πρώτη θέση	pro·ti the·si
2nd class	δεύτερη θέση	def·te·ri the·si

Driving & Cycling

I'd like to hire a ...	Θα ήθελα να νοικιάσω ...	tha i·the·la na ni·ki·a·so ...
car	ένα αυτοκίνητο	e·na af·ti·ki·ni·to
4WD	ένα τέσσερα επί τέσσερα	e·na tes·se·ra e·pi tes·se·ra
jeep	ένα τζιπ	e·na tzip
motorbike	μια μοτοσυκλέττα	mya mo·to·si·klet·ta
bicycle	ένα ποδήλατο	e·na po·dhi·la·to

Do I need a helmet?
Χρειάζομαι κράνος; khri·a·zo·me kra·nos

Is this the road to ...?
Αυτός είναι ο af·tos i·ne o
δρόμος για ... dhro·mos ya ...

Can I park here?
Μπορώ να παρκάρω bo·ro na par·ka·ro
εδώ; e·dho

The car/motorbike has broken down (at ...).
Το αυτοκίνητο/ to af·to·ki·ni·to/
η μοτοσυκλέττα i mo·to·si·klet·ta
χάλασε στο ... kha·la·se sto ...

I have a flat tyre.
Έπαθα λάστιχο. e·pa·tha la·sti·cho

I've run out of petrol.
Έμεινα από βενζίνη. e·mi·na a·po ven·zi·ni

For culinary terms, see Cretan Cuisine (p238).

Achaean civilisation – see *Mycenaean civilisation*

acropolis – highest point of an ancient city

agia (f), agios (m), agii (pl) – saint(s)

agora – commercial area of an ancient city; shopping precinct in modern Greece

amphora – large two-handled vase in which wine or oil was kept

basilica – early Christian church

bouzouki – stringed lute-like instrument associated with *rembetika* music

Byzantine Empire – characterised by the merging of Hellenistic culture and Christianity and named after Byzantium, the city on the Bosphorus that became the capital of the Roman Empire in AD 324; when the Roman Empire was formally divided in AD 395, Rome went into decline and the eastern capital, renamed Constantinople after Emperor Constantine I, flourished; the Byzantine Empire (324 BC–AD 1453) dissolved after the fall of Constantinople to the Turks in 1453

capital – top of a column

Classical period – era in which the Greek city-states reached the height of their wealth and power after the defeat of the Persians in the 5th century BC; the Classical period (480–323 BC) ended with the decline of the city-states as a result of the Peloponnesian Wars, and the expansionist aspirations of Philip II, King of Macedon (r 359–336 BC) and his son, Alexander the Great (r 336–323 BC)

Corinthian – order of Greek architecture recognisable by columns with bell-shaped capitals with sculpted elaborate ornaments based on acanthus leaves; see also *Doric* and *Ionic*

dark age (1200–800 BC) – period in which Greece was under Dorian rule

domatio (s), domatia (pl) – room, often in a private home; a cheap form of accommodation

Dorians – Hellenic warriors who invaded Greece around 1200 BC, demolishing the city-states and destroying the *Mycenaean civilisation*; heralded Greece's dark age, when the artistic and cultural advancements of the Mycenaean and *Minoan civilisations* were abandoned; the Dorians later developed into land-holding aristocrats, encouraging the resurgence of independent city-states led by wealthy aristocrats

Doric – order of Greek architecture characterised by a column that has no base, a fluted shaft and a relatively plain capital, when compared with the flourishes evident on *Ionic* and *Corinthian* capitals

Ellada or Ellas – see *Hellas*

ELPA – Elliniki Leschi Aftokinitou kai Periigiseon; Greek motoring and touring club

ELTA – Ellinika Tahydromia; Greek post office organisation

EOS – Ellinikos Orivatikos Syllogos; the association of Greek Mountaineering Clubs

EOT – Ellinikos Organismos Tourismou; main tourist office (has offices in most major towns), known abroad as *GNTO* (Greek National Tourist Organisation)

estiatorio – restaurant serving ready-made food as well as à la carte

Geometric period – the period (1200–800 BC) characterised by pottery decorated with geometric designs; sometimes referred to as Greece's *dark age*

GNTO – Greek National Tourist Organisation; see also *EOT*

Hellas – the Greek name for Greece; also known as Ellada or Ellas

Hellenistic period – prosperous, influential period (323–146 BC) of Greek civilisation ushered in by Alexander the Great's empire-building and lasting until the Roman sacking of Corinth

hora – main town, usually on an island

Ionic – order of Greek architecture characterised by a column with truncated flutes and capitals with ornaments resembling scrolls; see also *Doric* and *Corinthian*

kastro – walled-in town; also describes a fortress or castle

Koine – Greek language used in pre-Byzantine times; the language of the church liturgy

kouros – male statue of the Archaic period, characterised by a stiff body posture and enigmatic smile

kri-kri – endemic Cretan animal with large horns similar to a wild goat; also known as the *agrimi*

KTEL – Kino Tamio Eispraxeon Leoforion; national bus cooperative, which runs all long-distance bus services

leoforos – avenue

libation – in ancient Greece, wine or food that was offered to the gods

Linear A – Minoan script; so far undeciphered

Linear B – Mycenaean script; has been deciphered

lyra – small violin-like instrument or lyre, played

on the knee; common in Cretan and Pontian music

mantinadha (s), mandinadhes (pl) – a style of traditional Cretan rhyming couplets

megaron – central room or quarters of a Mycenaean palace

meltemi – dry northerly wind that blows throughout much of Greece in the summer

mezedhopoleio – restaurant specialising in *mezedhes*

Minoan civilisation – Bronze Age (3000–1200 BC) culture of Crete named after the mythical King Minos, and characterised by pottery and metalwork of great beauty and artisanship; it has three periods: Protopalatial (3400–2100 BC), Neopalatial (2100–1580 BC) and Postpalatial (1580–1200 BC)

mitata – round stone shepherd's huts

moni – monastery or convent

Mycenaean civilisation – first great civilisation (1900–1100 BC) of the Greek mainland, characterised by powerful independent city-states ruled by

kings; also known as the *Achaean civilisation*

New Democracy – Nea Dimodratia; conservative political party

necropolis – literally 'city of the dead'; ancient cemetery

nisi – island

nymphaeum – in ancient Greece, building containing a fountain and often dedicated to nymphs

odeion – ancient Greek indoor theatre

odos – street

OTE – Organismos Tilepikoinonion Ellados; Greece's major telephone carrier

ouzerie – place that serves ouzo and light snacks

Panagia – Mother of God or Virgin Mary; name frequently used for churches

paralia – waterfront

pediment – triangular section, often filled with sculpture above the columns, found at the front and back of a classical Greek temple

periptero (s), periptera (pl) – street kiosk

peristyle – columns surrounding a building, usually a temple or courtyard

pithos (s), pithoi (pl) – large Minoan storage jar or urn

plateia – square

propylon (s), propylaia (pl) – elaborately built main entrance to an ancient city or sanctuary; a propylon had one gateway and a propylaia more than one

prytaneion – the administrative centre of the city-state

rembetika – blues songs, commonly associated with the underworld of the 1920s

rhyton – another name for a *libation* vessel

rizitika – traditional, patriotic songs of western Crete

stoa – long colonnaded building, usually in an *agora*; used as a meeting place and shelter in ancient Greece

taverna – the most common type of traditional restaurant that serves food and wine

tholos – Mycenaean tomb shaped like a beehive

behind the scenes

SEND US YOUR FEEDBACK

We love to hear from travellers – your comments keep us on our toes and help make our books better. Our well-travelled team reads every word on what you loved or loathed about this book. Although we cannot reply individually to postal submissions, we always guarantee that your feedback goes straight to the appropriate authors, in time for the next edition. Each person who sends us information is thanked in the next edition – and the most useful submissions are rewarded with a free book.

Visit **lonelyplanet.com/contact** to submit your updates and suggestions or to ask for help. Our award-winning website also features inspirational travel stories, news and discussions.

Note: We may edit, reproduce and incorporate your comments in Lonely Planet products such as guidebooks, websites and digital products, so let us know if you don't want your comments reproduced or your name acknowledged. For a copy of our privacy policy visit lonelyplanet.com/privacy.

OUR READERS

Many thanks to the travellers who used the last edition and wrote to us with helpful hints, useful advice and interesting anecdotes:
B Leanne Beattie, Chris Biles, Wendy Bolt, Muriel Boselli, Paul Bryant C David Chubb, Mary Collins D Bavo Deneckere, F Seth Frantzman G Robyn Galloway H Jennifer Horne, Malcolm Hornsby K Mira Kautzky, Andrew P Kirk, Yvonne Kwakkestijn L Tassilo Lang M Sabrina Magnabosco, John Margaritsanakis, Chiara Mealli, Jacquelien Meijer, Peter Mynors N Janet Nicolas P Devid Paolini R Ewan Ross S Tami Shellef, Massimo Stefani, Pamela Stokes T Emma Tikunova W R Wakefield, Claire Waysand, Laura Woodman

AUTHOR THANKS

Andrea Schulte-Peevers

First up, a big thank you to Anna Tyler for giving me a shot at this book. A heartfelt thank you also to my husband David for being such good company while tooling around the island, and to Miriam Bers for her fruitful referrals. Big kudos to all the good folks who showed us amazing hospitality and generously shared their expertise and local insights, including the Papadospiridaki family, Vaggelis Alegakis, Nikos Miliarakis, Ioannis Giannoutsos, Marianna Founti-Vassi and Moin Sadiq.

Chris Deliso

Many Cretans provided good tips and good company. These include Manolis (Paleohora), Stavroula (Kissamos-Kastelli), Manolis, Rena and Ioanna (Hania), plus Leftheris and Giannis (Iraklio). The Lonely Planet crew, which helped steer the good ship *Crete* into harbour, also has my heartfelt appreciation: commissioning editor Anna Tyler, ever-patient coordinating author Andrea Schulte-Peevers, and the production and map-making teams. *Na eiste kala!*

Des Hannigan

My thanks to the many friends and passing strangers, both local and nonlocal, who have helped and advised me on my wanderings through the 'Great Island' over the years. They are too numerous to name, but I hope they have all been aware of my gratitude and affection.

ACKNOWLEDGMENTS

Climate map data adapted from Peel MC, Finlayson BL & McMahon TA (2007) 'Updated World Map of the Köppen-Geiger Climate Classification', *Hydrology and Earth System Sciences*, 11, 163344.

Cover photograph: Traditional Cretan Windmills, Ano Kera, Iraklio Province, Crete, Greece, Walter Bibikow/Corbis
Many of the images in this guide are available for licensing from Lonely Planet Images: www.lonelyplanetimages.com.

This Book

This 5th edition of Lonely Planet's *Crete* guidebook was re-searched and written by Andrea Schulte-Peevers, Chris Deliso and Des Hannigan. The previous two editions were written by Victoria Kyriakopoulos. The 1st edition was written by Jeanne Oliver and the 2nd by Paul Hellander. This guidebook was commissioned in Lonely Planet's London office, laid out by Cambridge Publishing Management, UK, and produced by the following:

Commissioning Editor Anna Tyler

Coordinating Editors Karen Beaulah, Gina Tsarouhas

Coordinating Cartographer Andras Bogdanovits

Coordinating Layout Designer Paul Queripel

Managing Editors Helen Christinis, Annelies Mertens, Tasmin Waby McNaughtan

Managing Cartographers Amanda Sierp, Shahara Ahmed

Senior Cartographer Anita Banh

Managing Layout Designer Chris Girdler

Assisting Editors Kathryn Glendenning, Michala Green, Kim Hutchins, Andi Jones, Hazel Meek, Martine Power, Saralinda Turner

Assisting Layout Designer Julie Crane

Cover Research Sabrina Dalbesio

Internal Image Researchers Rebecca Skinner, Aude Vauconsant

Illustrator Javier Martinez Zarracina

Colour Designer Tim Newton

Indexer Marie Lorimer

Language Content Laura Crawford

Thanks to Jessica Boland, Brendan Dempsey, Ryan Evans, Heather Howard, Trent Paton, Jessica Rose, Julie Sheridan, Gerard Walker

index